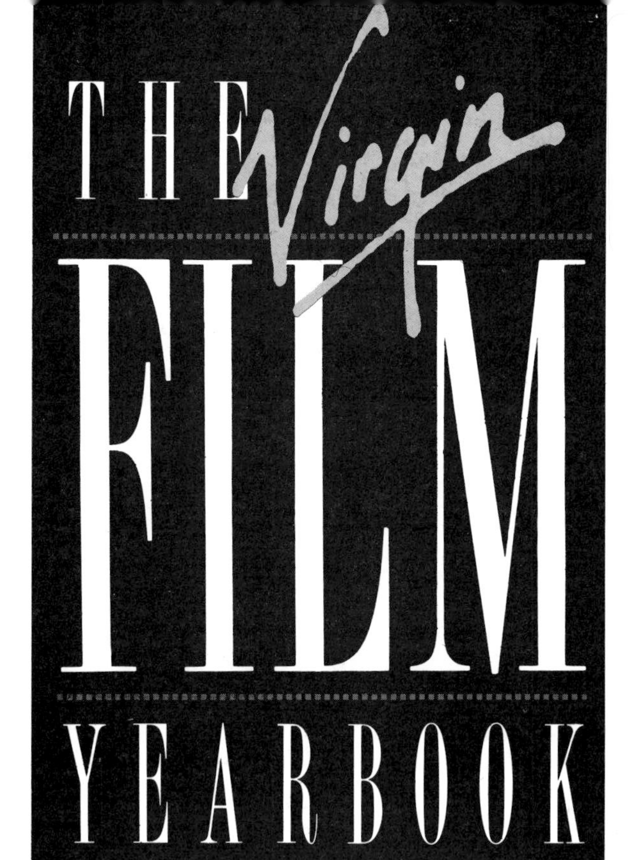

Virgin

VOLUME 7

EDITED BY JAMES PARK

In-house editor
CAT LEDGER

Editor's assistant and picture researcher
ALISON TAYLOR

Cover and design by
JERRY GOLDIE

THE FILM YEARBOOK VOLUME 7

A Virgin Book
Published in 1988
by the Paperback Division of
W.H. Allen & Co Plc
44 Hill Street
London W1X 8LB

ISBN 0 86369 279 6

Typeset by Avocet Ltd

Printed and bound in Great Britain by Scotprint, Musselburgh

ACKNOWLEDGEMENTS

Thanks to the distributors, publicity companies, publications and film archives which supplied the picture or information, or both.

Artificial Eye, Atlantic, Blue Dolphin, the British Film Institute, Cannon, Cinecom, Columbia, Dennis Davidson Associates, Electric Pictures, Enterprise, Entertainment, Goldcrest, Goldwyn, Guild, Hemdale, ICA Projects, Island, JAC, Mainline, the National Film Archive, Nelson Entertainment, The Other Cinema, PSA, Palace, Paramount, Premier Releasing, Rank, Recorded Releasing, Skouras, Twentieth-Century Fox, UIP, Universal, Variety, Vestron, Virgin, Walt Disney, Warner Bros.

CONTENTS

EDITOR

JAMES PARK writes screenplays and books about cinema. The author of *Learning to Dream: The New British Cinema*, he is working on a history of British film-making. This is the second time he has edited *The Film Yearbook*.

CONTRIBUTORS

MARK ADAMS covers the British film beat for *Variety*, making himself available for receptions, parties and other movie-associated events. Before coming to London he was a hack on a major Midlands evening newspaper. Originating from Cossington in Leicestershire, his interests include wine, P. G. Wodehouse, Sherlock Holmes, American comic books and Leicester City Football Club.

GEOFF ANDREW is joint editor of the film section of *Time Out* magazine. He also works as a freelance, contributes to the *Radio Times*, and has written a book, *Hollywood Gangster Movies*. Before becoming a journalist he was manager and co-programmer of London's Electric Cinema, and he keeps his hand in by organizing occasional seasons for the National Film Theatre.

ANNE BILLSON is a freelance writer and has contributed to such publications as *City Limits*, *The Independent*, *Monthly Film Bulletin*, *Sky*, *Tatler* and *The Times*. She is the author of two books: *Screen Lovers*, an illustrated study of love and lust in the cinema, and *Dream Demon*, a novelization of the upcoming feature film. She is currently working on her first novel.

TONY CRAWLEY is the author of *The Films of Sophia Loren*, *Bébé: The Films of Brigitte Bardot*, *Screen Dreams: The Hollywood Pin-Up* and *The Steven Spielberg Story*. He has written on films for publications throughout the world and now lives in France, where he has a franglais rock radio show and has co-authored *L'Age d'or du cinéma érotique*.

RAYMOND DURGNAT is a writer and lecturer on films and cultural history. His next books will be *King Vidor – American* and *Michael Powell and the British Genius*. He has been a visiting professor at UCLA, Columbia, Dartmouth College, Oklahoma and elsewhere, as well as a staff writer at Elstree Studios in the good old days of Pathe News.

QUENTIN FALK is author of *Travels in Greeneland: The Cinema of Graham Greene*, *Last of a Kind: The Sinking of Lew Grade* and *The Golden Gong: 50 Years of the Rank Organisation, Its Films and Its Stars*, and also a contributor to *Anatomy of the Movies* and *British Cinema Now*. A past editor of *Screen International* and assistant entertainments editor of the *Daily Mail*, he regularly writes reviews and articles for publications like *Punch*, *Radio Times*, *The Guardian*, *Today* and *Sight & Sound*. He is also editor of *Flicks*, Britain's first movie newspaper.

GRAHAM FULLER is a New York-based film journalist who writes regularly for *The Listener*, *The Village Voice*, *Film Comment*, *Premiere* and *American Film*. Formerly executive editor of *The Movie* and films editor of *Stills*, he has also contributed to *The Guardian*, *The Times*, *The Independent* and *Sight and Sound*.

TIMOTHY GEE became enthusiastic about movies after seeing *Mrs Wiggs of the Cabbage Patch*. In 1960 he started working in the British film industry. He has edited films for Ken Russell (*Salomé's Last Dance*), Bryan Forbes (*The Raging Moon*, *The Stepford Wives*, *The Slipper and the Rose*) and Desmond Davis (*Clash of the Titans*, *The Country Girls* and *Ordeal by Innocence*).

PHIL HARDY is the editor of a series of film encyclopedias and has just completed the *Faber Companion to Popular Music of the Twentieth Century*. He is also working on a book about the fifties, and writes for *Music Week*. He lives amongst the rolling hills of North London.

ADRIAN HODGES had a glittering early career as the assistant editor of *BP Forecourt News*, before moving to *Screen International*, the UK film trade magazine. He subsequently became a script executive at Thorn EMI Screen Entertainment. Following a year at Cannon Films (UK), he was appointed administrator of the NFDF, an independent body set up to develop British feature films.

HARLAN KENNEDY is the European editor of *Film Comment*. He is a member of the Critics' Circle and of FIPRESCI, the international federation of film critics. For four years he was the London contributing editor of *American Film* and now writes frequently for *Emmy* magazine, *American Cinematographer* and the *New York Times*.

THOMAS LLOYD is an American living in London who writes about theatre, cinema and the English for the folks back home.

TODD McCARTHY was the co-editor of *King of the Bs*. He has contributed to *Film Comment*, *American Film* and *Cahiers du Cinéma*. He is also a critic and reporter on *Variety*.

BART MILLS writes about films and television from Hollywood for such publications as *The Guardian*, the *Los Angeles Times* and *American Film*. He is also the author of a recent book on Mickey Rourke.

NANCY MILLS writes about films and television for the *Los Angeles Times* and numerous other newspapers in America, Canada and England.

MARKUS NATTEN is a retired poet and writer of four, to date unfilmed, screenplays, including *Watchdogs* and *Friday's Child*. He is also working on a graphic novel, *Hymns From Charnel Houses*. He lives in the New Forest.

TIM PULLEINE is deputy film editor of *The Guardian*. He contributes reviews and articles to various publications, including *Sight and Sound*, *Films and Filming* and *Monthly Film Bulletin*.

DAVID THOMPSON is the producer of the BBC's *Film Club* series. He is also a freelance journalist, writing for *Time Out*, *Films and Filming* and *The Independent*. A former programmer of the Electric Cinema, he recently organized a Martin Scorsese season at the National Film Theatre. His other passions include Mahler, steam locomotives and Rosanna Arquette.

A YEAR IN CINEMA

This was the year that America went soft. As the nation emerged from the blow-hard excesses of the Reagan years, movie-goers had less times for movies with simple answers. They preferred films that promoted parenthood but de-emphasized sex. Purely romantic movies pulled large crowds. Successful comedies often had hardly a gross joke. Dramatic scenes were less likely to be punctuated with gunfire. Parodies of cop movies often did better than straight cop movies.

Audiences were older as well as wiser. The demographics are skewing further into adult territory, so the mass of movie-goers are less inclined than formerly to support movies that pander to youth. Not a single big studio teenpic was a hit. The major studios have withdrawn from the exploitation market they had haunted for a decade. Aside from *Innerspace* and the Mel Brooks spoof *Spaceballs*, hardware science-fiction seems to be a dead genre. Fantasies like *Willow* and *The Princess Bride* had a harder than expected time finding an audience.

The movies that succeeded this year were the ones that left an after-image. When audiences left cinemas talking, instead of feeling stunned into submission, they were more likely to spread favourable word-of-mouth. More movies had something to say this year.

Women had more to watch. Babies have never played so many crucial roles in the movies as this year. And when actors got in the same shot as the babies, they were furthest from their guns and most appealing to female movie-goers. Other actors actually played children, a spectacle that confirmed many women's most firmly held view of men.

Stars, with few exceptions, couldn't infallibly draw their fans to a movie they didn't want to see. Attractive stories succeeded more often than concocted vehicles. Good matches of contrasting type generally fared better than solo efforts. Studios seemed to be moving back towards the values that prevailed in Hollywood's heyday; this year's top movies seemed more thoroughly and thoughtfully produced. Careful construction, rather than scattered strokes of genius, marked the movies emerging from this new studio system.

PROCESSED MOVIES

The year's two biggest hits, *Fatal Attraction* and *Three Men and a Baby*, were the best examples of how the most confident studios, Paramount and Disney, now machine-tool their movies. Both films had an idea behind the story - the same basic idea, in fact: men are putty in the hands of a woman (or a baby girl). Both were based on previously made movies, one a low-budget short, the other a French hit. Both productions were firmly controlled by the studio bosses right up to release, using thorough audience testing.

Years from now, film historians might say *Fatal Attraction* was Adrian Lyne's re-think of his flop *9½ Weeks*. This time, he gave his depiction of obsessive love a plot and a re-shot ending straight out of *Les Diaboliques*. The 'subtext' of the movie (this year's movies have a 'subtext'; last year's just had 'high concept') was a message about AIDS - if you sleep around, death will stalk you. 'Safe sex' in the AIDS age made its film début in a scene in *Dragnet* in which Tom Hanks passed up a quick one because his jumbo box of plonkers was empty.

BABYVISION

The subtext of the year's cycle of baby films was that parenthood is better than any number of quick ones. And some kind of movie-magic parthenogenesis is better than the standard method of procreation. *Three Men and a Baby* and *Baby Boom* by-passed the messy inconvenience of parturition, going straight to doorstep delivery. The films were clever satires on a generation of yuppies who have denied their biological destiny until it's almost too late. *Overboard* switched Goldie Hawn from yachtswoman to household drudge, to show that domesticity and parenthood offer rewards greater than luxurious ease.

YEAR OF THE CHILD

Children starred in more serious movies than ever before. Three top directors chose to make films about boys of twelve or so during World

Fatal Attraction

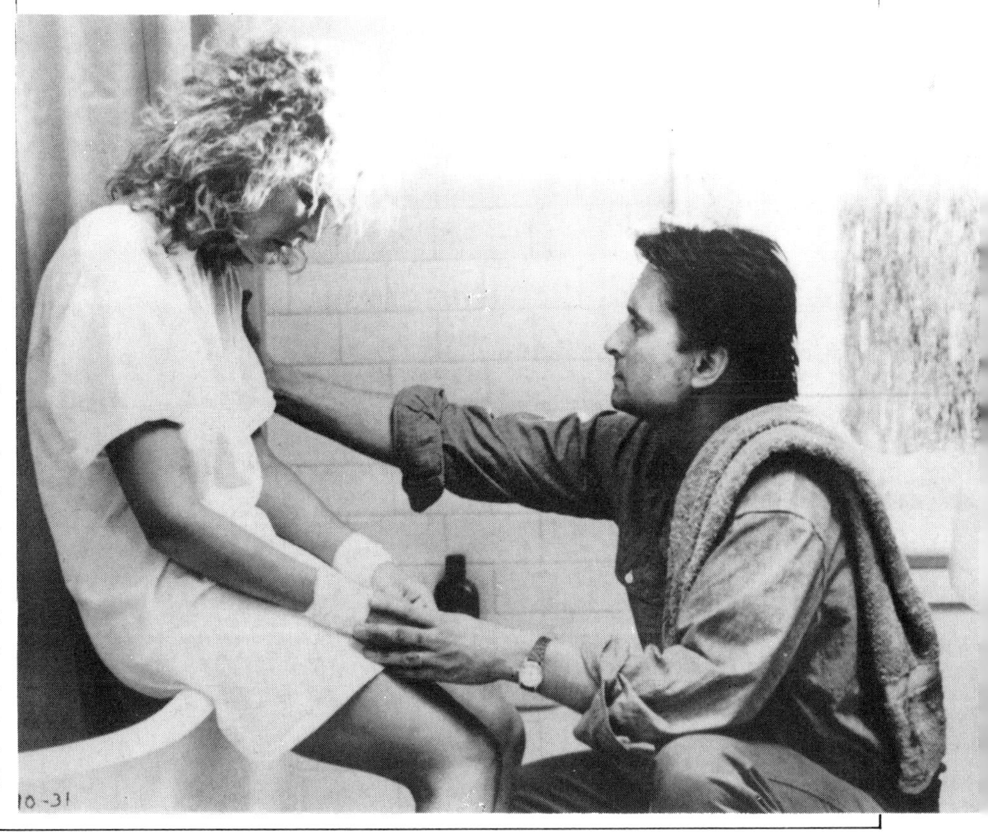

War II. Steven Spielberg's *Empire of the Sun* showed a boy choosing his own survival route over bad examples from British, American and Japanese adults. John Boorman's autobiographical *Hope and Glory* depicted wartime London as the jolliest playground ever. The most interesting of the three, Louis Malle's *Au revoir, les enfants* showed the reality of war intruding on boys' friendship. Bernardo Bertolucci's *The Last Emperor*, about a child-ruler who never grew up until Communist re-education showed him the true path, was a gorgeous spectacle that dazzled Oscar voters.

Children also starred in Hollywood's three movies that hoped to exploit Reagan's gestures towards accommodation with the Soviets. *Superman IV* took off from the Samantha Smith letter to Andropov to show the Man of Steel intervening in the Cold War. *Russkies* was a simple-minded kiddie adventure on the model of *The Russians Are Coming, The Russians Are Coming. Amazing Grace and Chuck* (*Silent Voice* in the UK) was too sweet a depiction of the implausible: athletes strike for peace. Damn the children! Full speed ahead for the Cold War in many other movies: *Red Heat, Little Nikita, Judgement in Berlin, The Living Daylights, No Way Out* and *Rambo III*.

OVERGROWN TEENPIX

The trouble with this year's movies starring children was that you couldn't take your children to most of them because they were aimed at adults. For the same reason many of this year's vastly diminished number of teen movies flopped. The Marek Kanievska-directed *Less Than Zero* had style and Robert Downey Jr.'s great performance as a junkie, but it lacked a convincing plot and seemed too moralistic. The similarly themed *Bright Lights, Big City* made the junkie the centre of the movie, but Michael J. Fox, the supposed coke-head, never did get convincingly strung out and the movie died of inanition.

John Hughes, always one step ahead of his teen fans, left the market. His *Planes, Trains and Automobiles* starred grown-ups Steve Martin and John Candy as mismatched travelling companions, while *The Great Outdoors* paired Candy and Dan Aykroyd as equally mismatched holiday-makers. In Hughes' absence, the top teen movie was a total surprise: *Dirty Dancing*. It scored in a vacuum because it unashamedly pushed all the right buttons - an exploitation title, a strong score, a decent amount of sweaty skin, a hypocritical authority figure, an Every-girl lead (Jennifer Grey). Plus, it had the X-factor, Patrick Swayze's sexy dancing. Other teen movies just seemed tired by contrast: *Can't Buy Me Love, Hiding Out, Summer School* and so on. Exceptions were teen movies starring Lou Diamond Phillips: *La Bamba* and *Stand and Deliver*, which drew audiences interested in fifties rock and eighties educational renewal.

Dirty Dancing *(top)*
Bright Lights, Big City *(right)*

Two films pitched at teens, *She's Having a Baby* and *For Keeps*, tried to rub the youthful audience's faces in the facts of life, showing parenthood as the acid test of true love. But teen movie-goers weren't ready to imagine themselves as parents. They preferred, along with the rest of the audience, to imagine parents as children. For this was the year in Hollywood when fathers were apt to become their own sons. *Like Father, Like Son* gave Dudley Moore and teen heart-throb Kirk Cameron equal time in each other's body. *Vice Versa* concentrated on Judge Reinhold's adventures as an eleven-year-old. *Eighteen Again*'s twist was to give George Burns his grandson's body. After all those movies on the theme, it was not just a big surprise but a colossal one that Penny Marshall's *Big* became the most gargantuan hit of the summer of 1988. Somehow Tom Hanks' depiction of pubescence summed up everything that could be said about little boys in men's bodies.

RAISING THE DEAD

A fantasy closely related to Male Maturity Mix-up is the reborn-to-love-again genre, in which romance subverts the usual balance of the celestial and the earthly. Hollywood made four resurrection comedies this year, *Date With an Angel, Made in Heaven, Hello Again* and *Beetlejuice*. All lacked the magic of Wim Wenders' *Wings of Desire*, though *Beetlejuice* did have the year's weirdest comedy performance in Michael Keaton as a semi-decomposed spectre.

TOUGH GIRLS

Hollywood's new inclination to favour softness and sensitivity involved ceding greater independence to movie heroines. Women were at the centre of more films set in the workaday world. Men were more apt to be lunkheads or putty in their hands, or, in the best reversal of all, empty-headed sex objects.

Cher was in control, in *Moonstruck* and *Suspect*, as an accountant and an attorney respectively. In *Moonstruck* it was the man, Nicolas Cage, who was high-strung and flighty, and in *Suspect* it was the woman who coped best with professional and personal stresses. *Baby Boom* cast Diane Keaton as a tigress in business, strong enough to succeed against men even on her own. *Broadcast News* presented the year's most interesting heroine, Holly Hunter, playing a TV producer not afraid to show her emotions but able to master them. Despite being attracted to the body of shallow William Hurt and to the mind of flop-sweaty Albert Brooks, she proved able to resist both temptations.

Glenn Close in Adrian Lyne's *Fatal Attraction* was the year's best villain, a sexually voracious professional unhinged by her biological clock and the need to possess the father of her child. Another New York movie directed by an Englishman, Ridley Scott's *Someone to Watch Over Me*, also offered a triangle in which the man was a puppy dog. Both Michael Douglas in *Fatal Attraction* and Tom Berenger in *Someone* had to be saved by the prompt gunplay of women (Anne Archer and Lorraine Bracco) willing to kill to keep them.

Barbra Streisand strutted and fretted in *Nuts*, another drama about a professional woman (a prostitute in this case) who vanquished every man in sight, even her defender Richard Dreyfuss. Rebecca DeMornay in *And God Created Woman* was a musician who saw men as objects for her to use. Juliette Binoche in *The Unbearable Lightness of Being* was strong enough to bring loverboy Daniel Day-Lewis to heel. Kelly McGillis in *The House on Carroll Street* was a humble magazine researcher who outsmarted an arch-conservative Nazi protector, Mandy Patinkin. Christine Lahti as an eccentric foster mother in *Housekeeping* didn't care what anyone thought of her sloppy ways. Lindsay Crouse in *House of Games* was a hyper-cool psychiatrist, beating con man Joe Mantegna at his own game.

GETTING NOIR

As ever in American movies, the rule remains generally that the better the roles for women, the more serious the movie. Several movies made by directors new to American film-making dabbled in *film noir* styles, but Annabel Jankel and Rocky Morton's *D.O.A.* and Ben Bolt's *The Big Town* paid too little attention to the female linchpin that *noir* requires. *Masquerade*, by American-from-Paris Bob Swaim, profited by making the heretofore virginal Meg Tilly a full-blown sensualist.

Suspect

RICH AND MACHO

The principal exceptions to the proposition that American movies are going soft are Eddie Murphy, Sylvester Stallone and Arnold Schwarzenegger. Their $10 million-plus salaries allow them to select and craft macho subjects that please the hard-core of male movie-goers who don't care what their wives or girlfriends think.

Beverly Hills Cop II was the major hit of the summer of 1987, despite being virtually a carbon copy of its predecessor. Again Eddie Murphy came to town and got his man, confounding the boss of the local police. What Tony Scott's sequel lost in originality and laughs though, it made up for in fast action and gunfire. When Murphy reappeared in movie houses at Christmas, in *Raw*, the only violence was verbal, and the victims were women. The concert film, an extraordinary misogynistic monologue, seemed to express the innermost ideals of Murphy's fans. However, they did follow him to his next offering, *Coming to America*, in which he played a simple prince from Africa who sought an independent-minded American bride.

Sylvester Stallone's long-awaited study of the geo-politics of South-West Asia, *Rambo III*, delivered all the expected rippling musculature and whizzing bullets. If the movie seemed badly timed to those aware that the Soviets began withdrawing from Afghanistan a fortnight before its opening, Rambo fans as usual ignored the reality gap. Curiously, Tri-Star attempted to market the movie as an all-audience phenomenon, with ads showing women saying, 'I believe in self-reliance, being aggressive and expressing anger openly. Kind of like Rambo.' Few females bought that come-on, and the movie seemed also to suffer from being released the same week as another pre-sold sequel, Paul Hogan's *Crocodile Dundee II*. Hogan's movie was considerably more action-oriented than the first *Dundee*, but the violence was muted by humour and cleverness.

Arnold Schwarzenegger, that living comic book figure, made three *übermensch* movies. *Predator* and *The Running Man* placed his awesome body in science-fiction settings. Walter Hill's *Red Heat*, a standard mismatched-buddies cop story, dared to use a contemporary American location and a business suit wardrobe, but made Schwarzenegger a Russian lug who hardly talked except in subtitles.

BACK TO NAM

In the action sphere, Vietnam now looms as a near-genre in itself, following the success of

Platoon. Stanley Kubrick's *Full Metal Jacket* achieved near-greatness. Its hour-long boot-camp sequence, with Lee Ermey as the profanest man in movie history, was a classic paranoid nightmare. The subsequent battle scenes, all too evidently shot in a London gasworks, suffered by comparison. The John Irvin-directed *Hamburger Hill* was straight-ahead action, with no particular point to make, except perhaps that bullets are best avoided. *Off Limits* (*Saigon* in the UK), merely a buddy-buddy cop movie seeking attention for its Saigon setting, starred Willem Dafoe ripping off his own performance in *Platoon*. *Braddock: Missing in Action III* featured Chuck Norris repeating himself again as a vet returning to Vietnam. The most popular re-creation of old Saigon - when will we admit that it's been Ho Chi Minh City for 13 years now? - was Robin Williams as a brass-defying Armed Forces Radio deejay in *Good Morning Vietnam*.

CLEANING THE STREETS

While many cop movies went soft, the strongest out-and-out, men-in-blue, kick-ass movie was Dennis Hopper's nasty and brutish *Colors*. Sean Penn played to his image as a punk with too much power, while Robert Duvall tried to tame him on the mean streets of gangland LA. *Above the Law* introduced smooth-cheeked martial artist Steven Seagal. His contribution to movies was showing the unflamboyant reality of actual hand-to-hand combat - though in *The Presidio* Sean Connery relied again on fantasy, vanquishing a redneck and demolishing a bar with the use of a single well-placed thumb.

Soft cop movies, following the lead of last year's *Lethal Weapon*, gave action heroes a context (another new buzzword) instead of making them lone wolves in the jungle. *Cop* cast James Woods as a borderline psychotic macho lawman who softened when he found himself drawn to feminist Lesley Ann Warren. Woods repeated as a secret softie in *Best Seller*, playing a hitman who ultimately sacrificed himself. *The Big Easy* (one of the year's half-dozen movies to follow market research findings that audiences are attracted to the word 'big') put New Orleans cop Dennis Quaid on the take, then took him off after throwing him in bed with Ellen Barkin. *Stakeout*, the year's most popular cop film, was far more interested in the comic and romantic possibilities in Richard Dreyfuss's voyeuristic

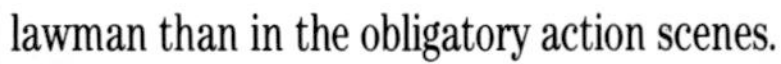
lawman than in the obligatory action scenes.

Even Paul Verhoeven's droll *Robocop*, full as it was of clashing machinery, took time to give mechanized Peter Weller a residual memory of his days as a human. For non-action fans, *Robocop* functioned as social satire, twitting the media and exposing big business as the ultimate villain. Oliver Stone's *Wall Street* and John Sayles' *Matewan* were the year's most heartfelt condemnations of capitalism. In Michael Douglas's characterization, *Wall Street*'s Gordon Gekko was a charismatic villain, nearly convincing Charlie Sheen and the audience that greed is good. *Matewan* triumphed over its earnest intention to show how bad greed is and how ordinary people can combine to fight it. Capitalism survived these thrusts, however, and imperialism lives despite Alex Cox's *Walker*, a would-be black comedy about America's first invasion of Nicaragua, which struck most as a messy trifle.

Frantic

ROLLING DICE

Those who preferred the softer, more adult turn that American movies seem to have taken were also heartened by how unpredictable box-office success has become. It's almost as if audiences are grown-up enough to figure out for themselves what they like. Jack Nicholson couldn't put a foot wrong - and along came *Ironweed*. William Hurt was on top in *Broadcast News*, but *A Time of Destiny* flopped dismally. Bill Cosby is the emperor of TV but on the evidence of *Leonard Part 6* he can't make a watchable movie. Harrison Ford has been in five of the top ten hits of all time, but even he couldn't draw crowds for Roman Polanski's Hitchcock homage *Frantic* (the year's other Hitchcock homage, *Throw Momma From the Train*, found laughs a better route to popularity). Woody Allen issued his tedious, twice-shot *September* and discovered how it feels to be Ciminoed by the critics. Cimino's own *The Sicilian* received the most antagonistic notices in intergalactic history.

IN THE WINGS

In this climate, many big stars sat the year out. Among the great unseen were Robert Redford, Clint Eastwood, Bill Murray, Al Pacino, Jane Fonda, Jessica Lange, Dustin Hoffman and Warren Beatty. All of them were perhaps stunned by the spectacle of the over-exposed and now hardly employable Burt Reynolds, who hasn't made a hit since he had hair.

BART MILLS

THE FILMS

July 1987 – 30 June 1988

Short reviews by Bart Mills, Tim Pulleine, Quentin Falk, David Thompson, James Park, Markus Natten, Harlan Kennedy, Graham Fuller and Anne Billson

ABOVE THE LAW

A grimly efficient action thriller, Andrew Davis's film is chiefly notable for its star, Steven Seagal. He's a martial arts instructor and one-time bodyguard who has never acted before. Rather smoother of face than most cinema roughnecks, Seagal does a lot of standing around with his arms folded, but turns out to know his onions when it comes to crunching criminals. Yes, this is a cop who kills without a gun. The baddies are the CIA again - you'd think they would learn. **BM**

Director *Andrew Davis* ***producer*** *Steven Seagal, Davis* ***exec*** *Robert Solo* ***script*** *Steven Pressfield, Ronald Shusett, Davis* ***camera*** *Robert Steadman* ***editor*** *Michael Brown* ***design*** *Maher Ahmad* ***music*** *David M. Frank* ***cast*** *Steven Seagal, Pam Grier, Henry Silva, Ron Dean, Daniel Faraldo, Sharon Stone, Nicholas Kusenko, Joe V. Greco, Chelcie Ross, Thalamus Rasulala*

Running time: 99 mins

US release: Warner, Apr 8, 1988

ACTION JACKSON

Cars flip, flames leap. People flip and leap in flames out of windows. Ex-stunt director Craig Baxley's movie is not called 'Stand Still Jackson'. Carl Weathers, a former football player who sparred with Sylvester Stallone in three Rocky movies, plays a cop who's too tough for his bosses, let alone Detroit's criminals. Without using his Harvard law degree even once, Action vanquishes industrialist/ drug Czar Craig T. Nelson and saves his girlfriend Vanity from heroin. State-of-the-art stunt work makes the movie a must for fans of lowbrow live-action cartoons. **BM**

Director *Craig R. Baxley* ***producer*** *Joel Silver* ***script*** *Robert Reneau* ***camera*** *Matthew F. Leonetti* ***editor*** *Mark Helfrich* ***design*** *Virginia Randolph* ***music*** *Herbie Hancock, Michael Kamen* ***cast*** *Carl Weathers, Craig T. Nelson, Vanity, Sharon Stone, Thomas F. Wilson, Bill Duke, Robert Dvi, Jack Thibeau, Nicholas Worth, Sonny Landham*

Running time: 118 mins

US release: Lorimar, Feb 12, 1988

UK release: Guild, Jul 1, 1988

ADVENTURES IN BABYSITTING

(Night on the Town in UK)

After a crude slapstick opening, this junior *After Hours* develops considerable charm and excitement. Teenager Elisabeth Shue arrives to take charge of a pair of brats, but following a distress call from her chum downtown, takes on nocturnal Chicago with the kids in tow. One disaster follows another as the ingratiating couple tangle with mobsters, street life and a black jazz club 'where nobody leaves unless they sing the blues.' After the bubble-gum of *Gremlins*, *Goonies* and *Young Sherlock Holmes*, which he wrote only, an auspicious directing début for Chris Columbus. **QF**

Adventures in Babysitting

Director *Chris Columbus* ***producers*** *Debra Hill, Lynda Obst* ***script*** *David Simkins* ***camera*** *Ric Waite* ***editors*** *Fredric Steinkamp, William Steinkamp* ***design*** *Todd Hallowell* ***music*** *Mike Gormley, Seth Kaplan* ***cast*** *Elisabeth Shue, Maia Brewton, Keith Coogan, Anthony Rapp, Calvin Levels, Vincent Phillip D'Onofrio, Penelope Ann Miller, George Newbern, John Ford Noonan, Bradley Whitford, Ron Canada, John Chandler, Dan Ziskie, Allan Aarons, Marcia Bennett, Rummy Bishop, David Blacker, Lolita David*

Running time: 102 mins

US release: BV, Jul 1, 1987

UK release: Warner, Feb 19, 1988

ALOHA SUMMER

Back in 1959, when the very idea of a bikini was just too stimulating, Hawaii was seething with racial disharmony, and distant law-makers were turning the islands into a State. Chris Makepeace came for a vacation with his parents and stayed to surf and make goggle-eyes at the girls. He made some friends, had a few beers, listened to the top tunes of the era and survived a hurricane.

You had to be there, though. Tommy Lee Wallace's film makes beach blanket life seem even direr than sitting through a Sandra Dee festival. **BM**

Director *Tommy Lee Wallace* ***producer*** *Mike Greco* ***exec*** *Warren Chaney* ***script*** *Greco, Bob Benedetto* ***camera*** *Steven Poster* ***editors*** *James Coblentz, Jack Hofstra, Jay Cassidy* ***design*** *Donald Harris* ***music*** *Jesse Frederick, Bennett Salvay* ***cast*** *Chris Makepeace, Yuji Okumoto, Don Michael Paul, Tia Carrere, Sho Kosugi, Lorie Griffin, Blaine Kia, Warren Fabro, Andy Bumatai, Ric Mancini, Scott Nakagawa*

Running time: 97 mins

US release: Spectrafilm, Feb 26, 1988

AMAZING STORIES

This TV fantasy anthology lacks the ingenuity promised by the directors' pedigrees and the superb opening credits. The first of the three episodes, *The Mission*, features World War II pilots Kevin Costner and Kiefer Sutherland engaged in a struggle to rescue a colleague trapped in a turret of their plane. The cumulative suspense orchestrated is nullified by an incredible dénouement. *Mummy Daddy*, Will Dear's parody of the Universal monster cycle is little more than an extended chase involving an actor/expectant father (Harrison), a TV crew and a genuine mummy. It's the most successful segment. The third instalment, *Go to the Head of the Class*, directed by Robert Zemeckis, is a tenuously macabre tale of classroom horror centred on a bitter teacher/pupil relationship. The story is redeemed only by the casting of the excellent Christopher Lloyd as a vindictive school teacher who castigates a boy for continual tardiness. **MN**

Directors *Steven Spielberg, William Dear, Robert Zemeckis* ***producer*** *David E. Vogel* ***exec*** *Steven Spielberg* ***script*** *Menno Meyjes (*The Mission*)*, *Earl Pomerantz (*Go to the Head of the Class*), Mick Garris, Tom McLoughlin, Bob Gale (*Mummy Daddy*)* ***camera*** *John McPherson (*The Mission, Go to the Head of the Class*), Robert Stevens (*Mummy Daddy*)* ***editor*** *Steven Kemper (*The Mission*), Joe Ann Fogle (*Mummy Daddy*), Wendy Greene Bricmont (*Go to the Head of the Class*)* ***design*** *Rick Carter* ***music*** *John Williams* ***cast*** The Mission*: Kevin Costner, Casey Siemaszko, Kiefer Sutherland, Jeffrey Jay Cohen, John Philbin, Gary Mauro, Glen Mauro, Terry Beaver, David Grant,* Mummy Daddy*: Tom Harrison, Bronson Pinchot, Brion James, Tracey Walter, Larry Hankin, Michael Zand, Lucy Lee Flipin,* Go to the Head of the Class*: Christopher Lloyd, Scott Cofffey, Mary Stuart Masterson, Tom Breznahan, Bill Beck*

Running time: 110 mins

UK release: UIP, Oct 9, 1987

AMAZON WOMEN ON THE MOON

This self-referential episodic attack on mass media and American pop culture sacrifices the potency of several good TV commercial satires to diluted parodies of various genres. A myriad of cult performers invest the only sporadically amusing proceedings with a surface gloss of credibility. The real fun (apart from a segment pontificating on whether or not Jack the Ripper's true identity was the Loch Ness Monster) is to watch this on a VCR in the US, then play regular TV and try to spot the difference. There isn't. Much. **MN**

Directors *Joe Dante, Carl Gottlieb, Peter Horton, John Landis, Robert K. Weiss* ***producer*** *Weiss* ***execs*** *Landis, George Folsey Jr.* ***script*** *Michael Barrie, Jim Mulholland* ***camera*** *Daniel Pearl* ***editors*** *Bert Lovitt, Marshall Harvey, Malcolm Campbell* ***design*** *Alex Hajdu* ***cast*** *Rosanna Arquette, Ralph Bellamy, Carrie Fisher, Griffin Dunne, Steve Guttenberg, Sybil Danning, Monique Gabrielle, Kelly Preston, Russ Meyer, Steve Forrest, Joey Travolta, Ed Begley Jr., Henny Youngman, Steve Allen, Paul Bartel, Arsenio Hall, Howard Hesseman, Lou Jacobi, B. B. King*

Running time: 85 mins

US release: Universal, Sep 18, 1987

UK release: UIP, Nov 27, 1988

AN AMERICAN TAIL

More Disney than Disney itself, this pleasing throwback was inspired and produced by Steven Spielberg. What more fitting memorial could there be to Spielberg's ancestors' voyage to America than a feature-length cartoon? Fievel Mousekewitz, immigrant extraordinaire, arrives in New York a century ago with a boatload of mice from many nations. Silly little Fievel! He loses his family and must search for them through streets that he discovers to his sorrow are not after all paved with cheese. **BM**

Director/design *Don Bluth* ***producers*** *Bluth, John Pomeroy, Gary Goldman* ***execs*** *Steven Spielberg, David Kirschner, Kathleen Kennedy, Frank Marshall* ***script*** *Judy Freudberg, Tony Geiss* ***camera*** *David R. Ankney, Joe Juiliano, Karl Bredendieck, Rocky Solotoff, Ralph Migliori, Stan Miller, Marlyn O'Connor* ***music*** *James Horner* ***voices*** *Cathianne Blore, Dom DeLuise, John Finnegan, Phillip Glasser, Amy Green, Madeline Kahn, Pat Musick, Christopher Plummer*

Running time: 80 mins

US release: Universal, Nov 21, 1986

UK release: UIP, Jul 17, 1987

AND GOD CREATED WOMAN

Roger Vadim returns to the scene of the crime, tamely re-making his 1957 shocker. But the brisk and un-sultry Rebecca DeMornay, pretty as she is, will make no one forget Brigitte Bardot. This time the heroine is no tease, just a modern woman with a career - in this case, boringly, rock 'n' roll. As for the story, she begins as a jailbird paroled with the aid of a local politico (Langella) because she convinces a handy carpenter (Spano) to enter into a marriage of convenience. As for sex, she has it whenever the urge strikes, as a more conventional woman might blow her nose, and with as much apparent pleasure. **BM**

Director *Roger Vadim* ***producers*** *George G. Braunstein, Ron Hamady* ***execs*** *Steven Reuther, Mitchell Cannold, Ruth Vitale* ***script*** *R. J. Stewart* ***camera*** *Stephen M. Katz* ***editor*** *Suzanne Pettit* ***design*** *Victor Kempster* ***music*** *Thomas Chase, Steve Rucker* ***cast*** *Rebecca DeMornay, Vincent Spano, Frank Langella, Donovan Leitch, Judith Chapman, Jaime McEnnan, Benjamin Mouton, David Shelley, Einstein Brown, David Lopez*

Running time: 94 mins

US release: Vestron, Mar 4, 1988

Amazing Stories

ANGEL DUST (Poussière d'ange)

French *policier* of a somewhat strenuously offbeat sort, where the plot is complicated enough to defy synopsis but mainly takes a back seat to perverse atmosphere and detail. Sometimes this is rather engaging, as with the put-upon police inspector (Giraudeau) at the centre of the tale being obliged by domestic vicissitudes to sleep in his car, and the director has a good eye for urban landscape (the settings randomly juxtapose locations from several different cities). The final effect, however, tends to be of an unreconciled relationship between generic convention and its subversion. **TP**
Director *Edouard Niermans* ***exec*** *Jacques-Eric Strauss* ***script*** *Jacques Audiard, Alain Le Henry, Niermans, Didier Haudepin* ***camera*** *Bernard Lutic* ***editors*** *Yves Deschamps, Jacques Witta* ***design*** *Dominique Maleret* ***music*** *Léon Senza, Vincent-Marie Bouvot* ***cast*** *Bernard Giraudeau, Fanny Bastien, Fanny Cottençon, Michel Aumont, Jean-Pierre Sentier, Luc Lavandier, Gérard Blain, Yveline Ailhaud, Louis Audubert, James Bakech, Pierre Belot, Patrick Bonnel, Bertie Cortez, Valerie Deronzier, Max Fournel, François Giombini*
Running time: 95 mins
UK release: Palace, Feb 12, 1988

ANGEL HEART

What starts as if it is to be a sub-Chandler murder mystery, with Mickey Rourke as a seedy New York private eye hired to trace a missing person and stumbling over bodies galore as the trail leads down to New Orleans, gradually turns into something altogether more extravagant in the way of a gothic tale, finally landing the hapless dick in Hades itself. For much of the time the picture is enjoyably done after a lurid fashion, with a suavely demonic cameo from Robert De Niro, but the central plot twist

involves a questionable act of deception and Rourke's designer stubble hardly accords with the supposed fifties setting. **TP**
Director/script *Alan Parker* ***producers*** *Alan Marshall, Elliott Kastner* ***execs*** *Mario Kassar, Andrew Vajna* ***camera*** *Michael Seresin* ***editor*** *Gerry Hambling* ***design*** *Brian Morris* ***music*** *Trevor Jones* ***cast*** *Mickey Rourke, Robert De Niro, Lisa Bonet, Charlotte Rampling, Stocker Fontelieu, Brownie McGhee, Michael Higgins, Elizabeth Whitcraft, Elliott Keener, Charles Gordone, Dann Florek, Kathleen Wilhoite, George Buck, Judith Drake, Gerald L. Orange, Peggy Severe*
Running time: 113 mins
US release: Tri-Star, Mar 6, 1987
UK release: CCW, Oct 2, 1987

Angel Dust *(above)*
Angel Heart *(left)*

ANNA

The story of a former Czech movie star reduced to crummy stage auditions in New York turns from bittersweet to plain bitter as she rescues her only fan - a naïve creature with terrible teeth who's come across the ocean to see her - and the ugly duckling becomes a swan at her surrogate mother's expense. Sally Kirkland was Oscar-nominated for her bravura performance as the big, blonde, bruised heroine who sacrifices her self-worth and her boyfriend while her protégée (model Pauline Porizkova) becomes a spoiled brat. *Anna*, however, becomes sillier the longer it goes on, director Yurek Bogayevicz being unable to resist overblown homages to *A Star Is Born* and *All About Eve*. Best bit - writer Agnieszka Holland at her most acerbic - has Kirkland watching one of her old movies in a rep house, only for the celluloid to crinkle up before her eyes. **GF**
Director *Yurek Bogayevicz* ***producers*** *Bogayevicz, Zanne Devine* ***script*** *Agnieszka Holland* ***camera*** *Bobby Bukowski* ***editor*** *Julie Sloane* ***design*** *Lester Cohen* ***cast*** *Sally Kirkland, Robert Fields, Pauline Porizkova, Gibby Brand, John Robert Tillotson, Joe Aufiery, Charles Randall, Mimi Wedell, Larry Pine, Lola Pashalinksi, Stefan Schnabel, Steven Gilborn*
Running time: 95 mins
US release: Vestron, Oct 30, 1987

APPOINTMENT WITH DEATH

Hopefully the final nail in the coffin of Agatha Christie big-screen adaptations. The usual star-packed whodunit but directed without wit, pace or the remotest jot of excitement. Set in 1937 British

Mandate Palestine, it could as easily have taken place in Godalming. Makes the last Agatha Christie entry, *Ordeal by Innocence*, look like *Citizen Kane*. **QF**
Director/producer *Michael Winner* ***execs*** *Menahem Golan, Yoram Globus* ***script*** *Anthony Shaffer, Peter Buckman, Winner, based on novel by Agatha Christie* ***camera*** *David Gurfinkel* ***editor*** *Arnold Crust (Winner)* ***design*** *John Blezard* ***music*** *Pino Donaggio* ***cast*** *Peter Ustinov, Lauren Bacall, Carrie Fisher, John Gielgud, Piper Laurie, Hayley Mills, Jenny Seagrove, David Soul, Nicholas Guest, Valerie Richards, John Terlesky, Amber Bezer, Douglas Sheldon*
Running time: 102 mins
US release: Cannon, Apr 8, 1988
UK release: Cannon, May 26, 1988

APPRENTICE TO MURDER

Donald Sutherland is apt to pop up in anything, anywhere. In R. L. Thomas's movie, shot in Norway with Norwegian money, Sutherland is a witch doctor in small-town Pennsylvania 60 years ago. He practises a sort of faith healing he calls 'pow-wow medicine', involving the kind of devil-defying hexagrams you can see today all over rural Pennsylvania. Sutherland ensnares young Chad Lowe with his apparent unearthly powers. Lovely Mia Sara turns Lowe's head, however, and seeks to take him away from all this. The story, minus the satanic special effects, is true, and the telling, which carefully avoids shots of the fjords, is convincing. **BM**
Director *R.L. Thomas* ***producer*** *Howard K. Grossman* ***exec*** *Michael Jay Rauch* ***script*** *Alan Scott, Wesley Moore* ***camera*** *Kelvin Pike* ***editor*** *Patrick McMahon* ***design*** *Gregory Bolton* ***music*** *Charles Gross* ***cast*** *Donald Sutherland, Chad Lowe, Mia Sara, Knut Husebo, Rutanya Alda, Eddie Jones*
Running time: 94 mins
US release: New World, Feb 5, 1988

Aria

ARIA

Seemingly an attempt to do for opera what promotional videos have done for rock, producer Don Boyd's collection of name directors illustrating their favourite arias results in diminishing returns. Linked (in the UK version) by an irritatingly actorish John Hurt as a fantasy Pagliacci, the disparate collection largely reveals the favourite mannerisms of each *auteur*. Altman's camera flies all over a Hogarthian audience and fails to sustain interest. Godard drolly undresses teenage girls and cuts up Lully; Franc Roddam gives us a glitzy *Liebestod* of lovers apparently dying becuase they are just *too* beautiful. While Julien Temple's Tashlin pastiche would have worked well without Verdi, it is left to sometime opera producer Ken Russell to deliver a coherent, if characteristically OTT, visual fantasy out of Puccini. Just who the film was supposed to appeal to is anyone's guess - judging by the extensive nudity, more dirty raincoats than hat and tails. **DT**
Producer *Don Boyd* ***execs*** *Jim Mervis, Tom Kuhn, Charles Mitchell*
1. Director/script *Nicolas Roeg* ***camera*** *Harvey Harrison* ***editor*** *Tony Lawson* ***design*** *Diana Johnstone* ***music*** Un Ballo in Maschera *by Giuseppe Verdi* ***cast*** *Theresa Russell, Stephanie Lane*
2. Director/script *Charles Sturridge* ***camera*** *Gale Tattersall* ***editor*** *Matthew Longfellow* ***design*** *Andrew McAlpine* ***music*** La Forza del Destino *by Giuseppe Verdi* ***cast*** *Nicola Swain, Jackson Kyle, Marianne McLoughlin*
3. Director/script *Jean-Luc Godard* ***camera*** *Carolyn Champeter* ***design*** *Stephen Altman* ***music*** Armide *by Jean Baptiste Lully* ***cast*** *Marion Peterson, Valerie Allain*
4. Director/script *Julien Temple* ***camera*** *Oliver Stapleton* ***editor*** *Neil Abrahamson* ***design*** *Piers Plowden* ***music*** Rigoletto *by Giuseppe Verdi* ***cast*** *Buck Henry, Beverly D'Angelo, Gary Kasper, Anita Morris, John Hostetter*
5. Director/script *Bruce Beresford* ***camera*** *Dante Spinotti* ***editor*** *Marie Thérèse Boiché* ***design*** *Andrew McAlpine* ***music*** Die Tote Stadt *by Eric Wolfgang Korngold* ***cast*** *Elizabeth Hurley, Peter Birch*
6. Director/script *Robert Altman* ***camera*** *Pierre Mignot* ***editor*** *Jennifer Augé* ***design*** *Scott Bushnell, John Gay* ***music*** Les Boréades *by Jean Philippe Rameau* ***cast*** *Bertrand Bonvoisin, Cris Campion, Anne Canovas, Sandrine Dumas, Jody Guelb, Julie Hagerty, Philipine Leroy-Beaulieu, Geneviève Page, Delphine Rich, Louis-Marie Taillefer*
7. Director/script *Franc Roddam* ***camera*** *Fred Elmes* ***editor*** *Rick Elgood* ***design*** *Matthew Jacobs* ***music*** Tristan und Isolde *by Richard Wagner* ***cast*** *Bridget Fonda, James Mathers*
8. Director/script *Ken Russell* ***camera*** *Gabriel Beristain* ***editor*** *Michael Bradsell* ***design*** *Paul Dufficey* ***music*** Turandot *by Giacomo Puccini* ***cast*** *Linzi Drew*
9. Director/script *Derek Jarman* ***camera*** *Mike Southon, Christopher Hughes* ***editors*** *Peter Cartwright, Angus Cook* ***design*** *Christopher Hobbs* ***music*** Louise *by Gustave Charpentier* ***cast*** *Amy Johnson, Tilda Swinton, Spencer Leigh*
10. Director/script *Bill Bryden* ***camera*** *Gabriel Beristain* ***editor*** *Marie Thérèse Boiché* ***design*** *Rossella Scanagatta* ***music*** I Pagliacci *by Ruggero Leoncavallo* ***cast*** *John Hurt, Sophie Ward*
Running time: 89 mins
US release: Miramax, Mar 4, 1988
UK release: Virgin, Oct 30, 1987

ASTERIX IN BRITAIN: THE MOVIE (Astérix chez les Bretons)

Apparently successful in capturing the charm of the original Goscinny-Uderzo cartoons, *Asterix in Britain's* main joke is that the British are a nation addicted to their afternoon refreshment breaks. But, when tea is substituted for hot water and milk, they find the strength needed to drive away the Roman hordes.
Director *Pino Van Lamsweerde* ***producer*** *Yannick Piel* ***script*** *Pierre Tchernia, based on the cartoon strip by René Goscinny Alberto Uderzo* ***camera*** *Philippe Laine* ***editors*** *Robert Isnardon, Monique Isnardon* ***design*** *Michel Guérin* ***music*** *Vladimir Cosma* ***voices*** *Jack Beaber, Bill Kearns, Graham Bushnell, Herbert Baskind, Jimmy Shuman, Ed Marcus, Sean O'Neil, Gordon Heath*
Running time: 89 mins
UK release: Palace, Mar 25, 1988

AU REVOIR, LES ENFANTS

Restrained, slightly muffled but ultimately moving semi-autobiographical account of Malle's life in a Catholic boarding school during WWII. A Jewish boy fleeing the Gestapo (Fejtö) is initially an object of jealousy to Malle's alter ego (Manesse), but eventually they become friends. Manesse, however, discovers evil when the Jews are betrayed by the lame orphan boy discharged from the kitchens after some black marketeering, and feels guilt at having played an accidental part in betraying his friend. Malle says it's the film he has wanted to make since the beginning of his career. **JP**
Director/producer/script *Louis Malle* ***camera*** *Renato Berta* ***editor*** *Emanuelle Castro* ***design*** *Willy Holt* ***cast*** *Gaspard Manesse, Raphaël Fejtö, Francine Racette, Stanislas Carrée de Malberg, Philippe Morier-Genoud, François Berleand, François Negret, Peter Fitz, Pascal Rivet, Benoit Henriet, Richard Leboeuf, Xavier Legrand*
Running time: 104 mins
US release: Orion Classics, Feb 12, 1988

Barfly

·B·B·B·B·B·B·B·B·B·B·B·B

BABETTE'S FEAST

Film of the Year

Director *Gabriel Axel* ***producer*** *Just Betzer, Bo Christensen* ***exec*** *Claes Kastholm Hansen* ***script*** *Axel, based on story by Isak Dinesen* ***camera*** *Henning Kristiansen* ***editor*** *Finn Henriksen* ***design*** *Sven Wichman* ***music*** *Per Nørgård* ***cast*** *Stéphane Audran, Jean-Philippe Lafont, Gudmar Wivesson, Jarl Kulle, Bibi Andersson, Hanne Stensgaard, Bodil Kjer, Vibeke Hastrup, Birgitte Federspiel, Bendt Rothe, Lisbeth Movin, Preben Lerdorff Rye, Axel Strøbye, Ebbe Rode, Ebba With, Pouel Kern, Erik Petersen, Holger Perfort, Aster Esper Andersen, Else Petersen, Finn Neilsen*
Running time: 103 mins
US release: Orion Classics, Mar 4, 1988
UK release: Artificial Eye, Mar 4, 1988

BABY BOOM

Diane Keaton as a stereotypical yuppie executive whose life suddenly changes when a relative's baby is almost literally dumped on her. The implausibility and exaggeration of the early sequences give way to a more pleasing vein of neo-Capraesque fantasy after the surrogate mother decamps to the countryside and proves that single parenthood can mix with small (if not big) business, especially given the romantic encouragement of an eligible local bachelor like Sam Shepard. There's a nice cameo from Sam Wanamaker as the kind of boss whose iron fist is always apt to peek through his velvet glove. **TP**

Director *Charles Shyer* ***producer*** *Nancy Meyers* ***script*** *Meyers, Shyer* ***camera*** *William A. Fraker* ***editor*** *Lynzee Klingman* ***design*** *Jeffrey Howard* ***music*** *Bill Conti* ***cast*** *Diane Keaton, Harold Ramis, Sam Wanamaker, James Spader, Pat Hingle, Britt Leach, Kristina & Michelle Kennedy, Sam Shepard, Kim Sebastian, Mary Gross, Patricia Estrin, Elizabeth Bennett, Peter Elbling, Shera Danese,*
Running time: 111 mins
US release: UA, Oct 7, 1987
UK release: UIP, Mar 18, 1988

BACK TO THE BEACH

It's hard to imagine who Lyndall Hobbs thought would love her parody of early sixties beach movies like *How to Stuff a Wild Bikini* and *Beach Blanket Bingo* - kids who mercifully are too young to have seen the originals or ancient dodos who remember the old films with fondness. Frankie Avalon and Annette Funicello are together again as Ohio parents who return to the scene - you know, where it's at: Malibu. The oldsters' offspring are as tamely rebellious as they themselves were in days of yore. Kookie Byrnes, Don Adams and the cast of *Leave It to Beaver* walk on, and the audience gasps. Pee-wee Herman does 'Surfin' Bird'. Man, oh, man: at least Bobby Darin isn't around to see this. **BM**

Director *Lyndall Hobbs* ***producer*** *Frank Mancuso Jnr.* ***execs*** *Frankie Avalon, Annette Funicello* ***script*** *Peter Krikes, Steve Meerson, Christopher Komack, based on characters created by Lou Rusoff* ***camera*** *Bruce Surtees* ***editor*** *David Finfer* ***design*** *Michael Helmy* ***music*** *Steve Dorff* ***cast*** *Annette Funicello, Frankie Avalon, Connie Stevens, Lori Loughlin, Tommy Hinkley, Demian Slade, John Calvin, Joe Holland, Pee-wee Herman, Don Adams*
Running time: 92 mins
US release: Paramount, Aug 7, 1987

BAD DREAMS

The popularity of knife movies was one of the most dispiriting trends of the eighties, and developing a critical perspective on that parade of garbage was a real challenge to film writers. Now that the genre is mercifully subsiding back into the cobwebby corners it crawled out of, it's a pleasure to blast writer/director Andrew Fleming's derivative sleaze-pile. A girl (Rubin) spends 13 years in a coma after a mass suicide session commanded by cultist Richard Lynch. She recovers consciousness and Lynch returns into the hallucinations of the others in Rubin's therapy group, whose gory deaths are instigated by another madman, Harris Yulin. **BM**

Director *Andrew Fleming* ***producer*** *Gale Ann Hurd* ***script*** *Fleming, Steven E. de Souza* ***camera*** *Alexander Gruszynski* ***editor*** *Jeff Freeman* ***design*** *Ivo Cristante* ***music*** *Jay Ferguson* ***cast*** *Jennifer Rubin, Bruce Abbott, Richard Lynch, Dean Cameron, Harris Yulin, Susan Barnes, Elizabeth Daily, Sy Richardson, Missy Francis*
Running time: 84 mins
US release: Fox, Apr 8, 1988

BAGDAD CAFE

Percy Adlon goes to America and, following the hilarious and humane spirit of *Zuckerbaby*, shows us more of society's loose ends coming together. A large German lady tourist (the irrepressible Marianne Sägebrecht) is dropped by her husband at a rundown motel and slowly integrates herself, using her magic set, with its tough black owner and her family. Cultural peculiarities are matched by Adlon's playful use of colour, and Jack Palance's unexpected return to the screen is a gentle reminder of how the mythology of the New World is being recast here. **DT**

Director *Percy Adlon* ***producers/script*** *Percy Adlon, Eleonore Adlon* ***camera*** *Bernd Heinl* ***editor*** *Norbert Herzner* ***design*** *Bernt Amadeus Capra, Byrnadette di Santo* ***music*** *Bob Telson* ***cast*** *Marianne Sägebrecht, C.C.H. Pounder, Jack Palance, Christine Kaufman, Monica Calhoun*
Running time: 108 mins
US release: Island, Apr 22, 1988

LA BAMBA

Very traditional Hollywood biopic covering the rise to fame of Richie Valens, the Mexican-born rock star whose eight months of success were cut short when he took a fateful plane ride with Buddy Holly in 1959. Valens is persuasively played by angelic newcomer Lou Diamond Phillips, but since he is characterized as such a good-hearted innocent it is left to his sinful, delinquent brother to provide the sleazy fun. A neat package that is content to be breezily superficial, and sneaks in most of Valens's's hits. **DT**

Director/script *Luis Valdez* ***producers*** *Taylor Hackford, Bill Borden* ***exec*** *Stuart Benjamin* ***camera*** *Adam Greenberg* ***editors*** *Sheldon Kahn, Don Brochu* ***design*** *Vince Cresciman* ***music*** *Carlos Santana, Miles Goodman* ***cast*** *Lou Diamond Phillips, Esai Morales, Rosana De Soto, Elizabeth Peña, Danielle von Zerneck, Joe Pantoliano, Rick Dees, Marshall Crenshaw, Howard Huntsberry, Brian Setzer, Daniel Valdez, Felipe Cantu, Eddie Frias, Mike Moroff, Geoffrey Rivas, Sam Anderson, Maggie Gwinn, Jeffrey Alan Chandler*
Running time: 108 mins
US release: Columbia, Jul 24, 1987
UK release: CCW, Sep 25, 1987

BARFLY

Nearly 100 minutes of drinking, screaming, fighting and more drinking weave a sporadic fascination when two actors like Mickey Rourke and Faye Dunaway visit the lower depths. But even occasional, refreshing blasts of black comedy cannot relieve an overall, unredeeming ugliness tinged uncomfortably with a screwball sort of sentimentality. Certainly Rourke inhabits the role of Henry Chinaski, a thinly disguised version of scriptwriter Charles Bukowski, author-poet and stupendous drunk, as he totters between the neon-lit drinkeries of central Los Angeles. But there remains the nagging concern that here are a couple of stars merely shamming seedy. **QF**

Director *Barbet Schroeder* ***producers*** *Schroeder, Fred Roos, Tom Luddy* ***execs*** *Menahem Golan, Yoram Globus* ***script*** *Charles Bukowski* ***camera*** *Robby Müller* ***editor*** *Eva Gardos* ***design*** *Bob Ziembicki* ***music*** *Jack Baran* ***cast*** *Mickey Rourke, Faye Dunaway, Alice Krige, J.C. Quinn, Frank Stallone, Jack Nance, Sandy Martin, Roberta Bassin, Gloria Leroy, Joe Unger, Harry Cohn, Pruitt Taylor Vince, Joe Rice, Julie 'Sunny' Pearson, Donald L. Norden, Wil Albert, Hal Shafer, Zeek Manners, Pearl Shear, Rick Colitti*
Running time: 100 mins
US release: Cannon, Oct 16, 1987
UK release: Cannon, Mar 4, 1988

BABETTE'S FEAST

A Danish art movie largely concerned with the preparation and consumption of a lavish banquet doesn't, perhaps, sound particularly enticing, especially when one learns that it's directed by a virtual unknown and set, almost throughout, in a remote religious community during the latter half of the last century. To describe Gabriel Axel's *Babette's Feast* in such stark terms conjures up a dismal vision of a would-be Carl Dreyer attempting to render cinematic a Fanny Craddock cookery lesson. But nothing could be further from the truth. This adaptation of a delightfully funny story by Isak Dinesen, better known (especially since *Out of Africa*) as Karen Blixen, is one of the most sensual, warming and witty movies to emerge from Europe in years.

The story, taken from the Dinesen collection *Anecdotes of Destiny*, is rather slim. On the windswept coast of Jutland in the 1870s, two elderly sisters - Filippa and Martine - supervise the spiritual welfare of the similarly aged members of an austere Lutheran community founded by their dear departed father, himself a man of ascetic piety who was deeply suspicious of anything or anybody tainted by the excesses of Papism. Devout and spinsterly, the two women administer to the villagers' physical needs with a mixture of kindness and simple country cooking: gruel, cod and more cod.

But Martine and Filippa, strangely, have a French house-keeper, Babette, and the film not only sets out to explain how this refugee from persecution in Paris came to arrive on the sisters' doorstep one dark and wintry night, but also reveals how the woman - a Communard, a Papist, and most relevantly, a once famous chef - comes to perform her own very special miracle at a supper that will briefly bring radiant grace to the Brotherhood's simple, sparse lives.

Babette's presence in the village is explained by two seemingly irrelevant flashbacks. Years earlier, a dissolute cavalry officer, Lieutenant Löwenhielm, had been sent to stay with his ancient aunt in the Jutland region in the hope that this would improve his manners; the young man had fallen for the beautiful Martine, but, intimidated by her father the Dean's puritanical fervour, had abandoned his courtship and

opted for an ambitious military life. Filippa, too, had attracted an admirer, a year or so later, in the form of a French opera singer, Achille Papin, whose interest in the girl focussed on the pure, golden tones of her singing voice; sadly, his plans for her future career as a diva had foundered on her inherited suspicion of physicality, brought to a head during the rehearsal of a duet from Mozart's *Don Giovanni*, a rehearsal that had ended with a chaste, theatrical kiss. And what have these tales of lost love and self-denial to do with Babette? She was an acquaintance of Monseur Papin, who had sent her to Jutland out of a desire to help both the sisters and the fugitive Communard.

The climax of the film is the feast itself. After serving the sisters for over a decade, obediently restricting herself to the cooking of gruel and cod, Babette wins 10,000 francs in a lottery and asks a single favour of her employers: that to commemorate the hundredth anniversary of the Dean's birth, she might cook a meal, at her own expense, for the Brotherhood. Reluctantly, the sisters agree, although fearing an orgy of exotic and pagan culinary excess; indeed, their suspicions would seem to be confirmed when Babette imports her ingredients - including quails, a turtle, and crates of wine and champagne (none of which the villagers have ever encountered before) - from France. Wary both of upsetting their well-intentioned maid and of giving way to sensual decadence, the sisters extract a promise from all the villagers that not a word about the food shall be uttered during the meal.

The night of the feast: the former Lieutenant Löwenhielm, now a General and a disillusioned man of the world, returns with his aunt to pay tribute to the Dean's piety and to discover if his decision to leave Jutland, so many years ago, was an act of wisdom or folly. He is startled to find that the villagers seem quite accustomed to eating food of the very highest order; while he expresses his unbridled admiration for the turtle-soup, the Veuve Clicquot and the *cailles en sarcophage*, his fellow diners blithely discuss the weather, refusing to notice the grandeur of what is placed before them. At the end of the banquet, however, he is not alone in his discovery of peace of mind, a realization that anything is possible in this strange world; the ancient villagers too are reborn, their hostilities and jealousies swept aside by the tide of fine wine and food. They dance their way home in the snow beneath the stars like innocent children.

The preceding synopsis may seem rather lengthy for such a slim tale, but it is the wealth of detail, nuance and irony that transforms both Dinesen's story and Axel's film into major delights. Indeed, Axel's achievement appears all the greater if one returns to the original source. Rarely has so much been made of so little, with single phrases and sentences expanded into full-blooded scenes. Axel fleshes out five pages of the writer's terse, wry prose account of the dinner into a major set-piece running to nigh on 30 minutes. Of course, much of this sequence is devoted simply to the depiction of the food itself, but Axel also revels in the human reactions to the feast. The General, registering a mixture of bewilderment, nostalgia, and sheer, unabashed enjoyment as he savours the vintage Burgundy or exclaims, with all the hushed surprise of an atheist suddenly witnessing a divine epiphany, *'Blinis Demidoff!'*; an ancient woman smirking quietly to herself as she realizes that red wine is an altogether more uplifting beverage than plain, simple water; two old rivals succumbing to the magic of the moment and dissolving in an explosion of smiles and well-wishing. In the spirit of Dreyer, Axel focuses on faces, the indomitable human souls shining forth from beneath the wrinkles that trace the passing of the years.

But it is Babette, of course, who makes all this possible. This culinary alchemist is played by Stéphane Audran, former wife and regular lead actress for that other noted gourmet, Claude Chabrol. Over how many meals have we seen this epitome of French bourgeois life preside! The choice of actress is impeccable: Audran's gaunt, chic face has hardened, her dark eyes evoke the hardships and pain Babette must have endured through losing her son and husband in the struggle of the Communards; at the same time, however, the actress knows intuitively how to reveal, with a twitch of the mouth or a raised eyebrow, that rare, barely definable blend of detached intellectual consideration and private, sensuous indulgence that accompanies a master chef's subtle tasting of food and drink.

Axel's film also impresses for its starkly beautiful imagery. The order's austerity is mirrored in the landscape of grey-green dunes and pale, bare cottages, in contrast to which the sumptuous feast appears as a miracle, a sublime confirmation of human artistry verging on the divine. In this respect, *Babette's Feast* is entirely different from other celebrated food-movies - *The Discreet Charm of the Bourgeoisie* (in which, of course, Audran also appeared), *La Grande bouffe*, *Tampopo* - in that cooking and eating are equated not with sex and the more fundamental bodily functions but with a cerebral and spiritual capacity. And therein lies the film's greatest achievement. Babette is a wizard, a creator, destined (as one of the sisters finally realizes) to enchant Paradise with the artistry that has been so long neglected in this far-flung spot on the harsh Danish coast; the feast becomes her annunciation, her epiphany, and as well as being a supreme act of self-sacrifice (Babette spends all her lottery winnings on the dinner, thus abandoning her chances of returning to France), it is also the final, triumphant assertion of her worth: like the opera singer who sent her to this strange corner of the world, she feels the need to give of her utmost. Her congregation may be unaware of her true identity - she was once the toast of Paris for her cooking at the Café Anglais - but her effect on their lives is indisputable. Ironically, it is the happiness derived from earthly deeds, from the gratification of the normally deprived body, that returns the lost flock to true love and charity.

All of which may sound horribly portentous. But Axel keeps his metaphysical subtext well below the surface and concentrates on simple human emotions. The film also concerns lost love, missed opportunities, dashed or misplaced ambitions. It is funny, charming and, ultimately, subtly uplifting. In translating the written word into the image, the director blends comedy and drama with an understatement that serves as the subtlest of fragrant seasonings. If you haven't seen *Babette's Feast*, check it out. But be sure to book yourself a table at a good restaurant for after the screening. You'll need it.

GEOFF ANDREW

BATTERIES NOT INCLUDED

The come-on credit of 'Steven Spielberg Presents' has never seemed so devalued as with this pathetic hybrid of *Cocoon* and *Close Encounters*. An unbearable bunch of New York tenement dwellers - dotty veterans, pregnant Hispanic, salt-of-the-earth Black, and caring bearded artists - are threatened with eviction. So Industrial Light and Magic races to the rescue with some lovable hardware from Outer Space. Entire sympathies go out to the property developers. **QF**

Director *Matthew Robbins* ***producer*** *Ronald L. Schwary* ***execs*** *Steven Spielberg, Kathleen Kennedy, Frank Marshall* ***script*** *Brad Bird, Robbins, Brent Maddock, S. S. Wilson, from a story by Mick Garris* ***camera*** *John McPherson* ***editor*** *Cynthia Scheider* ***design*** *Ted Haworth* ***music*** *James Horner* ***cast*** *Hume Cronyn, Jessica Tandy, Frank McRae, Elizabeth Peña, Michael Carmine, Dennis Boutsikaris, Tom Aldredge, Jane Hoffman, John DiSanti, John Pankow, MacIntyre Dixon, Michael Greene, Doris Belack, Wendy Schaal*

Running time: 106 mins
US release: Universal, Dec 18, 1987
UK release: UIP, Mar 25, 1988

BÉATRICE (La Passion Béatrice)

Embittered by constant humiliation in the Hundred Years War and the childhood memory of his mother's infidelity, French warlord François (Donnadieu) wreaks revenge on God by repeatedly raping his daughter Béatrice (Delpy) and pack-hunting his weak son (Tavernier *fils*) beyond his castle walls. But Béatrice's spirit cannot be broken: the conflict between father and daughter embodies the primal struggle between good and evil. The quest for the self is central to Tavernier's *œuvre* and here it finds its most radical expression yet - in an uncompromisingly bleak Shakespearian terrain, to which Bruno De Keyzer's relentless travelling shots bring a baleful lyricism. **GF**

Director *Bertrand Tavernier* ***exec*** *Adolphe Viezzi* ***script*** *Colo Tavernier O'Hagan* ***camera*** *Bruno de Keyzer* ***editor*** *Armand Psenny* ***design*** *Guy-Claude François* ***music*** *Ron Carter, Lili Boulanger* ***cast*** *Bernard-Pierre Donnadieu, Julie Delpy, Nils Tavernier, Monique Chaumette, Robert Dhery, Maxime Leroux, Jean-Claude Adelin*

Running time: 131 mins
US release: Goldwyn, Mar 18, 1988

THE BEEKEEPER

Latter-day road movie with Marcello Mastroianni, blending completely with the Greek surroundings, as an ageing schoolmaster who embarks on a relationship with a much younger woman, but fails either to bridge the generation gap or to obtain a new purchase on his ethical convictions. The absence of humour may sometimes risk making the film an oppressive experience, but the realization is masterly, not just in the characteristic use of long takes but in the capacity to put resolutely real surroundings to heightened expressive use. **TP**

Director *Thodorus Angelopoulos* ***exec*** *Nikos Angelopoulos* ***script*** *Thodorus Angelopoulos, Dimitris Nollas, Tonino Guerra* ***camera*** *Giorgos Arvanitis* ***editor*** *Takis Yannopoulos* ***design*** *Mikes Karapiperis* ***music*** *Eleni Karaindrou* ***cast*** *Marcello Mastroianni, Nadia Mourouzi, Serge Reggiani, Jenny Roussea, Dinos Iliopoulos, Vassia Panagopoulou, Dimitris Poulikakos, Nikos Kouos*

Running time: 122 mins
UK release: Artificial Eye, Jan 8, 1988

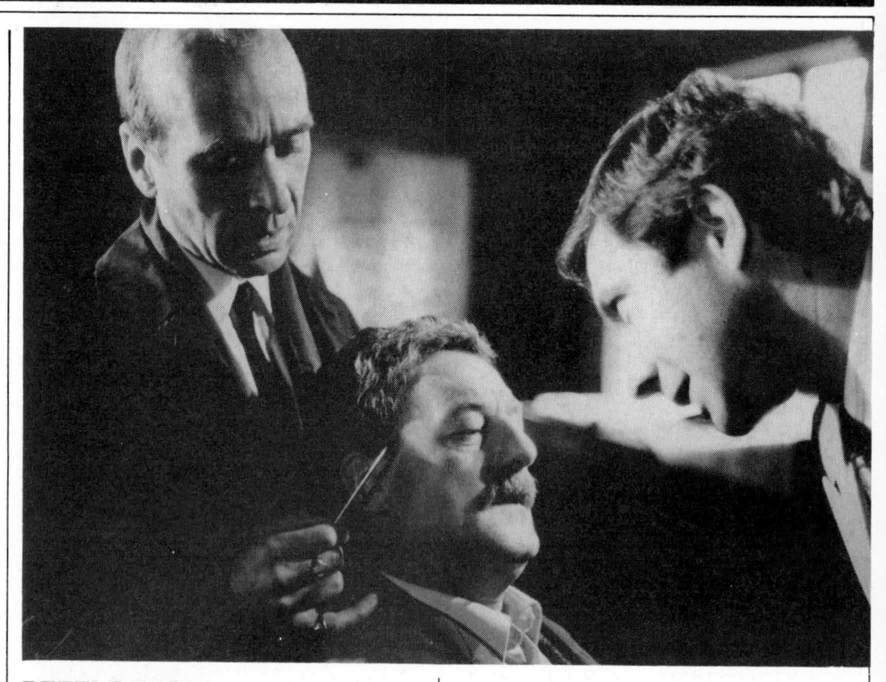

Bellman and True

BEETLEJUICE

Like a two-hour reel of cartoons, *Beetlejuice* has just too much novelty. A comic ghost-story from the ghosts' point of view, Tim Burton's film rivals Joe Dante for hyperactivity and over-plottedness. Alec Baldwin and Geena Davis go off a bridge and into a hellish after-life in which their dream home is occupied by Jeffrey Jones's unsuitable family. Trapped in the house, these ghosts turn out to be ineffective poltergeists. Death's bureaucracy forces them to call in corpse-like, bug-eating freelance bio-exorciser Michael Keaton. He gets big laughs but his role is too small to save the film from bittiness. **BM**

Director *Tim Burton* ***producers*** *Michael Bender, Larry Wilson, Richard Hashimoto* ***script*** *Michael McDowell, Warren Skaaren, Larry Wilson* ***camera*** *Thomas Ackerman* ***editor*** *Jane Kurson* ***design*** *Bo Welch* ***music*** *Dammu Elfman* ***cast*** *Alec Baldwin, Geena Davis, Michael Keaton, Catherine O'Hara, Glenn Shadix, Winona Ryder, Jeffrey Jones, Sylvia Sidney*

Running time: 92 mins
US release: Warner, Mar 30, 1988
UK release: Warner, Aug 12, 1988

THE BELIEVERS

A sad illustration of what can happen when a serious director pitches for the commercial big time. From the opening household accident, when Martin Sheen's wife gets fried, through multiple thunderstorms, power cuts and other such stock effects to the final confrontation between good and evil in a deserted factory, it's obvious John Schlesinger is all wrong for this sort of story. Sheen's a psychologist working for the police department who gets involved in investigating a series of child murders, only to find that his son is being prepared for sacrifice by followers of a voodoo-style religion. **JP**

Director *John Schlesinger* ***producers*** *Schlesinger, Michael Childers, Beverly Camhe* ***exec*** *Edward Teets* ***script*** *Mark Frost from the novel* The Religion *by Nicholas Conde* ***camera*** *Robby Müller* ***editor*** *Peter Honess* ***design*** *Simon Holland* ***music*** *J. Peter Robinson* ***cast*** *Martin Sheen, Helen Shaver, Harley Cross, Robert Loggia, Elizabeth Wilson, Harris Yulin, Lee Richardson, Richard Masur, Carla Pinza, Jimmy Smits*

Running time: 114 mins
US release: Orion, Jun 12, 1983
UK release: Rank, Apr 8, 1988

BELLMAN AND TRUE

Odd mixture of heist thriller and domestic drama with Bernard Hill as computer expert obliged to stir himself out of alcoholic stupor in order both to take care of his deserted young stepson and fend off the attentions of criminals to whom he is in debt. Some well judged performances and apt locations keep things quite watchable, and there is the nostalgic bonus of having the end credits accompanied by dear old Lonnie Donnegan carrolling a suitably offbeat version of 'John Peel', from which ditty the enigmatic title turns out to be a quotation. **TP**

Director *Richard Loncraine* ***producers*** *Michael Waring, Christopher Neame* ***execs*** *George Harrison, Denis O'Brien, John Hambley, Johnny Goodman* ***script*** *Desmond Lowden, Loncraine, Waring, based on the novel by Lowden* ***camera*** *Ken Westbury* ***editor*** *Paul Green* ***design*** *Jon Bunker* ***music*** *Colin Towns* ***cast*** *Bernard Hill, Derek Newark, Richard Hope, Ken Bones, Frances Tomelty, Kieran O'Brien, John Kavanagh, Arthur Whybrow, Jim Dowdall, Peter Howell, Kate McEnery, Anne Carroll*

Running time: 122 mins
US release: Island, Mar 11, 1988
UK release: Recorded Releasing, Apr 15, 1988

THE BELLY OF AN ARCHITECT

Peter Greenaway's games again, this time humanized by Brian Dennehy's impressive central performance. Dennehy arrives in Rome with his newly impregnated wife to direct an exhibition about proto-fascist architect Etienne-Louis Boullée. Dennehy has a growth in his belly, too, a malignant growth of jealousy, professional inadequacy and possibly also cancer. His co-director Caspasian Speckler is stealing his wife and his exhibition, and

Dennehy is becoming more and more obsessed with his belly. Never have a sour face and a flabby abdomen carried so much weight in a serious film. Greenaway's precision and detachment have at times made his films seem too distant, but Dennehy's pain is so real that Greenaway's geometry this time comes to life. **BM**
Director/script *Peter Greenaway* ***producers*** *Colin Callender, Walter Donohue* ***execs*** *Roberto Levi, Claudio Biondi* ***camera*** *Sacha Vierny* ***editor*** *John Wilson* ***design*** *Luciana Vedovelli* ***music*** *Wim Mertens* ***cast*** *Brian Dennehy, Chloe Webb, Lambert Wilson, Sergio Fantoni, Stefania Casini, Vanni Corbellini, Alfredo Varelli, Geoffrey Copleston, Francesco Carnelutti, Marion Mase, Marne Maitland, Claudio Spadaro*
Running time: 118 mins
UK release: Recorded Releasing, Oct 16, 1987

BERNADETTE

Technically well crafted, and with an engaging central performance from the American Sydney Penny as the French peasant girl whose visions led to the foundation of a shrine at Lourdes, *Bernadette* nevertheless remains earthbound. The title character never becomes interesting. Seemingly reluctant to focus on the dilemma facing a young innocent caught up in political issues, the script is diverted into portraits of the locals as they take up positions pro and anti. Rather more reverential than the Hollywood version, *The Song of Bernadette.* **JP**
Director *Jean Delannoy* ***producer*** *Giancarlo Parretti* ***exec*** *Jacques Quintard* ***script*** *Robert Arnaut, Delannoy* ***camera*** *Jean-Bernard Penzer* ***editor*** *Annick Charvein* ***design*** *Alain Paroutaud* ***music*** *Francis Lai* ***cast*** *Sydney Penny, Jean-Marc Bory, Jean-Marie Bernicat, Philippe Brigaud, Claude Buchvald, Bernard Cazassus, O. Alain Christie, François Dalou, Franck David, Roland Lesaffre, Michèle Simmonet, Jean Davy, Bernard Dheran, Arlete Didier, Michel Duchaussoy*
Running time: 119 mins
UK release: Cannon, Apr 15, 1988

BEST SELLER

While there's nothing particularly inspirational about casting Brian Dennehy as a massively honest Los Angeles cop and James Woods as a twitchy, violent psychopath, to then pair them as a kind of perverse buddy-buddy team leads to unpredictable results. Dennehy's a Wambaugh-style writer suffering from creative block and mounting debts. Woods is desperate to pin a former paymaster who's now parading as a public benefactor, and will tell his story. The two guys clearly needed each other. It's a shame that the producers couldn't have trusted to the built-in ingenuity of the script and the charisma of the actors without resorting to some of the most gratuitous violence doled out in recent movie memory. **QF**
Director *John Flynn* ***producer*** *Carter De Haven* ***execs*** *John Daly, Derek Gibson* ***script*** *Larry Cohen* ***camera*** *Fred Murphy* ***editor*** *David Rosenbloom* ***design*** *Gene Rudolf* ***music*** *Jay Ferguson* ***cast*** *James Woods, Brian Dennehy, Victoria Tennant, Allison Balson, Paul Shenar, George Coe, Ann Pitoniak, Mary Carver, Sully Boyar, Kathleen Lloyd, Harold Tyner, E. Brian Dean, Jeffrey Josephson, Edward Blackoff*
Running time: 110 mins (95 mins in UK)
US release: Orion, Sep 25, 1987
UK release: Rank, Nov 27, 1987

BEVERLY HILLS COP II

Detroit cop Eddie Murphy wings into LA again, to bust crime and tickle ribs, though this time there are two mysteries even he cannot solve. One, how do you tell the two cities apart under Tony Scott's golden-glow, TV commercial-style direction? Two, how can a witless script and a comedian on strident auto-pilot pull in $150 million worth of box-office business? The answer must lie either with Paramount's publicity machine or with the old adage that if you keep the gags coming fast enough no one will notice how few of them are any good. **HK**
Director *Tony Scott* ***producers*** *Don Simpson, Jerry Bruckheimer* ***execs*** *Robert D. Wachs, Richard Tienken* ***script*** *Larry Ferguson, Warren Skaaren, based on characters created by Danilo Bach, Daniel Petrie Jr.* ***camera*** *Jeffrey L. Kimball* ***editors*** *Billy Weber, Chris Lebenson, Michael Tronick* ***design*** *Ken Davis* ***music*** *Harold Faltermeyer* ***cast*** *Eddie Murphy, Judge Reinhold, Jürgen Prochnow, Ronny Cox, John Ashton, Brigitte Nielsen, Allen Garfield, Dean Stockwell, Paul Reiser, Gil Hill, Paul Guilfoyle, Robert Ridgley, Brian O'Connor, Alice Adair, Eugene Butler, Glenn Withrow, Stephen Liska, Gilbert Gottfried*
Running time: 102 mins
US release: Paramount, May 20, 1987
UK release: UIP, Oct 9, 1987

BEYOND THERAPY

Durang's delightfully skewed view of New York neurotics at play hits Robert Altman's soft spot for emotional cripples, resulting in one of those movies that you have to love or else you'll leave it. Goldblum is a love-hungry bisexual. Haggerty is his date from the personal column. They seek refuge from each other with shrinks even more demented than they, Jackson and Conti. Beyond therapy lies the will o' the wisp of personal fulfilment, and that's harder to find in Manhattan than a cab that will stop. Wait for the film's last shot, which justifies Altman's having made it entirely in Paris. **BM**
Director *Robert Altman* ***producer*** *Steven M. Haft* ***exec*** *Roger Berlind* ***script*** *Christopher Durang, Altman, based on the play by Durang* ***camera*** *Pierre Mignot* ***editors*** *Steve Dunn, Jennifer Augé* ***design*** *Stephen Altman* ***music*** *Gabriel Yared* ***cast*** *Julie Hagerty, Jeff Goldblum, Glenda Jackson, Tom*

Bernadette *(left)*
Best Seller *(below)*

Conti, Christopher Guest, Geneviève Page, Cris Campion, Sandrine Dumas
Running time: 93 mins
US release: New World, Feb 27, 1987
UK release: Entertainment, Oct 16, 1987

BIG

No, *Big* isn't exactly the same movie as *Like Father, Like Son* or *Vice Versa*, in each of which a father and son switch consciousnesses. *Big* is about a boy who wishes he were big and gets his wish. Waking up the next morning as 30-year-old Tom Hanks, he embarks on a stunning career as a toy industry mogul. He finds love in the person of Elizabeth Perkins, a former steely executive melted by his genuinely boyish charm. Eventually, though, maturity palls and he wishes he were little again. He duly shrinks and Perkins is left with memories of the future. Hollywood didn't make three versions of *Hamlet* this year, so be thankful there are three such stooges as Dudley Moore, Judge Reinhold and Tom Hanks to keep this plot funny. **BM**
Director *Penny Marshall* ***producers*** *James L. Brooks, Robert Greenhut* ***script*** *Gary Ross* ***camera*** *Barry Sonnenfeld* ***editor*** *Barry Malkin* ***design*** *Santo Loquasto* ***music*** *Howard Shore* ***cast*** *Tom Hanks, Elizabeth Perkins, John Heard, Jared Rushton, Robert Loggia, David Moscow*
Running time: 102 mins
US release: Fox, Jun 7, 1988

THE BIG BANG

This feature cartoon by Picha is 80-odd minutes of witless animated porn. Sometime in the future the USSSR, alias the USA merged with the Soviet Union, is at war with the all-female nation of 'Vaginia' (geddit?). Your chortles are invited as the two sides go up at it, and the screen fills up with phallic missiles, flying testicles, exploding buttocks, many-breasted women and other things too humorous to mention. It is all like being cornered in a Moroccan *casbah* by a dirty-postcard seller and not knowing the Arabic for 'Go away'. **HK**
Director *Jean-Marc Picha* ***producer*** *Boris Szulzinger* ***script*** *Picha, Tony Hendra* ***editor*** *Nicole Garnier-Klippel* ***music*** *Roy Budd* ***voices*** *David Lander, Carol Androfsky, Marshall Efron, Alice Playten*
Running time: 77 mins
UK release: Entertainment, Jul 17, 1987

BIG BUSINESS

Good comedians need little more than a novel set-up, and Bette Midler and Lily Tomlin get one in Jim Abrahams' solo début as a director (he previously formed part of the movies' only directing trio with the Zucker brothers). Midler is twins born to rich parents and Tomlin is twins born at the same time in the same hospital to poor parents. One of each pair is switched at birth, so that both mothers think they have non-identical twins. One Midler grows up poor and one rich, and likewise with the two separated Tomlins. All goes well until the mismatched poor pair go to New York to protest the sale of their home town factory by the rich pair. The film starts slow to establish the four leads and their *beaux*, but, once in its stride, it provides plenty of laughs. **BM**
Director *Jim Abrahams* ***producers*** *Steve Tisch, Michael Peyser* ***script*** *Dori Pierson, Marc Rubel* ***camera*** *Dean Cundey* ***editor*** *Harry Keramidas* ***design*** *William Sandell* ***music*** *Lee Holdridge* ***cast*** *Betty Midler, Lily Tomlin, Fred Ward, Edward Herrmann, Michele Placido, Daniel Gerroll, Barry Primus, Michael Gross, Deborah Rush, Nicolas Coster, Patricia Gaul, J.C. Quinn, Norma Macmillan, Joe Grifasi, John Vickery, John Hancock, Mary Gross, Seth Green*
Running time: 97 mins
US release: BV, Jun 10, 1988

THE BIG EASY

Film of the Year

Director *Jim McBride* ***producer*** *Stephen Friedman* ***exec*** *Mort Engelberg* ***script*** *Dan Petrie Jr.* ***camera*** *Alfonso Beato* ***editor*** *Mia Goldman* ***design*** *Jeannine Claudia Oppewall* ***music*** *Brad Fiedel* ***cast*** *Dennis Quaid, Ellen Barkin, Ned Beatty, John Goodman, Ebbe Roe Smith, Lisa Jane Persky, Charles Ludlam, Tom O'Brien, Marc Lawrence, Solomon Burke, Jim Garrison*
Running time: 108 mins
US release: Columbia, Aug 21, 1987
UK release: Recorded Releasing, Sep 4, 1987

THE BIG PARADE

From the director of *Yellow Earth*, Chen Kaige's second film finally emerged with alterations imposed by its very subject, the People's Liberation Army. Nevertheless this drama of conflict and character dealing with 400 volunteers from the Airborne Division in training for the Beijing National Day Parade confirmed Kaige's status as a considerable directing talent. Using the Scope screen to the full, he contrasts static, heat-drenched images on the parade ground with fluent, vibrant movement inside. The final scenes of the parade itself were not Kaige's intention, but the slow-motion massed movement is a remarkably subversive compromise. **DT**
Director *Chen Kaige* ***producer*** *Chen Liguo* ***script*** *Gao Lili* ***camera*** *Zhang Yimou* ***editor*** *Zhou Xinxia* ***design*** *He Qun* ***music*** *Qu Xiasong, Zhao Jiping* ***cast*** *Wang Xueqi, Sun Chun, Lu Lei, Wu Ruofu, Guan Qiang, Kang Hua*
Running time: 103 mins
UK release: ICA Projects, Mar 11, 1988

BIG SHOTS

Strictly for the under-twelves, Robert Mandel's preposterous buddy tale follows two fatherless boys on their journey to racial and inter-generational harmony. Sweet, innocent Ricky Busker grieves when his father dies after their fishing trip and some toughs steal the watch his dad had given him.

The Big Town

Streetwise Darius McCrary, a black boy Busker's own age, befriends him. Together they plot to retrieve the watch and find McCrary's missing father. The boys then share numerous adventures. No, they don't raft down the Mississippi, but they steal a car with a dead body in the trunk and drive 1,000 miles by themselves. **BM**
Director *Robert Mandel* ***producers*** *Joe Medjuck, Michael C. Gross* ***exec*** *Ivan Reitman* ***script*** *Joe Eszterhas* ***camera*** *Miroslav Ondricek* ***editors*** *Bill Anderson, Sheldon Kahn, Dennis Virkler* ***design*** *Bill Malley* ***music*** *Bruce Broughton* ***cast*** *Ricky Busker, Darius McCrary, Robert Joy, Robert Prosky, Jerzy Skolimowski, Paul Winfield*
Running time: 90 mins
US release: Fox, Oct 2, 1987

THE BIG TOWN

A botch from start to finish, *The Big Town* attempts to do for craps what *The Color of Money* did for nine-ball. Somehow, though, cubes lack the high drama of spheres. Matt Dillon is a young 'arm' who hits Chi-town in 1957 and rolls all the right numbers. Diane Lane, the first American star to spend large stretches of a movie lounging in front of the camera wearing a pair of pasties, leads the callow youth astray. Tommy Lee Jones provides the hissable opposition at the dice table. Ben Bolt inherited the director's chair after Harold Becker had already begun shooting and, for whatever reason, the film is riddled with implausibilities and discontinuities. Structural errors include splitting the function of the hero's mentor among four actors. All could have been redeemed if there were a spark of chemistry between Dillon and Lane, but she remains snake eyes to his boxcars. **BM**
Director *Ben Bolt* ***producer*** *Martin Ransohoff* ***exec*** *Gene Craft* ***script*** *Robert Roy Pool, based on the novel* The Arm *by Clark Howard* ***camera*** *Ralph D. Bode* ***editor*** *Stuart Pappe* ***design*** *Bill Kenney* ***music*** *Michael Melvoin* ***cast*** *Matt Dillon, Diane Lane, Tommy Lee Jones, Bruce Dern, Lee Grant, Tom Skerritt, Suzy Amis, David Marshall Grant*
Running time: 109 mins
US release: Columbia, Sep 25, 1987
UK release: Rank, Sep 4, 1987

BIGFOOT AND THE HENDERSONS

(Harry and the Hendersons in US)
Following *E.T.*, untold numbers of American features have centred on an appealing alien who charms a houseful of average suburbanites and survives to return to his native land. The trouble is, none of these follow-ons has been directed by a master like Steven Spielberg. *Bigfoot and the Hendersons* places the legendary North Woods monster Bigfoot in a household headed by gun-nut John Lithgow. Bigfoot galumphs through the movie growing more and more lovable, and for those who stick it out to the end, the inevitable tearful parting scene is affecting. **BM**
Director *William Dear* ***producers*** *Richard Vane, Dear* ***script*** *Dear, William E. Martin, Ezra D. Rappaport* ***camera*** *Allen Daviau* ***editor*** *Donn Cambern* ***design*** *James Bissell* ***music*** *Bruce Broughton* ***cast*** *John Lithgow, Melinda Dillon, Margaret Langrick, Joshua Rudoy, Kevin Peter Hall, David Suchet, Lainie Kazan, Don Ameche, M. Emmet Walsh*
Running time: 111 mins
US release: Universal, Jun 5, 1987
UK release: UIP, Dec 11, 1987

THE BIG EASY

In the opening few minutes of *The Big Easy* the camera skims over the Louisiana bayous and into New Orleans, backed by a foot-tapping tune, and comes to rest on a body lying in the fountain of the Piazza D'Italia. Lt. Remy McSwain (Dennis Quaid) arrives at the scene, his car radio pulsing to the Cajun music. The deejay reveals that it is 2 a.m. in New Orleans (pronounced N'Awlians by the locals) or The Big Easy as it is known.

The basic story of *The Big Easy*, that of corruption in the police department, is familiar. But the movie has so many stand-outs, whether in the acting, direction, script or music departments, that it sets itself apart from others of the genre.

The film came out at a time when film-makers seemed to have latched onto New Orleans as a prime location spot, with the likes of *No Mercy, Angel Heart, Down by Law* and *Avenging Force* all set there. But apart from its opening scene in the Piazza (hardly a typical New Orleans venue) director Jim McBride makes no obvious attempt to exploit such New Orleans elements as the white-washed verandas or Mardi Gras revels. Rather, his film has an underlying realism that, while it puts story above setting, melds into a tale that is *of* the South.

Alongside an excellent supporting cast, the film will also be remembered as having pushed both Dennis Quaid and Ellen Barkin securely into the 'star' bracket. Their pairing gives the film a screwball comedy atmosphere, and, until the obligatory explosive climax, the movie rests on a snappy battle-of-the-sexes routine that is abrasive, erotic and funny.

The Big Easy was not a great success on either side of the Atlantic. Maybe people just didn't know what to make of what appeared to be a routine cop thriller, with no topline names, but with a quirky quality that set it aside from other movies in the genre.

The film is also distinguished by its soundtrack. A moody score by Brad Fiedel is complemented by a host of Cajun tunes, including one penned and performed by Dennis Quaid himself. Evocative songs by the likes of Buckwheat Zydeco, Professor Longhair, Terrance Simien Zachary Richard and the Mallet Playboys should convert anyone still unaware of Cajun music.

The music is just one part of the film's rich texture, of which an important part is also played by the creole cooking, the peculiar French-orientated patois and even Dennis Quaid's toy 'Gator'. As Lt. Remy McSwain keeps reminding Anne Osborne (Barkin), 'folk have a different way of doing things down here' (in New Orleans). He takes her to Tipitina's restaurant, plans to romance her at a Neville Brothers concert, and generally tries to let her know that New Orleans is a sassy town with a character like no other.

At the first meeting of Quaid and Barkin - a D.A.'s officer on the trail of police corruption - she speaks lawyer-talk, forcing him to reach for a dictionary to find out what 'obstreperous' means. He annoys her with his mildly corrupt behaviour, like jumping a queue into a restaurant.

But, as in all good screwball movies, opposites attract. Despite the fact that he's essentially corrupt, she can't help being drawn to the charming homicide detective with an easy smile. The inevitable sex scene arrives and we are treated to a steamy grapple, interrupted by the bleeper which summons Quaid to yet another murder.

True love gets another hold-up when Quaid is caught taking a bribe and ends up being prosecuted by Barkin. The courtroom confrontation is played for laughs, which are helped along by Charles Ludlam's wonderful performance as Quaid's defence attorney. He plays the part with his eyes rolling.

Quaid manages to get the case abandoned by having a powerful magnet placed in the police storeroom next to a videotape of him accepting the bribe. The magnet erases the tape and a fuming Barkin has to admit there is no more evidence to be brought against Quaid.

At that point the film's tone begins to turn. Barkin won't have anything more to do with Quaid, but, when another killing provides evidence that a supposed Mafia drugs-war can be put down to corrupt policemen, he agrees to help her. His transition to honest cop comes a little suddenly (that's the power of love for you), but the screenwriters throw in the shooting of Quaid's brother, just to make sure he will head down the right plot path.

The actual climax is nothing special; millions of dollars-worth of cocaine is stashed in a boat moored at the police docks. The two bad guys die in the gunfight, and Quaid and Barkin escape just before the boat explodes - basically an ordinary wham-bang climax. Over the end credits Quaid and Barkin return to their love-nest with the confetti still in their hair - the typical happy ending.

But that tweeness doesn't really matter. It can't take away the fact that *The Big Easy* is a film of substance.

Director Jim McBride - whose last film was the underrated Richard Gere starrer *Breathless* - uses the local colour expertly, and, with the help of cinematographer Alfonso Beato, gives the film a rich, deep colour quality which never looks tacky. As with Richard Gere's character in *Breathless*, Quaid is always sharp, though the actor's personal charm and easy smile make Remy McSwain easier to like than Gere's frenetic thief.

In the supporting cast, the ever-fine Ned Beatty reprises another of his Southern sheriff roles, while John Goodman and Ebbe Roe Smith are constantly amusing as the bad cops. Lisa Jane Persky as Detective McCabe has a female role that is strong and witty. Offbeat casting also includes singer-preacher Solomon Burke as voodoo priest/black mobster Daddy Mention, and one-time Kennedy assassination conspiracy theorist Jim Garrison as Judge Noland.

The Big Easy is one of those films where all the combinations work. And if you're so perverse you don't like the acting, the story, or the direction, there's still the wonderful Cajun music.

MARK ADAMS

BILOXI BLUES

Number two in Neil Simon's autobiographical play trilogy reaches the screen. Under Mike Nichols' direction, this one is 'opened up' more than was *Brighton Beach Memoirs*, but its tale of cadet-training days in Boot Camp still seems all mouth and little movement, with lots of dim mirth and rites-of-passage moralizing. Matthew Broderick is the Neil Simon alter ego, negotiating ethnic tensions, japes in the dorm and the hurdles of a stagey script; but Christopher Walken steals the film as a flaky psycho of a Sergeant. **HK**
Director *Mike Nichols* ***producer*** *Ray Stark* ***execs*** *Joseph M. Carraciolo, Mary-kay Powell* ***script*** *Neil Simon, based on his play* ***camera*** *Bill Butler* ***editor*** *Sam O'Steen* ***design*** *Paul Sylbert* ***music*** *Georges Delerue* ***cast*** *Matthew Broderick, Christopher Walken, Matt Mulhern, Corey Parker, Markus Flanagan, Casey Siemaszko*
Running time: 106 mins
US release: Universal, Mar 25, 1988
UK release: UIP, Sep 9, 1988

THE BLACK CANNON INCIDENT

Chinese satire aimed at ideological intransigence and bureaucratic incompetence. Based around an enquiry into an engineer (Zifeng) who had been involved in negotiations with a German for the purchase of plant.
Director *Huang Jianxin* ***production*** *Xi'an Film Studio* ***execs*** *Wu Tianming, Manfred Durniok* ***script*** *Li Wei, based on the short story* Langman de Heipao *by Zhang Xianliang* ***camera*** *Wang Xinsheng, Feng Wei* ***editor*** *Chen Dali* ***design*** *Liu Yichuan* ***music*** *Zhu Shirui* ***cast*** *Liu Zifeng, Gerhard Olschewski, Gao Ming, Wang Yi, Yang Yazhou, Ge Hui, Zhao Xiuling, Wang Beilong*
Running time: 99 mins
UK release: ICA, Sep 25, 1987

BLACK WIDOW

Rafelson's determinedly old-fashioned thriller has Russell as the murderous, mantis-like *femme fatale* of the title, working her way through a series of wealthy husbands until crime investigator Winger discovers a common denominator behind the several, apparently unrelated killings. Cue for psychological power-games and puzzles, as Winger, fascinated by her prey, delves deep behind Russell's disguise to uncover a distorting mirror-image of herself. Despite a teasing script and solid acting, Rafelson never really delivers the goods with this knowing update of the classic forties *film noir* format: too slow and arty to be suspenseful, too schematically stereotyped to be revealing, it is also betrayed by a performance of immense inanity by Sami Frey as Russell's final millionaire victim. **GA**
Director *Bob Rafelson* ***producer*** *Harold Schneider* ***exec*** *Laurence Mark* ***script*** *Ronald Bass* ***camera*** *Conrad L. Hall* ***editor*** *John Bloom* ***design*** *Gene Callahan* ***music*** *Michael Small* ***cast*** *Debra Winger, Theresa Russell, Sami Frey, Dennis Hopper, Nicol Williamson, Terry O'Quinn, Lois Smith, D.W.Moffett, Leo Rossi, Mary Woronov, Rutanya Alda, James Hong, Diane Ladd*
Running time: 103 mins
US release: Fox, Feb 6, 1987
UK release: UKFD, Jul 24, 1987

Black Widow

BLIND DATE

Blake Edwards, no Martin Scorsese, takes the set-up of *After Hours* (a guy's worst night with a girl) and plays it for slapstick instead of dread. Basinger has a drinking problem - one drink and she's a problem. As Willis's blind date, she goes through every routine in Hollywood's long history of abusing bad drunk jokes. Basinger is blessed with no comic instincts, and it's painful to see her try and fail to extend her range beyond the blankly beautiful. As the schnook, Willis plays against his TV chutzpah shtick. Most of the film's gags were old in Hal Roach's day. No one misses Peter Sellers more than that old joke-thief Blake Edwards.
Director *Blake Edwards* ***producer*** *Tony Adams* ***execs*** *Gary Hendler, Jonathan D. Krane* ***script*** *Dale Launer* ***camera*** *Harry Stradling* ***editor*** *Robert Pergament* ***design*** *Rodger Maus* ***music*** *Henry Mancini* ***cast*** *Kim Basinger, Bruce Willis, John Larroquette, William Daniels, Phil Hartman, Stephanie Faracy, Alice Hirson, Graham Stark, Joyce Van Patten, Jeannie Elias, Sacerdo Tanney, Georgann Johnson, Sab Shimono, Momo Yashima, Armin Shimerman*
Running time: 93 mins
US release: Tri-Star, Mar 27, 1987
UK release: CCW, Aug 14, 1987

BLISS

Bizarre satirical comedy in which a four-square advertising executive drops dead, only to return to life with radically altered perceptions about his way of living and his unlikeable wife and adult children. Script and direction evince initial energy but invention progressively dries up to expose some dated sixties attitudes, typified by allusions to cancer as a metaphor for almost any of the world's ills and capped by the intrusion of the neo-hippy who becomes the reincarnated hero's soul-mate. **TP**

Director Ray Lawrence *producer* Anthony Buckley *script* Lawrence, Peter Carey, based on the novel by Carey *camera* Paul Murphy *editor* Wayne Le Clos *design* Owen Paterson *music* Peter Best *cast* Barry Otto, Lynette Curran, Helen Jones, Gia Carides, Miles Buchanan, Jeff Truman, Tim Robertson, Bryan Marshall, Jon Ewing, Kerry Walker, Paul Chubb, Sara De Teliga, Saski Post, George Whaley, Robert Menzies
Running time: 112 mins
UK release: Entertainment, Oct 30, 1987

BLUE IGUANA

Blue as in *noir*. Writer/director John Lafia's entertaining début borrows styles from all over, principally hard-boiled forties movies but also spaghetti Westerns. It even borrows from other tongue-in-cheek *neo-noirs*. Dylan McDermott is a bounty hunter sent south of the border by a neck brace-wearing Dean Stockwell to rescue some millions from a faulty money laundry run by preening banker Jessica Harper. There is a gunsel, a Mr Big, a brassy Dietrich-ish club owner and a few good lines like 'I used to have so many friends I didn't have to see anyone twice.' **BM**
Director/script John Lafia ***producers*** Steven Golin, Sigurjon Sighvatsson ***execs*** Michael Kuhn, Nigel Sinclair ***camera*** Rodolfo Sanchez ***editor*** Scott Chestnut ***design*** Cynthia Sowder ***music*** Ethan James ***cast*** Dylan McDermott, Jessica Harper, James Russo, Pamela Gidley, Tovah Feldshuh, Dean Stockwell, Katia Schkolnik, Flea, Yano Anaya, Michele Seipp, Don Pedro Colley
Running time: 90 mins
US release: Paramount, Apr 22, 1988

BORN IN EAST L.A.

Cheech Marin had a modest success a few years ago with a novelty song parodying Bruce Springsteen's 'Born in the USA'. His video for the song turned out to be the outline of this film, writer/director Marin's first without former partner Tommy Chong. Marin plays a native-born Californian whose life in the Hispanic section of Los Angeles is interrupted by an Immigration Service raid. Mistakenly deported to Tijuana, Marin scuffles to survive and return despite the considerable handicap of not speaking Spanish. Some of the film's scenes might make good videos, but the whole thing is a long sit. **BM**
Director/script Richard (Cheech) Marin ***producer*** Peter Macgregor-Scott ***exec*** Stan Coleman ***camera*** Alex Phillips ***editor*** Don Brochu ***design*** J. Rae Fox ***music*** Lee Holdridge ***cast*** Cheech Marin, Paul Rodriguez, Daniel Stern, Kamal Lopez, Jan-Michael Vincent, Neith Hunter, Alma Martinez, Tony Plana
Running time: 84 mins
US release: Universal, Aug 21, 1987

BOY MEETS GIRL

A shoe-string-budget first feature, made in 1984 when its director was only 22, this tale of romantic despair mixes a jagged edge of contemporaneity with something altogether more old-fashioned by way of not merely evoking the French cinema's long-running preoccupation with star-crossed young lovers but more specifically sounding echoes of early Godard - narrative dislocation, absurdist asides et al. The monochrome evocation of nocturnal Paris is affecting; and though the film outstays its welcome, it does fitfully communicate a real response to the medium. **TP**
Director/script Léos Carax ***producer*** Patricia Moraz ***exec*** Alain Dahan ***camera*** Jean-Yves Escoffier ***editor*** Nelly Meunier, Francine Sandberg ***design*** Serge Marzolff, Jean Bauer ***music*** Jacques Pinault ***cast*** Denis Lavant, Mireille Perrier, Carroll Brooks, Elie Poicard, Maïté Nahyr, Christian Cloarec, Lorraine Berger, Marc Desclozeaux, Anna Baldaccini, Evelyne Schmitt
Running time: 104 mins
UK release: Other Cinema, Jul 10, 1987

Boy Meets Girl

BRADDOCK: MISSING IN ACTION III

Chuck Norris's fans detect something, some earthbound unpretentiousness that in their eyes turns his stolid inexpressiveness into heroic magic. Norris is back again now as Braddock, the Vietnam vet with the wounded psyche and undemobbed trigger finger. Norris co-wrote and had his brother Aaron direct this story of Braddock's return to rescue his Vietnamese wife, whom he had thought dead, and their child, of whose existence he hadn't known until the need for another sequel arose. For good measure, Mad Braddock also brings back some 60 orphans from a Communist hell. **BM**
Director Aaron Norris ***producers*** Menahem Golan, Yoram Globus ***script*** James Bruner, Norris, based on characters created by Arthur Silver, Larry Levinson, Steve Bing ***camera*** Joao Fernandes ***editor*** Michael J. Duthie ***design*** Ladislav Wilheim ***music*** Jay Chattaway ***cast*** Chuck Norris, Aki Aleong, Roland Harrah 3d, Miki Kim, Yehuda Efroni, Ron Barker
Running time: 103 mins
US release: Cannon, Jan 22, 1988

BRIGHT LIGHTS, BIG CITY

Director James Bridges brings warmth and generosity but little personality to this vehicle for Michael J. Fox, faithfully adapted by Jay McInerney from his own Salingeresque novel. Fox plays the young fact-checker at an eminent Manhattan magazine (i.e. *The New Yorker*), whose night-time pursuits - clubs, coke, booze (with Kiefer Sutherland brilliant as the devil's advocate) - cost him his job and push him ever closer to the edge. He overdoes it a bit in one piece of Method madness with a bottle, but it's a thoroughly likeable performance, nicely supported by Swoosie Kurtz as his sympathetic colleague, Jason Robards Jr. as the office drunk, Phoebe Cates as his brattish ex-wife, Dianne Wiest as the mother whose cancer death explains his own disintegration and Tracy Pollan as the girl at the end of the rainbow. **GF**
Director James Bridges ***producers*** Mark Rosenberg, Sydney Pollack ***script*** Jay McInerney, based on his novel ***camera*** Gordon Willis ***editor*** John Bloom ***design*** Santo Loquasto ***music*** Donald Fagen ***cast*** Michael J. Fox, Kiefer Sutherland, Phoebe Cates, Swoosie Kurtz, Frances Sternhagen, Tracy Pollan, John Houseman, Charlie Schlatter, Jason Robards Jr., David Warrilow, Dianne Wiest, Alec Mapa, William Hickey
Running time: 110 mins
US release: UA, Apr 1, 1988
UK release: UIP, Jun 10, 1988

BROADCAST NEWS
Film of the Year

Director/producer/script James L. Brooks ***exec*** Polly Platt ***camera*** Michael Ballhaus ***editor*** Richard Marks ***design*** Charles Rosen ***music*** Bill Conti ***cast*** William Hurt, Albert Brooks, Holly Hunter, Jack Nicholson, Robert Prosky, Lois Chiles, Joan Cusack, Peter Hackes, Christian Clemenson, Robert Katims, Ed Wheeler
Running time: 132 mins
US release: Fox, Dec 16, 1987
UK release: Fox, Apr 8, 1988

BROADCAST NEWS

There are not many new and lasting screen characters to fuel any sequel to David Thomson's book *Suspects*. We know the stars: or at least think we do. The roles, less so; apart from Rambo and Rocky repeaters. Try it ... ! What was William Hurt's name in *Altered States*? Who was Kelly McGillis in *Witness*, or Tom Cruise in *Top Gun* ...?

Thank heavens for James L. Brooks. Having locked us into Aurora Greenway, Emmy Horton and Garrett Breedlove in 1983, he's done it again with *Broadcast News*. Creating not merely lasting, pithy dialogue ('I'm beginning to repel people I'm trying to seduce') but memorable human beings in Tom Grunick, Jane Craig and Aaron Altman. Despite being played by one star, one slightly familiar face and a crackerjack newcomer, they remain Tom, Jane and Aaron.

Curiously enough, despite their deliberately unresolved love story, it is the mechanics of their jobs that rest in the mind, like their names. You just don't expect a person's job to be memorable - not in a Hollywood film. Not unless he, she or it is a private eye, space jockey, robot or Barney, the *Mission Impossible* engineer.

Brooks's second movie is my film of the year for another reason. Quite simply, it is the first film I've seen since - well, 1983 - where, even after 132 minutes, I could have done with another half hour. (So, of course, could Brooks: In order to finish with more of a bang than a whimper.) You're not able to feel that way about films any more, most movies being more greatly flashed, than fleshed, out to a ritual two hours, in order to assist future TV schedules.

With his big black beard, Jim Brooks was once described as Mephistopheles playing a stand-up comic. His comedy is more subtle than that; more so than the fast crumbling Woody Allen. But then Woody tests his films, clinically, in the cutting room - and then he re-shoots. Brooks is a great believer in testing his at sneak previews. 'There's no kidding yourself when they're not laughing.'

In fact, Jim Brooks could be said to be the man who forged the return of adult cinema. Or, at least, the return of adults to the cinema in America. All part of the plan when releasing *Terms of Endearment* in 1983: 'I hope it will make Them listen more to somebody with a passion to make a particular picture, instead of just the demographics.'

'Don't get me wrong,' he said. 'I love people who write for children, but the way they do it is not healthy. They're always thinking of short-cuts to making the kind of film people want to see. Getting 15 year olds into a room - do you like this, do you like that? - and making decisions on what film to make on the basis of it. That scares me! And it doesn't work. How do you get up in the morning and try and think like a 15 year old? The answer is to do the film you really want to do and just try to be good at it.'

With his background in television - from CBS News copy boy and radio news writer to 16 award-winning years of creating the brightest TV comedies, including two set in newsrooms, *The Mary Tyler Moore Show* and *Lou Grant* - the subject of his second movie should have seemed an obvious one for Jim Brooks. He might have written it before adapting Larry McMurtry's *Endearment* for the screen. Not so.

TV news was the last thing on his fertile mind after winning three of the five *Endearment* Oscars. (One wonders if TV news is really on

anyone's mind in America.) Back then, he was sure of one thing only - no *Terms of Endearment II*. If he could unearth the right book or play, he had considered slipping his winner into a vice-versa mode - and exploring a father-son relationship. But he left that to Oliver Stone, who does it each time he comes to bat.

Brooks knows nothing of such relationships - beyond his love of *Death of a Salesman*. Once his mother announced she was expecting, his father left New York and simply sent a postcard home: 'If it's a boy, name him Jim.'

And yet Brooks writes relationships best. 'I just feel a real hunger for that.' And watching the TV newshounds at work and play during the 1984 Democratic Convention in San Francisco was the genesis of Jane, Aaron and Tom.

Things having changed greatly since his day. Brooks researched TV news fully at all three major US networks, selected his all-important triangle - two to one in favour of grits over glitz - and got to work. On the characters more than their continually controversial domain. The newsroom remained his (energetic) backcloth. It could as well have been big business, science, education, politics.

Hence the film is in no way as trenchant - nor livid - an expose of TV as Paddy Chayefsky's *Network*. This could explain its lack of Oscars: it didn't hit the enemy hard enough! But Brooks gets in his chief concerns - and his barbs - as we watch the rise of an ingratiating sportscaster in the ratings-dictated TV news world. This is Tom Grunick, loved and hated by Jane, his producer, and Aaron, his rival - for both job and gal.

Casting was the usual headache. Even after sweating out the script for three years, Brooks swears he would never have made the movie if he hadn't been able to land William Hurt's WASP-ish charisma for Tom. Finding Jane took most time, but he always had a promised cameo from Nicholson, and in from the start as Aaron had been Albert Brooks - a close pal, not kin. There are, in fact, five Hollywood directors named Brooks and they're all unrelated: Bob, Jim, Joe, Mel, Richard. Albert has been known to make it six. He gave James Brooks a role in his latest movie, *Modern Romance*.

And the casting was endearing. William Hurt superbly captures Grunick's slow wits, always one beat behind everything until he's on camera. Then, he's a wiz. Smart, too, in his way: charisma over brain power, flash over substance. Holly Hunter, making Tom a star with her urgent orders in his earpiece during a News special, adores his looks, despises his lack of professionalism. Journalistic professionalism, that is, for he's a perfect TV pro, from the way he sits on his jacket to make sure his collar is seen, sheds a tear on camera and looks good enough to eat. Albert Brooks, suddenly joining in a Francis Cabrel song in perfect French, is the expert Aaron. He has everything but the cool it takes to be an anchor - sweating more profusely than Nixon. Naturally, he couldn't stand Tom's handsome devil, and felt he might even be Satan ...

'What do you think the devil is going to look like if he's around?' he asks Jane, as Brooks warns America. 'He'll be attractive and he'll be nice and helpful and he'll get a job where he influences a great God-fearing nation and ... he will just, bit by bit, lower standards where they are important ... And he will talk about all of us really being salesmen. And he'll get all the great women.'

If Oliver Stone keeps putting both sides of the paternal coin on film, Brooks divides himself, his dreams. He is Aaron wishing to be Tom - with Aaron's competence. Or, without might even be easier. As Shirley Maclaine once commented, Jim Brooks is an 'intensely brilliant, complicated man with a mercurial sense of humorous cynicism, born out of a unique twist of mind.' Then she added: 'If he were a little dumber, he'd be a lot happier.'

Americans doubtless have more of an angle on the characters. Holly Hunter's hurricane named Jane is felt to be based on her (also *très petite*) equivalent in the CBS Washington bureau, Susan Zirinsky. But Brooks insists Jane is a composite portrait. Jack Nicholson's top tele-gun, Bill Rorish, is generally agreed to be a nod to Chet Huntley.

Which then of The Big Three Anchors-cum-zillionaires is Grunick - Tom Brokaw, Peter Jennings or Dan Rather? None, I thought, just a clever satirical mix. Until learning that the Aaron-competent (and uncomfortable) Rather employs folks to do his writing for him. People like Peggy Noonan, also a George Bush speech-writer, who recently came up with the following for Rather, 'Autumn has dropped like a fruit.' Not even the acerbic James Brooks could have come up with a soppier line for Grunick than that.

Finally the penny dropped. Tom Grunick is really that other dim, well-meaning, sportscaster who surprised himself by netting the top job - Ronald Reagan.

TONY CRAWLEY

BULL DURHAM

Bull Durham differs from previous baseball movies in glorifying and sending up the game itself instead of turning it into a metaphor for success, American life or anything else. Kevin Costner is convincing as a career second-rater, the minor league catcher who never made the majors but kept his pride. In his last year in the game, he imparts seasoning to self-centred but endearingly goofy Tim Robbins and challenges ageing ball-park groupie Susan Sarandon's assumption that the game is best played, and her bed is best occupied, by the immature. **BM**

Director/script *Ron Shelton* **producers** *Thom Mount, Mark Burk* **exec** *David V. Lester* **camera** *Bobby Byrne* **editors** *Robert Leighton, Adam Weiss* **design** *Armin Ganz* **music** *Michael Convertino* **cast** *Kevin Costner, Susan Sarandon, Tim Robbins, Trey Wilson, Robert Wuhl, Jenny Robertson, Max Patkin, William O'Leary*
Running time: 108 mins
US release: Orion, Jun 24, 1988

BUSINESS AS USUAL

Blatant political polemic and pure entertainment rarely make comfortable screen bedfellows but this committed, low-budget, drama of sexual harassment in Liverpool nearly made it. That is thanks to the passion of first-time director Lezli-An Barrett and a cast of committed actors who, if unable wholly to flesh out the characters, do manage to elevate the enterprise beyond mere agitprop. **QF**

Business As Usual

Director/script *Lezli-An Barrett* **producer** *Sara Geater* **execs** *Menahem Golan, Yoram Globus* **camera** *Ernest Vincze* **editor** *Henry Richardson* **design** *Hildegard Bechtler* **music** *Paul Weller* **cast** *Glenda Jackson, John Thaw, Cathy Tyson, Mark McGann, Eamon Boland, James Hazeldine, Buki Armstrong, Stephen McGann, Philip Foster, Natalie Duffy, Jack Carr, Mel Martin, Michelle Byatt, Robert Keegan, Angela Elliot, Craig Charles, Christine Moore, Stephen Dillon, Lucy Sheen, Eithne Brown, Roland Oliver*
Running time: 89 mins
UK release: Cannon, Sep 11, 1987

·C·C·C·C·C·C·C·C·C·C·C·C

CAN'T BUY ME LOVE

Yes you can. This moralistic Disney fable seems to follow through on the title, but at the end the buyer and the seller stick to the original bargain. Nerdish Patrick Dempsey moons after cheerleader Amanda Peterson and her clique. Peterson, desperate for Dempsey's $1,000, agrees to pretend to pair off with him so he can pal around with the popular crowd. Popularity goes to Dempsey's head, and, when he moves on to other girls, she reveals the deal that raised him up from nerdity. His fall is instant and complete, but, after a suitable interval, she sees that Dempsey really is a bitchin' guy, even if he was born a nerd and will remain a nerd. Very uncomfortable viewing for the over-17s. **BM**

Director *Steve Rash* ***producer*** *Thom Mount* ***execs*** *Jere Henshaw, Ron Beckman* ***script*** *Michael Swerdlick* ***camera*** *Peter Lyons Collister* ***editor*** *Jeff Gourson* ***design*** *Donald L. Harris* ***music*** *Robert Folk* ***cast*** *Patrick Dempsey, Amanda Peterson, Courtney Gains, Tina Caspary, Seth Green, Sharon Farrell, Darcy De Moss, Dennis Dugan, Cloyce Morrow, Devin Devasquez, Eric Bruskotter, Gerardo Mejia, Cort McCown, Ami Dolenz, Max Perlich*

Running time: 94 mins (93 mins in UK)
US release: BV, Aug 14, 1987
UK release: Warner, May 27, 1988

CASUAL SEX?

As ill-conceived as any Hollywood comedy about a pair of Californian cuties trying to avoid AIDS could possibly be, *Casual Sex?* - or 'Stacy and Melissa Get Laid' - stars Lea Thompson as a reformed sleep-around and Victoria Jackson as her ditsy mate. They vacation at a plush health farm in search of 'clean' boyfriends. Thompson catches an unctuous singer who turns out to be a slob, and eventually winds up with a macho New Jersey greaseball (newly self-taught in sensitivity); Jackson catches a sickly sweet blond physio. Six years later they're still playing happy families with kids and dogs in tow. True love, after all, is the only answer to the Big A. Presumably aimed at teens, Genevieve Roberts' movie is dumb and reactionary, with only Andrew Dice Clay's lovable 'Joisey' hunk capable of raising a laugh. **GF**

Director *Genevieve Roberts* ***producers*** *Ilona Herzberg, Sheldon Kahn* ***exec*** *Ivan Reitman* ***script*** *Wendy Goldman, Judy Toll, based on their play* ***camera*** *Rolf Kesterman* ***design*** *Randy Ser* ***music*** *Van Dyke Parks* ***cast*** *Lea Thompson, Victoria Jackson, Stephen Shellen, Jerry Levine, Andrew Dice Clay, Mary Gross*

Running time: 97 mins
US release: Universal, Apr 15, 1988

LE CAVIAR ROUGE

If a thriller is a movie with spies and gunshots, this ultra-slow, one-room-set, made-for-TV talkabout is a thriller. Robert Hossein directs himself and his wife Candice Patou from a script he co-wrote, which was based on a novel he co-wrote. The Hosseins play Russian spies, once lovers and now estranged. She is actually an ex-spy, but she has witnessed a meeting that might compromise a KGB plan to assassinate a Sakharov-like dissident scientist. The clever spymasters reunite Hossein and Patou, confining them to a safe house on the shores of Lake Geneva, where they discuss degrees of guilt all night. **BM**

Director *Robert Hossein* ***producer*** *Philippe Dussart* ***script*** *Hossein, Frederic Dard, from their novel* ***camera*** *Edmond Richard* ***editor*** *Sophie Bhaud* ***design*** *Jacques D'Ovidio* ***music*** *Jean-Claude Petti, Claude-Michel Schonberg* ***cast*** *Hossein, Candice Patou, Ivan Desny*

Running time: 91 mins
US release: Galaxy Intl, Mar 25, 1988

CHINA GIRL

Romeo and Juliet, or perhaps a non-musical *West Side Story*, relocated to the New York border of Little Italy and Chinatown in a garishly concocted piece of hokum from the director of *The Driller Killer*. A cross-cultural teenage romance loses out to Triad vs. Mafia rivalry, with buckets of make-up blood getting spilled as the younger hoodlums on either side try to carve one another to pieces, and their elders but not betters weigh in with some sanguinary retribution. A few striking visuals provide inadequate compensation for the ineptitude of script and performances. **TP**

Director *Abel Ferrara* ***producer*** *Michael Nozik* ***execs*** *Mitchell Cannold, Steven Reuther* ***script*** *Nicholas St John* ***camera*** *Bojan Bazelli* ***editor*** *Anthony Redman* ***design*** *Dan Leigh* ***music*** *Joe Delia* ***cast*** *James Russo, Richard Panebianco, Sari Chang, David Caruso, Russell Wong, Joey Chin, Judith Malina, James Hong, Robert Miano, Paul Hipp, Doreen Chan, Randy Sabusawa, Keenan Leung, Lum Chang Pan, Sammy Lee, Johnny Shia, Stephen Chen, Raymond Moy, Josephina Gallego-Diaz, Caprice Benedetti, Anthony Dante*

Running time: 90 mins
US release: Vestron, Sep 25, 1987
UK release: Vestron, Jan 29, 1988

Cobra Verde

COBRA VERDE

Herzog's latest - and supposedly last - collaboration with his regular lead Klaus Kinski finds the wrinkled demon playing once again a misunderstood crazy. Loosely adapted from Bruce Chatwin's *The Viceroy of Ouidah*, the South American peasant-turned-slave-trader Cobra Verde is despatched to the West African coast to engage with the mad King of Dahomey. An incoherent narrative structure and a grotesquely voyeuristic approach to native culture reveal Herzog as once more an undisciplined opportunist who makes films to meet the challenges of nature, and never mind the audience. **DT**

Director *Werner Herzog* ***producer*** *Luigi Stipetic* ***execs*** *Walter Saxer, Salvatore Basile* ***script*** *Herzog, based on the novel* The Viceroy of Ouidah *by Bruce Chatwin* ***camera*** *Viktor Ruzicka* ***editor*** *Maximiliane Mainka* ***design*** *Ulrich Bergfelder, Fabrizio Carola* ***music*** *Popol Vuh* ***cast*** *Klaus Kinski, King Ampaw, José Lewgoy, Salvatore Basile, His Royal Highness Nana Agyefi Kwame II of Nsein*

Running time: 111 mins
UK release: Palace, Apr 22, 1988

Coming Up Roses

COLORS

Documentarist in its intention to alert the authorities to LA's escalating gang wars, Dennis Hopper's *Colors* male-bonds Robert Duvall's non-violent veteran cop and Sean Penn's swaggering rookie - given to spray-gunning young suspects in the face - in the LAPD's campaign to crack the mounting violence. As virtual war breaks out between the red-clad Bloods and the blue Crips, so the narrative becomes increasingly indecipherable - although *Colors* rides along on a high-octane aggression, at times reminiscent of Samuel Fuller in its tabloid immediacy, that makes plot complications redundant. The film surely completes Hopper's Hollywood rehabilitation, but it should be noted that his take on women - Maria Conchita Alonso's sultry 'homegirl' is marriage material for Penn until he alienates her with his uniformed brutality - is unreservedly misogynistic. **GF**
Director *Dennis Hopper* ***producer*** *Robert H. Solo* ***script*** *Michael Schiffer* ***camera*** *Haskell Wexler* ***editor*** *Robert Estrin* ***design*** *Ron Foreman* ***music*** *Herbie Hancock* ***cast*** *Sean Penn, Robert Duvall, Maria Conchita Alonso, Randy Brooks, Grand Bush, Don Cheadle, Gerardo Mejia, Glenn Plummer, Rudy Ramos, Sy Richardson, Trinidad Silva, Charles Walker, Damon Wayans*
Running time: 120 mins
US release: Orion, Apr 15, 1988

COMING TO AMERICA

Eddie Murphy as straight man? Oddly enough, he wrote the story for John Landis's film and cast himself as a goody-goody who speaks perfectly stilted English, instead of standard scatological Murphy-ese. In this reactive role, he is an African prince who comes to America pretending to be poor because he's seeking a bride who would love him for himself alone. He gives dozens of Paul Hogan-ish deadpan looks and allows his lackey Arsenio Hall and other characters to get the laughs. Many of these other characters are in fact himself playing cameos; e.g., three-fourths of a barbershop quartet of gabbling fools. **BM**
Director *John Landis* ***producers*** *George Folsey Jr., Robert D. Wachs* ***execs*** *Mark Lipsky, Leslie Belzberg* ***script*** *David Sheffield, Barry W. Blaustein* ***camera*** *Woody Omens* ***editors*** *Malcolm Campbell, George Folsey Jr.* ***design*** *Richard MacDonald* ***music*** *Nile Rodgers* ***cast*** *Eddie Murphy, Arsenio Hall, John Amos, James Earl Jones, Shari Headley, Madge Sinclair, Eriq LaSalle, Allison Dean, Paul Bates, Louie Anderson, Clint Smith, Vanessa Bell*
Running time: 116 mins
US release: Paramount, Jun 29, 1988

COMING UP ROSES

(Rhosyn a Rhith)

Stephen Bayly's touching low-budget comedy is a Welsh *Last Picture Show*. How does a small-town projectionist (Hywel) in a closed and demolition-threatened cinema hold off the property tycoons and make a few pounds on the side? Answer: by growing mushrooms in the stalls and selling them on the Q.T. Business booms and so do the story's comic complications. Bayly directs Ruth Carter's script with beatific understatement, and Hywel and Iola Gregory excel as the hero and his usherette girlfriend. The film is in Welsh with subtitles: three cheers for a language and culture that refuse to bow to demolition. **HK**
Director *Stephen Bayly* ***producer*** *Linda James* ***script*** *Ruth Carter* ***camera*** *Dick Pope* ***editor*** *Scott Thomas* ***design*** *Hildegard Bechtler* ***music*** *Michael Story* ***cast*** *Dafydd Hywel, Iola Gregory, Olive Michael, Mari Emlyn, W.J. Phillips, Glan Davies, Gillian Elisa Thomas, Ifan Huw Dafydd, Rowan Griffiths*
Running time: 93 mins
US release: Skouras, Sep 11, 1987
UK release: Mainline, Feb 20, 1987

COMRADES

Bill Douglas's lengthy tribute to the Tolpuddle Martyrs gives every indication of being a labour of love, which makes all the more frustrating the amorphousness of the resulting film. Despite atmospheric location shooting in both Dorset and Australia, the course of events remains fatally muddled; some of the social commentary (such as Freddie Jones's drunkenly hypocritical cleric) is surprisingly crude; and the deployment of a network of distancing devices manages not so much to provide a stylistic armature as to compound the confusion. **TP**
Director/script *Bill Douglas* ***producer*** *Simon Relph* ***camera*** *Gail Tattersall* ***editor*** *Michael Audsley* ***design*** *Michael Pickwoad* ***music*** *Hans Werner Henze, David Graham* ***cast*** *Robin Soans, William Gaminara, Philip Davis, Stephen Bateman, Keith Allen, Patrick Field, Jeremy Flynn, Robert Stephens, Michael Hordern, Freddie Jones, Barbara Windsor, Murray Melvin, Imelda Staunton, Amber Wilkinson, Katy Behean, Sandra Voe, Valerie Whittington, Harriet Doyle, Heather Page, Patricia Healey, Shane Down, Joanna David, Collette Barker, Vanessa Redgrave, James Fox, Arthur Dignam, John Hargreaves, Simon Parsonage, Charles Yunipingu, Simon Landis, Anna Volska, Brian MacDermott, Shane Briant, Tim Eliot, David Netheim, Ralph Cotterill, David McWilliams, Lynette Curran, Alex Norton*
Running time: 183 mins
UK release: Curzon, Aug 28, 1987

CONSUMING PASSIONS

Semi-Python is better than no Python at all, but *Consuming Passions* strays too far from the Python aesthetic of fast and furious offensiveness.
Based on a play by Michael Palin and Terry Jones, *Consuming Passions* uses the familiar device of cannibalism as a metaphor for over-indulgence in other appetites. Jonathan Pryce, who has surrendered to greed, and Vanessa Redgrave, a prisoner of her libido, embroil innocent Tyler Butterworth in a scheme to perpetuate sales of a sweet that's six per cent human. Redgrave is funny, Pryce isn't and Butterworth just stands there. **BM**
Director *Giles Foster* ***producer*** *William Cartlidge* ***script*** *Paul D. Zimmerman, Andrew Davies, from the play* Secrets *by Michael Palin, Terry Jones* ***camera*** *Roger Pratt* ***editor*** *John Grover* ***design*** *Peter Lamont* ***music*** *Richard Hartley* ***cast*** *Vanessa Redgrave, Jonathan Pryce, Tyler Butterworth, Freddie Jones, Sammi Davis, Prunella Scales, Thora Hird, William Rushton, John Wells, Timothy West, Mary Healey, Andrew Sachs, Bryan Pringle*
Running time: 98 mins
US release: Goldwyn, Apr 6, 1988

COP

James Woods is such an intimidating presence that the only obvious casting choice is to give him bad-guy parts. But instead of going down that dead end, Woods has been smart enough to create a new type in the movies: the despicable hero. In writer-director James B. Harris's slick, meaty action film, Woods is a maverick cop obsessed with identifying a serial killer his bosses say doesn't exist. To get his man, he abuses his friendship with cop-shop higher-up Charles Durning and exploits his own affection for feminist Lesley Ann Warren. The final showdown - not with crooked cop Charles Haid, who turns out to be just a subsidiary villain - is a routine stalk 'n' shoot. **BM**

Comrades

Director *James B. Harris* **producers** *Harris, James Woods* **execs** *Thomas Coleman, Michael Rosenblatt* **script** *Harris, based on the novel* Blood on the Moon *by James Ellroy* **camera** *Steve Dubin* **editor** *Anthony Spano* **design** *Gene Rudolf* **music** *Michel Colombier* **cast** *James Woods, Lesley Ann Warren, Charles Durning, Charles Haid, Raymond J. Barry, Randi Brooks, Steve Lambert, Annie McEnroe, Vicki Wauchope*
Running time: 110 mins
US release: Atlantic, Jan 8, 1988
UK release: Entertainment, Jun 10, 1988

THE COUCH TRIP

Dan Aykroyd is in his element as a bull-mouse loony on the loose in Beverly Hills. Escaping from a strait-jacket in Illinois by impersonating his shrink, Aykroyd takes a job in Los Angeles subbing for radio call-in adviser, Charles Grodin. To the consternation of the tight-buttocked Grodin, Aykroyd's profane directness sends ratings soaring. Stunts like taking hundreds of callers to a ball game ('Nymphomaniacs in bus three with me!') and lines like bit player Walter Matthau's 'A man never stands so tall as when he stoops to pet a plant' give *The Couch Trip* a more than adequate laugh count. **BM**
Director *Michael Ritchie* **producer** *Lawrence Gordon* **script** *Steven Kampmann, Will Porter, Sean Stein, from novel by Ken Kolb* **camera** *Donald E. Thorin* **editor** *Richard A. Harris* **design** *Jimmy Bly* **music** *Michel Colombier* **cast** *Dan Aykroyd, Walter Matthau, Charles Grodin, Donna Dixon, Richard Romanus, Mary Gross, David Clennon, Arye Gross, Citoria Jackson, Chevy Chase*
Running time: 98 mins
US release: Orion, Jan 15, 1988

THE COURIER

Dublin as a not so fair, and disappointingly anonymous, city is the background for a stereotyped crime yarn, with Gabriel Byrne as the white-suited king of the dope pedlars, eventually (and to the surprise of nobody) meeting his fate by being shot on a fire escape and crashing on to the pavement from a great height. Even Ian Bannen as the lugubrious tec on his trail cannot breathe any life to speak of into an undertaking disfigured elsewhere by a particularly objectionable display of gratuitous sadism entailing a broken bottle jabbed into a stool-pigeon's face. **TP**
Directors *Joe Lee, Frank Deasy* **producer** *Hilary McLoughlin* **execs** *Neil Jordan, Nik Powell, John Hambley, Michael Algar* **script** *Deasy* **camera** *Gabriel Beristain* **editors** *Derek Trigg, Annette D'Alton* **design** *David Wilson* **music** *Declan MacManus (Elvis Costello)* **cast** *Gabriel Byrne, Ian Bannen, Cait O'Riordan, Kevin Doyle, Mary Ryan, Michelle Houlden, Mark Flanagan, Andrew Connolly, Patrick Bergin, Anne Enwright, Padraig O'Loingsigh, Lucy Vigne Welsh, Ger Ryan, Owen Hyland, Martin Dunne, Dave Duffy*
Running time: 85 mins
US release: Vestron, Sep, 1988
UK release: Palace, Feb 19, 1988

The Courier

CRAZY MOON

As his father Donald does occasionally, Kiefer Sutherland pays his Canadian dues too. In Allan Eastman's slight hymn to weirdness, the cuter the better, Sutherland plays a maladjusted rich boy with an innocent and pure heart. It's Sutherland's awful parents and dangerous brother who have driven him to seek solace in all the *outré* props the film's art director could find, from mannequins to motorcycles. Sutherland also swoons over sentimental old tunes like 'Boo Hoo'. And he pays court to the wildly unsuitable Vanessa Vaughan, who is lovely but deaf and works in a shop. Romance triumphs over reality ... but then what's a movie for? **BM**
Director *Allan Eastman* **producers/script** *Tom Berry, Stefan Wodoslawky* **camera** *Savas Kalogeras* **design** *Guy Lalande* **cast** *Kiefer Sutherland, Peter Spence, Vanessa Vaughan, Ken Pogue, Eve Napier, Harry Hill, Sean McCann, Bronwen Mantel*
Running time: 87 mins
US release: Miramax, Jul 24, 1987

CREEPSHOW II

Three segments of Stephen King-inspired portmanteau schlock-horror (compared with five in the altogether superior George Romero-directed original) that range from execrable to bearable. Best of a mediocre trio is *The Hitch-Hiker* about a persistent thumb-tripper who simply refuses to die despite being repeatedly rammed and run over by desperate driver Lois Chiles, returning home after an adulterous liaison. **QF**
Director *Michael Gornick* **producer** *David Ball*

***exec** Richard P. Rubinstein **script** George A. Romero, based on short stories by Stephen King **camera** Richard Hart, Tom Hurwitz **editor** Peter Weatherley **design** Bruce Miller **music** Les Reed* **cast** Old Chief Wood'nhead: *George Kennedy, Dorothy Lamour, Don Harvey, David Holbrook, Holt McCallany, Frank S. Salsedo, Maltby Napoleon, Tyrone Tonto, Dan Kamin, Deane Smith, Shirley Sonderegger;* The Raft: *Daniel Beer, Jeremy Green, Page Hannah, Paul Satterfield;* The Hitch-Hiker: *Lois Chiles, Stephen King, Tom Wright, David Beercroft, Richard Parks, Cheré Bryson;* Linking Sequences: *Tom Savini, Dominick John, Philip Doré, Joe Silver*
Running time: 90 mins
US release: New World, May 1, 1987
UK release: Entertainment, Nov 20, 1987

CRITTERS 2: THE MAIN COURSE

Apparently amusing sequel, with outer space hunters dispatched to the village of Grovers End to complete their earlier attempt to obliterate the vicious, but yet lovable, killers.
***Director** Mike Garris **producer** Barry Opper **exec** Robert Shaye **script** D. T. Twohy, Mick Garris **camera** Russell Carpenter **editor** Charles Bornstein **design** Philip Dean Foreman **music** Nicholas Pike **cast** Scott Grimes, Liane Curtis, Don Opper, Barry Corbin, Tom Hodges, Sam Anderson, Lindsay Parker, Herta Ware, Lin Shaye, Terrence Mann, Roxanne Kernohan, Doug Rowe*
Running time: 87 mins
US release: New-Line, Apr 29, 1988

CROCODILE DUNDEE II

Paul Hogan ambles back on to the screen, a little older, a little less funny, and a lot richer. The script he co-wrote with his son Brett gives him plenty of opportunity to look blankly at civilization's foolishness. But John Cornell's début as a director is paced so torpidly that the lack of inspiration in the story soon becomes apparent. This time, outbacker Dundee, still costumed as if for a fancy dress ball, starts off in Manhattan as Linda Kozlowski's house-husband. Soon she is menaced by crazed Colombian drug-dealers. These thugs unwisely pursue the couple to Oz, where Dundee picks them off one by one. **BM**
***Director** John Cornell **producer** Cornell, Jane Scott **exec** Paul Hogan **script** Paul Hogan, Brett Hogan **camera** Russell Boyd **editor** David Stiven **design** Lawrence Eastwood **music** Peter Best **cast** Paul Hogan, Linda Kozlowski, Charles Dutton, Hechter Ubarry, Juan Fernandez, John Meillon*
Running time: 111 mins
US release: Paramount, May 25, 1988
UK release: UIP, Jun 17, 1988

CROSS MY HEART

A date is a period of time a man and a woman spend together auditioning - for marriage, for sex or even for just another date. Playing parts is what Martin Short and Annette O'Toole do in Armyan Bernstein's sometimes witty, often interminable tale of one bad date that, of course, ends happily. Short pretends to be a success and O'Toole pretends not to be a mother already, and so after protracted negotiations they make it to bed. But the truth will out. They argue, they make up. The movie aims to be funny and heart-warming, but the draggy real-time pace and contrived embarrassing situations produce more discomfort than anything. **BM**

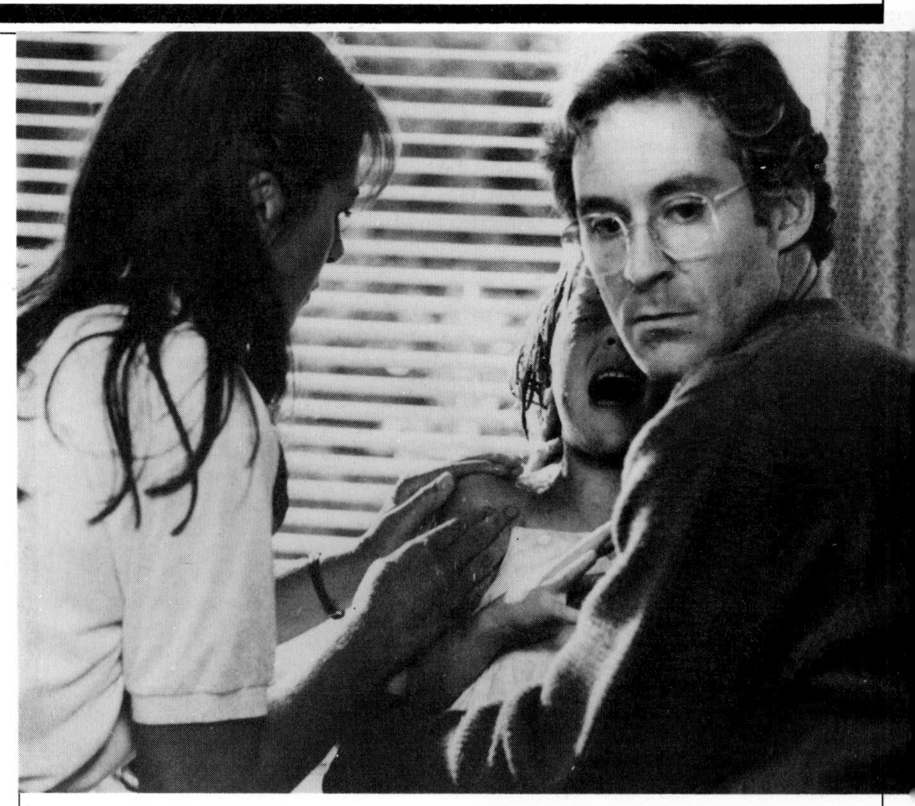

Cry Freedom

***Director** Armyan Bernstein **producer** Lawrence Kasdan **execs** Aaron Spelling, Alan Greisman **script** Bernstein, Gail Parent **camera** Thomas Del Ruth **editor** Mia Goldman **design** Lawrence G. Paull **music** Bruce Broughton **cast** Martin Short, Annette O'Toole, Paul Reiser, Joanna Kerns, Jessica Puscas, Lee Arenberg*
Running time: 90 mins
US release: Universal, Nov 13, 1987

CRY FREEDOM

It's ironic that a film starting out to be the story of martyred black South African Steve Biko should wind up being the story of a white man who did nothing except write about Biko. Richard Attenborough couldn't get finance for a film truly about apartheid, so he settled for this film about editor Donald Woods' education at Biko's hands and his eventual flight from the regime that killed Biko. Denzel Washington gives a moving portrait of the soft-spoken Biko, and Kevin Kline is effective as the stalwart Woods, but the film is fatally marred by foreshortening its depiction of apartheid in favour of long stretches of mini-peril faced by Woods and his family. **BM**
***Director/producer** Richard Attenborough **exec** Terence Clegg **script** John Briley, based on* Biko *and* Asking for Trouble *by Donald Woods **camera** Ronnie Taylor **editor** Lesley Walker **design** Stuart Craig **music** George Fenton, Jonas Gwangwa **cast** Kevin Kline, Penelope Wilton, Denzel Washington, John Hargreaves, Alec McCowen, Kevin McNally, Zakes Moke, Ian Richardson, Josette Simon, John Thaw, Timothy West, Miles Anderson, Tommy Buson, Jim Findley, Julian Glover, Kate Hardie, Alton Kumalo*
Running time: 158 mins
US release: Universal, Nov 6, 1987
UK release: UIP, Nov 27, 1987

·D·D·D·D·D·D·D·D·D·D·D

DA

Hugh Leonard's imaginative rewrite of his popular play retains the sprightly humour of the original but loses its pathos. Martin Sheen is a middle-aged New Yorker who returns to Ireland to bury his father, Barnard Hughes. The old man keeps popping up and reminding Sheen of heart-warming and hilarious episodes from his early years. In the play the son despairs of ever reconciling his feelings towards 'Da', but here Sheen merrily transports the old ghost to New York. Hughes is adorable and Sheen is an adequate straight man. **BM**
***Director** Matt Clark **producer** Julie Corman **execs** William R. Greenblatt, Martin Sheen, Sam Grogg **script** Hugh Leonard, from his play **camera** Alan Kivilo **editor** Nancy Nuttal Beyda **music** Elmer Bernstein **cast** Barnard Hughes, Martin Sheen, William Hickey, Karl Hayden, Doreen Hepburn, Hugh O'Conor, Ingrid Craigie*
Running time: 102 mins
US release: Film Dallas, Apr 29, 1988

DANCERS

The Red Shoes allegedly inspired an entire generation of gels to take up ballet. This backstage (and some exciting on-stage) drama of a touring company in Southern Italy is so routine by comparison that it's unlikely to inspire anyone except already committed balletomanes. Herbert Ross was probably hoping lightning would strike twice when he re-united his *The Turning Point* stars Mikhail Baryshnikov and Leslie Browne. But the story is trite and insubstantial, the screenplay laughable. **QF**
***Director** Herbert Ross **producers** Menahem Golan, Yoram Globus **execs** Nora Kaye, Jack Brodsky **script** Sarah Kernochan **camera** Ennio Guarnieri **editor** William Reynolds **design** Gianni Quaranta **music** Pino Donaggio **cast** Mikhail Baryshnikov,*

Alessandra Ferri, Leslie Browne, Thomas Rall, Lynn Seymour, Victor Barbee, Julie Kent, Mariangela Melato, Leandro Amato, Gianmarco Tognazzi, Desmond Kelly, Chrisa Keramidas, Amy Werba, Jack Brodsky
Running time: 99 mins
US release: Cannon, Oct 9, 1987
UK release: Cannon, Dec 8, 1987

DARK EYES

An ingenious conflation of several Chekhov stories, Nikita Mikhalkov's film gives Marcello Mastroianni every comic and romantic opportunity to play his patented rueful roué character. The kept man of Silvana Mangano, Mastroianni capers through his wife's parties and ploughs through her friends. Retreating to a mud-bath spa, he meets Elena Sofonovo. This time it's for real, and Mastroianni finds himself following Sofonovo to her all-but-inaccessible home in Russia. Many promises are made, but none are kept, and Mastroianni is left with his memories. The film's tone is elegiac, interrupted by snickers. **BM**
Director *Nikita Mikhalkov* ***producers*** *Silvia D'Amico Benedico, Carlo Cucchi* ***script*** *Alexander Adabakhian, Mikhalkov, with collaboration from Suso Cecchi D'Amico, based on short stories by Anton Chekhov* ***camera*** *Franco Di Giacomo* ***editor*** *Enzo Meniconi* ***design*** *Mario Garbuglia, Adabakhian* ***music*** *Francis Lai* ***cast*** *Marcello Mastroianni, Silvana Mangano, Marthe Keller, Elena Sofonova, Vsevolod Larionov, Innokenti Smoktunovsky*
Running time: 117 mins
US release: Island, Sep 26, 1987

THE DARK SIDE OF THE MOON
(Manden I Månen)

The sort of film that seems to have been designed to conform to everybody's most clichéd notions about the Scandinavian propensity for gloom, *The Dark Side of the Moon*, recounting the travails of a wife-killer who emerges from literal confinement in jail into a symbol-laden imprisonment of the spirit on the outside, is crammed with expressionistic effects which remain obstinately divorced from any thematic concept. An incoherent sub-plot concerning off-screen murders gives way to a glum form of 'happy' ending via the protagonist's reconciliation with his daughter, but not in such a way as to mitigate the wrap-around tedium. **TP**
Director/script *Erik Clausen* ***producer*** *Per Årman* ***exec*** *Tivi Magnusson* ***camera*** *Morten Bruus* ***editor*** *Ghita Beckendorff* ***design*** *Leif Sylvester Petersen* ***music*** *John Høybe* ***cast*** *Peter Thiel, Catherine Poul Jpont, Christina Bengtsson, Kim Jansson, Yavuzer Cetinkaya, Royt Richards, Berthe Qvistgaard, Erik Truxa, Anne Nøjgard, Marianne Mortensen, Stig Hoffmeyer*
Running time: 94 mins
UK release: Cannon, Mar 18, 1988

DATE WITH AN ANGEL

Not since the *Benji* movies has there been such a bucket of sick as *Date With an Angel*, one of a spate of recent American movies about what heaven demands of the best of us, and how wonderful it really is. A Voice commands, 'His time has come,' and an angel is dispatched to bring Michael E. Knight to his final reward. But he's just about to marry exquisite Phoebe Cates, who doesn't get it when she finds the angel, Emmanuelle Béart, in Knight's flat. Beart can't carry Knight off to the Pearly Gates just yet, because Comsat or Sputnik broke her wing on the way earthward. Beart's got the cutest little baby face but for some reason she is totally tongue-tied, like the movie is brain-tied. Send a kid you hate to this one. **BM**
Director/script *Tom McLoughlin* ***producer*** *Martha Schumacher* ***camera*** *Alex Thomson* ***editor*** *Marshall Harvey* ***design*** *Craig Stearns* ***music*** *Randy Kerber* ***cast*** *Michael E. Knight, Phoebe Cates, Emmanuelle Béart, David Dukes, Phil Brock, Albert Macklin, Pete Kowanko, Vinny Argiro, Bibi Besch*
Running time: 105 mins
US release: DEG, Nov 20, 1987

THE DEAD
Film of the Year

Director *John Huston* ***producers*** *Wieland Schulz-Keil, Chris Sievernich* ***script*** *Tony Huston, based on the short story from* Dubliners *by James Joyce* ***camera*** *Fred Murphy* ***editor*** *Roberto Silvi* ***design*** *Stephen Grimes, Dennis Washington* ***music*** *Alex North* ***cast*** *Anjelica Huston, Donal McCann, Helena Carroll, Cathleen Delany, Ingrid Craigie, Rachael Dowling, Dan O'Herlihy, Donal Donnelly, Marie Kean, Frank Patterson, Maria McDermottroe, Seán McClory, Katherine O'Toole, Maria Hayden, Bairbre Dowling, Lyda Anderson, Colm Meany, Corma O'Herlihy, Paul Grant*
Running time: 83 mins
US release: Vestron, Dec 17, 1987
UK release: Vestron, Dec 11, 1987

Dark Eyes

THE DEAD

'Why do I feel this riot of emotion?' Gabriel Conroy (Donal McCann) asks himself in the haunting interior monologue that closes *The Dead*, as images of a wintry landscape - 'Snow was general all over Ireland' - echo his intimations of mortality. Beside him in their hotel room, his wife Gretta (Anjelica Huston) has cried herself to sleep. The last movement of John Huston's valedictory masterpiece, adapted by his eldest son Tony from James Joyce's not-so-short story from *Dubliners* (1914), has forsaken the living for a walk with the ghost of her old, unconsummated love, one such as Gabriel has never known.

Borne back into her Galway girlhood - from this evening early in the New Year of 1904 - by the tenor Bartell D'Arcy's mournful rendition of 'The Lass of Aughrim' as she and Gabriel were leaving his aunts' annual Twelfth Night supper party, Gretta has confessed her friendship with the delicate, dark-eyed boy who used to serenade her with the song. His health did not withstand a journey through the snow to see her on the eve of her departure from the village. 'I think he died for me ...'

As Gabriel, through whose eyes we witness Gretta transfixed on the stairs while she experiences her private epiphany, has moved gradually to the centre of the film, genuinely Joycean in its timbre and the way it elaborates its themes, so our sense of his personal crisis has grown: he looks particularly grim after the morbid recitation by Mr Grace (Seán McClory) of Lady Gregory's poem 'Broken Vows', about love's terrible thrall: 'You promised me a thing that is not possible.' His own lovely tribute to his three hostesses - with Fred Murphy's camera tracking down on the deeply-moved spinsters; elderly Aunt Julia (Cathleen Delany), hearty Aunt Kate (Helena Carroll), and the younger Mary Jane (Ingrid Craigie) - even admits that 'in gatherings such as this, sadder thoughts will occur to our minds. Thoughts of the past, of youth, of changes, absent friends that we miss here tonight.'

No matter that the evening proceeds harmoniously, with all the guests enjoying themselves and even dear, drunken Freddy Malins (Donal Donnelly) not overly incurring the wrath of his crabby, infirm mother (Marie Kean), or that Huston (who directed mostly from a wheelchair) jauntily unfurls the action in an unassuming comic-lyric style sometimes more reminiscent of Ford, it's a mood of bittersweet nostalgia and regret that prevails. Gretta's romantic pain instils in Gabriel an overwhelming sense of life's ephemerality, coupled with the dawning realization that his marriage is empty and that the truncated love of Gretta's long-dead, 17-year-old admirer was greater than all his years of marital worship. 'How poor a part I played in your life,' he laments. 'What were you like then?' (No wonder she harbours a wish to see Galway again.) Thus afflicted, Gabriel imagines Aunt Julia, so game but so feeble in her singing of 'Arrayed for the Bridal' at the party, laid out in her coffin in the not-so-distant future.

With melancholy solitude replacing communal warmth at the end of *The Dead*, why then do we feel a riot of emotion when watching this movie? Gabriel's thought - as supplied by Joyce - at this moment is crucial, since it evokes both the transcendent, uplifting nature of the boy's abstracted death and the spectre of Old John Huston himself: 'One by one they were all becoming shades. Better to pass boldly into that other world, in the full glory of some passion than fade and wither dismally with age.' Huston died at the age of 81 on 28 August 1987, having completed his 41st film as director that spring and screened it for his friends and colleagues, but forced by emphysema to withdraw from his second son Danny's directorial début, *Mr. North*, which he'd co-written, was co-producing, and had a major role in.

It would be an oversimplification to say that Huston died with his boots on, but not bathetic to allow that he himself succumbed at a moment of catharsis. Not only can *The Dead* be regarded as Huston's rueful reckoning with his own approaching death (for its lucid, unaffected style alone it might be the single most impressive epitaph of a dying American film-maker), but a vocational triumph (he had wanted to film it as long ago as 1956, when a visitor to the set of *Moby Dick* had suggested it to him), and a spiritual if not a physical homecoming: he exiled himself to Ireland after the McCarthy hearings, raised his children and roistered there as an Irish gentleman for two decades, becoming a citizen in 1964 but living latterly in Mexico. (*The Dead*'s interiors were all shot in Southern California, although the house which Joyce wrote about - 15 Usher's Island, Dublin - was filmed for the exteriors by a second unit.)

In auteurist terms, meanwhile, *The Dead* was a culmination less of a career popularly regarded as a Hemingwayesque romp through an eccentric lexicon of modern authors, but of a

bookish man's dedication to preserving the letter and spirit of his sources. Huston was one of the most prolific purveyors of literary fiction in the post-war American cinema. Sometimes that instinct had a 'Book of the Month' feel about it, but one is bound to stand by his assertion that 'I loved the books and rightly or wrongly saw a picture in them.' There were major failures, and I must confess a lack of enthusiasm for much of Huston's work, which has a 'sacred cow' status without any shaping vision. But *The Red Badge of Courage* (despite its notorious production history), *The Unforgiven* and *The Man Who Would Be King* are all fine films, while *The Dead* now sits beside *Fat City* and *Wise Blood* to comprise Huston's great late trio.

Huston first read Joyce's *Ulysses* in 1928 when his journalist mother, Reah Gore, smuggled it into the US. He would later admit that 'Joyce was and remains the most influential writer in my life ... *Ulysses* influenced not only me and the things I did afterwards, but my whole generation. He was the most important writer of that time and his influence has continued to this day, even to people who don't realize it.' Of *The Dead*: 'There's a theme, and while you are hardly prepared for it, that's the real value of the ending. When you reach the finish and hear Gabriel's words, you realize you've come unerringly there. And you realize as well that what he says goes also for yourself, so it is not only a self-discovery on Gabriel's part, but reveals something of yourself to you.'

The extent to which *The Dead* bears out this notion demonstrates that Huston's reverence for Joyce and love for Ireland did not impair his ability to read beyond Joyce's famous 'surfaces' and transcribe their meanings. Rather, the handsome period production design and elegant middle-class costumes, the good food, wine and music, the social niceties and finesses that sidestep conflicts of character and opinion (even though Dan O'Herlihy, as the cantankerous Protestant Mr Browne, is eventually rude to Mrs Malins), provide a veneer of politeness and *bonhomie* that dissolves into a palpable meaninglessness as Gabriel contemplates our mutual fate: 'Think of all those back in time ... this solid world dwindling ... snow falling in that lonely graveyard ... upon all the living and the dead.' In his jealous contemplation of the simple perfection of Gretta's impossible love - pure because it could never be - its abiding beauty evades him. But, in his desolation, McCann leaves Gabriel with a certain sense of reconciliation - his is a towering performance among a dozen that are superb. Thanks to the Hustons, all three of them, meanwhile, Gretta's tragic rapture finds a wider and more sympathetic audience.

GRAHAM FULLER

DEAD OF WINTER

What has happened to Arthur Penn? Disaster tends to come in threes; so perhaps it was predictable that this absurd sub-Hitchcock chiller would always prove a clinker coming in the wake of *Four Friends* and *Target*. There's no hint of a once-great director in this painfully old-fashioned gothic melodrama about an innocent actress sucked into a plot of blackmail and revenge. Full of script inconsistencies, further devalued by performances of eye-rolling absurdity, it unfolds at interminable length. Like the latterday spawn of an unholy union between *Gaslight* and *The Spiral Staircase*, this too belongs to the monochrome mists of late night TV. **QF**

Director *Arthur Penn* ***producers*** *John Bloomgarden, Marc Shmuger* ***script*** *Schmuger, Marc Malone* ***camera*** *Jan Weincke* ***editor*** *Rick Shaine* ***design*** *Bill Brodie* ***music*** *Richard Einhorn* ***cast*** *Mary Steenburgen, Roddy McDowall, Jan Rubes, William Russ, Wayne Robson, Mark Malone*

Running time: 100 mins

US release: MGM, Feb 6, 1987

UK release: UIP, Feb 5, 1988

DEADLINE (War Zone in UK)

This bleak little story of a cynical American journalist assigned to cover Beirut, who is subsequently exploited by the various factions for their own news-gathering, is not half bad. Shot entirely in Israel on a modest budget - which too often shows - it contains a terrifying and convincing portrait of chaos and casual killing. Walken is a fine actor and tends to rise above often banal material which, in between fast-moving action, gets bogged down in speechifying, presumably for balance's sake. Not as effective as Schlöndorff's 1981 *Circle of Deceit*, set in the same Zone. **QF**

Director *Nathaniel Gutman* ***producer*** *Elisabeth Wolters-Alfs* ***script*** *Hanan Peled* ***camera*** *Ammon Salomon, Thomas Mauch* ***editor*** *Peter Przygodda* ***design*** *Jürgen Henze* ***music*** *Jacques Zwart, Hans Jansen* ***cast*** *Christopher Walken, Marita Marschall, Hywel Bennett, Arnon Zadock, Amos Lavie, Etti Ankri, Martin Umbach*

Running time: 99 mins

US release: Skouras, Sep 11, 1988

UK release: Guild, Mar 20, 1987

DEATH WISH 4: THE CRACKDOWN

Bronson's veteran vigilante is brought back into business when he's blackmailed by a mysterious tycoon into rubbing out two sets of drug dealers. The tycoon proves actually to be a rival crook out to clear the field of the opposition, but his belief that he can play Bronson for a sucker is predictably ill-founded. More immediately to the point than doubts over the status of a protagonist who guns down opponents without any prior challenge is the extraordinary lack of either tension or conviction in the ragbag of a narrative, which permits its 'hero' to stroll into the homes and business fronts of the drug barons with scarcely a by-your-leave. **TP**

Director *J. Lee Thompson* ***producer*** *Pancho Kohner* ***execs*** *Menahem Golan, Yoram Globus* ***script*** *Gail Morgan Hickman, based on characters created by Brian Garfield* ***camera*** *Gideon Porath* ***editor*** *Peter Lee-Thompson* ***design*** *Whitney Brooke Wheeler* ***music*** *Paul McCallum, Valentine McCallum, John Bisharat* ***cast*** *Charles Bronson, Kay Lenz, John P. Ryan, Perry Lopez, George Dickerson, Soon-Teck Oh, Dana Barron, Jesse Dabson, Peter Sherayko,*

James Purcell, Michael Russo, Dannie Trejo, Daniel Sabia, Mike Moroff, Dan Ferro, Tom Everett, David Fonteno, Michael Wise, Irwin Keyes, Tim Russ
Running time: 99 mins (98 mins in UK)
US release: Cannon, Nov 6, 1987
UK release: Cannon, Apr 15, 1988

DEMONS 2

Lamberto Bava's infatuation with pseudo-*grand guignol* excess continues with this sequel to his 1985 picture. The father of Italian gore, Dario Argento, produced this incestuous tale of demonic beings emerging (courtesy of some effectively ghoulish SFX from Sergio Stivaletti) from a TV set to plague yet more fashionably juvenile party animals in an apartment block. The usual cacophonic Argento soundtrack of avant-garde rock is incongruously applied, but the final product is too derivative of American genre entries and lacks the opulent grandiosity Argento has conferred upon his own work. **MN**
Director *Lamberto Bava* ***producer*** *Dario Argento* ***script*** *Bava, Argento, Franco Ferrini, Dardano Sacchetti* ***camera*** *Gianlorenzo Battaglia* ***editor*** *Franco Fraticelli, Pietro Bozza* ***design*** *Davide Bassan* ***music*** *Simon Boswell, The Smiths, The Cult, Art of Noise, Peter Murphy, Dead Can Dance* ***cast*** *David Knight, Nancy Brilli, Coralina Cataldi Tassoni, Bobby Rhodes, Asia Argento, Virginia Bryant, Anita Bartolucci*
Running time: 91 mins
UK release: Avatar, Sep 18, 1987

DIRTY DANCING

Jennifer Grey stars in this coming-of-age story set in a Catskills resort in the summer of 1963. She is college-bound but still daddy's little girl. Patrick Swayze, the resort's dance instructor, electrifies Grey, who leaps out of the nest a bit too soon for daddy (Jerry Orbach). Grey overcomes the rich-girl-poor-girl barrier, learning how to dance and love from the graceful Swayze, (a one-time ballet artiste who finally gets to strut his stuff on film). Despite some preposterous plot turns, Emile Ardolino's film conveys many tender moments and faithfully captures the end of an innocent era. **BM**
Director *Emile Ardolino* ***producer*** *Linda Gottlieb* ***execs*** *Mitchell Cannold, Steven Reuther* ***script*** *Eleanor Bergstein* ***camera*** *Jeff Jur* ***editor*** *Peter C. Frank* ***design*** *David Chapman* ***music*** *John Morris* ***cast*** *Jennifer Grey, Patrick Swayze, Jerry Orbach, Cynthia Rhodes, Jack Weston, Jane Bruckner, Kelly Bishop, Lonny Price, Max Cantor, Charles Honi Coles, Neal Jones, 'Cousin Brucie' Morrow, Wayne Knight, Paula Trueman, Alvin Myerovich, Miranda Garrison, Garry Goodrow, Antone Pagan*
Running time: 100 mins
US release: Vestron, Aug 21, 1987
UK release: Vestron, Oct 16, 1987

DISORDERLIES

Comedy vehicle for obese rap singers, The Fat Boys. Starting out at a rundown convalescent hospital, they're hired as incompetent orderlies to care for an ailing millionaire his nephew wants in the grave as quickly as possible. But, thanks to their loving care, he recovers.
Director *Michael Schultz* ***producers*** *Schultz, George Jackson, Michael Jaffe* ***execs*** *Charles Stettler, Joseph E. Zynczak* ***script*** *Mark Feldberg, Mitchell Kelbanoff* ***camera*** *Rolf Kesterman* ***editor*** *Ned Humphreys* ***design*** *George Costello* ***cast*** *Damon Wimbley, Darren Robinson, Mark Morales, Ralph Bellamy, Tony Plana, Anthony Geary, Marco Rodriguez, Troy Beyer*
Running time: 96 mins
US release: Warner, Aug 14, 1987

D.O.A.

The *Max Headroom* team of Rocky Morton and Annabel Jankel stamp their style on this remake of a classic B *noir* from 1949. Too much nervous eighties humour, however, vitiates the tension of the forties story. In black and white, a dying professor, Dennis Quaid, staggers into a cop-shop to tell how he got poisoned. In colour, his story unfolds. It involves Meg Ryan as a somewhat over-age college freshman, Daniel Stern as a jealous professor in Quaid's department and Charlotte Rampling as a devious benefactress. Several people fall to their deaths at different times on the same pavement, and another meets his doom in a tar pit. **BM**
Directors *Rocky Morton, Annabel Jankel* ***producers*** *Ian Sander, Laura Ziskin* ***script*** *Charles Edward Pogue, based on the 1949 screenplay by Russell Rouse and Clarence Greene* ***camera*** *Yuri Neyman* ***editor*** *Michael R. Miller* ***design*** *Richard Amend* ***music*** *Chaz Jankel* ***cast*** *Dennis Quaid, Meg Ryan, Charlotte Rampling, Daniel Stern, Jane Kaczmarek, Christopher Neame, Robin Johnson, Rob Knepper, Jay Patterson, Brion James, Jack Kehoe, Elizabeth Arlen*
Running time: 96 mins
US release: BV, Mar 18, 1988

Dragnet

DOGS IN SPACE

Set in Melbourne in 1978, Richard Lowenstein's second feature is a wild, piercingly observant homage to the height of the punk era down under. Shifting his camera around one chaotic household with all-embracing Scope images and a motley crowd of characters (a stylistic ploy reminiscent of Altman in his glory days), Lowenstein finally focuses on a love story and ends with an explicit anti-drug note. With expert playing from a mainly unknown cast including the lead singer of INXS, the mixture of youthful energy, fraught emotions and a blasting soundtrack make this the freshest new Australian movie in years. **DT**
Director/script *Richard Lowenstein* ***producer*** *Glenys Rowe* ***execs*** *Robert Le Tet, Dennis Wright* ***camera*** *Andrew de Groot* ***editor*** *Jill Bilcock* ***design*** *Jody Borland* ***music*** *Iggy Pop, Stamphyl-Revega, Sam Sejavka/Mike Lewis, Ollie Olsen, The Marching Girls, Brian Eno, Royland S. Howard, The Primitive Calculators, The Birthday Party, Gang of Four, Chuck Rio* ***cast*** *Michael Hutchence, Saskia Post, Nique Needles, Deanna Bond, Tony Helou, Chris Haywood, Peter Walsh, Laura Swanson, Adam Briscomb, Sharon Jessop, Edward Clayton-Jones, Martii Coles, Chuck Meo, Caroline Lee, Fiona Latham, Stephanie Johnson, Gary Foley, Glenys Osborne*
Running time: 109 mins
US release: Skouras, Oct 9, 1987
UK release: Recorded Releasing, Jun 10, 1988

Dogs in Space

DOMINICK AND EUGENE

Tom Hulce's superb performance as a retarded young man outweighs this drama's weak storyline. Ray Liotta plays Hulce's non-identical twin, a promising medical student whose expenses are being paid by Hulce's insurance money. Hulce, meanwhile, enjoys his work as a dustman. The sweet-tempered Hulce doesn't even mind when Liotta brings over a girlfriend, Jamie Lee Curtis (who has little to do except look understanding). When Hulce on his daily round witnesses a child's murder, he and his brother must face the truth about the cause of his disability. Once they do that, why, everything is wonderful. **BM**

Director *Robert M. Young* ***producers*** *Marvin Minoff, Mike Farrell* ***script*** *Alvin Sargent, Corey Blechman* ***camera*** *Curtis Clark* ***editor*** *Arthur Coburn* ***design*** *Doug Kraner* ***music*** *Trevor Jones* ***cast*** *Tom Hulce, Ray Liotta, Jamie Lee Curtis, Todd Graff, Mimi Cecchini, Robert Levine, Bill Cobbs, David Strathairn, Tommy Snelsire, Mary Joan Negro, Tom Signorelli, Joe Maruzzo*

Running time: 111 mins

US release: Orion, Mar 18, 1988

DRAGNET

Dum-de-dum-dum, this irreverent spoof of the famous, strait-laced TV cop series of the fifties and sixties turns out to be really quite good fun, which has less to do with blatantly poking fun at the quaintness of the original and exploiting a mega-budget (the usual round of car smashes) than with Dan Aykroyd's performance as the splendidly (and literally) buttoned-up LAPD nephew of Jack Webb's Sgt. Joe Friday. Aykroyd is perfect at the staccato delivery whether in his by-the-book routines or pompous moralizing about his hip partner Tom Hanks's shortcomings. **QF**

Director *Tom Mankiewicz* ***producers*** *David Permut, Robert K. Weiss* ***exec*** *Bernie Brillstein* ***script*** *Dan Aykroyd, Alan Zweibel, Mankiewicz* ***camera*** *Matthew F. Leonetti* ***editor*** *Richard Halsey, William D. Gordean* ***design*** *Robert F. Boyle* ***music*** *Ira Newborn* ***cast*** *Dan Aykroyd, Tom Hanks, Christopher Plummer, Harry Morgan, Alexandra Paul, Jack O'Halloran, Elizabeth Ashley, Dabney Coleman, Kathleen Freeman*

Running time: 106 mins

US release: Universal, Jun 26, 1987

UK release: UIP, Mar 11, 1988

DUDES

Dudes falls between the two stools of new-wave comedy and conventional thriller. Penelope Spheeris has cocked a snook at Hollywood styles more successfully before. Here, three New York punkers light out for Hollywood but meet disaster in the desert. Waylaid by rednecks who snuff their pal and take their dough, Jon Cryer and Daniel Roebuck seek vengeance. Local filling station attendant Catherine Mary Stewart gives them a hand when they're unjustly clapped behind bars. Many urban wits have come to the badlands and lost their way, and Spheeris is the latest. The threadbare plot and lame dialogue give the project a disastrous home-movie look. **BM**

Director *Penelope Spheeris* ***producers*** *Herb Jaffe, Miguel Tejada Flores* ***exec*** *Mort Engelberg* ***script*** *John Randal Johnson* ***camera*** *Robert Richardson* ***editor*** *Andy Horvitch* ***design*** *Robert Ziembicki* ***music*** *Charles Bernstein* ***cast*** *Jon Cryer, Catherine Mary Stewart, Daniel Roebuck, Lee Ving, Flea, Pete Willcox, Read Morgan, Wycliffe Young, Calvin Bartlett, Billy Ray Sharkey, Glenn Withrow, Michael Melvin, Axel G. Reese, Marc Rude, Vance Colvig*

Running time: 97 mins

US release: New Century, Aug 28, 1987

UK release: Recorded Releasing, May 6, 1988

·E·E·E·E·E·E·E·E·E·E·E·E·

EAT THE PEACH

Inevitably dubbed an Irish western because of its proliferation of frontier references, this amiable, whimsical and eccentric comedy is less Ford and more Forsyth. After seeing the Elvis Presley film *Roustabout*, out-of-work Vinnie dreams of building his own motorcycling Wall of Death. To finance the scheme, he and his friend Arthur must smuggle a variety of goods across the border - everything and anything from drinks to pigs. Despite the intervention of Provos and the British army, it's all resolutely good-natured and a considerable strike for Irish cinema. **QF**

Director *Peter Ormrod* ***producer*** *John Kelleher* ***exec*** *David Collins* ***script*** *Peter Ormrod, Kelleher* ***camera*** *Arthur Wooster* ***editor*** *J. Patrick Duffer* ***design*** *David Wilson* ***music*** *Donal Lunny* ***cast*** *Stephen Brennan, Eamon Morrissey, Catherine Byrne, Niall Toibin, Joe Lynch, Tony Doyle, Takashi Kawahara*

Running time: 95 mins

US release: Skouras, Jul 17, 1987

UK release: UIP, Dec 5, 1986

EAT THE RICH

The Comic Strip's follow-up to *The Supergrass*, intended as an acidic attack on eighties Britain, failed to generate any more significance than its deafening heavy metal soundtrack. Nosher Powell (a veteran stunt man and heavy) lets rip at the leading role of a Home Secretary popular for dealing with national crises as if they were tiffs between East End crooks. But the parallel plot involving an anarchist revolt led by black transsexual Lanah Pellay is tedious in the extreme, and the film's scatter-shot approach to satire renders it finally as toothless as an old *Carry On*. **DT**

Director *Peter Richardson* ***producer*** *Tim Van Rellim* ***exec*** *Michael White* ***script*** *Richardson, Peter Richens* ***camera*** *Witold Stock* ***editor*** *Chris Ridsdale* ***design*** *Caroline Amies* ***music*** *Simon Brint, Roland Rivron* ***cast*** *Ronald Allen, Sandra Dorne, Jimmy Fagg, Lemmy, Lanah Pellay, Nosher Powell, Fiona Richmond, Ron Tarr, Robbie Coltrane, David Beard, Angie Bowie, Katrin Cartlidge, Sean Chapman, Miles Copeland, Hugh Cornwell, Neil Cunningham, Robert Davis, Neil Dickson, Adrian Funnell, Adrian Edmondson, Norman Fisher, Bob Flagg, Peter Fontaine, Dawn French, Fran Fullenwider, Joanne Good, Cathryn Harrison, Jools Holland, Debbie Lindon, Christopher Malcolm, Rik Mayall, Miranda Richardson, Nigel Planer, Marika Rivera, Jennifer Saunders, Sandy Shaw, Koo Stark, Rupert Vansittart, Ruby Wax, Bill Wyman, Daniel Peacock, Paul McCartney*

Running time: 89 mins

US release: New Line, Oct 23, 1987

UK release: Recorded Releasing, Oct 23, 1987

EIGHTEEN AGAIN

Was this movie necessary? Among America's four movies this year about mind-body switches between men of different generations, Paul Flaherty's is the most obviously unoriginal. The claim to uniqueness here is that the switch occurs not between father and son, but between grandfather and grandson! Charlie Schlatter is the boy who takes over gramps's mind after an auto crash, and George Burns is the senior citizen who becomes 18 again. The other movies in this narrow genre have relied mostly on following the older (and more famous) body as it flounders through boyhood, but here George Burns is neglected in favour of too many flat jokes featuring the forever-smiling Schlatter. **BM**

Director *Paul Flaherty* ***producer*** *Walter Coblenz* ***execs*** *Irving Fein, Michael Jaffe* ***script*** *Josh Goldstein, Jonathan Prince* ***camera*** *Stephen M. Katz* ***editor*** *Danford B. Greene* ***design*** *Dena Roth* ***music*** *Billy Goldenberg* ***cast*** *George Burns, Charlie Schlatter, Tony Roberts, Anita Morris, Miriam Flynn, Jennifer Runyon, Red Buttons, George DiCenzo, Bernard Fox, Kenneth Tigar, Anthony Starke, Pauly Shore*

Running time: 100 mins

US release: New World, Apr 8, 1988

EMPIRE OF THE SUN

Film of the Year

Director *Steven Spielberg* ***producers*** *Spielberg, Kathleen Kennedy, Frank Marshall* ***exec*** *Robert Shapiro* ***script*** *Tom Stoppard, based on the novel by J.G. Ballard* ***camera*** *Allen Daviau* ***editor*** *Michael Kahn* ***design*** *Norman Reynolds* ***music*** *John Williams* ***cast*** *Christian Bale, John Malkovich, Miranda Richardson, Nigel Havers, Joe Pantoliano, Leslie Phillips, Masato Ibu, Emily Richard, Rupert Frazer, Peter Gale, Takatoro Kataoka, Ben Stiller, David Neidorf, Ralph Seymour, Robert Stephens, Zhai Nai She, Guts Ishimatsu, Emma Piper, James Walker, Jack Dearlove*

Running time: 152 mins

US release: Warner, Dec 9, 1987

UK release: Warner, Mar 11, 1988

EMPIRE OF THE SUN

Steven Spielberg cannot win. As producer or director of comic-strip fantasies, he's dismissed as a little boy who refuses to grow up. When he wears his more serious head, they tell him he's bitten off more than he can chew.

The approach of most American critics to Spielberg's *Empire of the Sun* was patronizing. At last they could say out loud what they've been threatening to say for years: that he is David Lean *manqué*. Thus *Premiere* magazine's Peter Kaplan suggests: 'There is a whiff of another director in this picture'. He then takes six paragraphs to formulate his carefully preconceived notion: 'Lean's triumph was combining the epic and the intimate, elements that are for Spielberg somehow irreconcilable ... Steven Spielberg, don't call home; call David Lean.'

It is not, of course, difficult to make connections between Spielberg and Lean. Given that the latter's *A Passage to India* seemed to substitute length and detail for pace and power, I tend to agree with those critics who argue that Spielberg has revitalized Lean's epic format.

J. G. Ballard's *Empire of the Sun* was first published in 1984, attracting reviews like 'the greatest British novel about the last war' and 'unforgettably haunting in its pictures and atmosphere.'

Basically, it recounts the terrifying events that the young Jim Graham lives through after the armed forces of Imperial Japan - the Empire of the Sun - march into Shanghai following the bombing of Pearl Harbour in December 1941. The story is loosely based on Ballard's own experiences as a boy interned with his parents in a Japanese prison camp at Lunghua near Shanghai from 1942 to 1945.

With hindsight, it's easy to see the attraction to Spielberg of a drama about the adult world of war seen through the eyes of a young boy. Additionally, the novel is littered with the kind of cinematic references that register with a post-war movie-brat.

When Spielberg was introduced to the book, it turned out that Warner Bros was already developing it with writer Tom Stoppard. There was talk of, yes, David Lean coming on board as director. When Lean lost interest, Warner's offered the project to Spielberg, with whom they had done *The Color Purple*.

'I identified,' said Spielberg, 'with, and was inspired by, Jim's character. He's the youngest hero in recent literature, a survivor in a world that doesn't allow survival. *Empire of the Sun* is an anti-war story about the effect of war on impressionable kids who are becoming adults; a human interest story woven within an epic tapestry.'

Warned that obtaining permission to shoot in China might entail four years of negotiations, the producers began the proverbial 'worldwide search' for a location that might double for the harbour city of Shanghai. This led to such places as Buenos Aires, Vienna, Liverpool, Stockholm, Hong Kong and Lisbon.

However, with help from the Shanghai Film Studios and the China Film Co-Production Corporation, they were able to complete the negotiations within a year, winning permission to bring crew and cameras to China for three weeks. The city has changed little in the past 40 years, enabling the film-makers to go on Shanghai's roof-tops and match shots from old photographs. Around 10,000 extras were recruited to people the Bund - the city's main waterfront highway - and to re-stage the mass flight from a besieged city.

Although the luxurious Tudor-style homes, which comprised the British quarter of the International Settlement, still stood with the same imposing façades, the producers found that, with 14 to 15 Chinese families now living in each house, they could use the once-exclusive neighbourhood for exterior shots only. 'Stand-ins' were found in Sunningdale, Berkshire and Knutsford, near Manchester.

Despite an un-starry cast which included John Malkovich, Joe Pantoliano, Miranda Richardson and Nigel Havers, the budget eventually weighed in, unsurprisingly for such an enormous logistical undertaking, at around $30 million. For an intelligent spectacle without recourse to endless effects, such a figure would always pose something of a box-office hurdle. In America, the film performed 'disappointingly'; in the rest of the world, considerably better.

The real success of *Empire of the Sun* isn't just in its fidelity to the incidentals of such uncompromising material - if not as stark and bloodthirsty as Ballard's original - but in taking as a central character a spoilt little English expatriate schoolboy, and giving him genuine anti-heroic status.

The rest of the characters, from parents to POW pirates, are shadowy in comparison as the hyperactive boy moves from shrill innocent to cynical adolescent during this extraordinary wartime rite of passage. Christian Bale gives a remarkable performance in the central role. His eyes constantly dart about and only, wearily, close as the security of family reunion is eventually achieved. For Jim, the sun has finally set.
QUENTIN FALK

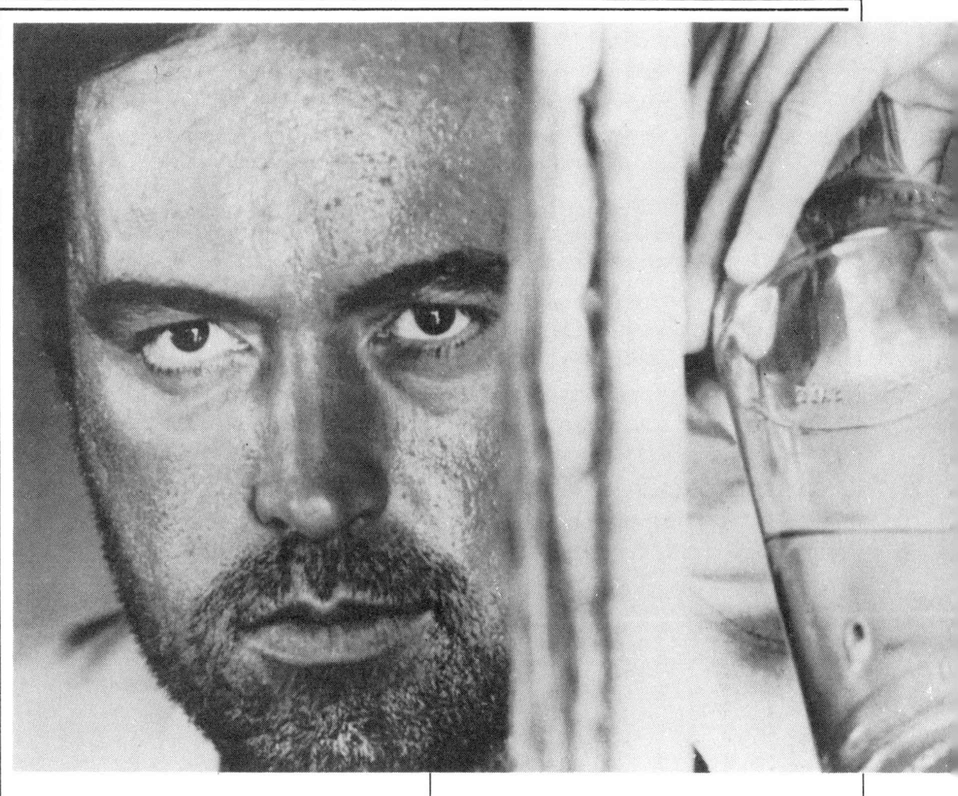

Extreme Prejudice

END OF THE LINE

Threatened with the loss of their jobs, Arkansas railroaders Wilford Brimley and Levon Helm hijack a loco and head for the company HQ in the Big City, where they find their train-loving president has been shunted into retirement by an opportunist yuppie. Despite good intentions all round, Columbia Film School graduate Jay Russell's directorial début is a lukewarm social comedy that needed the fuel and fire of a *Matewan* to give it some steam. Executive producer Mary Steenburgen (an old neighbour of Russell's in Little Rock) provides the best turn as Helm's slatternly, chain-smoking beautician wife, reminding us how good she was in *Melvin and Howard*. **GF**

***Director** Jay Russell **producers** Lewis Allen, Peter Newman **exec** Mary Steenburgen **script** Russell, John Wohlbruck **camera** George Tirl **editor** Mercedes Danevic **design** Neil Spisak **music** Andy Summers **cast** Wilford Brimley, Levon Helm, Mary Steenburgen, Barbara Barrie, Henderson Forsythe, Bob Balaban, Kevin Bacon, Michael Beach, Holly Hunter*

Running time: 105 mins

US release: Orion Classics, Aug 28, 1987

EXTREME PREJUDICE

A Tex meets Mex and buddy love turns sour with Nolte as a US Ranger engaged in a covert CIA operation to uncover the activities of his former partner, now turned drug baron. Hill's direction is characteristically lean and mean, but little room is left for characterization when the shoot-outs become relentlessly repetitive. With a finale that even tries to outdo *The Wild Bunch*, this was a potential gem that ricochets off into a barrel load of clichés whenever bullets start to fly. **DT**

***Director** Walter Hill **producer** Buzz Feitshans **execs** Mario Kassar, Andrew Vajna **script** Deric Washburn, Harry Kleiner **camera** Matthew F. Leonetti **editor** Freeman Davis **design** Albert Heschong **music** Jerry Goldsmith **cast** Nick Nolte, Powers Boothe, Michael Ironside, Maria Conchita Alonso, Rip Torn, Clancy Brown, William Forsythe, Matt Mulhern, Larry B. Scott*

Running time: 104 mins

US release: Tri-Star, Apr 24, 1987

UK release: Guild, Sep 25, 1987

·F·F·F·F·F·F·F·F·F·F·F·F·F·

THE FAMILY

Spanning 80 years in the lives of four generations of an Italian upper-middle-class family, from 1906 to the present, Scola's new film echoes his earlier *Le Bal* in confining itself to a single interior, in this case the family's Roman apartment. With an ostensibly more realistic screenplay, however, this convention begins to seem something of a stumbling block and the artificiality of style starts to rub off on the material. Despite the starry cast and elegant production values, the 127 minute duration feels over-generous. **TP**

***Director/editor** Ettore Scola **producer** Franco Committeri **script** Ruggero Maccari, Furio Scarpelli, Scola **camera** Ricardo Aronovich **design** Luciano Ricceri **music** Armando Trovajoli **cast** Vittorio Gassman, Fanny Ardant, Stefania Sandrelli, Andrea Acchipinti*

Running time: 127 mins

US release: Vestron, Jan 22, 1988

FAMILY BUSINESS

Costa-Gavras slums unsuccessfully in this ironic comedy celebrating criminality. Abandoning his usual *métier* of left-leaning political thrillers, Costa-Gavras here tells the ponderous story of a burglar who teaches his son too well. Johnny Hallyday, back from a stretch in the pen, is blackmailed by his son into teaching him the safe-cracking dodge. The

well-born loving wife and mother (Ardant) is happy with the bourgeois Riviera lifestyle bought by thievery. Eventually the son has a change of heart and betrays Hallyday and his partner (Marchant) to the police. **BM**
Director *Constantin Costa-Gavras* ***producer*** *Michèle Ray* ***script*** *Costa-Gavras, from the novel by Francis Ryck* ***camera*** *Robert Alazraki* ***editor*** *Marie-Sophie Dubus* ***design*** *Eric Simon* ***music*** *Georges Delerue* ***cast*** *Johnny Hallyday, Fanny Ardant, Guy Marchant, Laurent Romor, Remi Martin, Juliette Rennes, Caroline Pochon*
Running time: 123 mins (original version)
US release: European Classics, Sep 6, 1987

FATAL ATTRACTION
Film of the Year
Director *Adrian Lyne* ***producers*** *Stanley R. Jaffe, Sherry Lansing* ***script*** *James Dearden* ***camera*** *Howard Atherton* ***editors*** *Michael Kahn, Peter E. Berger* ***design*** *Mel Bourne* ***music*** *Maurice Jarre* ***cast*** *Michael Douglas, Glenn Close, Anne Archer, Ellen Hamilton Latzen, Stuart Pankin, Ellen Foley, Fred Gwynne, Meg Mundy, Tom Brennan, Lois Smith, Mike Nussbaum, J. J. Johnston, Michael Arkin, Sam J. Coppola, Eunice Prewitt, Jane Krakowski, Justine Johnston*
Running time: 120 mins
US release: Paramount, Sep 18, 1987
UK release: UIP, Jan 15, 1988

FATAL BEAUTY
When is this woman going to make a good movie? In her latest disaster, Whoopi Goldberg plays an unorthodox police-woman, *à la Beverly Hills Cop*, going after a drug-pushing villain with a German name (Yulin). Goldberg's character, inexplicably, has an Italian name. Ultra-WASP Sam Elliott plays a bodyguard with a Jewish name. Goldberg throws out multiple anti-man witticisms while following the trail of some bad dope that is knocking off yuppie snorters all over LA. The jokes and action in Tom Holland's film will entertain only those who thought *Dirty Harry* was soft on crime. **BM**
Director *Tom Holland* ***producer*** *Leonard Kroll* ***script*** *Hilary Henkin, Dean Riesner* ***camera*** *David M. Walsh* ***editor*** *Don Zimmerman* ***design*** *James William Newport* ***music*** *Harold Faltermeyer* ***cast*** *Whoopi Goldberg, Sam Elliott, Rubén Blades, Harris Yulin, John P. Ryan, Jennifer Warren, Brad Dourif, Mike Jolly, Charles Hallahan, Neil Barry, Richard (Cheech) Marin, Ebbe Roe Smith*
Running time: 104 mins
US release: MGM, Oct 30, 1987

FIVE CORNERS
The Bronx in 1964 is the setting for Tony Bill's low-key movie - enlivened by such surreal touches as the killing of a spiteful teacher by an unknown archer - about a bunch of young adults, mostly misfits, trying to sort out their lives. Marvellous as usual, Jodie Foster is the realistic neighbourhood angel, loved by a cripple, protected by a strong, silent pacifist involved in the Civil Rights movement, and stalked by a sad psychotic (Turturro) who eventually throws his mad old momma out of a window. Jodie and a penguin survive. Bill and writer John Patrick Shanley (responsible for *Moonstruck*) sympathize with, rather than judge, their characters and, despite the eruptions of violence, reflect poignantly on small people already overtaken by the cataclysmic events of the decade. **GF**
Director *Tony Bill* ***producers*** *Forrest Murray, Bill* ***execs*** *George Harrison, Denis O'Brien* ***script*** *John Patrick Shanley* ***camera*** *Fred Murphy* ***editor*** *Andy Blumenthal* ***design*** *Adrianne Lobel* ***music*** *James Newton Howard* ***cast*** *Jodie Foster, Tim Robbins, Todd Graff, John Turturro, Elizabeth Berridge, Rose Gregorio, Gregory Rozakis, John Seitz, Kathleen Chalfant, Rodney Harvey, Cathryn de Prume, Carl Capotorto, Daniel Jenkins, Michael R. Howard, Pierre Epstein*
Running time: 94 mins
US release: Cineplex, Jan 22, 1988

A FLAME IN MY HEART
(Une Flamme dans mon cœur)
Turkey of the Year
Director *Alain Tanner* ***exec*** *Dominique Vignet* ***producer*** *Paulo Branco* ***script*** *Myriam Mézières, Tanner* ***camera*** *Acacio de Almeida* ***editor*** *Laurent Uhler* ***cast*** *Myriam Mézières, Benoît Régent, Aziz Kabouche, André Marcon, Jean-Gabriel Nordman, Jean-Yves Berteloot, Anne Rucki, Douglas Ireland*
Running time: 110 mins
UK release: Mainline, Apr 22, 1988

FLOWERS IN THE ATTIC
V.C. Andrews' horticultural horror books have sold millions, but, like Stephen King's stories, they don't seem to provide the same frissons when filmed. Writer/director Jeffrey Bloom (not a pseudonym) fails to inject much suspense into Andrews' story of four kids carrying names that start with 'C' who are victimized by their own family. Cathy, Chris, Cory and Carrie are locked up by their evil grandmother (Fletcher) while their fortune-hunting mother (Tennant) tends rich and dying grandpa, and adds arsenic to their cookies. **BM**
Director *Jeffrey Bloom* ***producers*** *Sy Levin, Thomas Fries* ***execs*** *Charles Fries, Mike Rosenfeld* ***script*** *Bloom, based on novel by V.C. Andrews* ***camera*** *Frank Byers, Gil Hubbs* ***editor*** *Gregory F. Plotts* ***design*** *John Muto* ***music*** *Christopher Young* ***cast*** *Louise Fletcher, Victoria Tennant, Kristy Swanson, Jeb Stuart Adams, Ben Ganger, Lindsay Parker, Marshall Colt, Nathan Davis, Brooke Fries, Alex Koba, Leonard Mann, Bruce Neckels*
Running time: 95 mins
US release: New World, Nov 20, 1987
UK release: Entertainment, Apr 22, 1986

FOR KEEPS (Maybe Baby in UK)
Possibly useful for propaganda purposes, John G. Avildsen's comedy about teen parents falls flat as believable storytelling. Molly Ringwald and newcomer Randall Batinkoff are honour students who come from nice homes. They're destined for glittering prizes in college and afterwards - until pregnancy, true love and aversion to abortion turn them into poverty-line parents. Their own parents, as always in American films about teens, 'just don't understand'. All the difficulties and rewards of the situation are mechanically trotted out, including such facts as the truth about pre-natal haemorrhoids. **BM**
Director/editor *John G. Avildsen* ***producers*** *Jerry Belson, Walter Coblenz* ***script*** *Tim Kazurinsky, Denise DeClue* ***camera*** *James Crabe* ***design*** *William J. Cassidy* ***music*** *Bill Conti* ***cast*** *Molly Ringwald, Randall Batinkoff, Kenneth Mars, Miriam Flynn, Conchata Ferrell, Sharon Brown*
Running time: 98 mins
US release: Tri-Star, Jan 15, 1988
UK release: Columbia, Jun 17, 1988

FOUR ADVENTURES OF REINETTE AND MIRABELLE
(4 aventures de Reinette et Mirabelle)
A footnote to the 'Comédies et Proverbes' series, this delightfully modest quartet of stories - *The Blue Hour, The Waiter, The Beggar, The Kleptomaniac, The Hustler, Selling the Picture* - takes its cue from the confrontation between loquacious country girl Reinette and cool Parisian student Mirabelle. Moving from the fields to the big city, each episode is a little 'moral tale' in itself, made with an eloquent simplicity that curiously suggests the important début of a young talent rather than the Indian summer of a *grand seigneur*. **DT**
Director/producer/script *Eric Rohmer* ***camera*** *Sophie Maintigneux* ***editor*** *Marie-Luisa Garcia* ***music*** *Ronan Girre, Jean-Louis Valero* ***cast*** *Joëlle Miquel, Jessica Forde, The Housseua Family, Philippe Laudenbach, Yasmine Haury, Marie Rivière, Beatrice Romand, Gérard Courant, David Rocksavage, Jacques Auffray, Haydée Caillot, Fabrice Luchini, Marie Bouteloup, Françoise Valier*
Running time: 99 mins
UK release: Artificial Eye, Jan 8, 1988

THE FOURTH PROTOCOL
Civilization as we know it can only be saved by Michael Caine. Will our man from the British Secret Service stop Russian agent Pierce Brosnan assembling and detonating a nuclear bomb on British soil? Frederick Forsyth's novel bravely strove to keep the Cold War freezing, but this tepid movie version defrosts it at a stroke. The Russian accents are an embarrassment, the script (by Forsyth himself) is shapeless, and in Caine's currently erratic career this film is only a step away from *Jaws the Revenge*. **HK**
Director *John Mackenzie* ***producer*** *Timothy Burrill* ***execs*** *Frederick Forsyth, Michael Caine, Wafic Said* ***script*** *Frederick Forsyth* ***camera*** *Phil Meheux* ***editor*** *Graham Walker* ***design*** *Allan Cameron* ***music*** *Lalo Schifrin* ***cast*** *Michael Caine, Pierce Brosnan, Joanna Cassidy, Ned Beatty,*

Friendship's Death

Betsy Brantley, Peter Cartright, David Conville, Matt Frewer, Ray McAnally, Ian Richardson, Anton Rodgers
Running time: 119 mins
UK release: Rank, Mar 20, 1987
US release: Lorimar, Aug 28, 1987

FRANTIC

Trouble in Paris for American Dr Harrison Ford when his wife is kidnapped on the eve of a medical conference. Whodunit? Through an assault course of false trails, McGuffins, language perplexities and dead bodies, Ford sleuths. Roman Polanski proves that the minor career setback of *The Pirates* can now be forgotten. This is a major career setback. Diffuse, stilted, humourless and implausible, the movie seems the work of an exiled film-maker dying from lack of Hollywood oxygen. **HK**
Director *Roman Polanski* ***producers*** *Thom Mount, Tim Hampton* ***script*** *Gérard Brach, Polanski* ***camera*** *Witold Sobocinski* ***editor*** *Sam O'Casten* ***design*** *Pierre Guffroy* ***music*** *Ennio Morricone* ***cast*** *Harrison Ford, Emmanuelle Seigner, Betty Buckley, John Mahoney, Jimmie Ray Weeks, Yorgo Voyagis, David Huddleston, Gérard Klein, Jacques Ciron, Dominique Pinon, Thomas M. Pollard, Alexandra Stewart*
Running time: 120 mins
US release: Warner, Feb 26, 1988

FRIDAY THE THIRTEENTH PART VII - THE NEW BLOOD

Body count for this hardy annual, set in the forests of Alabama, is a dozen teenagers and two adults.
Director *John Carl Buechler* ***producer*** *Iain Paterson* ***script*** *Daryl Haney, Manuel Fidello* ***camera*** *Paul Elliott* ***editors*** *Barry Zetlin, Maureen O'Connell, Martin Jay Sadoff* ***design*** *Richard Lawrence* ***music*** *Harry Manfredini, Fred Mollin* ***cast*** *Jennifer Banko, John Otrin, Susan Blu, Lar Park Lincoln, Terry Kiser, Kevin Blair, Susan Jennifer Sullivan, Heidi Kozak, Kane Hodder*
Running time: 90 mins
US release: Paramount, May 13, 1988

FRIENDSHIP'S DEATH

Film-maker/theorist Peter Wollen's first solo outing depicts the brief relationship between Sullivan (Paterson), a cynical British journalist, and Friendship (Swinton), an alien robot in human female guise who has fetched up in Amman, Jordan, during Black September, 1970, instead of her intended destination, the Massachusetts Institute of Technology. Herself dispossessed, she identifies with the PLO and decides to stay when Sullivan leaves, giving him a crystal which years later yields a revelatory message. Wollen's two-hander is a complex conceptual tract, filtered through the sci-fi genre, which examines the state of political homelessness and, self-reflexively, the potency of the cinematic image. Beautiful to look at, it succeeds as a polemic and - because Friendship is unavoidably humanized through Swinton's hypnotic playing - as more of a love story than perhaps Wollen intended. **GF**
Director/script *Peter Wollen* ***producer*** *Rebecca O'Brien* ***exec*** *Colin MacCabe* ***camera*** *Witold Stock* ***editor*** *Robert Hargreaves* ***design*** *Gemma Jackson* ***music*** *Barrington Pheloung* ***cast*** *Bill Paterson, Tilda Swinton, Patrick Bauchau, Ruby Baker, Joumana Gill*
Running time: 78 mins
UK release: BFI, Nov 20, 1987

FATAL ATTRACTION

Fatal Attraction is an adept thriller about adultery, vengeance and madness which plugged into America's AIDS hysteria and the nation's new misogyny to achieve its nine-figure gross. Like *Platoon* the year before, its success was the result of lucky timing.

Platoon, which showed how the best soldiers go bad first, happened to come out just after the revelations about Col. Oliver North. *Fatal Attraction* was released right after the first wave of publicity about heterosexuals' susceptibility to AIDS. Both films achieved blockbusterdom by staying distant from the audience's real concerns, yet getting close enough to serve as metaphor. Americans prefer not to face facts directly.

If a cure is found, maybe there will be a major studio film about AIDS. Meanwhile, we have a sturdy drama, written by James Dearden and directed by Adrian Lyne, that delivers an AIDS-like warning against promiscuity. One false move, one night in the wrong bed, one wish that shouldn't be fulfilled, and you can be marked for death.

Lawyer Michael Douglas has it all: a good job, big money, a beautiful wife, a lovely kid. But, one layer down, he's no different from any of us - he's slightly bored without knowing it.

When unattached Glenn Close looms, he looks. She looks back, and soon they're having a meal together, strictly business of course. Close pierces Douglas's double-think, forcing the idea of sex out into the open. Once acknowledged, his desire won't be denied, and he succumbs.

Lyne must have learned something about sex scenes when he misfired on *9½ Weeks*. Instead of adding up to a comic book of soft porn, his scenes of sexual behaviour involving Douglas and Close are motivated by their characters. Douglas's awkwardness and Close's obsessiveness are even better played in their overwrought love-making than out of bed.

One hot weekend is all Douglas wanted. What she wants, it becomes increasingly clear, is all of him. He wants to kiss her off with a polite see-you-never, but she uses every dirty trick to stay in his life. She even shows up as a prospective buyer of the Douglas family flat after he decides to move to the suburbs.

This is the point where *Fatal Attraction* loses most of the serious critics. Close's increasingly eccentric schemes to retrieve Douglas play as melodrama. What seemed like a romance with overtones of comedy suddenly becomes a horror movie. When Close grabs Douglas's daughter, and Mrs Douglas (Anne Archer) drives off hysterically to find her, and her car crashes, and she lands in hospital, bandaged but all right, and Douglas resolves ever more strongly to protect his family - yes, it's soap.

But superior soap. The film's derivative but effective climax, with its water dripping through the floorboards and its 'dead' woman emerging menacingly out of the water, whitened the knuckles of any movie-goers who hadn't distanced themselves by declaring the story preposterous.

And most people did buy the whole story. Douglas's vacillation evidently seemed realistic even to those who had thrilled to his Indiana Jones-style exploits in *Romancing the Stone* and its sequel. His slightly weak chin and twitchy eyes make him something less than a total hero at the best of times.

Completing the double turnabout on the stereotypes, Close plays hard-nosed siren to Douglas's passive lover-boy. The much-lauded actress has previously played mothers and victims but here shows such an evil glint in her eye that she seems believable clutching a butcher's knife. So many actresses playing mad, bad and scantily-clad seem to be thinking a mantra, 'It's only a movie, it's only a movie.' But Close can convey the reality of such scenes as her wicked-witch kidnapping of Douglas's only child without lapsing into stock characterization.

Dearden's original version of the script kept the situation ambiguous to the end: Close commits suicide with a knife bearing Douglas's fingerprints. Paramount tested the film with that ending and ran into a buzzsaw of protest against villainy succeeding, even so obliquely. The American audience, it seems, demands victory for the good guys. Today, Butch Cassidy and the Sundance Kid would survive that hail of Bolivian bullets, and Peter Fonda and Dennis Hopper would vanquish the rednecks at the end of *Easy Rider*. Paramount considered *Fatal Attraction* unreleasable without retribution. Close had to die for her sins.

Lyne had re-cut *9½ Weeks* to suit MGM, perhaps to the detriment of that film. He seemed happy to call the *Fatal Attraction* principals together to re-shoot the end. Although he let Douglas off the hook, Lyne didn't allow the two-timer the satisfaction of being the hero who saves the situation. He gave Anne Archer the gun that blows Close away after she rises out of the tub.

The film's success quickly provoked a cogent feminist critique. Many denounced the film for making a man the victim, and a woman the villain. They argued that, driven to dementia by the need for a child from a man who doesn't want her any more, a woman might break down, but she wouldn't suddenly turn into a homicidal maniac. These critics pointed out that, in reality, women are much less likely than men to react violently to romantic disappointment. Pick up any big-city American newspaper, and the odds are that there will be an article about a man who has killed his wife or girlfriend, and perhaps their children as well. A film that reverses the truth so comprehensively, feminists complained, could only make the real-life gender war worse.

These critics tried to avoid answering the question of why a movie that was so irritating could be so damned popular. Cornered, they suggested that men liked *Fatal Attraction* because it showed Douglas ultimately having his cake and eating it too. Women went along, they said, because the kind of man who likes this movie is the kind of man who decides which movie a couple will see. And these chauvinists' domesticated women actually wound up liking the movie because, in the end, the home-wrecker eats lead and the wife reclaims her straying man.

But then *Fatal Attraction* was never meant to be a movie for liberated women. The film entertained: the characters were well drawn and the leading actors stretched ably to play them, their love scenes were out of the ordinary, the suspense was expertly ratcheted to breaking-point, and the climax was surprising. There aren't many movies of which that can be said.

The phrase used in America for the eagerly-awaited AIDS cure is 'magic bullet'. In our hearts, we know that stressing monogamy won't save us. Tainted blood and contaminated needles apart, the disease will continue to spread through sexual contact. It's satisfying, then, to go to the cinema and see the old-style American solution to a problem: Anne Archer's magic bullet slaying the contagion that has invaded her home.

BART MILLS

A FLAME IN MY HEART

We should, of course, be able to tell at once from the opening credits, accompanied as they are by the plangent but simultaneously austere tones of a solo violin: melancholy, deeply spiritual, classical in the extreme. Not a down-market sound, this sublime sonata by Johann Sebastian Bach. Here is film that's meant to have class.

Then there's the grim, grainy black-and-white photography. Memories stir: vintage art-movies, *cinéma vérité*. Monochrome, these days, tends to signify serious in a big way: honesty, integrity, realism, in high-flying contrast to the commercial compromises inevitably suggested by colour. Bach in black-and-white, melancholia in monochrome: by the time we've reached the opening shots of Mercedes, an actress embarking upon rehearsals for her role as Racine's *Berenice* (well, we've had the musical and visual guarantees thrust upon us, so what's wrong with a bit of lofty drama to add to a recipe that oozes respectability?) - by this time we must surely realize, unless we're totally, idiotically illiterate about basic film semiotics, that heavy depression is in the offing.

Class and depression: they're both there, to be sure. The class derives from *A Flame in My Heart*'s auteurist credentials: the film is directed by *éminence Suisse* Alain Tanner, the man responsible for *The Salamander*, *Jonas Who Will Be 25 in the Year 2000*, *The Middle of the World*, *Messidor* and *In the White City*. The depression ... well, that's a little different. Admittedly there's more than enough moody posturing on screen to last a lifetime, but mostly the depression is yours and mine. How in hell does a film-maker of Tanner's sensitivity and standing get to make a movie as shoddy, voyeuristic, misogynist, and downright risible as this?

Let's take the movie stage by stage. This Mercedes character, played by Myriam Mézières - who also wrote the film - is one of those French types seen so often in the most cliché-ridden movies: she pouts a lot, shakes her head a lot, smokes a lot. And she whinges, on and on, but really doesn't seem to know what she wants. At the start of the film, she's fed up, she says, with her Arab lover Johnny and wants their relationship to end; understandably, since Johnny is a cartoon caricature of swarthy macho chauvinism, given to breaking into her flat making violent threats, using emotional blackmail, and ripping up her dresses. Whatever her intentions, however, Mercedes' response to such outrageously self-centred behaviour is simply to give way, time and time again: she strips for him (and, naturally, the camera), and goes to bed with him in return for blatantly dishonest promises that he will leave her alone. One can't help thinking that this masochistic misery and her strutting, sadistic Arab (the film verges dangerously on racism) are made for each other, and as such barely deserve our attention, let alone sympathy.

But wait: Mercedes finally escapes to the privacy of a hotel, and all should be well. Trouble is, this profoundly passionate woman can't exist without *amour* and plenty of it, so off she trundles to the Métro to pick up a shy young journalist whom she quickly ushers back to her bed. Pierre, a veritable Prince Charming of tenderness and tolerance, is a mite too good to be true; indeed the implausibility is only increased when he feels the urge to announce his name in mid-orgasm. It's that sort of movie.

What with all the bonking on view, Mercedes is happy in her immediate conviction that Pierre will love and protect her. She moves in with him, and gets down to further bonking, interspersed - for the sake of art, we presume - with deeply meaningful conversations that merely serve to confirm our suspicion that the woman is a complete and utter fruit cake. Pierre is a politi-

cal correspondent: has she ever read his work? No, of course not; to Mercedes, only *amour* and the theatre are of interest. She exists at the centre of the world where, apparently, it burns; he, on the other hand, only flies around it. Why Pierre, presumably fairly articulate given his fashionable status as a globe-trotting journo, doesn't kick her out forthwith remains a mystery.

Instead, he goes off on a brief business trip. At once Mercedes cracks up: even though her lover sends her a lyrical epistle extolling the virtues of oral sex, she loses her job, cuts the telephone wire, eats cereals all day, and lounges semi-naked in front of the television, masturbating for the sake of the camera's unblinking gaze. Some fun, huh? Never mind, after a fortnight Pierre returns, and she is so overjoyed she finds herself a job as a fairground stripper: her rather less than modest routine with a large toy monkey, conducted before an audience of leering, understandably zombiefied blacks (watch out for that racism again), provokes poor Pierre, the gentle sweetie, to remark with a *sang-froid* that suggests he's British, 'That was a little vulgar, wasn't it?'

If you've got a body - and most of us have - show it, seems to be Mercedes/Myriam's philosophy. But not, of course, all the time. She does find the space to accompany Pierre to Cairo, where, despite being madly in love, she wanders off into the suburban slums and sinks into a trance, staring at a child. Maybe the reason she doesn't return to Pierre is because, as she insists, he's afraid of women. Well, maybe he is, but in this case it's highly understandable.

So what's it all about? Mézières has spoken of her desire to make a film in which a woman's desire was portrayed in ways that were not pornographic but poetic, sensitive. It's strange then that so much of the film should linger on the exhibitionist and narcissistic presentation of her body. Is such self-confidence the mark of a strong woman? Hardly, when Mercedes is such a miserable victim figure, whose brief moments of happiness are totally dependent on the presence of men. At the same time, in a movie featuring so much pseudo-philosophical discussion of *amour*, it's odd that the passion depicted never once transcends the purely physical. In all these respects, the film is barely different from its counterparts in the straight porn industry; as *un film d'Alain Tanner* it's a woeful experience, bereft of integrity, not to mention dramatic subtlety. Simultaneously tedious, laughable, pretentious and offensive, *A Flame in My Heart* is a pain in the neck, proving once and for all that a veneer of artistic respectability - that music, that camera-work, those literary references - makes for duplicitous sign-posting, nothing more.

GEOFF ANDREW

FULL METAL JACKET

The phrase 'theatre of war' takes on new implications in the wake of Kubrick's astonishing film. The first third, treating Marine Corps basic training, is a gruelling *tour de force*, taking the director's recurring theme of dehumanization to new limits. The remainder, set in Vietnam at the time of the Tet offensive, may at first appear not to be organically linked to what has preceded it; yet - scripted with grim humour and realized with unflagging bravura - it comes to create a sort of fiery, hot-blooded mirror image of the abstracted brutality of the opening. Never has the cerebral rigour of Kubrick's cinema coexisted more startlingly with a capacity for visceral elaboration, and never has his work left so powerfully ambiguous a reflection on humanism. **TP**

Director/producer *Stanley Kubrick* ***exec*** *Jan Harlan* ***script*** *Kubrick, Michael Herr, Gustav Hasford, based on the latter's novel* The Short-Timers ***camera*** *Douglas Milsome* ***editor*** *Martin Hunter* ***design*** *Anton Furst* ***music*** *Abigail Mead* ***cast*** *Matthew Modine, Adam Baldwin, Vincent D'Onofrio, Lee Ermey, Dorian Harewood, Arliss Howard, Kevyn Major Howard, Ed O'Ross, John Terry, Keiron Jecchinis, Kirk Taylor, Tim Colceri, John Stafford, Bruce Boa, Ian Tyler, Sal Lopez, Gary Landon Mills, Papillon Soo Soo*

Running time: 116 mins
US release: Warner, Jun 26, 1987
UK release: CCW, Sep 11, 1987

THE FUNERAL

Solemnly magnificent comedy on the Japanese way of dying by Juzo (*Tampopo*) Itami. A family gathers to honour a late-lamented member and gets involved in yards of po-faced protocol, several dubious off-the-coffin incidents (involving sex and food) and a general air of earnest, spiralling bewilderment. Highlights include a masterly variation on the *Ben Hur* chariot race (how to pass a TV dinner from car to car in the pouring rain); a slyly hilarious teach-yourself video on How To Behave at a Funeral: and a scene involving eel and avocados that no *Tampopo* fan should miss. **HK**

Director/script *Juzo Itami* ***camera*** *Yonezo Maeda* ***editor*** *Akira Suzuki* ***design*** *Hiroshi Tokuda* ***music*** *Joji Yuasa* ***cast*** *Tsutomu Yamazaki, Nobuko Miyamoto, Kin Sugai*

Running time: 123 mins
US release: New Yorker, Oct 23, 1987

FUNNY FARM

Funny Farm is hardly one and not at all the other: there is no farm in this virtually joke-free Chevy Chase vehicle. Chase is a sportswriter who rusticates himself to seek his muse. He fails to write a publishable novel while his wife (Madolyn Smith) succeeds by simply parodying Chase's problems adjusting to the country. As depicted, these problems are too predictable to raise a laugh. When a bird chirps outside Chase's window, he douses it with hot coffee. When he enjoys a local delicacy, it turns out that he's been eating lamb testicles. George Roy Hill, how low you've sunk. **BM**

Director *George Roy Hill* ***producer*** *Robert L. Crawford* ***execs*** *Patrick Kelley, Bruce Bodner* ***script*** *Jeffrey Boam, based on the book by Jay Cronley* ***camera*** *Miroslav Ondricek* ***editor*** *Alan Heim* ***design*** *Henry Bumstead* ***music*** *Elmer Bernstein* ***cast*** *Chevy Chase, Madolyn Smith*

Running time: 101 mins
US release: Warner, Jun 3, 1988

·G·G·G·G·G·G·G·G·G·G·

GABY - A TRUE STORY

The overcoming of a handicap is generally a good movie subject if the handicap is cute, like Rocky's stupidity or The Karate Kid's weakness. Luis Mandoki succeeds in making a paralytic's struggle towards full womanhood not just appealing but also inspiring. Rachel Levin, an actress who overcame a temporarily crippling disease herself, plays the real-life victim of cerebral palsy, Gaby Brimmer. Brimmer's parents, played by Liv Ullmann and Robert Loggia, are understanding and supportive, and her nanny (Aleandro) helps her achieve literacy. **BM**

Director *Luis Mandoki* ***producer*** *Pinchas Perry* ***script*** *Martin Salinas, Michael James Love* ***camera*** *Lajos Koltai* ***editor*** *Garth Craven* ***design*** *Alejandro Luna* ***music*** *Maurice Jarre* ***cast*** *Liv Ullmann, Norma Aleandro, Rachel Levin, Robert Loggia, Lawrence Monoson, Robert Beltran*

Running time: 110 mins
US release: Tri-Star, Oct 30, 1987
UK release: Columbia, Jun 10, 1988

The Glass Menagerie

GARDENS OF STONE

Coppola returns to the Vietnam War, but (though the setting is the military one of the honour guard responsible for burials at Arlington Cemetery) on the home front and on an intimate scale which tends to suggest that the grand gesture is his real forte. Despite, or even because of, the careful mounting and nuanced performances, there is something remote and academic about this study of the relationship between a veteran sergeant (Caan) and the son of an ex-comrade who, under the old man's avuncular tutelage, gains a commission but also, with fatal results, achieves his ambition of seeing active service. The circular structure, beginning and ending with the young man's funeral, holds out a fatalistic reverberation which the intervening events somehow fail to justify. **TP**

Director *Francis Coppola* ***producers*** *Michael I. Levy, Francis Coppola* ***execs*** *Stan Weston, Jay Emmett, Fred Roos* ***script*** *Ronald Bass, based on the novel by Nicholas Proffitt* ***camera*** *Jordan Cronenweth* ***editor*** *Barry Malkin* ***design*** *Dean Tavoularis* ***music*** *Carmine Coppola* ***cast*** *James Caan, James Earl Jones, Anjelica Houston, D.B. Sweeney, Dean Stockwell, Mary Stuart Masterson, Dick Anthony Williams, Lonette McKee, Sam Bottoms, Elias Koteas, Larry Fishburne, Casey Siemaszko, Peter Masterson, Carlin Glynn, Erik Holland, Bill Graham, Terence Currier, Terry Hinz, Lisa-Marie Felter*

Running time: 111 mins
US release: Tri-Star, May 8, 1987
UK release: Columbia, Jan 22, 1988

Good Morning Babylon

THE GLASS MENAGERIE

Using a cast that had already worked together on the stage, Paul Newman has fashioned from Tennessee Williams' first masterpiece a film of utter fidelity to the theatrical text which still eschews staginess in favour of cinematic fluidity. Aided by the virtuoso lighting of Michael Ballhaus, he skilfully elucidates both the play's wistful humour and its Depression background. John Malkovich is especially fine as the narrator figure; one's slight reservations attach to the way that Joanne Woodward's playing of the mother threatens to become over-florid. **TP**

Director *Paul Newman* ***producer*** *Burt Harris* ***script*** *Tennessee Williams* ***camera*** *Michael Ballhaus* ***editor*** *David Ray* ***design*** *Tony Walton* ***music*** *Henry Mancini* ***cast*** *Joanne Woodward, John Malkovich, Karen Allen, James Naughton*

Running time: 135 mins
US release: Cineplex, Oct 23, 1987
UK release: Columbia, Jan 15, 1988

GOOD MORNING BABYLON

(Good Morning Babilonia)

Symbiotic directing team the brothers Taviani picked up an engagingly *simpatico* idea. Two Tuscan brothers leave home for America to continue their craft of stonemasonry and end up working on the set of D. W. Griffith's epic *Intolerance*. Unfortunately the concentrated naïve style that worked so well on home soil only results abroad in soggy wish-fulfilment, with Charles Dance as an uncharismatic D.W.G. and hazily romantic interludes for the boys with two beautiful dancers. **DT**

Directors *Paolo Taviani, Vittorio Taviani* ***producer*** *Giuliani G. De Negri* ***execs*** *Edward Pressman, Marin Karmitz* ***script*** *Paolo Taviani, Vittorio Taviani, Tonino Guerra, based on idea by Lloyd Fonvielle* ***camera*** *Giuseppe Lanci* ***editor*** *Roberto Perpignani* ***design*** *Gianni Sbarra* ***music*** *Nicola Piovani* ***cast*** *Vincent Spano, Joaquim De Almeida, Greta Scacchi, Désiré Becker, Omero Antonutti, Charles Dance, Bérangère Bonvoisin, David Brandon, Brian Freilino, Margarita Lozano, Massimo Venturiello, Andrea Prodan*

Running time: 117 mins
US release: Vestron, Jul 15, 1987
UK release: Artificial Eye, Aug 28, 1987

GOOD MORNING, VIETNAM

Robin Williams was Oscar-nominated for his incredible vocal gymnastics and sane-beneath-the-zany portrayal of real-life Armed Forces Radio DJ Adrian Cronauer - whose irreverent rock 'n' roll broadcasts earned him the adulation of the GIs and the wrath of the authorities in Saigon at the start of the Vietnam War. Indeed, the star never palls in Barry Levinson's straight comedy, and the scene in which Cronauer greets a convoy of troops is deeply affecting - less so his sentimental attachment to a Vietnamese girl and the schmaltzy interplay with her people. **GF**

Director *Barry Levinson* ***producers*** *Mark Johnson, Larry Brezner* ***script*** *Mitch Markowitz* ***camera*** *Peter Sova* ***editor*** *Stu Linder* ***design*** *Roy Walker* ***music*** *Alex North* ***cast*** *Robin Williams, Forest Whitaker, Tun Thanh Tran, Chintara Sukapatan, Bruno Kirby, Robert Wuhl, J.T. Walsh, Noble Willingham, Richard Edson, Juney Smith*

Running time: 120 mins

US release: BV, Dec 23, 1987

THE GOOD WIFE

It turns out that Australian lumberjacks are no more okay than Monty Python's Canadians. Ken Cameron's moral tale never recovers from a hesitant start, in which Bryan Brown is discovered felling mighty timbers while Rachel Ward scrubs floors. This idyllic vision of maleness is shattered when Brown's gormless brother asks to sleep with Ward and Brown lets him. Once loosed from domestic constraints, Ward then goes off the deep-end for local dandy Sam Neill. Neill steals the film with his sharp and funny portrait of a slimeball who lives to corrupt women but can't handle one who responds unreservedly. **BM**

Director *Ken Cameron* ***producer*** *Jan Sharp* ***script*** *Peter Kenna* ***camera*** *James Bartle* ***editor*** *John Scott* ***design*** *Sally Campbell* ***music*** *Cameron Allen* ***cast*** *Rachel Ward, Bryan Brown, Sam Neill, Steven Vidler, Jennifer Claire, Bruce Barry*

Running time: 92 mins

US release: Atlantic, Jan 16, 1987

UK release: Entertainment, Sep 25, 1987

THE GRAND HIGHWAY

(Le Grand chemin)

The top-grossing French film in France in 1987 is about a meek little nine year old (Antoine Hubert, son of writer/director Jean-Loup) who stays in a small Breton village in the summer of 1958 and gradually heals the fractured marriage of his mother's friend (Anémone) and her husband (Bohringer), the coarse local carpenter - whose own son was still-born. Little Louis even finds his own girlfriend in Vanessa Guedji's sexually precocious ten year old, who stuffs eels down his shorts and teaches him to piss on the church roof. Birth, death and regeneration are the themes (Anémone greets Louis by skinning a fetal rabbit), but this is mostly a film of plain rural delights. **GF**

Director/script *Jean-Loup Hubert* ***producers*** *Pascal Hommais, Jean-François Lepetit* ***camera*** *Claude Lecomte* ***editor*** *Raymonde Guyot* ***design*** *Thierry Flamand* ***music*** *Georges Granier* ***cast*** *Antoine Hubert, Anémone, Richard Bohringer, Vanessa Guedji, Christine Pascal, Raoul Billery, Pascale Roberts, Marie Matheron, Daniel Rialet*

Running time: 107 mins

US release: Miramax, Jan 22, 1988

The Good Wife

THE GREAT OUTDOORS

Since John Belushi died, Dan Aykroyd has paired off with many other screen comics in a search for another perfect foil for his precise sense of parody. John Candy comes closest in girth to Belushi, and John Hughes' script for *The Great Outdoors* aims to come close to *Neighbours*. Howard Deutch's film misses the mark, nevertheless. It's a boring collection of gags for pre-teens who like profanity. Family man Candy is enjoying a happy holiday in a mountain cabin when his brother-in-law, con man Aykroyd, drops in with his own less-than-ideal family and plays a series of cruel pranks on the hapless Candy. **BM**

Director *Howard Deutch* ***producer*** *Arne L. Schmidt* ***execs*** *John Hughes, Tom Jacobson* ***script*** *Hughes* ***camera*** *Ric Waite* ***editor*** *Tom Rolf, William Gordean, Seth Flaum* ***design*** *John W. Corso* ***music*** *Thomas Newman* ***cast*** *Dan Aykroyd, John Candy, Stephanie Faracy, Annette Bening, Chris Young, Ian Giatti, Hilary Gordon, Rebecca Gordon, Robert Prosky, Lucy Deakins*

Running time: 90 mins

US release: Universal, Jun 24, 1988

A GREAT WALL

(The Great Wall Is a Great Wall in US)

Sneaking in quietly while major Western producers wrangled with the authorities to set up their epics, actor and former documentary film-maker Peter Wang shot this first American-Chinese production in 1984. Charming and quaint as far as it goes, *A Great Wall* has computer executive Wang leading his very Westernized family over to Peking where he has relatives. Whimsically attentive to cute cultural differences, the film rigorously avoids all ideological and political issues, and seems stuck in the era of ping-pong diplomacy. Pleasing as an eager-to-please travelogue, this is a disappointment on every other level. **TM**

Director *Peter Wang* ***producer*** *Shirley Sun* ***script*** *Wang, Sun* ***camera*** *Peter Stein, Robert Primes* ***editor*** *Grahame Weinbren* ***design*** *Wing Lee, Feng Yuan, Ming Ming Cheung* ***music*** *David Liang, Ge Ganru, Paul Mesches* ***cast*** *Wang Xiao, Peter Wang, Sharon Iwai, Kelvin Han Yee, Li Qinqin, Hu Xiaoguang, Shen Guanglan, Xiu Jian, Ran Zhijuan, Han Tan, Jeanette Pavini, Howard Frieberg, Bill Neilson, Teresa Roberts*

Running time: 102 mins

US release: Orion Classics, Jan 31 1986

UK release: Mainline, Jul 10, 1987

·H·H·H·H·H·H·H·H·H·H·H·H

HAIRSPRAY

John Waters goes respectable without sacrificing bad taste in a film which has proved his most accessible (to a mainstream audience) yet and, sadly, was Divine's swansong. The big man rasps out his last lines as the outsize mom of plump newcomer Ricki Lake, whose Tracy Turnblad is desperate to become the queen of a TV teen dance show in early sixties Baltimore - and to dethrone the pampered daughter (Fitzpatrick) of Sonny Bono and a fantastically coiffured Debbie Harry. Waters slickly enfolds an integrationist theme as Lake champions the inclusion of black kids in the white supremacist show. Pia Zadora and Ric Ocasek (of The Cars) check in as a beatnik chick and cat, the soundtrack throbs, the hair explodes. Divine dances off into the sunset, and fat is beautiful. **GF**

Director/script *John Waters* ***producer*** *Rachel Talalay* ***execs*** *Robert Shaye, Sara Richer* ***camera*** *David Insley* ***editor*** *Janice Hampton* ***design*** *Vincent Peranio* ***cast*** *Sonny Bono, Ruth Brown, Divine, Colleen Fitzpatrick, Michael St Gerard, Debbie Harry, Ricki Lake, Leslie Ann Powers, Clayton Prince, Jerry Stiller, Mink Stole, Shawn Thompson, Ric Ocasek, Pia Zadora*

Hairspray

Running time: 90 mins

US release: New Line, Feb 26, 1988

UK release: Palace, Jul 1, 1988

HALF OF HEAVEN

(La Mitad del Cielo)

Abruptly widowed country girl Rosa - the beguiling Molina on top form - leaves with her daughter for the city and rises from maid to restaurant owner in Gutiérrez Aragón's most assured film to date. A witty, wry and delicately surreal depiction of Spain under Franco in the sixties, with a fine supporting cast of suitors to the bewitching but determinedly independent central character, who refuses to marry for fear that there is a curse on her family. In Spain the roots go deep. **DT**

Director *Manuel Gutiérrez Aragón* ***producer*** *Luis Megino* ***script*** *Aragón, Megino* ***camera*** *José Luis Alcaine* ***editor*** *José Salcedo* ***music*** *Milladoiro* ***cast*** *Angela Molina, Fernando Fernán Gómez, Margarita Lozano, Antonio V. Valero, Nacho Martinez, Santiago Ramos*

Running time: 127 mins

US release: Skouras, Jan 21, 1988

HAMBURGER HILL

A straightforward documentary-style account of a real-life bloody Vietnam action. There is a distinct sense of ho-hum here, compared to either the heightened realism or the overt surrealism that lifted such potentially ordinary 'Nam' epics as *Apocalypse Now*, *Platoon* or *Full Metal Jacket*. That said, it's astonishingly well-made with a cast of unknowns and a British director bearing a residue of guilt from the days he was filming conflict footage, but could easily retreat to a comfortable hotel away from the guns. **QF**

Director *John Irvin* ***producers*** *Marcia Nasatir, James Carabatsos* ***execs*** *Jerry Offsay, David Korda* ***script*** *James Carabatsos* ***camera*** *Peter MacDonald* ***editor*** *Peter Tanner* ***design*** *Austen Spriggs* ***music*** *Philip Glass* ***cast*** *Anthony Barrile, Michael Patrick Boatman, Don Cheadle, Michael Dolan, Don James, Dylan McDermott, M.A. Nickles, Harry O'Reilly, Daniel O'Shea, J.C. Palmore, Tim Quill, Tommy Swerdlow, Courtney B. Vance, Steven Weber, Tegan West, Kieu Chinh, Doug Goodman, J. C. Palmore, J. D. Van Sickle*

Running time: 110 mins

US release: Paramount, Aug 28, 1987

UK release: Palace, Aug 21, 1987

A HANDFUL OF DUST

After a recent stream of literary adaptations mostly celebrating the stuffy, arid world of E.M. Forster, classics illustrated have been renewed in altogether livelier style with this elegant, but above all moving, version of Evelyn Waugh's most personal novel, about uppercrust adultery and betrayal. Faithful without being slavish, the screenwriters have pared some of the original's less attractive incidentals while keeping fully intact Waugh's emotion, wit and dark irony. In Kristin Scott-Thomas, playing Lady Brenda, cinema has a radiant new star.

A Handful of Dust

Waugh, badly mistreated by previous big-screen adaptations (*The Loved One, Decline and Fall*), might well have approved this time round. **QF**
Director *Charles Sturridge* ***producer*** *Derek Granger* ***execs*** *Jeffrey Taylor, Kent Walwin, Nick Elliott* ***script*** *Tim Sullivan, Granger, Sturridge, based on the novel by Evelyn Waugh* ***camera*** *Peter Hannan* ***editor*** *Peter Coulson* ***design*** *Eileen Diss* ***music*** *George Fenton* ***cast*** *James Wilby, Kristin Scott-Thomas, Rupert Graves, Anjelica Huston, Alec Guinness, Judi Dench, Pip Torrens, Cathryn Harrison*
Running time: 118 mins
US release: New Line, Jun 10, 1988
UK release: Premier, Jun 10, 1988

HAPPY NEW YEAR

Crime pays off for two middle-aged jewel thieves who go for the big score on a visit to Palm Beach. Based on Claude Lelouch's 1973 release which featured Lino Ventura.
Director *John G. Avildsen* ***producer*** *Jerry Weintraub* ***exec*** *Allan Ruban* ***script*** *'Warren Lane' (Nancy Dowd), based on film* La Bonne année *by Claude Lelouch* ***camera*** *James Crabe* ***editor*** *Jane Kurson* ***design*** *William J. Cassidy* ***music*** *Bill Conti* ***cast*** *Peter Falk, Charles Durning, Wendy Hughes, Tom Courtenay, Joan Copeland, Tracy Brooks Swope, Daniel Gerroll, Bruce Malmuth, The Temptations, Peter Sellars, Anthony Heald, Claude Lelouch*
Running time: 85 mins
US release: Columbia, Aug 7, 1987

HARRY AND THE HENDERSONS

(See Bigfoot and the Hendersons)

HE'S MY GIRL

This drag comedy targets the Los Angeles rock and video scene but misfires on most cylinders. David Hallyday, son of French singer Johnny Hallyday, is a Missouri boy who wins a free trip to LA to perform on TV. He wants to bring along his pal, a grease monkey called Reggie (Carter) but only a female companion is permitted. So Carter discards Reggie's overalls, slips on Regina's dress and immediately turns on the station's honcho, who just loves black women. Some of these routines raise chuckles, as does Warwick Sims's turn as a heavy metaller, but too much is flat and predictable. **BM**
Director *Gabrielle Beaumont* ***producers*** *Lawrence Taylor Mortorff, Angela Schapiro* ***script*** *Taylor Ames, Charles F. Bohl* ***camera*** *Peter Lyons Collister* ***editor*** *Roy Watts* ***design*** *Cynthia Kay* ***cast*** *T. K. Carter, David Hallyday, Jennifer Tilly, Warwick Sims, David Clennon, Monica Parker*
Running time: 104 mins
US release: Scotti, Sep 11, 1987

HEARTS OF FIRE

Turkey of the Year

Director *Richard Marquand* ***producers*** *Marquand, Jennifer Miller, Jennifer Alward* ***script*** *Scott Richardson, Joe Eszterhas* ***camera*** *Alan Hume* ***editor*** *Sean Barton* ***design*** *Roger Murray-Leach* ***music*** *John Barry* ***cast*** *Fiona Flanagan, Bob Dylan, Rupert Everett, Suzanne Bertish, Julian Glover, Susannah Hoffmann, Larry Lamb, Maury Chaykin, Tony Rosato, Richie Havens, Tim Cappello, Ian Dury*
Running time: 95 mins
US release: Lorimar, Mar 11, 1988
UK release: UKFD, Oct 9, 1987

HELLO AGAIN

Put a sitcom actress in a sitcom story and you've got a movie that's an hour too long. Disney chose a situation that was old when Noël Coward used it in *Blithe Spirit*: a suburban housewife (Long) suffocates on a Korean chicken ball and, through a medium (Ivey), comes back to haunt her husband (Bernsen). The resulting social satire, pitched at an audience that's supposed to think everything Long does is golden, doesn't rival director Frank Perry and writer Susan Isaacs' previous collaboration, *Compromising Positions*. At least Irishman Gabriel Byrne gets to play an Irishman for once. **BM**
Director/producer *Frank Perry* ***exec*** *Salah M. Hassanein* ***script*** *Susan Isaacs* ***camera*** *Jan Weincke* ***editor*** *Peter C. Frank, Trudy Ship* ***design*** *Edward Pisoni* ***music*** *William Goldstein* ***cast*** *Shelley Long, Judith Ivey, Gabriel Byrne, Corbin Bernsen, Sela Ward, Austin Pendleton, Carrie Nye, Robert Lewis, Madeleine Potter, Thor Fields, John Cunningham, I.M. Hobson, Mary Fogarty*
Running time: 96 mins
US release: BV, Nov 6, 1987
UK release: Warner, Jun 10, 1988

HELLRAISER

Confidently handled début feature by horror writer Clive Barker, in which an American (Robinson) and his English second wife (Higgins) move into a north London house only to find it possesses defects which no estate agent's jargon could gloss over. But while the exposition cleverly trails hints of sexual hysteria, subsequent developments, with first the husband's reprobate brother literally coming out of the woodwork from the infernal regions, and then his teenage daughter turning up at quite the wrong moment, rather sacrifice thematic concision to a grab-bag of macabre effects, and some of the humour has an unintentional ring. **TP**
Director *Clive Barker* ***producer*** *Christopher Figg* ***execs*** *David Saunders, Christopher Webster, Mark Armstrong* ***script*** *Barker, based on his story* The Hellbound Heart ***camera*** *Robin Vidgeon* ***editor*** *Richard Marden* ***design*** *Jocelyn James* ***music*** *Christopher Young* ***cast*** *Andrew Robinson, Clare Higgins, Ashley Laurence, Sean Chapman, Oliver Smith, Robert Hines, Antony Allen, Leon Davis, Michael Cassidy, Frank Baker, Kenneth Nelson, Gay Barnes, Niall Buggy, Dave Atkins, Oliver Parker, Pamela Sholto, Doug Bradley, Nicholas Vince, Simon Bamford, Grace Kirby, Sharon Bower, Raul Newney*
Running time: 93 mins
US release: New World, Sep 18, 1987
UK release: Entertainment, Sep 11, 1987

Hellraiser

HEARTS OF FIRE

Despite the promise of its title, this was a film that set no one's heart on fire. I saw it on the second day of its exclusive London opening, and the audience barely reached double figures. But then success never seemed to be on the cards.

The script, initially penned by ex-*Rolling Stone* writer Joe Eszterhas, dealt with the rise of a talented young American female singer - from slaving in a tollbooth to pounding it out on stage. First, she is supported by a reclusive middle-aged rhythm 'n' blues hero who's making a desultory comeback, then taken under the wing of a flash English rocker who's become bored with his fame and wealth.

The director was Richard Marquand, a former BBC man who had impressed by handling all manner of crazy flying objects in *Return of the Jedi* and who, along with Eszterhas, scored an audience bull's-eye with *Jagged Edge*. In his less than big-budget days he had even made *The Birth of the Beatles*, an affectionate look at the rise of the Fab Four. But *Hearts of Fire* called for the creation of persuasive fictional rock stars - a casting minefield.

For the ageing rocker, Billy Parker, Marquand went to work on a personal hero of his, Bob Dylan. Dylan may not have stopped (he still tours relentlessly) but his creative juices flow much less freely than they once did. His one previous acting role, in Peckinpah's *Pat Garrett and Billy the Kid* revealed an awkward, if sweet, screen persona. For some reason best known to him, Dylan took the part.

The role of James Colt, eighties superstar, was given to preening giraffe Rupert Everett, at the time planning to launch himself into a rock career (of which nothing later). Finally, a 'discovery' was needed for Molly. Enter Fiona, a fresh-faced moppet full of all-American energy, whose c.v. included one LP (I did come across it once) and a guest role as a sex-performer in a *Miami Vice* episode.

An all-star press conference held at London's National Film Theatre before shooting commenced probably did the film some harm. While various hacks asked a reluctant Dylan if he would contribute any 'protest songs' to the film, others studiously ignored Fiona and chortled at Everett, who seemed uncertain whether he would be allowed to employ his own sweet vocal cords on the soundtrack. Marquand denied that the story was a re-hash of *A Star Is Born*, and assured us it would be an 'authentic' depiction of the rock world.

When was the last time you saw an authentic fictional film on the subject? *This Is Spinal Tap*, perhaps? There is something so intrinsically cliché-ridden about the lives of rock stars - the self-abuse, the drugs, the groupies, the sell-out for commercial gain - that it was impossible to imagine Eszterhas and Marquand could offer any new insights. A brief look at the script put paid to any residual optimism, what with Billy Parker pontificating cynically on the way it is, James Colt living in luxurious boredom in a country mansion with, yes, a butler, and Molly continually gasping her enthusiasm while falling for them both. All with a few rock gigs and an attempted assassination to stir things up.

The finished film proved to be a dull patch-up job on the footage from what had clearly been an uninspiring shoot. Fast cutting in a wasted Cinemascope format made it appear that none of the three principals were acting in the same film. Poor Bob looked mostly very cuddly, and went about wrecking a hotel room with all the enthusiasm of a drugged tortoise. Fiona squeaked and bubbled, put on a brave show of imitating Pat Benatar on stage, and remained pleasantly unmemorable. Rupert Everett's cockney accent slid all the way to Eton and back, and his stage presence wouldn't have won him the Eurovision Song Contest, but he did his best to be deeply unlikeable while swigging vodka from a bottle and neglecting to shave (well, I suppose that's what rock stars do, don't they?).

Even the soundtrack album proved to be a bummer. Dylan failed to come up with any bright new songs (his supposed classic in the film, *The Usual*, was an old John Hiatt number), and Everett's version of *Tainted Love* revealed no voice to speak of. Fiona's gutsy vocalizing has yet to be heard again, to my knowledge. Perhaps she's collecting tolls on some mid-Western highway.

Saddest of all, director Marquand, still in his forties, died of a heart attack before the première. Evidently the shoot had been a trying experience, not helped by Marquand's self-confessed awe of Dylan, whose extraordinary charisma has floored more than a few. On the strength of *Jagged Edge* at least, there were certainly better things to come. One sequence in *Hearts of Fire*, when a blind fan holds a gun to James Colt, did show Marquand's expertise in handling suspense. Trouble was, by then most of the audience were only too happy for her to pull the trigger.

DAVID THOMPSON

Michael Knue **design** *C. J. Strawn, Mick Strawn* **music** *Michael Convertino* **cast** *Michael Nouri, Kyle MacLachlan, Ed O'Ross, Clu Gulager, Claudia Christian, Clarence Felder, William Boyett, Richard Brooks, Catherine Cannon, Larry Cedar, John McCann, Chris Mulkey*
Running time: 96 mins
US release: New Line, Oct 20, 1987

HIDDEN CITY

'What the hell's going on?' asks Charles Dance halfway through Stephen Poliakoff's directorial début, and well he might, this being a conspiracy thriller in search of both a conspiracy and some thrills. Dance is a statistician who becomes embroiled with a strident young film researcher obsessed with a revelation of something nasty hidden in old government propaganda shorts. Their quest leads to some revelatory London locations but the script's pretensions soon lapse into a muddled bore. **DT**
Director/script *Stephen Poliakoff* **producer** *Irving Teitelbaum* **camera** *Witold Stok* **editor** *Peter Coulson* **design** *Martin Johnson* **music** *Michael Storey* **cast** *Charles Dance, Cassie Stuart, Bill Paterson, Richard E. Grant, Alex Norton, Tusse Silberg, Richard Ireson, Saul Jephcott, Michael Mueller*
Running time: 108 mins
UK release: Other Cinema, Jun 24, 1988

Horse Thief *(above)*
High Season *(right)*

HEY BABU RIBA

The funeral of the woman they loved 30 years before reunites four Yugoslavian expats in Belgrade and we flash back to 1953 when Esther (Videnovic), the tomboy beauty of their teens, coxed for their rowing team and tactfully parried their declarations of love. The foursome is sexually initiated by older women: Esther by their enemy, a crass Party comrade who impregnates her. This heavy-handed anti-communist diatribe and sentimental wallow in nostalgia wouldn't be so dull - there are some sweet jokes about political allegiances - if writer/director Jovan Acin had imposed a sense of style and rhythm. **GF**
Director *Jovan Acin* **producer** *Dragoljub Popovic, Nikola Popovic* **execs** *George Zecevic, Petar Jankovic* **script** *Acin, from the memories of Petar Jankovic, George Zecevic, Acin* **camera** *Tomislav Pinter* **editor** *Snezana Ivanovic* **design** *Sava Acin* **music** *Zoran Simjanovic* **cast** *Gala Videnovic, Relja Bacic, Nebojsa Bakocevic, Marko Todorovic, Dragan Bjelogrilic, Srdjan Todorovic, Milos Zutic, Djordje Nenadovic, Goran Radakovic, Milan Strljic, Dragomir Bojanic-Gidra*
Running time: 109 mins
US release: Orion Classics, Sep 18, 1987

HIBISCUS TOWN

Veteran Chinese director Xie Jin, of *Two Stage Sisters*, joins his younger colleagues in putting the boot into the Cultural Revolution. But unlike their austere fables (*Yellow Earth, The King of Children*) this film is a sumptuous old-fashioned melodrama. Set in a small town in South Hunan, it spans 20 years from 1963 and grandly juggles the fates of half-a-dozen main characters: pretty beancurd-seller Hu, oafish power-seeker Wang, disgraced lady commune leader Li, etc. Fine acting, fabulous wide-screen colour photography, and by the end you're in no doubt what modern China thinks about the old days of hard-line fanaticism under Chairman M. **HK**
Director *Xie Jin* **production** *Shanghai Film Studio* **exec** *Wu Yigong* **script** *Ah Cheng, Jin, based on the novel by Gu Hua* **camera** *Lu Junfu* **editor** *Zhou Dingwen* **design** *Jin Qifen* **music** *Ge Yan* **cast** *Liu Xiaoqing, Jiang Wen, Zheng Zaishi, Zhu Shibin, Xu Songzi, Zhang Guangbei, Xu Ning, Liu Linian, Li Moxian, Mai Wenyan*
Running time: 135 mins
UK release: ICA Projects, Jun 3, 1988

THE HIDDEN

A better title for Jack Sholder's low-budget sci-fi *policier* might have been 'Alien Starman Terminator Meets Dirty Harry'. Kyle MacLachlan is an inter-galactic executioner sent to Earth to terminate a hideous being that can take any form. MacLachlan aids tough cop Michael Nouri in his quest to nab the beast, which confusingly inhabits and discards various human bodies as it leaves a trail of murder and mayhem through Los Angeles. MacLachlan has some nice moments in the Jeff Bridges role of the being for whom nothing human is not alien. **BM**
Director *Jack Sholder* **producers** *Robert Shaye, Gerald T. Olson, Michael Meltzer* **execs** *Stephen Diener, Lee Muhl, Dennis Harris, Jeffrey Klein* **script** *Bob Hunt* **camera** *Jacques Haitkin* **editor**

HIDING OUT

This is an amusing take on the fish-out-of-water high school movie, although the hero (Cryer) is no exotic time-traveller, like *Back to the Future*'s Michael J. Fox or Kathleen Turner in *Peggy Sue Got Married*, but a yuppie broker on the run from the Mob. As teen comedies go, it's an unexpectedly violent thriller - in the first 15 minutes at least. Escaping murder when a vampiric assassin blows away the FBI man protecting him, Cryer disguises himself as a student with a two-tone haircut and heads for a Delaware classroom and an icky romance with Annabeth Gish. There he challenges a Nixonian civics teacher, sorts out his girl's dad's tax returns over some Scotch, and rediscovers his youthful idealism before the killer catches up with him. Cryer's engaging performance holds together a slight but neat début by Bob Giraldi. **GF**
Director *Bob Giraldi* **producer** *Jeff Rothberg* **script** *Joe Menosky, Rothberg* **camera** *Daniel Pearl* **editor** *Edward Waschilka* **design** *Dan Leigh* **music** *Anne Dudley* **cast** *Jon Cryer, Keith Coogan, Annabeth Gish, Gretchen Cryer, Oliver Cotton, Claude Brooks, Lou Walker, Tim Quill, Anne Pitoniak, Nancy Fish*
Running time: 98 mins
US release: DEG, Nov 6, 1987

HIGH SEASON

Jacqueline Bisset and James Fox are a separated English couple - she a photographer, he a sculptor - on the idyllic Greek island of Rhodes. Running out of cash, with a 13-year-old daughter (Baker) to provide for, Bisset decides to sell the priceless Grecian urn given to her by her adoring elderly mentor (Shaw). Trouble is, the pot gets smashed by the dippy wife (Manville) of an English agent (Branagh) posing as a holiday-maker while seeking to expose the art historian Shaw as an Anthony Blunt-type spy. Bisset and Branagh make it in the moonlit waves; Fox rogers a succession of Australian hikers; the Club 18-30 element lurch

about puking; and Irene Papas goes on the rampage to revenge her late Nationalist husband. But not even Chris Menges' glittering camerawork can save Clare Peploe's dated tourist-class satire from archness. Apart from the veteran Shaw's frisky, doting old Englishman, this is a package to forget. **GF**
Director *Clare Peploe* ***producer*** *Clare Downs* ***executive producer*** *Michael White* ***script*** *Clare Peploe, Mark Peploe* ***camera*** *Chris Menges* ***editor*** *Gabriella Cristiani* ***design*** *Andrew McAlpine* ***music*** *Jason Osborn* ***cast*** *Jacqueline Bisset, James Fox, Irene Papas, Sebastian Shaw, Kenneth Branagh, Lesley Manville, Robert Stephens, Paris Tselios, Geoffrey Rose, Ruby Baker, Mark Williams, Shelly Laurenti, George Diakoyorgio, Father Bassili, Captain Stelios*
Running time: 101 mins
US release: Hemdale, Mar 25, 1988
UK release: Curzon/Enterprise, Apr 29, 1987

The Hidden

HIGH TIDE

After the dull *Mrs Soffel*, Gillian Armstrong returned to Oz for another collaboration with Judy Davis, who plays a no-hope back-up singer accidentally stumbling across her estranged teenage daughter who never knew her true mother. Virtuoso photography and powerful performances - especially from newcomer Claudia Karvan - sustain the drama over some occasional weak scripting, and sentimentality is avoided in the clash of responsibilities and aspirations over three generations. **DT**
Director *Gillian Armstrong* ***producer*** *Sandra Levy* ***exec*** *Anthony I. Ginnane* ***script*** *Laura Jones* ***camera*** *Russell Boyd* ***editor*** *Nicholas Beauman* ***design*** *Sally Campbell* ***music*** *Mark Moffiatt, Ricky Fataar* ***cast*** *Judy Davis, Jan Adele, Claudia Karvan, Colin Friels, John Clayton, Frankie J. Holden, Monica Trapaga, Mark Hembrow*
Running time: 104 mins
US release: Tri-Star, Dec 18, 1987

HOLLYWOOD SHUFFLE

Financed on gifts, credit cards and promises, Townsend's beguiling comedy about the life of an aspiring black actor got guilt raves throughout the industry. Scenes showing an educated black actor trying to master a 'street' accent so he could work in a film satirized Hollywood's narrow view of black capabilities. How could a $100,000 film written, directed by and starring a total unknown get such warm reviews and draw such full houses? The answer is a rebuke to the American style of movie-making. **BM**
Director/producer *Robert Townsend* ***exec*** *Carl Craig* ***script*** *Townsend, Keenen Ivory Wayans* ***camera*** *Peter Deming* ***editor*** *W. O. Garrett* ***design*** *Melba Katzman Farquhar* ***music*** *Patrice Rushen, Udi Harpaz* ***cast*** *Townsend, Anne-Marie Johnson, Starletta Dupois, Helen Martin, Craigus R. Johnson, Dom Jack Irrera, Paul Mooney, Lisa Mende, Robert Shafer, John Witherspoon, Ludie Washington, Keenen Ivory Wayans*
Running time: 82 mins
US release: Goldwyn, Mar 20, 1987
UK release: Virgin, Mar 25, 1988

HOPE AND GLORY

Film of the Year

Director/producer/script *John Boorman* ***execs*** *Jake Eberts, Edgar F. Gross* ***camera*** *Philippe Rousselot* ***editor*** *Ian Crafford* ***design*** *Anthony Pratt* ***music*** *Peter Martin* ***cast*** *Sebastian Rice-Edwards, Geraldine Muir, Sarah Miles, David Hayman, Sammi Davis, Derrick O'Connor, Susan Wooldridge, Jean-Marc Barr, Ian Bannen, Annie Leon, Jill Baker, Amelda Brown, Katrine Boorman, Colin Higgins, Shelagh Fraser, Gerald James, Barbara Pierson, Nicky Taylor, Jodie Andrews, Nicholas Askew, Jamie Bowman, Colin Dale, David Parking, Carlton Taylor, Sara Langton, Susan Brown, Charley Boorman, Peter Hughes*
Running time: 112 mins
US release: Columbia, Oct 16, 1987
UK release: CCW, Sep 4, 1987

HORSE THIEF

Another remarkable film from the enterprising Xi'an Studios of China, dealing with a desperate horse thief who outlaws himself in his determination to provide for his family and then becomes a religious outcast. Though set in Tibet in 1923, the story is timeless and is told in scope images of a suitably hypnotic power. **DT**
Director *Tian Zhuangzhuang* ***exec*** *Wu Tianming* ***script*** *Zhang Rui* ***camera*** *Hou Yong, Zhao Fei* ***editor*** *Li Jingzhong* ***design*** *Huo Jianqi* ***music*** *Qu Xiaosong* ***cast*** *Tseshang, Rigzin, Dan Jiji, Jayang Jamco, Gaoba, Diaba*
Running time: 88 mins
UK release: ICA Projects, Aug 14, 1987

HOPE AND GLORY

'Written, produced and directed by John Boorman' declare the titles of *Hope and Glory*, but the film is a personal one to a greater extent than this may indicate. The small boy over whose face in a family snapshot the possessive credit appears may be called Bill Rohan, but to all intents and purposes he is Boorman's own younger self. And what follows, with the director's own voice providing the initial narration, is an exercise in autobiography, a dramatized recollection of childhood years in suburban South London during the earlier part of World War Two.

Bill's immature father has joined up; his mother Grace (Sarah Miles) is left to cope with Bill and his two sisters. This is a story of growing up, but one in which the drama of external events - barrage balloons, a captured parachutist, the onslaught of the Blitz - throws into heightened relief not simply the everyday horror of school but the boy's developing consciousness of the adult world, with its deceptions and contradictions.

The rhyming of public and private progression is made explicit. At the outset a newsreel commentator speaks of the country's being in 'the dim light between peace and war' and in the penultimate sequence a radio (or, rather, a wireless) retails Churchill's speech about the conflict reaching 'the end of the beginning.' Yet the effect remains unschematic.

Boorman has in the past seemed to be (save perhaps for Nicolas Roeg) the most eclectically international of British film-makers, and sometimes the undoubted brilliance of his work has felt over-calculated. Not so here: turning to his own family history has unlocked a fund of spontaneity, and of humour. For while *Hope and Glory* could not properly be described as a comedy, it is frequently rich in comic observation: 'Mind the Brussels sprouts,' the German aviator is solemnly cautioned by the policeman leading him into captivity from the allotment into which he has bailed out.

Moreover, the release into spontaneity which one senses in the film's style is also part of its subject. The eye that Boorman turns on this suburban scene is a fond one, quite without condescension. But the changes he observes the war bringing are not just in the sphere of domestic economy ('Now it's patriotic to be poor,' sighs Grace with relief at the second-hand clothing exchange) but in the realm of the emotions too.

On the one hand, there is the teenage Dawn (played with infectious vitality by Sammi Davis), whose burgeoning into womanhood, and indeed motherhood, via her romance with a Canadian serviceman, assumes an air of being giddily speeded up. The tone of these scenes is predominantly boisterous, but on one occasion shades into hysteria as a row between mother and daughter over the latter's going to meet her boyfriend ends in Grace's capitulating with the declaration, 'Don't kill love.' And what, more darkly, also emerges, to Bill's half-understanding, is that Grace was and still is in love with her husband's best friend, Mac, who had earlier felt himself unable to seek her hand because he was out of a job.

This wistful relationship comes to light during a sequence in which Mac takes Grace, Bill and his younger sibling Susie to the now heavily fortified seaside. In the blacked-out train on the way home, Mac and Grace talk in undertones about their past - Mac: 'We did the decent thing;' Grace: 'This war's put an end to decent things ... we did all the proper things and we lost love.' The elegiac sense of banked-down, thwarted feeling is suggestively counterpointed by an image of conflagration in the succeeding scene, as the group return to find the Rohans' house flames, the result not of a bomb but of a domestic fire ('It happens in wartime as well, you know,' says the fire chief). And it is at this point that the film's, and Bill's, horizons suddenly widen as the family move in to the Thames-side bungalow of Grace's parents, 'another world,' as Mac puts it, albeit 'not 20 miles from Piccadilly.'

The sequence of the seaside outing, lying at the heart of the film, is graced by a stylistic richness which unmistakably - not only in its imagery but in the soundtrack carry-over of Grace's voice singing 'The White Cliffs of Dover' - owes a debt to the wartime documentaries of Humphrey Jennings. The more surrealist aspect of Jennings's work is evoked elsewhere, in the superbly composed travelling shot over a bombed-out landscape, which begins with a postman methodically emptying a pillar box which stands isolated amid the rubble, offset on the soundtrack by the Chopin which Grace played on the piano in the preceding scene.

The allusions are appropriate, not merely because *Hope and Glory* is revisiting, 40-odd years on, the time and milieu which inspired the best work of the British cinema's own generally recognized native poet, but in the sense that Boorman has succeeded in achieving what fate, and perhaps temperament too, denied Jennings the chance to attempt, the extension of that poetic spirit into the domain of a popular commercial feature. For the poetic impulse of Boorman's film is complemented not just by imposing craftsmanship but by a commodity, made emblematic in the daunting exterior set of 'Rosehill Avenue', of which British cinema has sometimes seemed all too suspicious, that of showmanship; it has the capacity to sweep an audience up into an enlarged world of the imagination.

The film is English to the core. Indeed, the riverside community of the latter passages even risks comparison with the genteel never-never-land of bygone Rank comedies, just as Ian Bannen's grandfather, taking potshots at marauding rats in the cabbage patch and extolling the virtue of nettle soup as a subsistence diet, pleasurably offers a rip-roaring 'character' role in line of descent from James Robertson Justice or A. E. Matthews. The crucial difference is that here such elements are not artificial, but part and parcel of a creative design.

This is, after all, the childhood memoir of a film-maker. The point is never laboured, but again and again it imbues the movie's effect, most startlingly in the air raid episode, when Dawn, followed by Bill, runs exultantly out of the confinement of the house to revel in the *son et lumière* of the bombing, and the reality of the experience is transmuted into the dynamic spectacle of cinema itself. In a different way, the sequences of Dawn's wedding, with military police in attendance to take off the AWOL bridegroom straight after the ceremony, and its near-instant aftermath of the bride going into labour, testify to an instinct for style which permits Boorman to reshape the raw material of memory into comic set-pieces.

Earlier in the film, we have seen Bill at the pictures with his mother and sisters, watching a war film when an on-screen aerial dogfight is interrupted by the announcement of an air raid. When Bill begs to stay and see the outcome, Dawn retorts, 'They've got the real thing outside.' But for Bill this is poor inducement: 'It's not the same,' he protests. With *Hope and Glory*, though, the adult Boorman contrives to bridge the gap, and the real thing merges indissolubly and exhilaratingly into its cinematic representation.

TIM PULLEINE

Housekeeping

HOUSE OF GAMES

Film of the Year

Director/script *David Mamet* ***producer*** *Michael Hausman* ***camera*** *Juan Ruiz Anchia* ***editor*** *Trudy Ship* ***design*** *Michael Merritt* ***music*** *Alaric Jans* ***cast*** *Lindsay Crouse, Joe Mantegna, Mike Nussbaum, Lilia Skala, J.T. Walsh, Willo Hausman, Karen Kohlhaas, Steve Goldstein, Jack Wallace, Ricky Jay, G. Roy Levin, Bob Lumbra, Andy Potok, Allen Soule, Ben Blakeman, Scott Zigler, W.H. Macy, John Pritchett, Meshach Tayler*
Running time: 102 mins
US release: Orion, Oct 14, 1987
UK release: Rank, Nov 20, 1987

THE HOUSE ON CARROLL STREET

An evocatively suggested period background, 1951 when the HUAC proceedings were in full cry, lends added piquancy to an ingeniously plotted and nicely proportioned mystery thriller. Kelly McGillis, as a victim of the hearings, gets caught up in exposing a conspiracy to smuggle ex-Nazi war criminals into the US (a conspiracy in which, of course, her chief persecutor, played to oily effect by Mandy Patinkin, proves to be implicated). A well managed climax in the rafters of Grand Central Station testifies to the continuing cinematic efficacy of the Hitchcock line on private crime in public places. **TP**

Director *Peter Yates* ***producer*** *Yates, Robert F. Colesberry* ***execs*** *Arlene Donovan, Robert Benton* ***script*** *Walter Bernstein* ***camera*** *Michael Ballhaus* ***editor*** *Ray Lovejoy* ***design*** *Stuart Wurtzel* ***music*** *Georges Delerue* ***cast*** *Kelly McGillis, Jeff Daniels, Mandy Patinkin, Christopher Rhode, Jessica Tandy, Jonathan Hogan*
Running time: 100 mins
US release: Orion, Mar 4, 1988

HOUSEKEEPING

Dreamy but dark, funny but ultimately forlorn, Bill Forsyth's first American film is plugged right into the illusory heart of the cinema and its fleeting promise of escape. Based on Marilynne Robinson's metaphysical novel about the female progeny of a restless railroader out West, it offers a bleak view of family life, but one awash with the wry humour and bitten-back lyricism that inflect all of Forsyth's films. Capturing Aunt Sylvie's distraction, her lack of self-consciousness and her wild, unfettered beauty, Christine Lahti's performance is perfect, while Sara Walker and Andrea Burchill are equally moving, in their own way, as the abandoned nieces for whom this transient, unearthly woman is forced to keep house. An unsentimental, watery masterpiece. **GF**

Director *Bill Forsyth* ***producer*** *Robert Colesberry* ***script*** *Forsyth, based on the novel by Marilynne Robinson* ***camera*** *Michael Coulter* ***editor*** *Michael Ellis* ***design*** *Adrienne Atkinson* ***music*** *Michael Gibbs* ***cast*** *Christine Lahti, Sara Walker, Andrea Burchill, Anne Pitoniak, Barbara Reese, Margot Pinvidic, Bill Smillie, Wayne Robson*
Running time: 116 mins
US release: Columbia, Nov 25, 1987
UK release: Columbia, Dec 4, 1988

HOUSE II, THE SECOND STORY

Bearing little resemblance to the original *House* (apart from the same producer and a scenarist here turned director too) which had to do with a young man exorcizing Vietnam War traumas, this is more *Creepshow*-style comic-book schlock horror. Story tells of a young man returning to the old dark homestead where he starts digging for a priceless Aztec skull, which had caused the messy death of his folks 25 years earlier. All kinds of feeble diversions, including cute furry creatures, creaking stop-frame animation and western gunfights. More silly than scary, more crass than comic. **QF**

Director/script *Ethan Wiley* ***producer*** *Sean S. Cunningham* ***camera*** *Mac Ahlberg* ***design*** *Gregg Fonseca* ***music*** *Harry Manfredini* ***cast*** *Arye Gross, Jonathan Stark, Royal Dano, Bill Maher, Lar Park Lincoln, John Ratzenberger*
Running time: 94 mins (88 mins in UK)
US release: New World, Aug 28, 1987
UK release: Entertainment, May 15, 1987

HOUSE OF GAMES

Some writers should leave the staging of their work to others, but a few are superb at interpreting their own creations. Alan Ayckbourn is one, David Mamet another. *House of Games* is Mamet's witty, original and impressive directorial début.

Mamet's scripts for *The Postman Always Rings Twice* and *The Untouchables* acquainted cinema-goers with the playwright's skills in dialogue and dramatic construction, but neither suggested Mamet could make a film with the power *Games* has to fascinate. Its subject is an elaborate con-trick, with deceit piled upon deceit, which Mike (Joe Mantegna) perpetrates upon successful psychiatrist Margaret Ford (Lindsay Crouse), and her entrapment parallels the way in which we, the audience, are drawn into the story's multiple twists. Also, the degree of her, and our, desire to know how things are done removes any irritation one might otherwise feel at the character's failure to see what snares are being set up around her. Once she enters the poker hall, the House of Games, she sets going a process of self-discovery which she has to see through to its finish.

On the surface, *Games* is a suspense movie reminiscent of the Hollywood *films noirs* of the forties and fifties. The way it's lit, dressed, photographed and acted reeks of the genre. A sense of foreboding and menace is pervasive. But there's a crucial difference. For Mamet, genre atmosphere is the medium, not the message. His metaphoric concern in *Games*, as in such of his stage plays as *Glengarry Glen Ross* and the more recent *Speed-the-Plow* (about the packaging of movies), is with the corrupted values that constitute the normal way of doing business.

Given the harsh angle of his vision, Mamet is surely a moralist, though he doesn't moralize in an obvious voice. It's not his style, his art. He doesn't write homilies, and he doesn't depict 'good' and 'bad' types, which would constitute poor (though maybe populist) art. His characters are victims, delineated with an artful detachment. In *Games*, when Ford, the shrink repeatedly duped by Mike, goes off her nut and finally kills him, that's chilling irony, not flagrantly moral (or authorial) retribution.

Mamet's characters manipulate themselves. They are, at least implicitly, the manipulated victims of historical process and social conditioning. That's the whole point of Mamet's perception, his running theme - the lies, myths and conditioned impulses ordained by a corrupt value system.

In *Games* the lady psychiatrist and the con man are opposite sides of the same tarnished coin. They form an exquisite complement, and Mamet handles this relationship and its gathering tragedy with amusement and charm as well as subtle psychology and dramatic skill.

All that made it uncommonly exciting to watch. The one disappointment for me initially came when the psychiatrist corners and kills Mike. In a plot full of dazzling surprises, that one struck me as excessive, out of control, a dramatic cheat. On top of which (and here I betray rank sentiment) the con man not only had a certain winning charm but more honesty about himself and his motives than did his socially superior killer. I wanted him to survive - maybe even go straight, and maybe even with Dr Ford.

But Mamet is no sentimentalist, and in the light of retrospection I came to see that the way he played it was right after all.

In a story about deceits, the deceived putative innocent ironically becomes a great deceiver herself. All along the film hints at the corrupti-

bility of ostensible virtue, her's, and that's what finally happens.

First the psychiatrist, this model of success and object of esteem, is tempted to the House of Games, a gambling den, in an effort to get one of her patients off the hook for a sizeable poker debt. An elaborate con trick perpetrated on her assures her return, like a moth to flame. Irresistibly, she becomes entangled with Mike, the game's operator, and the subculture in which he moves. The film's big 'sting' operation is one more joke on her. Her sense of shame and humiliation is now so deep, her rage so great, that she manoeuvres Mike into a corner where, out of control, she kills him without so much as a visible twinge of remorse. Her corruption is complete.

Thereafter, in a coda of wry humour, she has no qualm about tricking its owner out of a measly cigarette lighter just for the sport of it. Corruption has now become whimsical routine, or normal business. The lady and the con man weren't coin opposites after all. It just seemed like it. That's the real point of the film.

And if Mamet was making a statement about his America, we should have no doubt about the wider truth of his metaphor.

The two stars are ideally cast. Joe Mantegna has the looks and style to make of Mike what he is, a flawed rogue with a code of honour. Lindsay Crouse (Mamet's wife), with the help of cropped hairdo, fairly crackles with the tailored self-confidence of an ambitious professional. Her's is the disturbed and disturbing character, not Mike.

It only remains to praise a pin-point supporting cast (especially the acting in that early poker game scene), ditto such technical contributions as the photography of Juan Ruiz Anchia, Trudy Ship's editing and Michael Merritt's production design.

THOMAS LLOYD

I DON'T GIVE A DAMN

If you're really against a war, show how it disfigures the combatants psychologically, as Shmuel Imberman does in this drama about an Israeli paraplegic. Young soldier Ika Zohar joins up idealistically and comes home from the front embittered by what the war has done to him. He takes out his self-pitying despair on his family and his fiancée (Waxman). He hates everyone who isn't crippled and many who are. The film was Israel's most popular last year but, despite a few optimistic moments, it makes tough viewing for those not personally involved. **BM**

***Director** Shmuel Imberman **producers** Yair Pradelsky, Israel Ringel **exec** Nissim Levy **script** Hanan Peled, based on the novel by Dan Ben Amotz **camera** Nissim Leon **editor** Atara Horenstein **music** Benny Nagari **cast** Ika Zohar, Anath Waxman, Liora Grossman, Shmuel Vilojni, Shlomo Tarshish*

Running time: 102 mins

US release: Transworld, Feb 19, 1988

IN THE MOOD

(The Woo Woo Kid in UK)

Adolescent male fantasies provide plots for half of America's movies, and *In The Mood* strikes the rich vein of 'young but irresistible'. Playing *Summer of '42* for goofy laughs, writer-director Phil Alden Robinson's film is based on a true story from 1944. It seems there was a 15-year-old Californian boy, dubbed the 'woo woo kid', who was apprehended after he had run off and married a 21-year-old mother of two, and then was caught again running off with the 25-year-old wife of a Marine. Patrick Dempsey is fine as the gawky but sweet young lad, though his accent is more New York than California. Talia Balsam is his first love and Beverly D'Angelo steals the movie as his salty but susceptible follow-up. **BM**

***Director/script** Phil Alden Robinson **producers** Gary Adelson, Karen Mack **camera** John Lindley **editor** Patrick Kennedy **design** Dennis Gassner **music** Ralph Burns **cast** Patrick Dempsey, Talia Balsam, Beverly D'Angelo, Michael Constantine, Betty Jinnette, Kathleen Freeman, Peter Hobbs, Tony Longo, Douglas Rowe, Ernie Brown, Kim Myers, Brian McNamara, Dana Short*

Running time: 98 mins

US release: Lorimar, Sep 16, 1987

UK release: Guild, Jan 8, 1988

INNERSPACE

This is the Spielberg formula again, but in good working condition. Joe Dante crams as much goofy, good-natured humour as he can into this playful extension of the *Fantastic Voyage* idea. Dennis Quaid finds himself in double jeopardy as, miniaturized and mistakenly injected into hapless Martin Short, he struggles to guide Short through a maze of external obstacles so they can both escape with their lives. Much of the comedy stems from Short's reactions to being spoken to from another man inside his body, and the film threatens to short-circuit on occasion from sheer overload of invention, but the overriding feeling is one of fun and goodwill, not the too-familiar one of a director pressing the buttons of audience manipulation. **TM**

***Director** Joe Dante **producer** Michael Finnell **execs** Steven Spielberg, Peter Guber, Jon Peters **script** Jeffrey Boam, Chip Proser **camera** Andrew Laszlo*

editor Kent Beyda *design* James H. Spencer *music* Jerry Goldsmith *cast* Dennis Quaid, Martin Short, Meg Ryan, Kevin McCarthy, Fiona Lewis, Vernon Wells, Robert Picardo, Wendy Schaal, Harold Sylvester, William Schallert, Henry Gibson, John Hora, Mark L. Taylor, Orson Bean, Kevin Hooks, Kathleen Freeman, Archie Hahn, Dick Miller, Kenneth Toby
Running time: 120 mins
US release: Warner, Jul 1, 1987
UK release: CCW, Dec 27, 1988

THE INVISIBLE KID

A long, long way after H. G. Wells, writer-director Avery Crounse goes for the gross in this raunchy teen comedy. Jay Underwood discovers that adding pigeon droppings to toilet cleaner produces an invisibility potion. He uses it to hide under the nasty school principal's desk to witness a monumental farting session. He doesn't neglect to look in on the girls' locker room, of course. Although his secret is jeopardized when he fails to observe the substance's time constraints, he remains at large to help decide the result of a supposedly fixed basketball game. Use of a subjective camera gave Underwood many days off. **BM**
Director/script *Avery Crounse* ***producer*** *Philip J. Spinelli* ***execs*** *Spinelli, Crounse* ***camera*** *Michael Barnard* ***editor*** *Gabrielle Gilbert* ***design*** *Charles Tomlinson* ***music*** *Steve Hunter* ***cast*** *Jay Underwood, Karen Black, Wally Ward, Chynna Phillips, Brother Theodore, Mike Genovese, Jan King*
Running time: 95 mins
US release: Taurus, Mar 30, 1988

Ishtar *(above)*
Ironweed *(right)*

IRONWEED

Elaborately wrought, rather in the manner of the bygone literary adaptations of Wyler and Stephens, this atmospheric version of William Kennedy's Pulitzer Prize-winning novel of life and mainly hard times in the late thirties suffers from being too faithful to its source, with the result that the predestined quality for which the director seems to be striving tends to be at odds with the digressive contours of the narrative. This leaves Meryl Streep rather stranded with a low-life character turn, though Jack Nicholson as the vagrant obscurely seeking redemption contributes a sterling performance, and there is some fine support, notably from Tom Waits as his moribund sidekick. **TP**
Director *Hector Babenco* ***producers*** *Keith Barish, Marcia Nasatir* ***execs*** *Joseph H. Kanter, Denis Blouin, Rob Cohen* ***script*** *William Kennedy, based on his novel* ***camera*** *Lauro Escorel* ***editor*** *Anne Goursaud* ***design*** *Jeannine C. Oppewall* ***music*** *John Morris* ***cast*** *Jack Nicholson, Meryl Streep, Carroll Baker, Michael O'Keefe, Diane Venora, Fred Gwynne, Margaret Whitton, Tom Waits, Jake Dengel, Nathan Lane, James Gammon*
Running time: 143 mins
US release: Tri-Star, Dec 18, 1987
UK release: Palace, May 20, 1988

ISHTAR

Ishtar already seems to have entered the history books as Beatty's Waterloo. On the debit side, it is true that this light comedy doesn't look anywhere near what it cost to make (Vittorio Storaro has certainly never been responsible for a less distinguished-looking film), that the jokes about Beatty's trouble finding women don't work, and that Isabelle Adjani is wasted. Less stinging than her previous pictures, this road movie about two untalented singer-songwriters muddling their way through North Africa is still very much an Elaine May film, full of nervous camaraderie, moment-to-moment combustion among the actors and some agreeably spontaneous foolishness. A perfectly pleasant, though far from memorable, entertainment. **TM**

Director/script *Elaine May* ***producer*** *Warren Beatty* ***camera*** *Vittorio Storaro* ***editors*** *Stephen A. Rotter, William Reynolds, Richard Cirincione* ***design*** *Paul Sylbert* ***music*** *John Strauss* ***cast*** *Warren Beatty, Dustin Hoffman, Isabelle Adjani, Charles Grodin, Jack Weston, Tess Harper, Carol Kane, Aharon Ipale, David Margulies*
Running time: 107 mins
US release: Columbia, May 15, 1987
UK release: CCW, Nov 13, 1987

I'VE HEARD THE MERMAIDS SINGING

Patricia Rozema's movie, made for $262,000, defines the difference between Canada and America: it's modest, it's meandering and it preaches that success is 'internally defined'. Rozema's heroine, Sheila McCarthy, cycles around Toronto taking photographs with no thought of selling them, supporting herself as a temp at a chic art gallery. An 'organizationally impaired' klutz, she worships the gallery's sophisticated lesbian director (Baillargeon). After Baillargeon denounces McCarthy's photos as 'the trite made flesh' and tries to take credit for someone else's painting, McCarthy learns to trust her own special talents. **BM**

Director/script/editor *Patricia Rozema* ***producers*** *Rozema, Alexandra Raffé* ***exec*** *Don Haig* ***camera*** *Douglas Koch* ***design*** *Valanne Ridgeway* ***music*** *Mark Korven* ***cast*** *Sheila McCarthy, Paule Baillargeon, Anne-Marie MacDonald, John Evans, Brenda Kamino, Richard Monette*
Running time: 83 mins
US release: Miramax, Sep 11, 1987
UK release: Electric, Feb 19, 1988

·J·J·J·J·J·J·J·J·J·J·J·J·

JANE AND THE LOST CITY

Writer-director Terry Marcel - last stop, *Hawk the Slayer* - revives another myth from Britain's darker ages: this time circa 1940. 'Jane' was the wartime strip-cartoon heroine who kept our lads at the Front amused by losing her clothes in every crisis. She keeps losing them again here, but the main crisis is the movie itself. Marcel's uninspired script and direction are joined by floundering comic performances from Maud Adams, Robin Bailey and Jasper Carrott, and the production values are strictly end-of-the-pier. **HK**

Director *Terry Marcel* ***producer*** *Harry Robertson* ***exec*** *Terry Ramsden* ***script*** *Mervyn Haisman, Marcel, Harry Robertson* ***camera*** *Paul Beeson* ***editor*** *Alan Jones* ***design*** *Michael Pickwoad* ***music*** *Harry Robertson* ***cast*** *Sam Jones, Maud Adams, Jasper Carrott, Kirsten Hughes, Graham Stark, Robin Bailey, Ian Roberts, Elsa O'Toole, John Rapley, Charlies Comyn, Ian Steadman*
Running time: 92 mins
UK release: Blue Dolphin, May 13, 1988

JASON LIVES: FRIDAY THE 13th PART VI (Friday the 13th Part VI: Jason Lives in US)

It appeared that Jason had died once and for all in Part V of this perennial money-making Paramount series, but a bolt of lightning is all it takes to revive him for one more go-round. Writer-director Tom McLoughlin, previously responsible for *One Dark Night*, manages to inject some clever, self-deprecating humour into the proceedings, which involves the Masked One threatening kids at a summer camp, but, despite a body count of eighteen, it's all quite forgettable and quite likely marks the end of the series. **TM**

Director/script *Tom McLoughlin* ***producer*** *Don Behrns* ***camera*** *Jon R. Kranhouse* ***editor*** *Bruce Green* ***design*** *Joseph T. Garrity* ***music*** *Harry Manfredini* ***cast*** *Thom Mathews, Jennifer Cooke, David Kagen, Kerry Noonan, Renee Jones, Tom Fridley, C.J. Graham, Darcy Demoss, Vincent Guastaferro, Tony Goldwyn, Nancy McLoughlin, Ron Palillo*
Running time: 87 mins
US release: Paramount, Aug 1, 1986

JAWS THE REVENGE

Turkey of the Year

Director/producer *Joseph Sargent* ***script*** *Michel de Guzman, based on characters created by Peter Benchley* ***camera*** *John McPherson* ***editor*** *Michael Brown* ***design*** *John J. Lloyd* ***music*** *Michael Small* ***cast*** *Lorraine Gary, Lance Guest, Mario Van Peebles, Karen Young, Michael Caine, Judith Barsi, Lynn Whitfield*
Running time: 100 mins (90 mins in UK)
US release: Universal, Jul 17, 1987
UK release: UIP, Aug 7, 1987

JEAN DE FLORETTE

First of a two-picture $17,000,000 adaptation of a little known novel by Provençal dramatist and film-maker Marcel Pagnol, *Jean de Florette* coasts affectingly on its utter subservience to Pagnol's superb rural yarn and original dialogue, and Berri's unerring casting of Montand and Auteuil as, respectively, an arrogant village elder and his rat-faced sub-intelligent nephew, who scheme together to obtain a piece of fertile land inherited by a naïve and (hump-backed) city slicker, by keeping secret the whereabouts of a subterranean spring. Gérard Depardieu struggles too visibly to give some density to the role of the idealistic hunchback, who wasn't quite genuine in the novel either. Film Two, *Manon des Sources*, recounts the vengeance exacted by Depardieu's daughter. **LB**

Director *Claude Berri* ***producer*** *Alain Poire* ***exec*** *Pierre Grunstein* ***script*** *Berri, Gérard Brach, based on the novel by Marcel Pagnol* ***camera*** *Bruno Nuytten* ***editors*** *Hervé de Luze, Noëlle Boisson, Arlette Langman* ***design*** *Bernard Vezat* ***music*** *Jean-Claude Petit* ***cast*** *Yves Montand, Gérard Depardieu, Daniel Auteuil, Elisabeth Depardieu, Ernestine Mazurowna, Marcel Champel, Armand Meffre, André Dupon, Pierre Nougaro, Marc Betton, Jean Maurel, Roger Souza, Bertino Benedetto, Margarita Lozano, Pierre Jean Rippert*
Running time: 121 mins
US release: Orion Classics, Jun 26, 1987
UK release: Cannon, Jul 24, 1987

Jean de Florette

JOHNNY BE GOOD

Unfunny satire leaves the audience with nothing to enjoy. Here the rot begins with casting Anthony Michael Hall as a champion football player. This gangly ex-youth resembles no quarterback who ever gained gridiron glory, yet he is sought avidly by battalions of college recruiters. He endures all the blandishments academe can thrust upon him but remains as pure of heart as he is sound of body. Scenes with Hall's sidekick Robert Downey Jr. are meant to call to mind Hollywood's one successful football satire, *Semi-Tough*, but don't. **BM**

Director *Bud Smith* ***producers*** *Adam Fields* ***execs/script*** *Steve Zacharias, Jeff Buhai, David Obst* ***camera*** *Robert D. Yeoman* ***editor*** *Scott Smith* ***design*** *Gregg Fonseca* ***music*** *Jay Ferguson* ***cast*** *Anthony Michael Hall, Robert Downey Jr., Paul Gleason, Uma Thurman, Steve James, Seymour Cassel, Michael Greene, Marshall Bell, Deborah May, Michael Alldredge*
Running time: 84 mins
US release: Orion, Mar 25, 1988

JAWS THE REVENGE

Jaws the Revenge is a classic example of how the tail can wag the fish in Hollywood. Most sequels are made more or less cynically to exploit a proven marketing hook, but few follow-ons had less artistic reason for being than this fourth shark saga from Universal.

Steven Spielberg's 1975 original *Jaws* stood on its own as a horror classic. But the world demanded *Jaws 2* in 1978, and Universal generously provided it: Roy Scheider dutifully dispatched another Great White, without the help of the departed Robert Shaw or the now-too-proud Richard Dreyfuss. No one demanded and not many saw *Jaws 3-D* in 1983, in which a new cast of humans and a new fish grappled in a new setting with the same outcome.

Despite declining grosses, *Jaws* had become one of Universal's franchises, like *Star Trek* at Paramount and James Bond at MGM/UA. The popularity of the *Jaws* stop on the studio tour proved that there remained a certain pre-sold audience for any new *Jaws* project. A fourth shark movie was inevitable.

Studio head Sidney Sheinberg vetoed another *Jaws 3-D*-style approach - keeping the shark concept, jettisoning everything else and upping the body count. The next *Jaws* would re-emphasize family and restrict death by shark bite to a select few. It so happens that Sheinberg's wife is Lorraine Gary, the actress who played Scheider's wife in the first two *Jaws* movies. So Sheinberg dictated a scenario that would remind the audience of the original *Jaws*.

This sequel would bring Gary back into the spotlight, as a plucky widow who protects her grandchildren from a seemingly innumerable and unstoppable family of sharks. Sheinberg pronounced: 'This won't be a shark picture, it will be a people picture. The more you care about the people, the more frightened you are of the shark.'

But the way it turned out, the fourth *Jaws* movie is Universal's revenge on audiences, who watch in open-mouthed disbelief that a big-budget picture could be so thoroughly botched. From casting to special effects to set design, this film is on an artistic level with *Ghidra Meets Godzilla*.

At the outset, Gary's now-grown son gets gobbled, convincing mum that she needs a change of scene. She decides to visit her other son (Lance Guest) in balmy Grand Bahama, where heat-shy Great Whites never venture. Here Guest, an ichthyologist, and his sculptor wife (Karen Young) have an idyllic life in a snug little beach-side bungalow, and the three generations celebrate Christmas in the sun.

This is supposed to be therapeutic for Gary, but she's whingeing and twitching with shark-fear. She knows the pearly whites are glistening somewhere in the nearby shallows, even though everyone else thinks she's a hopeless neurotic and tells her it's all in her head. She is momentarily distracted by a handsome British pilot: Michael Caine picking up a pay cheque in his last Hollywood role before retiring to England. Caine referred to the role as 'the Robert Shaw part'. But nothing comes of Gary's few encounters with Caine, where he wears a fat-concealing bush jacket and plies her with some pointless chit-chat. She's 50, and grandmas don't get love scenes.

The 'Richard Dreyfuss part' goes to Mario Van Peebles in a dashing sailor suit. He plays a chirpy Bahamian until he learns what the inside of a shark looks like. The film's climactic shark-vs.-woman confrontation must have story-boarded better than it shot, for it isn't on the screen and the film ends without any discernible climax. One moment Gary is sailing off alone to fight the fish, the winds parting as her distended nostrils seek the quarry. The next moment, after some by-play between supporting actors and the shark, the wicked fish is dead, leaving audiences to wonder if the film's last reel was lost in transit.

Part of the problem with *Jaws the Revenge* was the speed with which it had to be completed, to ensure its arrival in cinemas in time for summer audiences. The release date was selected before a word of the script was written. The film's director, Joseph Sargent, and writer, Michael de Guzman, have both operated previously in television, where speed is a virtue. But in the movies time is necessary to punch up a script, attract good actors and execute special effects.

Eight months wasn't enough, and the film shows the rush in every department. Perhaps the greatest flaw is the complete lack of frighteners. This shark can bend stiffly at the waist - big deal. This Bruce, like the other Bruces before it, has plenty of teeth, but it just doesn't seem to move in a menacing way.

The release date arrived, and the film sank without trace. Kids couldn't take Gary, and their parents couldn't watch Bruce. But what was this? Just a few days after the film's disastrous opening, patrons of the Universal studio tour were being treated to glimpses of further tinkering on the movie: a new ending. Sheinberg and Co. were explaining away the flop by saying the audiences hadn't wanted Mario Van Peebles to die, so they needed a new ending for foreign release in which young Peebles lived - perhaps to star in the inevitable next sequel, *Jaws the Ridiculous*.

BART MILLS

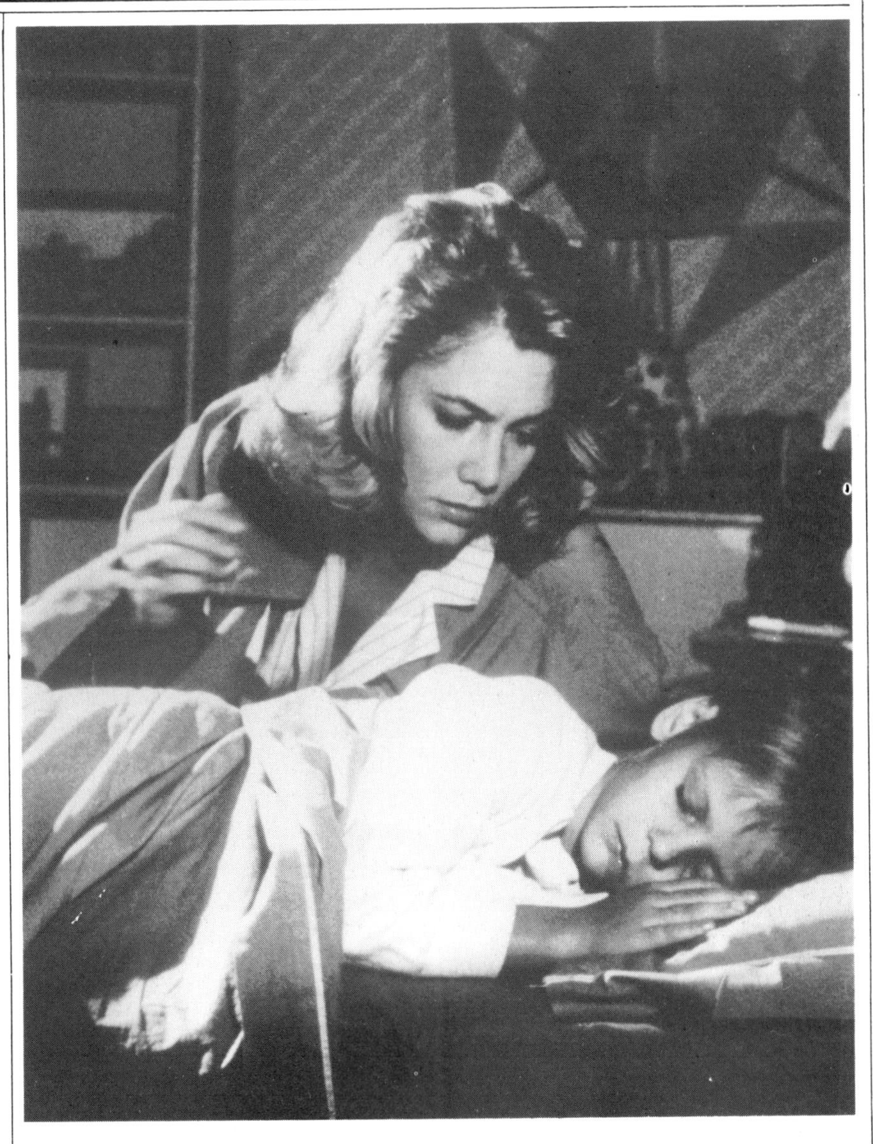

Julia & Julia

JUDGEMENT IN BERLIN

No *Judgement in Nuremberg, Judgement in Berlin* is an un-suspenseful dressed-up TV movie. It's co-produced and presided over by Mr Earnest Goodness himself, Martin Sheen, playing an American judge (Herbert Stern, upon whose memoir the film is based). Judge Sheen is picked to go to Berlin and try an East German held after hijacking an airliner to the West. Sheen ensures that, even on foreign soil, American ideals of justice and let's not forget freedom prevail. Sheen's Malibu neighbour Leon Penn directs and Sheen's sons' playmate Sean Penn offers a gripping cameo as an inadvertent defector. Penn's mum also appears. **BM**

Director *Leon Penn* ***producer*** *Joshua Sinclair, Ingrid Windisch* ***execs*** *Martin Sheen, William R. Greenblatt, Jeffery Auerbach* ***script*** *Sinclair, Penn, based on the book by Herbert J. Stern* ***camera*** *Gabor Pogany* ***editor*** *Teddy Darvas* ***design*** *Jan Schlubach* ***music*** *Peter Goldfoot* ***cast*** *Martin Sheen, Sam Wanamaker, Max Gail, Jürgen Heinrich, Heinz Hönig, Harris Yulin, Sean Penn, Carl Lumbly, Max Volkert Martens, Cristine Rose, Marie-Louise Sinclair, Joshua Sinclair*

Running time: 92 mins
US release: New Line, May 6, 1988

JULIA & JULIA

The first feature film shot on High Definition Video, and a pity they didn't get a high-definition script. This blurred and whimsical Italian fantasy about life and death - widow Kathleen Turner meets her ex-husband Gabriel Byrne in another dimension and Sting turns up to make it a triangle - is like a Mills and Boon story that's been done over by Pirandello. The performances droop under Peter Del Monte's direction, and an equally big disappointment is the HDV itself. Lacking the lustre and resolution of celluloid, and with the colours sometimes 'trailing' in pan-shots, it suggests the shape of technology-to-come still has a long way to go. **HK**

Director *Peter De Monte* ***script*** *Del Monte, Silvia Napolitano, Sandro Petraglia* ***camera*** *Giuseppe Rotunno* ***editor*** *Michael Chandler* ***design*** *Mario Garbuglia* ***music*** *Maurice Jarre* ***cast*** *Kathleen Turner, Sting, Gabriel Byrne, Gabriele Ferzetti, Angela Goodwin, Lidia Broccolino, Norman Mozzato*

Running time: 97 mins
US release: Cinecom, Feb 5, 1988

·K·K·K·K·K·K·K·K·K·K·

THE KILLING TIME

It's nearly always killing time in Hollywood. Rick King's attempt at neo-*noir* in small-town California includes most of the classic ingredients, but lacks that feeling of a vice shutting slowly and inevitably. Beau Bridges is perhaps too sunny as a deputy sheriff plotting to murder his mistress's monstrous spouse (Rogers). Joe Don Baker, as the town's departing sheriff, seems too straight for this town's crookedness. Kiefer Sutherland, who kills and then impersonates a new deputy in the film's opening scenes, skulks and scowls somewhat too often. **BM**

Director *Rick King* ***producer*** *Peter Abrams, Robert L. Levy* ***exec*** *J.P. Guerin* ***script*** *Dan Bohlinger, James Nathan, Bruce Franklin Singer* ***camera*** *Paul H. Goldsmith* ***editor*** *Lorenzo de Stefano* ***design*** *Bernt Amadeus Capra* ***music*** *Paul Chihara* ***cast*** *Beau Bridges, Kiefer Sutherland, Wayne Rogers, Joe Don Baker, Camelia Kath, Janet Carroll, Michael Madsen*

Running time: 95 mins

US release: New World, Oct 23, 1987

King Lear

KING LEAR

Godard's free (to the point of no relationship) version of the play throws out not just the poetry but virtually all the plot too. They are replaced by some predictable meanderings (in English, but none the easier to follow for that) on the power of the multi-nationals and the conundrum of adapting art and visual language to the nuclear age, complete with a character called William Shakespeare Junior the Fifth who comes wandering on to the scene, supposedly trying to reconstruct his ancestor's works in the aftermath of Chernobyl. Burgess Meredith and Molly Ringwald suggest that, given half a chance, they might not be at all bad as Lear and Cordelia, but the chance is not forthcoming. The total effect is more rebarbative than genuinely provocative. **TP**

Director *Jean-Luc Godard* ***producers*** *Menahem Golan, Yoram Globus* ***script*** *Jean-Luc Godard, based on the play by William Shakespeare* ***camera*** *Sophie Maintigneux* ***editor*** *Godard* ***cast*** *Burgess Meredith, Peter Sellars, Molly Ringwald, Jean-Luc Godard, Woody Allen, Norman Mailer, Kate Miller, Léos Carax*

Running time: 90 mins

US release: Cannon, Jan 22, 1988

UK release: Cannon, Jan 29, 1988

THE KITCHEN TOTO

Kenya was no place for a small native boy in 1950, with the Mau-Mau apt to murder your father, and your mother so needy she must send you off to labour in the kitchen of the police chief. Chief Bob Peck barely notices the boy as he struggles to stem the bloody rebellion. The boy's enchanting smile is seen less and less often as he gets sucked into the rebels' murderous designs, and the inevitable confrontation claims its innocent victims. Writer/director Harry Hook spends too much time at the edges of the real drama and fails to provide the leads with the character-defining scenes that might have made the story memorable. **BM**

Director/script *Harry Hook* ***producer*** *Ann Skinner* ***execs*** *Menahem Golan, Yoram Globus* ***camera*** *Roger Deakins* ***editor*** *Tom Priestley* ***design*** *Jamie Leonard* ***music*** *John Keane* ***cast*** *Edwin Mahinda, Bob Peck, Phyllis Logan, Nicholas Charles, Ronald Pirie, Robert Urquhart, Kirsten Hughes, Edward Judd, Nathan Dambuza Mdledle, Ann Wanjugu, Job Seda*

Running time: 95 mins

US release: Cannon, Apr 29, 1988

UK release: Cannon, Jul 8, 1988

The Kitchen Toto

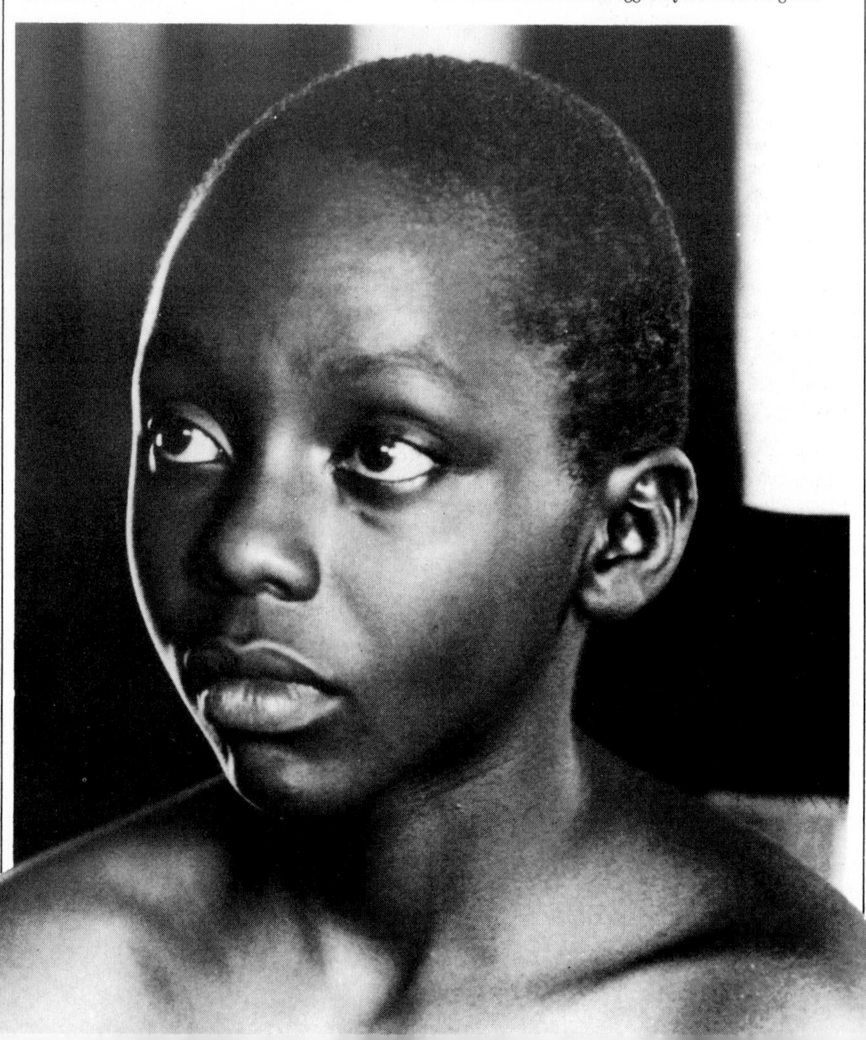

·L·L·L·L·L·L·L·L·L·L·L·

LADY BEWARE

Intended as a feminist statement about a woman combating a man who harasses her, *Lady Beware* was taken away from director Karen Arthur and recut by its financiers, Scotti Bros, into an explicit and crudely exploitative film few could comfortably watch. Diane Lane plays a department store window dresser whose *outré* designs excite perverted radiologist Michael Woods. He stalks her by phone and eventually in person, invading her mind to the point where she feels psychologically raped. The creep's sicko intrusions poison a promising relationship with nice guy Cotter Smith. Lane eventually vows revenge, and the voyeur winds up with his perversions on public display. The film's fairly ropy subject demanded sensitive treatment, but the Scottis' re-cut version, emphasizing nudity, should cause it to be placed in the soft-porn rack. **BM**

Director *Karen Arthur* ***producers*** *Tony Scotti, Lawrence Taylor Mortorff* ***script*** *Susan Miller, Charles Zev Cohen* ***camera*** *Tom Neuwirth* ***editor*** *Roy Watts* ***design*** *Tom Wells* ***music*** *Craig Safan* ***cast*** *Diane Lane, Michael Woods, Cotter Smith, Peter Nevargic, Edward Penn, Tyra Ferrell*

Running time: 108 mins

US release: Scotti Bros, Sep 18, 1987

LADY IN WHITE

In all too many American genre movies, the more hackneyed the subject, the more stylish the treatment. Frank LaLoggia layers his eerie ghost-

story over a realistic snuff thriller, manipulating the audience expertly between disbelief and terror. The victim of a schoolboy prank, jug-eared Lukas Haas gets locked inside the school cloakroom one moonlit night. He sees the ghost of a young girl his own age, and is menaced by a mysterious masked man. Who is real? Who is the murderer and who the murdered? Who is the Lady in White and does she really stalk the streets of the town at night? **BM**
Director/script/music *Frank LaLoggia* ***producers*** *Andrew G. La Marca, LaLoggia* ***execs*** *Charles M. LaLoggia, Cliff Payne* ***camera*** *Russell Carpenter* ***editor*** *Steve Mann* ***design*** *Richard K. Hummel* ***cast*** *Lukas Haas, Len Cariou, Alex Rocco, Katherine Helmond, Jason Presson, Renata Vanni, Angelo Bertolini, Jared Rushton, Gregory Levinson, Joelle Jacob*
Running time: 112 mins
US release: New Century/Vista, Apr 22, 1988

THE LAST EMPEROR
Film of the Year
Director *Bernardo Bertolucci* ***producer*** *Jeremy Thomas* ***script*** *Mark Peploe, Bertolucci* ***camera*** *Vittorio Storaro* ***editor*** *Gabriella Cristiani* ***design*** *Ferdinando Scarfiotti* ***music*** *Ryuichi Sakamoto, David Byrne, Cong Su* ***cast*** *John Lone, Joan Chen, Peter O'Toole, Ying Ruocheng, Victor Wong, Dennis Dun, Ryuichi Sakamoto, Maggie Han, Ric Young, Wu Jun Mei, Cary Hiroyuki Tagawa, Jade Go, Fumihiko Ikeda, Richard Vuu, Tijger Tsou, Wu Tao, Fan Guang, Henry Kyi, Alvin Riley III*
Running time: 163 mins
US release: Columbia, Nov 20, 1987
UK release: Columbia, Feb 26, 1988

THE LAST OF ENGLAND
After breaking through into a kind of cultural respectability with *Caravaggio*, Jarman threw caution and artistic restraint to the wind with this scream of anger at a contemporary Britain seen as a police state, with the ideals of the last war well and truly fossilized. Mixing in Super 8mm video and old home videos, the film has a frenzied intensity, but, stretched to an hour and a half, the obscurities and indulgences ultimately sink the potential poetry of Jarman's vision. **DT**
Director *Derek Jarman* ***producers*** *James Mackay, Don Boyd* ***camera*** *Jarman, Christopher Hughes, Cerith Wyn Evans, Richard Heslop, Tim Burke,* ***editors*** *Peter Cartwright, Angus Cook, John Maybury, Sally Yeadon* ***design*** *Christopher Hobbs* ***music*** *Simon Turner* ***cast*** *Spring, Gerrard McCarthur, John Phillips, Gay Gaynor, Matthew Hawkins, Tilda Swinton, Spencer Leigh, (voice of) Nigel Terry*
Running time: 91 mins
UK release: Tartan, Oct 23, 1987

LEONARD: PART VI
America is two nations - the TV audience and the film audience - and they don't often mix. Bill Cosby found that out making this stupid spy spoof that drew none of his fans from in front of their TV sets. Cosby plays a silly ex-operative enticed back into harness to combat a vegetarian (Gloria Foster) who employs animals in her attempt to take over the world. Tom Courtenay funds his retirement lampooning his role in *The Dresser* by playing Cosby's valet. British director Paul Weiland learned his craft making commercials, and directs quite a few plugs here (Coca Cola, Lava soap, etc.) **BM**
Director *Paul Weiland* ***producer*** *Bill Cosby* ***execs*** *Alan Marshall, Steve Sohmer* ***script*** *Jonathan Reynolds* ***camera*** *Jan DeBont* ***editor*** *Gerry Hambling* ***design*** *Geoffrey Kirkland* ***music*** *Elmer Bernstein* ***cast*** *Bill Cosby, Tom Courtenay, Joe Don Baker, Moses Gunn, Pat Colbert, Gloria Foster, Victoria Powell, Anna Levine, David Maier, Grace Zabriskie, Hal Bokar, George Maguire, John Hostetter, William Hall, George Kirby, Jane Fonda*
Running time: 85 mins
US release: Columbia, Dec 18, 1987

The Last of England

LESS THAN ZERO
Turkey of the Year
Director *Marek Kanievska* ***producers*** *Jon Avnet, Jordan Kerner* ***script*** *Harley Peyton, based on the novel by Bret Easton Ellis* ***camera*** *Edward Lachman* ***editor*** *Peter E. Berger* ***design*** *Barbara Ling* ***music*** *Thomas Newman* ***cast*** *Andrew McCarthy, Jami Gertz, Robert Downey Jr., James Spader, Michael Bowen, Nicholas Pryor, Tony Bill*
Running time: 98 mins
US release: Fox, Nov 6, 1987

LET'S HOPE IT'S A GIRL
(Speriamo Che Sia Femmina)
Mario Monicelli, one of the stalwarts of post-war Italian cinema, directs an international all-star cast in this Franco-Italian co-production which coalesces into a sprawling domestic drama with mild feminist undertones. Liv Ullmann presides as a hard-pressed matriarch struggling to look after her extended family and run-down Tuscan estate. Noiret plays her feckless husband, whose fatal car accident halfway through the film leads to the break-up, and eventual reunion, of the surviving members of the household. While Italian comedies have a tradition of undercutting the macho ethic, this one takes the idea to its logical conclusion by having its women refusing at last to cater to the whims of demanding, philandering menfolk, and knitting themselves instead into a cosy all-female unit. Lightweight, but rather charming in a leisurely sort of way, and the Tuscan landscape photography is a treat. **AB**
Director *Mario Monicelli* ***producer*** *Giovanni Di Clemente* ***script*** *Leo Benvenuti, Piero De Bernardi, Suso Cecchi D'Amico, Tullio Pinelli, Mario Monicelli* ***camera*** *Camillo Bazzoni* ***editor*** *Ruggero Mastroianni* ***design*** *Enrico Fiorentini* ***music*** *Nicola Piovani* ***cast*** *Liv Ullmann, Catherine Deneuve, Giuliana De Sio, Philippe Noiret, Giuliana Gemma, Bernard Blier, Stefania Sandrelli, Lucrezia Lante Della Rovere, Paolo Hendel, Athina Cenci*
Running time: 119 mins
UK release: Artificial Eye, Nov 6, 1987

LETHAL WEAPON
An action-adventure film that has more in common with *Witness* than just Danny Glover, *Lethal Weapon* depicts a cop's redemption through exposure to traditional family values. There's all the mayhem and murder a cop-movie enthusiast could desire, organized in the extravagant Donner manner. The pleasure of the movie, though, is watching suicidal Mel Gibson take the gun out of his mouth and learn to enjoy life the way Glover does in the bosom of his Cosby-ish family. Maybe *Lethal Weapon*, a big hit, will do for *policiers* what *Shane* did for Westerns. In any case, it made Gibson marketable in the States again after multiple non-*Max* misses. **BM**
Director *Richard Donner* ***producers*** *Donner, Joel Silver* ***script*** *Shane Black* ***camera*** *Stephen Goldblatt* ***editor*** *Stuart Baird* ***design*** *J. Michael Riva* ***music*** *Michael Kamen, Eric Clapton* ***cast*** *Mel Gibson, Danny Glover, Gary Busey, Mitchell Ryan, Tom Atkins, Darlene Love, Traci Wolfe, Jackie Swanson, Damon Hines, Ebonie Smith*
Running time: 110 mins
US release: Warner, Mar 6, 1987
UK release: CCW, Aug 28, 1987

THE LAST EMPEROR

The Last Emperor may not be the best film of the year, but it's certainly the one that leaves the heaviest impression. Evoking that phalanx of stiff clay warriors set up around an ancient Emperor's tomb, it's a $21 million tomb for an Emperor who had the bad luck to be both ancient and modern.

The film had me in two minds throughout, but that figures when you recall that earlier Bertolucci picture *Partner*, which showed The Artist being haunted by his double, The Political Terrorist. Still, Bertolucci's art obeys no politics. Which perhaps explains why the Hollywood élite threw enough Oscars to fill a sideboard at a movie which acquiesces in Chinese Communist brainwashing. It must be doing something unusually well.

Revolutions fascinate Bertolucci, and this sprawling epic piles one upon another. Pu Yi (1906-1967) succeeds to China's Manchu dynasty at the age of three, only to be always a prisoner: as infant despot, boy reformer, playboy-in-exile, puppet-ruler of Manchuria, prisoner of Mao, and finally simple gardener. Throughout it all he retains a sort of 'minimal self', symbolized by a pet cricket, which as a boy he secretes about his person, and which, as a ghost of 64 or so, he passes on to another little Chinese kid.

From one angle the film celebrates a baffled loner's psychic survival. As such it's like Scorsese's *Raging Bull*, with exotic ceremonial taking the place of funky boxing. It's also about adaptation, about change; the enigmatic Pu Yi evokes a modern uncertainty about character and how far change implies that it's really like Peer Gynt's onion; you peel successive layers from the 'real me' to find - nothing. It's also a rerun of Bertolucci's broodings, in *The Conformist*, about eerie osmoses between a man's character and his political functions. (Woody Allen's angle on all that was *Zelig*.)

Pu Yi himself is poignantly a non-entity, especially as he's played by four actors: three successive children and the sphinx-faced, aptly named, John Lone. Here is a sad fairy story, about a suckling plucked from his mother's

breast (that archaic phrase applies literally here). In eighties terms, he's in the same plight as E.T., trapped on an alien planet that happens to be ours. Moviewise, the year of *The Last Emperor* is also the Year of the Lost Child; *Empire of the Sun* and *Hope and Glory* also show boys freed-but-traumatized by social convulsions. All three films get snagged, in their different ways, on the problems of gearing the quirks and details of a kid's mind in with sprawling social events.

Bertolucci's Emperor isn't reduced to being 'just ordinary'; it's something he achieves; he comes to understand, against the grain, that being 'used', i.e. useful, as a witness to history, as a gardener, is nobler than being 'His Majesty the Baby' and freer than being a puppet of statecraft. In an age of exasperated individualism, it's quite a relief to think that, and that lifts the film's homage to conformity clear of a Communist party line. The film does accommodate Marxist sermonizing: about 'the personal being political', about Communism ending alienation, about the kindly wisdom of a Party prison governor, who, moreover, is played by an ex-film star now China's current Minister of Culture. (Imagine the reaction if Ronald Reagan took time off to play a prison governor whose inspirational ideology reformed Grenadan political criminals ...) But we're kept critically alert about Maoism's harsher possibilities; and the Prison Governor gets it, in his turn, from bullying young Red Guards, who, we don't forget, 'inspired' Western intellectuals during Bertolucci's youth, and the run-up to '1968'. So the ironies of history never end. The film's real topic is a universal problem: humility, belonging, and surviving history.

The Italian cinema, more than any other, stresses social scenery - crowds in landscapes. It's not *just* spectacle; sombre neo-realists like Rossellini and de Sica, and introverts like Antonioni, *think* like that too. Here Bertolucci's landscapes include Imperial Court-scapes, which, if they're wearisome in their vastness, are at least supposed to be. In a rare moment of refreshment, silken bedsheets ripple and glint over Emperor, wife and concubine 'making the wind and the rain'. But what really fascinates Bertolucci is Chinese court life as Spectacle and Theatre of Ritual. The 'littlest Emperor' has to *act out* a 'Baby God' role, scripted and directed by his aged courtiers, who really believe in their 'vision', even suffering for it. Later, Pu Yi's Western tutor prescribes *spectacles* for the poor lost boy - but only the Maoist theory of history can bring him to *see*.

As regards morality and social action, an especially intriguing character is the Scottish tutor, Reginald Johnston, who first wakens Pu Yi to Western democratic ideas. Peter O'Toole plays him in a semi-dotty style only describable as 'I Was Monty Python's Divinity Teacher'. His teaching aids are a media salad of politicians' portraits, dollar bills and magazine covers. His speech about becoming a 'gentleman' weirdly blends ethics, self-perfection and snobbery. He pedals his old sit-up-and-beg bone-shaker like a one-man avant-garde of Chinese massed bicycling. Is Bertolucci hinting that Democratic ideology is a gaga mix-up really, or that its very contradictions can ginger you up no end, or that individualism is only eccentricity? Or perhaps Johnston is such fun because Bertolucci just can't decide. However, Pu Yi's stabs at Johnston-inspired reform peter out once he expels the court eunuchs, bearing their private parts (previously sacrificed for him) in pickle jars. It laughs out of court any graft of Johnston-type gentleman ideal and Chinese collectivism, preparing the idea that Chinese Communism is just about right for modern China. Or else: since democracy, Chinoiserie, and Maoism all get weird, why not just survive, like Pu Yi ...

Bertolucci mocks, but isn't without sympathy for, that platoon of ancient Manchu courtiers, doing their grotesque best to father and mother the infant and bring him up properly while kowtowing to his every whim. Pu Yi's Wife No. 2 says it for polygamy and relates the ideology of monogamy to the bodyholds of ballroom dancing. The film doesn't 'explain' Fascism by vileness and madness, but grants it a kind of logic.

Bertolucci scarcely tries to get inside the Chinese mind. The only customs that interest him form a Freudian sex-and-infancy syndrome: prolonged wet-nursing, concubinage, pickled penises, and dieticians who perform an olfactory inspection of their patient's last stool before prescribing his next meal. The last is a bold transgression against the way costume films generally spare us the warts-and-all realities of their time.

The film's detractors will justly comment that spectators un-stunned by epic exotic spectacle will find the film cold, remote and ponderous. Pu Yi's thoughts are simple, slow and few. He has no confidant through whom to share his thinking with us. His various initiatives are too sporadic to get the drama rolling. As for the glamorous leather-clad lesbian Fascist lady spy, who places a wedding ring on Pu Yi's wife's toe, and lures her into drugs 'n' decadence, that clutter of cliché seems a very silly substitute for a sad, intimate story of a Chinese marriage splintering, like China herself ...

Come to think of it, *1900* got repetitious enough to make you scream, and the backbone of *Last Tango* was Brando's soliloquy, actually 'scripted' by the actor. At least this heavy-footed story exudes a sense of history coiled around the characters - a dragon that's treacherous, unforgiving, capricious.

That *The Last Emperor* presents unfamiliar history from an Asiatic point of view may sound off-putting, but these days it's a huge fascination, as *Gandhi* showed.

Bertolucci himself is that rarity, a well-off bourgeois brat who turned Marxist without becoming guilt-ridden or puritanical or unctuously accusatory or forever a-boil with indignation. His films suggest a shamelessly happy nature, and his friendly feeling to bourgeois parents shines through *La Luna* and *The Tragedy of a Ridiculous Man*. All his films tell one basic story: a lonely but lively rich kid gets the smell of togetherness from the labouring classes - be he the landowner's son in *1900*, Marlon Brando buttering up Maria Schneider, or Pu Yi, the Celestial Child, learning to cultivate the People's pot plants and love the Party. Over a streak of atonement to the masses, togetherness prevails. In Pu Yi's long sad life Maoist dogma is just another accident of history, and his better nature uses it, only because it's there, even more than it uses him.

Bertolucci is a Marxist like so many Italian peasants are Christians - that is to say, they're happy pagans underneath. A tale that, taken too literally, might read like *Last Foxtrot in Little-Red-Book-Land*, becomes more than the sum of its parts.

RAYMOND DURGNAT

LESS THAN ZERO

Even as the critical backlash against Jay McInerney's *Bright Lights, Big City* (1984), Bret Easton Ellis's *Less Than Zero* (1985) and Tama Janowitz's *Slaves of New York* (1986) gathered momentum, the rush was on to film the three mid-eighties cult novels most closely (and erroneously) identified with the American yuppie generation. Given the unlikelihood of these books outlasting the decade as classic pop literature, it seemed their chances of posterity would be linked to the movies that were being made of them.

On paper at least, *Slaves of New York* (originally an Andy Warhol project) seemed to be in the safest hands, those of James Ivory, who co-wrote the screenplay with Janowitz. They have discarded the scattered one-off short stories in the 'novel' to home in on the recurring problems of the floundering jewellery designer Eleanor (Bernadette Peters), her straying artist boyfriend Stash (Adam Coleman Howard), and the painter-with-more-ego-than-talent Marley (Nick Corri) in the milieu of the galleries and high-rent apartments of downtown Manhattan. The film is in post-production at the time of writing.

Bright Lights, Big City had been through six screenplays (the first three written by McInerney for Columbia) before James Bridges, hired by United Artists as a trouble-shooter when the original director Joyce Chopra was sacked, wrote his own version in seven days, going before the cameras on the eighth. Not only did he return to the novel and McInerney's original script, but he called in the author to rewrite scenes as he shot. The resulting film, about the pill-popping, young fact-checker at a Manhattan magazine who finds himself on the skids, was extraordinarily faithful to McInerney's original conception, and a rueful evocation of post-yuppie fallout.

Less Than Zero, the movie, unfortunately, is all fallout with no Big Bang to precede it. A *New York Times* production story revealed that Ellis, who'd sold the movie rights and had no part in the adaptation, anticipated it would be a failure, and it is. It actually begins promisingly enough with a cynical shot of the American flag and an azure Californian sky dotted with high-school mortar boards - jubilantly thrown into the air by the latest class of graduates, three of whom we are about to watch disintegrate. By the time we've reached two-thirds of the way through, the movie and its message have gone sadly astray. College-kid Clay (Andrew McCarthy) and his coked-up girlfriend Blair (Jami Gertz) drive through a glowing tunnel in Los Angeles and hit a coyote. It's another symbolic Bad Thing in their Christmas of disaffection, alienation and joyless hedonism. Blair flounces off and Clay runs bawling after her. 'Are we having fun? It doesn't feel like it.'

It certainly doesn't, either for them or for us. *Less Than Zero* is a frothing slurry of self-pity, tears and cocaine, all shot in candy colours. In the year of Tim Hunter's unyielding *River's Edge*, with its gang of morose, downmarket kids struggling to comprehend that the murdered girl by the water used to be their friend, one can't quite muster the sympathy for *Less Than Zero*'s expensive victims of excess. One of them, Julian (Robert Downey Jr.), a whining liability to his friends and family, has blown $50,000 on coke. This isn't so much the Blank Generation as the Blank Cheque Generation.

The novel is narrated, in an anaesthetized monotone, by Clay, back home in LA after four months in an Eastern university (the film shows him sitting on his bed in his college room, dumb and inert). Bored by too much sex, drugs and conspicuous consumerism, emotionally cut off from his parents, he and his mostly faceless friends are nonetheless trapped on an existential freeway of meaningless parties, clubs, gigs and random bisexual couplings. Clay is an impartial observer rather than a participant in his on-off relationship with Blair. He casually witnesses Julian's servicing of a middle-aged businessman in a hotel room to pay off his drug debts, the repeated rape of an underage girl staked out on a bed, his buddies mulling over a corpse in an alleyway. Unable to feel anything, he goes back East.

The most important idea in the book is expressed in its opening metaphor, 'People are afraid to merge on freeways in Los Angeles.' But the characters in the film merge in the foregrounded Clay/Blair/Julian friendship, which Julian (having slept with Blair) nervily over-justifies, and in Clay and Blair's attempts to rescue Julian from his drug addiction.

In imposing this fragile storyline and an old-fashioned Hollywood morality on Ellis's rigorously amoral novel, Peyton's adaptation has bypassed the book's greatest strengths. It may have been scarcely filmable in its original form, but one regrets the loss of the MTV-inspired rush of disconnected vignettes, in which Ellis married structure with content. Gone also is the unalleviated numbness, which in itself was cautionary. Striving to be more than zero when Clay and Blair rally round the hapless Julian, the movie topples into mawkish sentimentality.

This leads to at least one execrable scene between Downey, OD-ing on The Method and crazily reminiscent of a young Tony Curtis, and the histrionic Ms Gertz. 'Are you all right?' she twitters as he throws up. Suddenly the laughs come thick and fast, not all of them intended. 'Who's gonna take care of you guys when I'm gone?' frets Julian, genuinely concerned. Elegantly sleepwalking through the action, McCarthy comes closest to the atrophied spirit of the novel, although Downey won the most critical plaudits: an unshaven rag doll, he seems to be treading water.

Clay is straighter than straight in the film, his bisexuality in the pre-AIDS novel banished from the screen by the producers. The portrayal of Julian's gay pimp/dealer, played with oily malevolence by the excellent James Spader, is meanwhile tinged with homophobia. Again, this seems to me to be cheating on the source (although the film's makers have made no claims to fidelity). There are a few wicked delights. At a party, one pretty coke-fiend realizes her nose is bleeding and, not knowing what else to do, giggles stupidly. Julian tenderly play-acts a scene with a precocious little girl, pretending to be her spurned lover. And when Clay and Blair seize him at the end and he starts to withdraw, the three of them literally descend a building in a golden elevator. Trouble is, they've hit the bottom much too late.

Otherwise, *Less Than Zero* is less than relentless, except in its incandescent *mise-en-scène*. Marek Kanievska, the London-born director of *Another Country*, and his lighting cameraman Ed Lachman (*Desperately Seeking Susan*, *True Stories*) have flooded the film with icy swimming-pool blues and lurid infra-reds, turning LA into one big desensitized discorama. Desensitization was, indeed, the name of the game - *Less Than Zero* finished 87th in *Variety*'s annual list of big rental films for 1987. Its worth as a fable for the times was meanwhile reflected in its title.

GRAHAM FULLER

LETTERS FROM A DEAD MAN

This Soviet version of *The Day After* lacks the bludgeoning power of the American original and executes its restricted vision more artistically. As usual with films from the Eastern bloc, the story unfolds very slowly. We are in the bowels of a museum after Russia has been nuked. A few curators remain, using cycle-powered generators to light their last days. One writes letters to the son who he hopes, groundlessly, has survived. The managers of the central bunker, where plentiful food supplies are stored, ruthlessly weed out damaged survivors. The letter-writer, dying himself, seeks to save a few orphans who have been rejected. His concern enables the children to face the future, blind but determined. **BM**

Director *Konstantin Lopushansky* ***production*** *Lenfilm* ***execs*** *Raisa Proskuryakova, Yuri Golinchik* ***script*** *Lopushansky, Vyacheslav Ribakov* ***camera*** *Nikolai Pokoptsev* ***editor*** *T. Pulinoi* ***design*** *Elena Amshinskaya, Viktor Ivanov* ***music*** *Alexander Zhurbin* ***cast*** *Rolan Bikov, I. Riklin, V. Mikhailov, A. Sabinin, N. Gryakalova, V. Maiorova, V. Dvorzhetsky, V. Lobanov, S. Smirnova*

Running time: 87 mins

UK release: Artificial Eye, Sep 25, 1987

THE LIGHTHORSEMEN

Connoisseur of horse flesh Simon Wincer (*Phar Lap*) pays elaborate homage to the 800 cavalry of the Australian Light Horse in a superbly mounted re-creation of its famous charge on Turkish- and German-held Beersheba in southern Palestine in 1917 - a turning point in the Allies' Middle East campaign. The human drama - about three 'mates' and a young volunteer (Phelps) who lacks the killer instinct and leaves their ranks for the field hospital and a nurse's embrace - is altogether less successful than in Peter Weir's sharper *Gallipoli*. There are some bathetic homo-erotic scenes of naked riders romping with their horses in the sea and Anthony Andrews enjoys himself as a flamboyant British officer with a German name. Despite too many expository titles, the battle footage - a cacophony of clattering hooves and ringing harness against the backdrop of cannon - is truly thrilling. **GF**

Director *Simon Wincer* ***producers*** *Ian Jones, Wincer* ***exec*** *Antony I. Ginnane* ***script*** *Jones* ***camera*** *Dean Semler* ***editor*** *Adrian Carr* ***design*** *Bernard Hides* ***music*** *Mario Millo* ***cast*** *Jon Blake, Peter Phelps, Tony Bonner, Bill Kerr, John Walton, Gary Sweet, Tim McKenzie, Sigrid Thornton, Anthony Andrews, Anthony Hawkins, Gerard Kennedy, Shane Briant, Serge Lazareff, Ralph Cotterill*

Running time: 128 mins

US release: Cinecom, Apr 8, 1988

The Lighthorseman

LIKE FATHER LIKE SON

This well-worn Hollywood plotline, in which a father and his teenage son switch identities, is an ideal vehicle for Dudley Moore. He's a heart surgeon, and his son (TV star Kirk Cameron) is a high school goof. One fix of a peculiar substance imported from an Indian reservation, however, and they've switched brains. Moore's body suddenly has a kid's brain - which has seemed to be the case

Letters From a Dead Man

anyway in most of his movies. He disrupts the hospital while Cameron suddenly becomes a pompous know-it-all at school. Some scenes induce helpless laughter but too many fall very flat. Directed by TV veteran Rod Daniel, the movie will play better on the small screen. **BM**
Director *Rod Daniel* ***producers*** *Brian Grazer, David Valdes* ***script*** *Lorne Cameron, Steven L. Bloom* ***camera*** *Jack N. Green* ***editor*** *Lois Freeman-Fox* ***design*** *Dennis Gassner* ***music*** *Miles Goodman* ***cast*** *Dudley Moore, Kirk Cameron, Sean Astin, Patrick O'Neal, Margaret Colin, Catherine Hicks*
Running time: 98 mins
US release: Tri-Star, Oct 2, 1987

LIONHEART

Apparently less-than-epic adventure yarn set in the 12th century when a gang of orphans set out to protect the downtrodden and innocent while searching for the elusive King Richard II on his quest to recapture the Holy Land from the Moslems.
Director *Franklin J. Schaffner* ***producers*** *Stanley O'Toole, Talia Shire* ***execs*** *Francis Coppola, Jack Schwartzman* ***script*** *Menno Meyjes* ***camera*** *Alec Mills* ***editors*** *David Bretherton, Richard Haines* ***design*** *Gil Parrondo* ***music*** *Jerry Goldsmith* ***cast*** *Eric Stoltz, Gabriel Byrne, Nicola Cowper, Dexter Fletcher, Deborah Barrymore, Nicholas Clay, Bruce Purchase, Neil Dickson, Chris Pitt*
Running time: 104 mins
US release: Orion, Aug 14, 1987

Little Dorrit *(above and left)*

LITTLE DORRIT
Part I: Nobody's Fault
Part II: Little Dorrit's Story

Nobody's Fault is the story of Arthur Clennam, newly returned to London from China in the 1820s to find his destiny still decreed by the religious mania and withered spirit of his crippled mother, and further tormented by the Circumlocution Office's appalling red tape, before bad investment spirals him into the Marshalsea Debtor's Prison. The one bright spot in his life is his mother's seamstress, Amy, subject of *Little Dorrit's Story*, whose quiet determination and solicitude have succoured her father through his 23 years of incarceration at the Marshalsea - until Arthur effected their liberty. Christine Edzard's masterstroke in bringing Charles Dickens' teeming novel of corruption, capitalism and greed to the screen is in the overlapping of the two parts so that the suffocating world seen by Arthur is a place of hope and comfort for the unsentimental heroine. A great screen adaptation, as well as a cautionary fable for Mrs Thatcher's England, *Little Dorrit*'s definitive performances - from a cast of 211 - include those of Derek Jacobi as Arthur, Sarah Pickering as Amy, the late Joan Greenwood as Mrs Clennam, Max Wall as the gnarled Flintwinch, and Alec Guinness as William Dorrit, the vain, feckless embodiment of shabby gentility. **GF**

Director Christine Edzard **producers** *John Brabourne, Richard Goodwin* **script** *Edzard, based on the novel by Charles Dickens* **camera** *Bruno De Keyzer* **editors** *Oliver Stockman, Fraser Maclean* **design** *John McMillan, Peter Feroze, Mary McGowan, Charlie McMillan, Peter Seater, Hugh Doherty* **music** *Verdi, arranged by Michael Sanvoisin* **cast** *Derek Jacobi, Joan Greenwood, Max Wall, Patricia Hayes, Luke Duckett, Miriam Margolyes, Bill Fraser, Roshan Seth, Mollie Maureen, Diana Malin, Janice Cramer, Roger Hammond, Sophie Ward, Kathy Staff, Julia Lang, Pip Torrens, Graham Seed, John Savident, Brian Pettifer, John Hardin, Alec Wallis, Michael Meers, Edward Burnham, Harold Innocent, David Pugh, Alec Guinness, Cyril Cusack, Sarah Pickering, Amelda Brown, Daniel Chatto, Howard Goorney, Liz Smith, Gwenda Hughes, Celia Bannerman, Eleanor Bron, Michael Elphick, Simon Dormandy, Ian Hogg, Robert Morley, Alan Bennett, Brenda Bruce, Edward Jewesbury, Jonathan Cecil, Brian Poyser, Malcolm Tierney, Trevor Ray, Rosalie Crutchley, Betty Marsden, Paul Rhys*
Running time: 176 mins (part one), 181 mins (part two)
UK release: Curzon, Dec 11, 1987

LITTLE NIKITA

If Sidney Poitier were going to return to film acting in the part of an FBI agent, why shouldn't he return to play two FBI agents? As in *Shoot to Kill*, Poitier here is a lone wolf facing high odds with only a reluctant civilian to help. River Phoenix is an all-American boy whose parents are Russian 'sleepers'. Their happy life in America ends when their spy-master activates them against a murderous rogue agent. Poitier's job seems to be to put a spanner in all these works while keeping Phoenix American. Poitier's light moments are enjoyable but count for little against the muddled plot. **BM**
Director *Richard Benjamin* ***producer*** *Harry Gittes* ***script*** *John Hill, Bo Goldman* ***camera*** *Laszlo Kovacs* ***editor*** *Jacqueline Cambas* ***design*** *Gene Callahan* ***music*** *Marvin Hamlisch* ***cast*** *Sidney Poitier, River Phoenix, Richard Jenkins, Caroline Kava, Richard Bradford, Richard Lynch, Loretta Devine, Lucy Deakins*
Running time: 98 mins
US release: Columbia, Mar 18, 1988

THE LIVING DAYLIGHTS

James Bond again roams the world in search of ever more comic stunts and implausible baddies. The Commies again provide the antagonists but the protagonist this time is Timothy Dalton. Dalton, as young and virile as Sean Connery of blessed memory, is the George Lazenby of our era in his stolid, stalwart boringness. Maryam d'Abo is the Bond girl, a Czech cellist (if she were Polish, she'd be a Polish pianist). Joe Don Baker provides the villainy and reliable old John Glen directs this fifteenth in an evidently unending series. **BM**
Director *John Glen* ***producers*** *Albert R. Broccoli, Michael G. Wilson* ***script*** *Richard Maibaum, Michael G. Wilson, from a story by Ian Fleming* ***camera*** *Alec Mills* ***editors*** *John Grover, Peter Davies* ***design*** *Peter Lamont* ***music*** *John Barry* ***cast*** *Timothy Dalton, Maryam d'Abo, Joe Don Baker, Art Malik, Jeroen Krabbé, John Rhys-Davies, Andreas Wisniewski, Thomas Wheatley*
Running time: 130 mins
US release: UA, Jul 31, 1987
UK release: UIP, Jun 30, 1987

Living on Tokyo Time

LIVING ON TOKYO TIME

Dealing with a culturally mismatched couple, *Living on Tokyo Time* is a film with just enough sly humour to keep most art-house patrons awake. Minako Ohashi, a Japanese girl, leaves home for San Francisco. Ken Nakagawa is an aspiring Bay Area rocker who marries Ohashi so she won't have visa problems. He falls quietly in love with her while she pines for the peaks and chasms. Quiet Ken can barely get up the nerve to declare his passion. She seems unable to experience any kind of emotion, speaks quietly in well-schooled, totally uninflected English, and persists in calling her spouse Mr Ken. Eventually the inevitable happens, quietly, and the movie ends. **BM**
Director/editor *Steven Okazaki* ***producers*** *Lynn O'Donnell, Dennis Hayashi* ***script*** *John McCormick, Okazaki* ***camera*** *Okazaki, Zand Gee* ***cast*** *Minako Ohashi, Ken Nakagawa, Mitzie Abe, Bill Bonham, Brenda Aoki, Kate Connell, John McCormick, Sue Matthews, Jim Cranna, Alex Herschlag, Keith Choy, Judi Nihei, Lane Nishikawa*
Running time: 83 mins
US release: Skouras, Aug 14, 1987

THE LONELY PASSION OF JUDITH HEARNE

Quietly directed by Jack Clayton, this very human drama centres on a heart-rending portrayal by Maggie Smith of the unloved Irish spinster, whose natural mirth was curbed in childhood by a selfish Victorian aunt (Hiller). Judith's tippling accelerates when the spivvy Americanized brother (Hoskins) of her landlady (Kean) courts and then discards her when he finds she's penniless. The title is ironic: her Catholic devotion is unable to help her in her hour of need, which makes her retreat from the well of madness utterly compelling. Clayton meanwhile delineates a grey cheerless Dublin peopled by mean-spirited middle-class citizens nursing their own disappointments. **GF**
Director *Jack Clayton* ***producers*** *Peter Nelson, Richard Johnson* ***execs*** *George Harrison, Denis O'Brien* ***script*** *Peter Nelson, based on the novel by Brian Moore* ***camera*** *Peter Hannan* ***editor*** *Terry Rawlings* ***design*** *Michael Pickwoad* ***music*** *Georges Delerue* ***cast*** *Maggie Smith, Bob Hoskins, Wendy Hiller, Marie Kean, Ian McNeice, Alan Devlin, Rudi Davies, Prunella Scales, Aine Ni Mhuiri, Sheila Reid*
Running time: 116 mins
US release: Island, Dec 23, 1987

THE LOST BOYS

Dracula meets The Goonies in a raucous, brat-packing horror comic which is all surface style and very little comment. Okay, there's the germ of an idea in designer vampires, prowling the Californian boardwalk for prey, drinking château-bottled blood against a throbbing rock soundtrack and MTV images. But it all becomes rapidly wearing except

The Lonely Passion of Judith Hearne

perhaps to those who can stand the different-image-a-second world of pop videos. Lugosi would turn in his urn. **QF**
Director *Joel Schumacher* ***producer*** *Harvey Bernhard* ***exec*** *Richard Donner* ***script*** *Janice Fischer, James Jeremias, Jeffrey Boam* ***camera*** *Michael Chapman* ***editor*** *Robert Brown* ***design*** *Bo Welch* ***music*** *Thomas Newman* ***cast*** *Jason Patric, Corey Haim, Dianne Wiest, Barnard Hughes, Edward Herrmann, Kiefer Sutherland, Jami Gertz, Corey Feldman, Jamison Newlander, Brooke McCarter, Billy Wirth, Alexander Winter, Chance Michael Corbitt, Alexander Bacon Chapman, Nori Morgan*
Running time: 97 mins
US release: Warner, Jul 31, 1987
UK release: Warner, Jan 29, 1988

THE LOVE CHILD

Low-budget British comedy in which the promise of a setting in workaday Brixton gives way all too soon to second-hand whimsy as its strait-laced youthful hero comes all too predictably to terms with his legacy as offspring of (now deceased) flower-power drop-outs. Sheila Hancock is largely wasted as the lad's sensible old gran, and the less said the better about the 'joke' of a talking toilet equipped with the voice of Alexei Sayle. **TP**
Director *Robert Smith* ***producer*** *Angela Topping* ***script*** *Gordon Hann* ***camera*** *Thaddeus O'Sullivan* ***editor*** *John Davies* ***design*** *Caroline Hanania* ***music*** *Colin Gibson, Kenny Craddock* ***cast*** *Sheila Hancock, Peter Capaldi, Percy Herbert, Lesley Sharp, Alexei Sayle, Arthur Hewlett, Cleo Sylvestre, Stephen Lind, Ajaykumar, Andrew Seear, Kevin Allen, Robert Blythe, Cathy Murphy*
Running time: 100 mins
UK release: BFI, Oct 16, 1987

The Love Child

·M·M·M·M·M·M·M·M·M·

MADE IN HEAVEN

A delicate celestial fantasy that marked a return for independent stylist Alan Rudolph to studio backing, with some resultant compromises (a changed ending for one). In 1948 an ex-serviceman (Hutton) dies in a brave rescue attempt and upstairs meets an unborn soul (McGillis). They fall in love, but, when her time comes, she vanishes earthwards and Hutton is given 30 years to find her. With exquisite visuals and soundtrack, Rudolph keeps this romantic whimsy afloat and bubbling against all the odds. **DT**
Director *Alan Rudolph* ***producers*** *Raynold Gideon, Bruce A. Evans, David Blocker* ***script*** *Evans, Gideon* ***camera*** *Jan Kiesser* ***editor*** *Tom Walls* ***design*** *Paul Peters* ***music*** *Mark Isham* ***cast*** *Timothy Hutton, Kelly McGillis, Maureen Stapleton, Ann Wedgeworth, James Gammon, Don Murray, Timothy Daly, Emmett Humbird (Debra Winger), Lucille (Ellen Barkin), David Rasche, Amanda Plummer, Willard Pugh, Vyto Ruginis, Neil Young, Tom Petty, Ric Ocasek, Marj Dusay, Ray Gideon, Zack Finch*
Running time: 102 mins
US release: Lorimar, Nov 6, 1987
UK release: UKFD, Oct 23, 1987

THE MAGIC TOYSHOP

This clumsily pretentious adaptation of Angela Carter's novella flirts with the author's pantheon of feminism, Marxism, puberty and folklore. The tale of three children who assent to live with their late mother's sadistic toy shop owner brother (Bell), also indulges the familiar Carter predilection for sexual allusiveness (pretty Milmoe is covertly desired by both her uncle and cousin McKenna) and fairytale iconography, yet fails to achieve the cross-over appeal of *Company of Wolves*. Occasional images successfully highlight the transient border between hallucination and reality. However, the whole is too deliberately evasive and thematically confusing to procure any lasting interest. **MN**
Director *David Wheatley* ***producer*** *Steve Morrison* ***script*** *Angela Carter, based on her novel* ***camera*** *Ken Morgan* ***editor*** *Anthony Ham* ***design*** *Stephen Fineren* ***music*** *Bill Connor* ***cast*** *Tom Bell, Caroline Milmoe, Kilian McKenna, Patricia Kerrigan, Lorcan Cranitch, Gareth Bushill, Marlene Sidaway, Georgina Hulme, Marguerite Porter, Lloyd Newson*
Running time: 107 mins
US release: Skouras, Apr 22, 1988
UK release: Palace, Jul 31, 1987

MAID TO ORDER

Amy Jones's flimsy comedy turns *Cinderella* upside down as spoiled daddy's girl Ally Sheedy skids off the fast lane into the gutter before fairy godmother Beverly D'Angelo takes her in hand. The obnoxious darling ends up below stairs in the Malibu mansion of a tacky *nouveau riche* couple (Perrine and Shawn), where she overcomes her distaste for domestic chores and learns about real life from the Salvadorean servant, the black cook, and the working-class mechanic - who blossoms into a rock star and Ally's Prince Charming. This is mushy, moralizing, thoroughly disposable Hollywood dross and a warning to Sheedy that she has outgrown Brat Pack roles. Perrine is blowsily funny. **GF**
Director *Amy Jones* ***producers*** *Herb Jaffe, Mort Engelberg* ***script*** *Jones, Perry Howze, Randy Howze* ***camera*** *Shelly Johnson* ***editor*** *Sidney Wolinski* ***design*** *Jeffrey Townsend* ***music*** *Georges Delerue* ***cast*** *Ally Sheedy, Beverly D'Angelo, Michael Ontkean, Valerie Perrine, Dick Shawn, Tom Skerritt, Merry Clayton, Begona Plaza*
Running time: 96 mins
US release: New Century/Vista, Aug 28, 1987

MAKING MR. RIGHT

A romance masquerading as sci-fi, Seidelman's pleasant *Making Mr. Right* is a woman's-eye view of the currently popular wish-I-had-an-ideal-mate genre. Malkovich plays an emotionless scientist who creates a robot (also played by Malkovich) that malfunctions, displaying all the feelings his creator lacks. Ann Magnuson is an image consultant hired to guide the robot's entry into the world, and naturally the robot's capacity for love fixes on her. The duality of the two Malkovich characters mirrors that of the two women in Seidelman's *Desperately Seeking Susan*, but this follow-up falls a little short of the earlier film's enchantment. **BM**
Director *Susan Seidelman* ***producers*** *Mike Wise, Joel Tuber* ***execs*** *Seidelman, Dan Enright* ***script*** *Floyd Byars, Laurie Frank* ***camera*** *Edward Lachman* ***editor*** *Andrew Mondshein* ***design*** *Barbara Ling* ***music*** *Chaz Jankel* ***cast*** *John Malkovich, Ann Magnuson, Glenn Headly, Ben Masters, Laurie Metcalf, Polly Bergen, Harsh Nayyar*
Running time: 98 mins
US release: Orion, Apr 10, 1987
UK release: Rank, May 6, 1988

MALA NOCHE

Micro-budgeted feature set in Portland, Oregon and following a shabby grocery store owner's quest for the perfect boy lover.
Director/producer/editor *Gus Van Sant* ***script***

The Magic Toyshop

Van Sant, based on the story by Walt Curtis **camera** John Campbell **music** Creighton Lindsay **cast** Tim Streeter, Doug Cooeyate, Ray Monge, Nyla McCarthy, Sam Downey, Bob Pitchlynn, Eric Pedersen, Marty Christiansen, Bad George Connor, Don Chambers, Walt Curtis, Kenny Presler, Conde Benavides
Running time: 78 mins
US release: Gus Van Sant, May 4, 1987
UK release: Other Cinema, Jul 24, 1987

THE MAN FROM MAJORCA
(Mannen från Mallorca)

Swedish police thriller concerning a crime covered up from within the Justice Department. A pair of Swedish vice cops discover that a routine post-office raid is connected with a couple of subsequent deaths, a hit-and-run accident involving a teenage thief, and the murder of a garrulous wino.
Director *Bo Widerberg* ***exec*** *Göran Lindström* ***script*** *Widerberg, based on the novel* Grisfesten *by Leif G. W. Persson* ***camera*** *Thomas Wahlberg, Gunnar Nilsson, Hans Welin* ***editor*** *Widerberg* ***design*** *Jan Öquist* ***music*** *Björn Jason Lindh* ***cast*** *Sven Wollter, Tomas von Brömssen, Håkan Serner, Ernst Günther, Thomas Hellberg, Tommy Johnson, Sten Lonnert, Tord Nordlund, Margreth Weivers, Nina Gunke, Niels Jensen, Marie Delleskog*
Running time: 105 mins
UK release: Cannon, Aug 14, 1987

A MAN IN LOVE
(Un Homme amoureux)

Diane Kurys sidesteps the overt autobiography of her previous features and goes for big screen romance in a slight story of movie star (Coyote) meets beautiful ingénue (Scacchi) in exotic Rome while making a film on writer Cesare Pavese. Her leads score high on charisma and there are some sumptuous sex scenes, but the emotional core really comes from a beautiful cameo by Claudia Cardinale as Scacchi's mother. **DT**
Director/script *Diane Kurys* ***producer*** *Michel Seydoux, Kurys* ***exec*** *Seydoux* ***camera*** *Bernard Zitzermann* ***editors*** *Joëlle Van Effenterre, Nathalie Le Guay, Michèle Robert, Valérie Longeville* ***design*** *Dean Tavoularis* ***music*** *Georges Delerue* ***cast*** *Peter Coyote, Greta Scacchi, Jamie Lee Curtis, Claudia Cardinale, Peter Riegert, John Berry, Vincent Lindon, Jean Pigozzi, Elia Katz, Constantin Alexandrov, Jean Claude de Goros, Michèle Melega, Iole Silvani*
Running time: 111 mins
US release: Cinecom, Jul 31, 1987

MAN ON FIRE

A soft-headed story about a 12-year-old girl and her world-weary bodyguard suddenly becomes a hard-edged, brutal thriller when the girl is kidnapped. Eli Chouraqui's film divides too neatly into halves for either part to be fully effective - especially since the beginning appears to have been severely cut for US release. In this version, Brooke Adams as the girl's mother and Jonathan Pryce as Adams' lover have hardly two lines between them. Maybe they wanted a paid holiday on Lake Como. Scott Glenn is excellent as the burned-out ex-CIA man whose hand curls naturally around a gun again when the chips are down. **BM**
Director *Eli Chouraqui* ***producer*** *Arnon Milchan* ***script*** *Chouraqui, Sergio Donati, based on the novel by A.J. Quinnell* ***camera*** *Gerry Fisher* ***editor*** *Noëlle Boisson* ***design*** *Giantito Burchiellaro* ***music*** *John Scott* ***cast*** *Scott Glenn, Jade Malle, Joe Pesci, Brooke Adams, Jonathan Pryce, Paul Shenar, Danny Aiello, Laura Morante, Giancarlo Prati, Inigo Lezzi, Alessandro Haber, Franco Trevisi, Lou Castel, Lorenzo Piani*
Running time: 92 mins
US release: Tri-Star, Oct 9, 1987
UK release: Rank, Jun 17, 1988

MANON DES SOURCES

Those expecting the sequel to *Jean de Florette* to be a simple tale of wrongs righted may have been surprised by this twist on the Oedipus legend, about the discovery by the childless César (Montand) that his hunchback Jean, whose death he encouraged, was his own son. A touch heavy-handed in its

A Man in Love

mythological allusions, and suffering from some slack dramatization, the film starts as comedy with Montand encouraging nephew Ugolin (Auteuil) to declare his passion for Jean's daughter, now an earthy beauty who tends goats on the mountains. But she seeks revenge by blocking the village water-supply. The distraught farmers look for a scapegoat, causing the noose to tighten literally around Ugolin's neck - he hangs himself from a tree - and metaphorically around that of César. **JP**
Director *Claude Berri* ***exec*** *Pierre Grunstein* ***script*** *Berri, Gérard Brach, based on the novel* L'Eau des collines *by Marcel Pagnol* ***camera*** *Bruno Nuytten* ***editors*** *Geneviève Louveau, Hervé de Luze* ***design*** *Bernard Vezat* ***music*** *Jean-Claude Petit* ***cast*** *Yves Montand, Daniel Auteuil, Emmanuelle Béart, Hippolyte Girardot, Margarite Lozano, Elisabeth Depardieu, Gabriel Bacquier, Armand Meffre, André Dupon, Pierre Nougaro, Jean Maurel, Roger Souza, Didier Pain*
Running time: 120 mins (114 mins in UK)
US release: Orion Classics, Nov 6, 1987
UK release: Cannon, Nov 30, 1987

Manon des Sources

MASCARA

A tacky slice of Euro-sleaze which leaves a nasty taste in the mouth. Outwardly respectable police superintendent harbours incestuous leanings towards sister, leads secret life at transvestite club and strangles some transsexuals in a fit of pique. Sister's boyfriend, framed for the murders, is beaten to death. Charlotte Rampling gives the drag artists a run for their money in the ludicrous get-up stakes, but sartorial interest appears to be centred on the opera diva's frock (with neon trimmings) which Michael Sarrazin wears for his climactic Raving Loony Scene. **AB**
Director *Patrick Conrad* ***producers*** *Pierre Drouot, Rene Solleveld, Henry Lange* ***execs*** *Menahem Golan, Yoram Globus* ***script*** *Hugo Claus, Conrad, Pierre Drouot* ***camera*** *Gilberto Azevedo* ***editor*** *Susana Rossberg* ***design*** *Dirk Debou, Misjel Vermeiren* ***music*** *Egisto Macchi* ***cast*** *Charlotte Rampling, Michael Sarrazin, Derek De Lint, Jappe Claes, Herbert Flack, Harry Cleven, Serge-Henri Valcke, Romy Haag, Eva Robbins, John Van Dreelen, Norma Christine Deumner, Pascale Jean-Louis Berghe, Charlotte Berden, Marie-Luce Bonfanti, Carmela Locantore, Lois Chacon*
Running time: 98 mins
UK release: Cannon, Oct 9, 1987

MASQUERADE

An old-fashioned money-for-murder thriller can still work today if the suspense grows tighter and tighter amid believable turnabouts and revelations. Bob Swaim proves an expert manipulator of the audience's emotions and minds in this story of love and death among the hyper-rich on the Hamptons of Long Island. Meg Tilly is an orphaned heiress who falls heavily for youthful yachtsman Rob Lowe. She marries this penniless Apollo after experiencing the same greased-body treatment he's simultaneously giving his boss's wife, Kim Cattrall. Tilly's stepfather and her former beau look askance - or do they? **BM**
Director *Bob Swaim* ***producer*** *Michael I. Levy* ***exec/script*** *Dick Wolf* ***camera*** *David Watkin* ***editor*** *Scott Conrad* ***design*** *John Kasarda* ***music*** *John Barry* ***cast*** *Rob Lowe, Meg Tilly, Doug Savant, Kim Cattrall, John Glover, Dana Delany*
Running time: 91 mins
US release: MGM, Mar 11, 1988

MASTERS OF THE UNIVERSE

A 106-minute advert for a hideous line of fascist toys is unlikely to have much merit as a film. Gary Goddard's lavish display of bright and noisy destructiveness stars the splendidly muscled Dolph Lundgren as He-Man and the sepulchrally evil-voiced Frank Langella as Skeletor. These brand-names battle across the universe for a key to ultimate power which some young earthlings take for a novel musical instrument. Tedious laser battles doom a tonnage of nasties while He-Man's solemn mission to save the universe proves too weighty for Lundgren's attempts at repartee. **BM**
Director *Gary Goddard* ***producers*** *Menahem Golan, Yoram Globus* ***exec*** *Edward R. Pressman* ***script*** *David Odell* ***camera*** *Hanania Baer, William Neil (Boss Film Corp.)* ***editor*** *Anne V. Coates* ***design*** *William Stout* ***music*** *Bill Conti* ***cast*** *Dolph Lundgren, Frank Langella, Meg Foster, Bill Barty, Courteney Cox, James Tolkan, Christina Pickles, Robert Duncan McNeill, Jon Cypher, Chelsea Field, Tony Carroll, Pons Maar, Anthony DeLongis, Robert Towers, Barry Livingston, Jessica Nelson*
Running time: 106 mins
US release: Cannon, Aug 7, 1987
UK release: Cannon, Dec 26, 1987

MATEWAN

John Sayles' most ambitious film to date dramatizes the Matewan Massacre of 1920, when striking miners even won over scab immigrants and blacks to fight with them against the coal company. A scrupulously controlled gallery of mainly non-professionals in a very handsome setting underline the pro-Union thrust with an irresistible humanism. **DT**
Director/script *John Sayles* ***producers*** *Peggy Rajski, Maggie Renzi* ***execs*** *Amir Jacob Malin, Jerry Silva* ***camera*** *Haskell Wexler* ***editor*** *Sonya Polonsky* ***design*** *Nora Chavooshian* ***music*** *Mason Daring* ***cast*** *Chris Cooper, Will Oldham, Mary McDonnell, Bob Gunton, James Earl Jones, Kevin Tighe, Gordon Clapp, Josh Mostel, Ken Jenkins, Jace Alexander, Nancy Motto, Gary McCleery, David Strathairn, Joe Grifasi, James Kizar, Michael Preston*
Running time: 130 mins
US release: Cinecom, Aug 28, 1987

Matewan *(right)*

MAURICE

James Ivory's film of E.M. Forster's long suppressed novel of homosexual desire is perforce less frilly, more masculine in its *mise-en-scène* than *A Room With a View*. As the smug, middle-class Maurice (Wilby) finds and is then forced to forsake his Cambridge love (Grant) for a ferrety gamekeeper (Graves), so Pierre Lhomme's cinematography increasingly suffuses the screen with the cold, regretful light of a passing era. If some of the Cambridge scenes are wearily *Brideshead*, once Maurice is absorbed into a world of stifling propriety and gay persecution, the film evokes a uniquely complex mood of twilight despair, with Wilby touching despite his self-absorption. **GF**
Director *James Ivory* ***producer*** *Ismail Merchant* ***script*** *Ivory, Kit Hesketh-Harvey, based on the novel by E. M. Forster* ***camera*** *Pierre Lhomme* ***editor*** *Katherine Wenning* ***design*** *Brian Ackland-Snow* ***music*** *Richard Robbins* ***cast*** *James Wilby, Hugh Grant, Rupert Graves, Denholm Elliott, Simon Callow, Billie Whitelaw, Ben Kingsley, Judy Parfitt, Phoebe Nichols, Mark Tandy, Helena Michell, Kitty Aldridge, Patrick Godfrey, Michael Jenn, Barry Foster, Peter Eyre, Catherine Rabett, Orlando Wells, Helena Bonham Carter*
Running time: 140 mins
US release: Cinecom, Sep 18, 1987
UK release: Enterprise, Nov 6, 1987

MAYBE BABY (See For Keeps)

MIDNIGHT CROSSING

To high heaven, this one stinks. For a start, Faye Dunaway is a blind eye-doctor. Her husband, Daniel J. Travanti, is a mild-mannered insurance man with

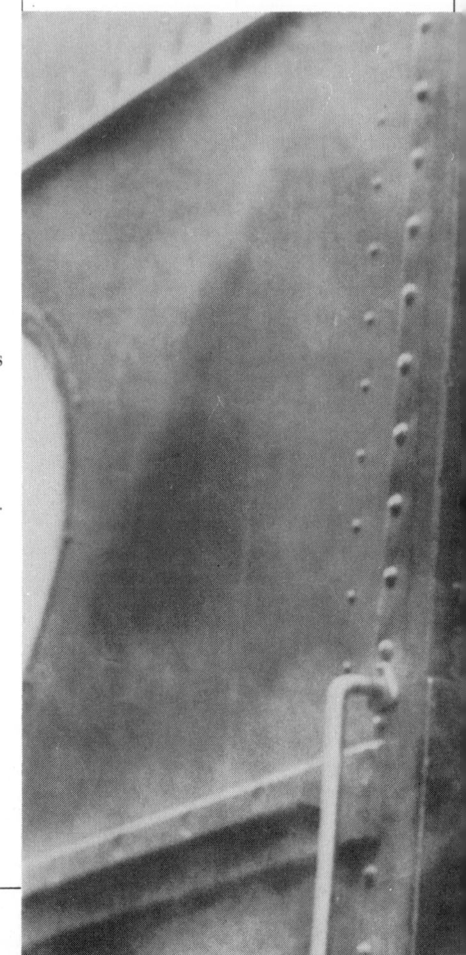

Maurice

a murderous secret. Travanti entices John Laughlin and Kim Cattrall to sail to an island off Cuba to reclaim some treasure left behind when Castro took over in 1959. On the voyage they meet old sea-dog Ned Beatty in the phoniest Robert Shaw part ever written. Soon after landfall, there are as many corpses as palm trees. Dunaway is the last one left, but things are not what they seem. Yes, with every scene, it gets worse. **BM**

***Director** Roger Holzberg **producer** Matthew Hayden **execs** Dan Ireland, Gary Barber, Gregory Cascante, Wanda Rayle **script** Holzberg, Doug Weiser **camera** Henry Vargas **editor** Earl Watson **music** Steve Tyrell **cast** Faye Dunaway, Daniel J. Travanti, Kim Cattrall, John Laughlin, Ned Beatty*

Running time: 104 mins

US release: Vestron, May 15, 1988

THE MILAGRO BEANFIELD WAR

An air of sprightly (New) Mexican magic infests Robert Redford's painstaking second feature as director, otherwise routine in its adaptation of John Nichols' bloodier novel about a struggle between a tiny community and ruthless big business. The people of Milagro are mobilized into saving their beautiful valley from being turned into a luxury estate by state-supported property tycoon Richard Bradford (married to a frowsy Melanie Griffith) when Robert Carricart's chuckling old ghost fixes it up for unemployed bean farmer Chick Vennera to irrigate his dried-up field. It becomes a Western in the middle (shades of *Tell Them Willie Boy Is Here*) with the arrival of Christopher Walken's scowling heavy, but finally dissolves into a sunlit populist party. Redford gets satisfying work from Rubén Blades, Sonia Braga and John Heard - all on the side of the angels - but this is a curiously insubstantial meal. **GF**

***Director** Robert Redford **producers** Redford, Moctesuma Esparza **exec** Gary J. Hendler **script** David Ward, John Nichols, based on Nichols' novel **camera** Robbie Greenberg **editors** Dede Allen, Jim Miller **design** Joe Aubel **music** Dave Grusin **cast** Rubén Blades, Richard Bradford, Sonia Braga, Julie Carmen, James Gammon, Melanie Griffith, John Heard, Carlos Riquelme, Daniel Stern, Chick Vennera, Christopher Walken, Freddy Fender, Robert Carricart, M. Emmet Walsh, Tony Genaro, Jerry Hardin*

Running time: 117 mins

US release: Universal, Mar 18, 1988

UK release: UIP, Aug 19, 1988

MISS MARY

The demise of the Galtieri crowd opened the gates to a new Argentine cinema, not all of which is world-class. Mariá Luisa Bemberg's *The Official Story* was an impressive feminist look at the country the death squads left behind. Now, in *Miss Mary*, Bemberg covers an earlier male-dominated Argentine era with less success. Julie Christie is a governess who has an affair with the son and heir - unforgivable from mother's point of view. Worse, from Christie's point of view, World War II comes along and she can't go home. That's all there is, I'm afraid. **BM**

***Director** Mariá Luisa Bemberg **producer** Lita Stantic **script** Bemberg, Jorge Goldemberg **camera** Miguel Rodriguez **editor** Cesar D'Angiolillo **design** Esmeralda Almonacid **music** Luis Mariá Serra **cast** Julie Christie, Sofia Viruboff, Donald McIntyre, Barbara Bunge, Nacha Guevara*

Running time: 102 mins (100 mins in UK)

US release: New World, Dec 19, 1986

UK release: Entertainment, Sep 18, 1987

THE MODERNS

Film of the Year

***Director** Alan Rudolph **producer** Carolyn Pfeiffer **exec** Shep Gordon **script** Rudolph, John Bradshaw **camera** Toyomichi Kurita **editors** Debra T. Smith, Scott Brock **design** Steven Legler **music** Mark Isham **cast** Keith Carradine, Linda Fiorentino, John Lone, Wallace Shawn, Geneviève Bujold, Geraldine Chaplin, Kevin J. O'Connor, Elsa Raven, Ali Giron, Gailard Sartain, Michael Wilson*

Running time: 126 mins

US release: Alive, Apr 15, 1988

THE MONSTER SQUAD

Some revoltingly precocious schoolboys band together to defeat Count Dracula, the Werewolf, the Mummy and the Creature from the Black Lagoon when these creatures emerge from their various hidey-holes to launch an all-out assault on Los Angeles. Frankenstein's Monster also arrives on the scene, but turns out to be a Good Guy. Like Fred Dekker's début, *Night of the Creeps*, this is a none too serious romp through horror film conventions. It is debatable as to whether the age group at which it is aimed will be familiar with the classic creature features from which the monsters are borrowed. **AB**

***Director** Fred Dekker **producer** Jonathan A. Zimbert **execs** Peter Hyams, Rob Cohen, Keith Barish **script** Shane Black, Dekker **camera** Bradford May **editor** James Mitchell **design** Albert Brenner **music** Bruce Broughton **cast** Andre Gower, Robby Kiger, Stephen Macht, Duncan Regehr, Tom Noonan, Brent Chalem, Ryan Lambert, Ashley Bank, Michael Faustino, Mary Ellen Trainor*

Running time: 81 mins

US release: Tri-Star, Aug 14, 1987

UK release: Columbia, 15 Jul, 1988

THE MODERNS

No other recent American film has polarized critics and audiences as much as Alan Rudolph's deliberately eccentric portrait of American expatriates in the Paris art scene of the twenties, *The Moderns*. A romantic and unsentimental send-up of that legendary world, the film has excited viewers responsive to Rudolph's adventurous risk-taking and sumptuous visuals, but horrified those antagonistic to a strong degree of stylization in film, notably the *New York Times*'s Vincent Canby, who may have written the single nastiest, most destructive review of his entire career in an attempt once and for all to rid himself, and the cinema, of Rudolph. Even after reading such reviews, it remains difficult to figure out exactly what could be so upsetting about *The Moderns*, which does go off its tracks every so often, particularly in its final section, but would seem to merit considerable attention for its daring approach to a usually idealized subject, and its many beauties.

At its core is the sort of multi-faceted melodramatic situation that could propel any conventional picture about a group of artists, anytime, anywhere: a talented painter, admired by *aficionados* but, at 33, on the brink of being considered a never-was, runs into his alluring ex-wife, who is now married to the wealthiest, most ruthless art dealer in town. The artist would like to win his old flame back, which establishes the triangle as one that will also affect his artistic standing. Strictly for cash, the painter is asked to execute three forgeries, which he is capable of doing expertly and, after resisting, finally does. The town, of course, ultimately proves too small for the two men; the artist prevails and, chucking it all, travels with his journalist friend to New York, where he meets up with his ex-wife, on the way to Hollywood.

Like Rudolph's previous films, *The Moderns* very quickly presents a finite, highly compressed world, a closed system in which a limited number of characters are banked off the edges of the story's frame and bounced into one another like so many billiard balls. Although Rudolph still betrays a debt to mentor Robert Altman in his gently roving camera style and oblique approach to narrative, he persistently calls to mind, in a less disciplined but similarly sumptuous manner, the extreme stylization of Von Sternberg and Hawks: John Lone slowly shaving, then brutally taking Linda Fiorentino in the bathtub, represents an expression of vaguely twisted, unpleasant sexuality that Victor Mature and Gene Tierney might easily have enacted in Von Sternberg's version of *The Shanghai Gesture*, while the knowing familiarity and moral complicity of Rudolph's characters intensely resembles that always written by Jules Furthman for both Von Sternberg and Hawks, and finally made his own by the latter.

Rudolph, who wrote the script with the late John Bradshaw, establishes the majority of his critical connections in the brilliantly orchestrated opening sequence: although a serious

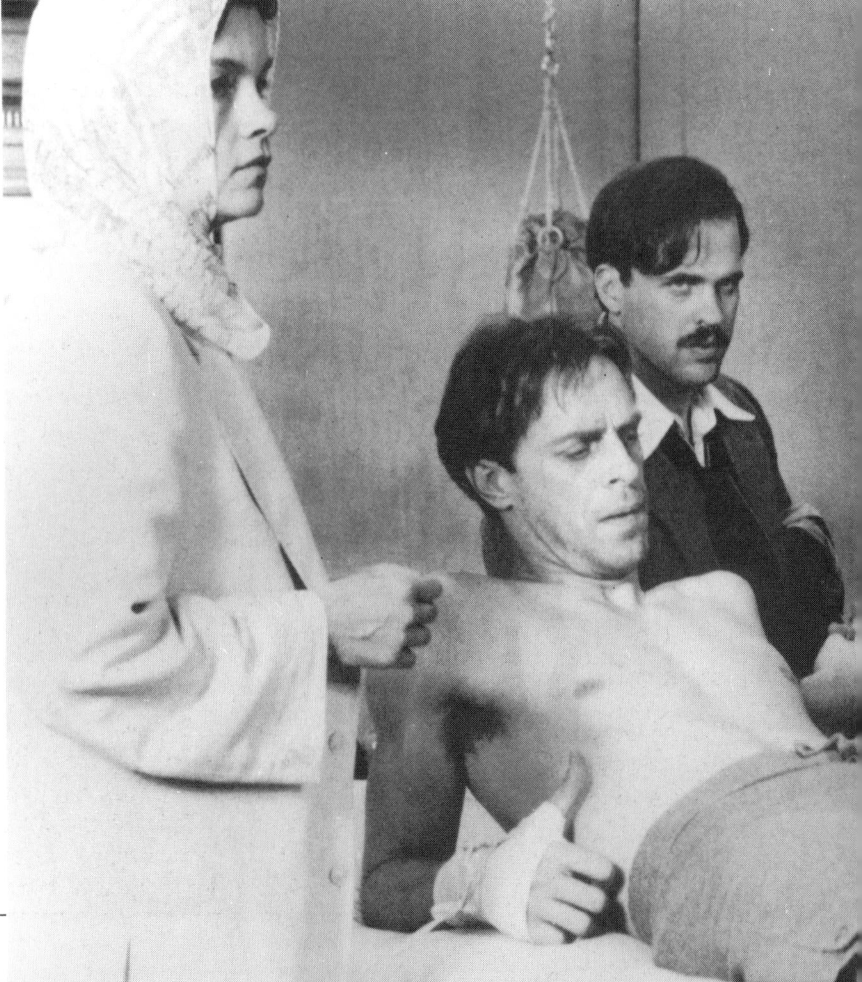

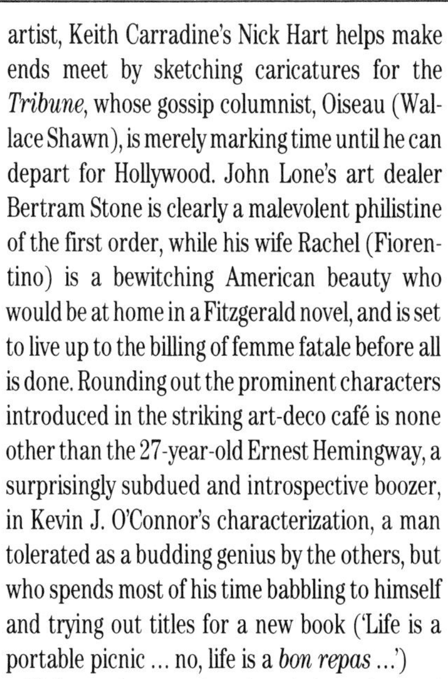

artist, Keith Carradine's Nick Hart helps make ends meet by sketching caricatures for the *Tribune*, whose gossip columnist, Oiseau (Wallace Shawn), is merely marking time until he can depart for Hollywood. John Lone's art dealer Bertram Stone is clearly a malevolent philistine of the first order, while his wife Rachel (Fiorentino) is a bewitching American beauty who would be at home in a Fitzgerald novel, and is set to live up to the billing of femme fatale before all is done. Rounding out the prominent characters introduced in the striking art-deco café is none other than the 27-year-old Ernest Hemingway, a surprisingly subdued and introspective boozer, in Kevin J. O'Connor's characterization, a man tolerated as a budding genius by the others, but who spends most of his time babbling to himself and trying out titles for a new book ('Life is a portable picnic ... no, life is a *bon repas* ...')

Nick receives continual artistic and moral support from the discerning but impoverished gallery owner Libby (Geneviève Bujold), and is the beneficiary of a different sort of backing from Nathalie (Geraldine Chaplin), a patroness of the arts who likes Nick's art and body, and rewards him handsomely for painting copies of a Cézanne, Modigliani and Matisse. In the midst of all this, Stone puts Nick in his place, both in the boxing ring and on the art circuit, but Nick manages to win back Rachel while Stone meets an unexpected fate.

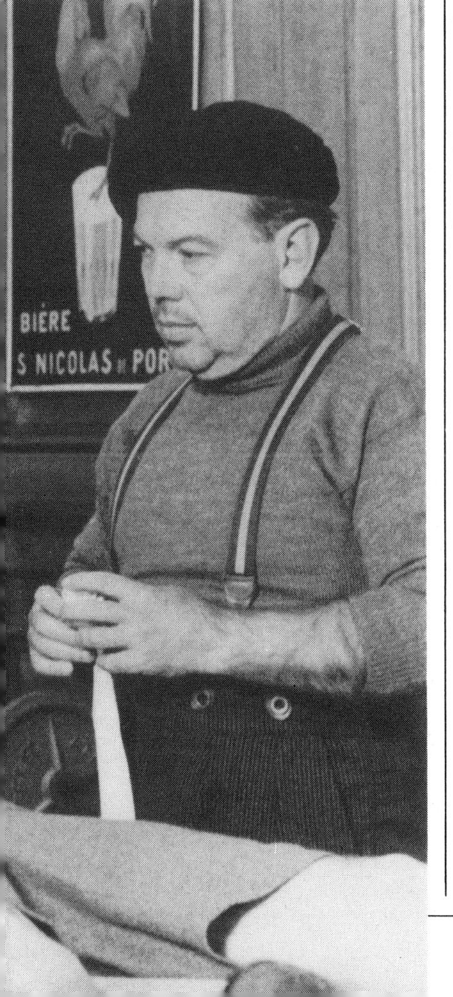

The studied casualness of Rudolph's characters and style makes his films emotionally cool, but enough is at stake here to draw one into the personal destinies put on the line. Most of the characters ultimately get what they want, or deserve, but some of the attitudes they and, by inference, Rudolph betray do seem quite curious. While conjuring up a heady atmosphere of intoxicating physical beauty via the actors and the man-made element of paintings, décor, clothes and music, and mining the Paris of the twenties legend for at least some of its worth, Rudolph increasingly subverts normal expectations and sends up the fixation - both the viewer's and his own - on the rarefied nature of life at that time and place. He does this through a variety of means, emphasizing the bluntly commercial, even crass, nature of the art business and the undisguised greed of its leading arbiter, exposing most of its denizens as duplicitous, corrupt or corruptible, and portraying the legendary salon of Gertrude Stein and Alice B. Toklas as a distinctly unpleasant place to visit, an address where outsiders are entirely unwelcome and even the gifted can expect insults and put-downs. Rudolph sets up, but then refuses to take too seriously, the issue of real vs. false art, leaving all to the eye of the beholder and the suspect whims of the expert.

Most perplexing, however, is the impulse of Oiseau and, finally, Nick and Rachel to head for Hollywood. Nowhere in the literature or history of that period can one recall characters, fictional or real, wanting to abandon Le Boulevard Saint Germain for Sunset Boulevard: for a gossip columnist to aspire to the world headquarters of same may be understandable, but what is one to imagine an outstanding artist will do there - fill in the backgrounds and do matte paintings? Rudolph may be making valid points to the effect that people's mental picture of Paris, or any imagined artistic haven, is unduly idealized and romanticized, but he seems on his shakiest ground when trying to push the parallels between Paris and Hollywood on the one hand, and the twenties and the eighties on the other, as epitomized by the shock cut to some modern punks in the Parisian bistro. If the characters couldn't express themselves to their satisfaction in Paris, they are certainly unlikely to be able to do so in Hollywood. Furthermore, in the context of Rudolph's difficult, hard-won career, there is something odd about the innocent, eager embrace Hollywood receives herein, unless an irony was intended that does not succeed in coming across. Rudolph has endured

nothing but grief at the hands of the major studios, and *The Moderns*, for so long a dream project, proved so terribly difficult to finance, that the director's introduction of Hollywood as a desired destination stands as one of the head-scratchers of the season.

Despite all this and other, less ponderable eccentricities, the film is richly seductive and satisfying in a vast number of ways. Astonishingly, given the severely limited budget and fact that it had to be shot in Montreal rather than on authentic locations, it manages to create a convincing Paris, a world even more constricted than those in *Choose Me* and *Trouble in Mind*, that consists mostly of cafés, galleries and lofts. Combined with the vintage sepia documentary footage, it captures a dream Paris, but with verisimilitude, which may be the key to the film's appeal for those who find its wavelength to begin with. *The Moderns* neither represents Paris as it was in 1926, nor as it should have been, but Rudolph has long since been such an assured stylist that he can paint a portrait as idiosyncratic and personal as this and still make it seem emotionally and iconographically valid. Whatever games of artistic relativity Rudolph may indulge within the film, there is no doubt that *The Moderns* itself is an original.

TODD McCARTHY

A MONTH IN THE COUNTRY

A scrupulously sensitive study of the trauma caused by the Great War, in which two young men - an archaeologist and a restorer - meet at a Yorkshire village church and together come to re-evaluate their lives. Undeniably well made and acted, the film nevertheless is stiflingly British in detailing every little quiver of repressed feeling and guilt. **DT**

Director *Pat O'Connor* ***producer*** *Kenith Trodd* ***execs*** *John Hambley, Johnny Goodman* ***script*** *Simon Gray, based on the novel by J. L. Carr*

A Month in the Country

camera *Kenneth MacMillan* ***editor*** *John Victor Smith* ***design*** *Leo Austin* ***music*** *Howard Blake* ***cast*** *Colin Firth, John Atkinson, Jim Carter, Patrick Malahide, Kenneth Branagh, Richard Vernon, Tim Barker, Vicki Arundale, Martin O'Neil, Natasha Richardson, Tony Haygarth, Eileen O'Brien*

Running time: 96 mins
US release: Orion Classics, Feb 19, 1988
UK release: CCW, Nov 30, 1987

MOONSTRUCK

John Patrick Shanley, New York's new poet of the neighbourhoods, writes powerfully about obsessive love in Manhattan's Little Italy. Nicolas Cage is a one-handed baker whose brother is betrothed to Cher, an accountant who would rather be grey than fall in love. The ardent Cage wins her, his every move the subject of many shrieks in the neighbourhood and much amusement for the audience. Veteran Vincent Gardenia outdoes himself as Cher's father and Olympia Dukakis is a refreshingly different Italian mother. In this operatic story, skilfully told by Norman Jewison, every member of both families has a big moment, almost an aria. **BM**

Director *Norman Jewison* ***producers*** *Jewison, Patrick Palmer* ***script*** *John Patrick Shanley* ***camera*** *David Watkin* ***editor*** *Lou Lombardo* ***design*** *Philip Rosenberg* ***music*** *Dick Hyman* ***cast*** *Cher, Nicolas Cage, Vincent Gardenia, Olympia Dukakis, Danny Aiello, Julie Bovasso, John Mahoney, Louis Guss, Feodor Chaliapin, Anita Gillette*

Running time: 102 mins
US release: MGM, Dec 16, 1987
UK release: UIP, Mar 25, 1988

MOVING

Richard Pryor has had a rough couple of years since Eddie Murphy came along and stole his thunder. Alan Metter's dim comedy continues the collapse of Pryor's popularity. Pryor plays an 'honorary white'-type whose deracination has made him terminally mild-mannered. Fired, he secures a new engineering job in faraway Idaho but must contend with a daughter (Dash) who's reluctant to leave New Jersey, a neanderthal neighbour (Quaid) and an intimidating team of removal men. When Pryor eventually explodes, it's too late and too straight. **BM**

Director *Alan Metter* ***producer*** *Stuart Cornfeld* ***script*** *Andy Breckman* ***camera*** *Donald McAlpine* ***editor*** *Alan Balsam* ***design*** *David L. Snyder* ***music*** *Howard Shore* ***cast*** *Richard Pryor, Beverly Todd, Dave Thomas, Dana Carvey, Randy Quaid, Stacey Dash, Raphael Harris, Ishmael Harris, Robert La Sardo, Ji-Tu, King Kong Bundy, Morris Day, Rodney Dangerfield*

Running time: 89 mins
US release: Warner, Mar 4, 1988

MY GIRLFRIEND'S BOYFRIEND

(L'Ami de mon amie)

Eric Rohmer's sixth (and last) entry in his 'Comédies et Proverbes' series is a more dramatically styled comedy of relationships than its predecessors, but none the worse for that. Lonely Blanche befriends self-obsessed Lea. Despite Lea's attempts at match-making, Blanche finds herself falling for her friend's partner. A round of emotional misunderstandings ensue, all delivered with Rohmer's astoundingly consistent direction of another superb young cast. **DT**

Director/script *Eric Rohmer* ***producer*** *Margaret Ménégoz* ***camera*** *Bernard Lutic* ***editor*** *Maria Luisa Garcia* ***music*** *Jean-Louis Valero* ***cast*** *Emmanuelle Chaulet, Sophie Renoir, Eric Veillard, François-Eric Gendron, Anne-Laury Meury*

Running time: 103 mins
UK release: Artificial Eye, Jun 24, 1988

MY SWEET LITTLE VILLAGE

(Vesnicko má stredisková)

Disarming satire on Czech parochialism, from the maker of *Closely Observed Trains*. Tougher in tone than its title might suggest, it progresses from a slow start to gradually uncover the adultery, corrupt intrigue and deep-seated prejudices that inform the lives of a number of eccentric inhabitants of a seemingly idyllic rural hamlet. Menzel flirts with bad taste in his characterization of the local idiot - one half of a delightful Laurel and Hardy twosome - but finally opts for gentle farce. Running gags provide the laughs; careful, detailed observation supplies the film's power to touch the heart. **GA**

Director *Jirí Menzel* ***producer*** *Jan Suster* ***script*** *Sdenek Sverák* ***camera*** *Jaromír Sofr* ***editor*** *Jirí Brozek* ***music*** *Jirí Sust* ***cast*** *János Bán, Marian Labuda, Rudolf Hrusínsky, Petr Cedak, Evzen Jegorov*

Running time: 101 mins
US release: Circle, Jan 9, 1987
UK release: Cannon, Dec 4, 1987

Moonstruck

·N·N·N·N·N·N·N·N·N·N·N·N

NADINE

Benton seems to have gone off the boil since the good old days of *The Late Show* and *Kramer vs. Kramer*. This is a thoroughly innocuous romantic comedy that in an earlier era might have been described as 'screwball'. A funny thing happens on the way to the divorce of Kim Basinger and Jeff Bridges in fifties Texas; a slight case of murder and mistaken identity. Result is the lovable warring couple join forces to try and make the authorities see sense while thwarting a dangerous property developer. Pleasant but disappointingly blah. **QF**

Director/script *Robert Benton* ***producer*** *Arlene Donovan* ***exec*** *Wolfgang Glattes* ***camera*** *Nestor Almendros* ***editor*** *Sam O'Steen* ***design*** *Paul Sylbert* ***music*** *Howard Shore* ***cast*** *Jeff Bridges, Kim Basinger, Rip Torn, Gwen Verdon, Glenne Headly, Jerry Stiller, Jay Patterson, William Youmans, Gary Grubbs, Mickey Jones*

Running time: 83 mins
US release: Tri-Star, Aug 7, 1987

NEAR DARK

After her collaboration on *The Loveless*, Kathryn Bigelow strikes out on her own in this gripping contemporary vampire yarn, developing the current trend of the small-town something-seedy-under-the-surface genre. A farmhand finds himself drawn into a band of roving vampires whose leader is a

Civil War veteran! One of the few recent horror movies that could be said to inject real blood into the old myths. **DT**
Director *Kathryn Bigelow* ***producer*** *Stephen Charles Jaffe* ***execs*** *Edward S. Feldman, Charles R. Meeker* ***script*** *Eric Red, Bigelow* ***camera*** *Adam Greenberg* ***editor*** *Howard Smith* ***design*** *Stephen Altman* ***music*** *Tangerine Dream* ***cast*** *Adrian Pasdar, Jenny Wright, Lance Henriksen, Bill Paxton, Joshua Miller, Marcie Leeds, Tim Thomerson, Kenny Call, Ed Corbett, Troy Evans, Bill Cross, Roger Aaron Brown, Thomas Wagner, Robert Winley, James LeGros, Ian King, Danny Kopel, Billy Beck, S. A. Griffin*
Running time: 95 mins
US release: DEG, Oct 2, 1987
UK release: Entertainment, Jan 8, 1988

THE NEST

Mayor of small West Coast island resort does a deal with a major corporation which results in the place being overrun by a gang of rapidly-mutating cockroaches.
Director *Terence H. Winkless* ***producer*** *Julie Corman* ***script*** *Robert King, based on the novel by Eli Cantor* ***camera*** *Ricardo Jacques Gale* ***editors*** *James A. Stewart, Stephen Mark* ***design*** *Carol Bosselman* ***music*** *Rick Conrad* ***cast*** *Robert Lansing, Lisa Langlois, Franc Luz, Terri Treas, Stephen Davies, Diana Bellamy, Jack Colins, Nancy Morgan, Jeff Winkless, Steve Tannen, Heidi Helmer, Karen Smyth, Noel Steven Geray*
Running time: 88 mins
US release: Concorde, Jan 22, 1988

A NEW LIFE

Writer-director-star Alan Alda returns to *Four Seasons* form in this sharply observant dramatic comedy of adults uncoupling and re-coupling in New York. Alda writes himself the best part, a greying but manic stock-trader whose egotism has driven shrinking violet Ann-Margret into mid-life divorce. After a few disastrous dates, both find new partners who turn out to be too much of a good thing. Veronica Hamel feistily demands a baby. John Shea is smotheringly sensitive. Alda adapts, Ann-Margret doesn't, for a trademark Alda bittersweet ending. **BM**
Director/script *Alan Alda* ***producer*** *Martin Bregman* ***exec*** *Louis A. Stroller* ***camera*** *Kelvin Pike* ***editor*** *William Reynolds* ***design*** *Barbara Dunphy* ***music*** *Joseph Turrin* ***cast*** *Alan Alda, Ann-Margret, Hal Linden, Veronica Hamel, John Shea, Mary Kay Place, Beatrice Alda, David Eisner*
Running time: 104 mins
US release: Paramount, Mar 25, 1988

A NIGHT IN THE LIFE OF JIMMY REARDON

There's something about a 17 year old who thinks he's God's gift to women that makes everybody older want to put their fist through the screen - yet writer-director William Richert claims the story is autobiographical. River Phoenix, back in the pre-Beatles *Stand by Me* era, is the precocious brat in question. He's making it with the same older woman (Ann Magnuson) who is servicing his father, and he scores with two other young ladies who are not his girlfriend. It's a mess worthy of the worst teen-pic, but Richert's higher aspirations make the film doubly disappointing. **BM**
Director *William Richert* ***producer*** *Russell Schwartz* ***execs*** *Mel Klein, Noel Marshall* ***script*** *Richert, based on his novel* Aren't You Even Gonna Kiss Me Goodbye? ***camera*** *John J. Connor* ***editor*** *Suzanne Fenn* ***design*** *Norman Newberry* ***music*** *Bill Conti* ***cast*** *River Phoenix, Ann Magnuson, Meredith Salenger, Ione Skye, Matthew L. Perry, Paul Koslo, Jane Hallaren, Jason Court*
Running time: 92 mins
US release: Fox, Feb 26, 1988

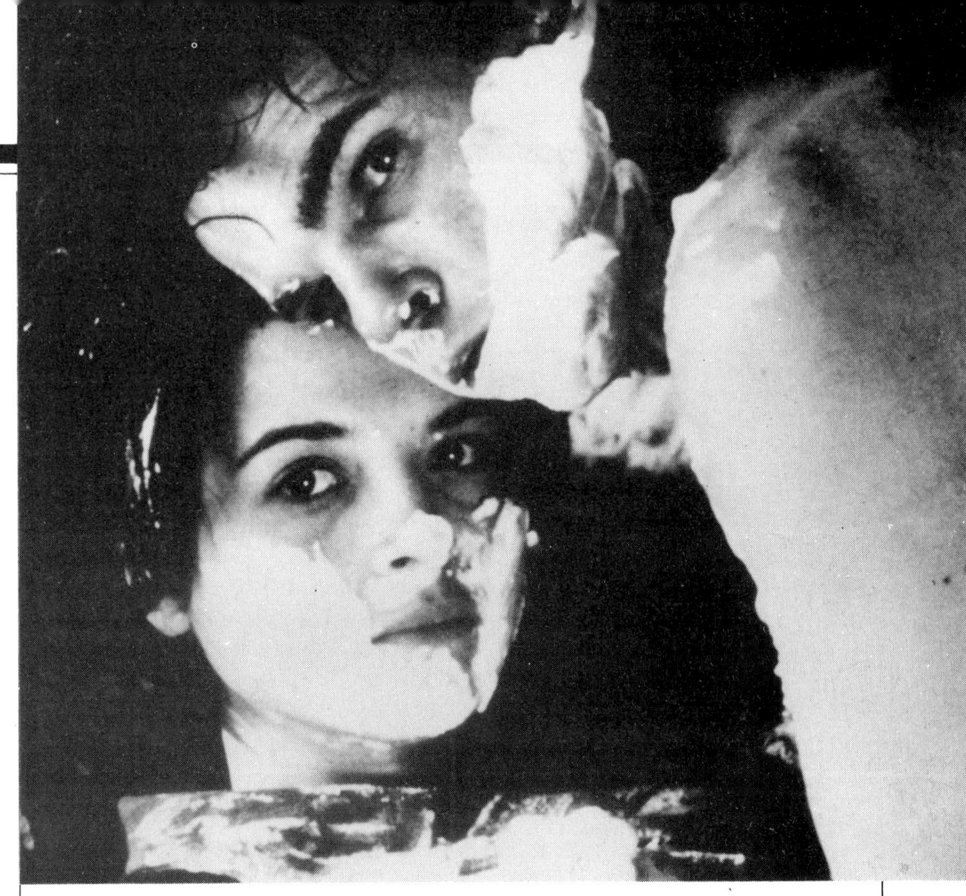
The Night Is Young

THE NIGHT IS YOUNG

(Mauvais sang)
Léos Carax's follow-up to his striking début *Boy Meets Girl* employs colour, a star name (Piccoli) and a larger budget, but does not signal much development from this director still in his twenties. The setting is Paris around the year 2000, when the world is riddled with a disease which afflicts those who make love when not *in* love (and yes, there's even a condom on view). An unlikely team set out to steal a cure developed in Switzerland, but this narrative is frequently sidestepped for Carax to indulge his extended fantasies and point the camera adoringly at the beautiful Binoche. **DT**
Director/script *Léos Carax* ***producer*** *Philippe Diaz* ***exec*** *Alain Dahan* ***camera*** *Jean-Yves Escoffier* ***editor*** *Nelly Quettier* ***design*** *Michel Vandestien* ***cast*** *Michel Piccoli, Juliette Binoche, Denis Lavant, Hans Meyer, Julie Delpy, Carroll Brooks, Hugo Pratty, Mireille Perrier, Serge Reggiani, Jérôme Zucca, Charles Schmitt*
Running time: 119 mins
UK release: Artificial Eye, Sep 18, 1987

NIGHT ON THE TOWN

(See Adventures in Babysitting)

NIGHT ZOO (Zoo ... La Nuit)

Jean-Claude Lauzon risks all in switching his sordid crime thriller into a lyrical love story between a father and son halfway through - the miracle is that he pulls it off. Vicious small-time hoodlum Marcel (Maheu), raped in prison prior to his release, returns to the ugly Quebec underworld where he is pursued by two bent cops on the hunt for some missing loot. Marcel is delivered from evil as, seeking to bring some joy into the days of his ailing, melancholy old dad (Le Bel), he takes him on a fishing trip in the mountains. Leaving the foul human menagerie behind, Lauzon even sends the pair on a hunting expedition to a zoo at night, but not even that contrived ending can spoil the tender mood which finally prevails in this bold offering from the Canadian new wave. **GF**
Director/script *Jean-Claude Lauzon* ***producers*** *Roger Frappier, Pierre Gendron* ***camera*** *Guy Dufaux* ***editor*** *Michel Arcand* ***design*** *Jean-Baptiste Tard* ***music*** *Jean Corriveau* ***cast*** *Roger Le Bel, Gilles Maheu, Lynne Adams, Lorne Brass, Germain Houde*
Running time: 115 mins
US release: Film Dallas, Mar 4, 1988

NIGHTFLYERS

Some scientists rent an old spaceship for a fact-finding mission to the unexplored planet of Volcryn and find they have unpleasant company.
Director *T.C.Blake (Robert Collector)* ***producer*** *Robert Jaffe* ***exec*** *Herb Jaffe* ***script*** *Robert Jaffe, based on novella by George R. R. Martin* ***camera*** *Shelly Johnson* ***editor*** *Tom Siiter* ***design*** *John Muto* ***music*** *Doug Timm* ***cast*** *Catherine Mary Stewart, Michael Praed, John Standing, Lisa Blount, Glenn Withrow, James Withrow, James Avery, Hélène Udy, Annabel Brooks, Michael Des Barres*
Running time: 89 mins
US release: New Century/Vista, Oct 23, 1987

NIGHTMARE ON ELM STREET 3: DREAM WARRIORS

Although, when narrative explication takes over in the second half, this further instalment in the saga of the terrifying razor-clawed Freddy becomes rather tiresomely fabricated, the imagination of the special effects which dominate the earlier part of

the picture is far above the norm for this sort of thing. Both in the visual elaboration of the nightmares and the eeriness with which the transitions from waking to dream are negotiated, the feeling is less of down-market pop cinema than of something genuinely experimental. **TP**
Director *Chuck Russell* ***producer*** *Robert Shaye* ***execs*** *Wes Craven, Stephen Diener* ***script*** *Craven, Bruce Wagner, Russell, Frank Darabont* ***camera*** *Roy H. Wagner* ***editors*** *Terry Stokes, Chuck Weiss, (effects) Cliff Hutchison* ***design*** *Mick Strawn, C. J. Strawn* ***music*** *Angelo Badalamenti* ***cast*** *Heather Langenkamp, Patricia Arquette, Larry Fishburne, Priscilla Pointer, Craig Wasson, Robert Englund, Brooke Bundy, Rodney Eastman, Bradley Gregg, Ira Heiden, Ken Sagoes, Penelope Sudrow, Jennifer Rubin*
Running time: 96 mins
US release: New Line, Feb 27, 1987
UK release: Palace, Oct 30, 1987

NO END (Bez Konca)
Actually made in 1984 but only released to foreign audiences two years later, Kieslowski's dark and brooding story of a widow's attempt to come to terms with the activities of her lawyer husband evidently carried a little too much political resonance. The deceased - played by Wajda's Man of Marble, Jerzy Radziwilowicz - is on hand as a commentator and overseer while his wife becomes involved in the uncompleted case of a strike organizer and hopelessly attempts to stave off sexual frustration. Although bleak and sometimes meandering, the film's inexorable tread towards her final suicidal resolution packs a real punch. **DT**
Director *Krzysztof Kieslowski* ***producer*** *Ryszard Chutkowski* ***script*** *Kieslowski, Krzysztof Piesiewic* ***camera*** *Jacek Petrycki* ***editor*** *Krystyna Rutkowska* ***design*** *Allan Starski* ***music*** *Zbigniew Preisner* ***cast*** *Grazyna Szapolowska, Maria Pakulnis, Aleksander Bardini, Jerzy Radziwilowicz, Artur Barcis, Michal Bajor, Krzysztof Krzeminski, Marek Kondrat, Tadeusz Bradecki, Daniel Webb*
Running time: 107 mins
UK release: Artificial Eye, Mar 11, 1988

Nightmare on Elm Street 3 *(above)*
No Way Out *(left)*

NO MAN'S LAND
Charlie Sheen grows up in Peter Werner's well-made cops and robbers story, demonstrating that there's a lot more to him than the callowness he had to show in every scene of *Platoon*. D. B. Sweeney is a rookie cop chosen by the lieutenant (Randy Quaid) to go undercover inside a Porsche-stealing ring headed by suspected cop-killer Sheen. The high-living Sheen takes Sweeney under his wing and the two become bosom buddies, never more so than when Sweeney romances Sheen's sister. Sweeney can't believe Sheen is a killer and is in danger of 'going native' until the tense final showdown. **BM**
Director *Peter Werner* ***producers*** *Joseph Stern, Dick Wolf* ***execs*** *Ron Howard, Tony Ganz* ***script*** *Wolf* ***camera*** *Hiro Narita* ***editor*** *Steve Cohen* ***design*** *Paul Peters* ***music*** *Basil Poledouris* ***cast*** *Charlie Sheen, D. B. Sweeney, Randy Quaid, Lara Harris, Bill Duke, Arlen Dean Snyder, M. Emmet Walsh*
Running time: 106 mins
US release: Orion, Oct 23, 1987

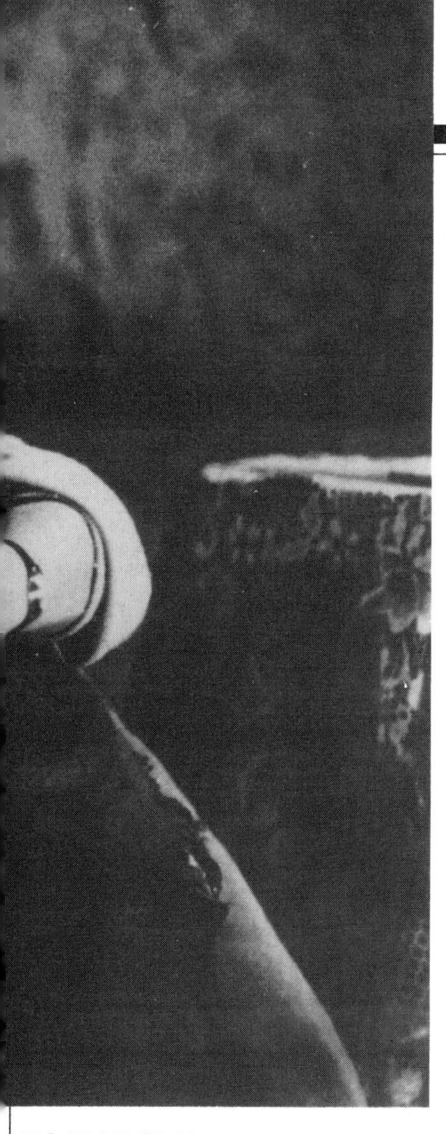

NO WAY OUT

A glossy remake of *The Big Clock*, previously filmed with Ray Milland and Charles Laughton in 1948, when it was set in a vast newspaper office block. This time it's the Pentagon, with Costner as a decorated US Navy Lieutenant helping out the CIA over a Communist conspiracy. A ludicrous sex scene in a limo and Gene Hackman wasted as a miserably weak Secretary of Defence are two examples of the confusion and compromise on display in what should have been an exciting hi-tech thriller. **DT**
Director *Roger Donaldson* ***producers*** *Laura Ziskin, Robert Garland* ***exec*** *Mace Neufeld* ***script*** *Garland, based on novel* The Big Clock *by Kenneth Fearing* ***camera*** *John Alcott, Alun Bollinger* ***editor*** *Neil Travis* ***design*** *Dennis Washington, Kai Hawkins* ***music*** *Maurice Jarre* ***cast*** *Kevin Costner, Gene Hackman, Sean Young, Will Patton, Howard Duff, George Dzundza, Jason Bernard, Iman, Fred Dalton Thompson, Leon Russom, Dennis Burkley, Marshall Bell, Chris D., Michael Shillo, Nicholas Worth, Leo Geter, Matthew Barry, John DiAquino, Peter Bell, Tony Webster, Matthew Evans*
Running time: 115 mins
US release: Orion, Aug 14, 1987
UK release: Rank, Jan 15, 1988

NOIR ET BLANC

Claire Devers' first feature, made on a tiny budget in grainy monochrome, details a timid accountant's involvement in a sado-masochistic relationship with a muscular black masseur. Devers conveys an

Nuts

oppressive atmosphere without showing any direct violence, and demonstrates an intense compassion for her obsessive characters. Less is more, and when the mutually desired violence becomes greater and the film descends (ascends?) into fantasy, Devers' discretion certainly pays off. **DT**
Director/script/design *Claire Devers* ***camera*** *Daniel Desbois, Christopher Doyle, Alain Lasfargues, Jean-Paul de Costa* ***editor*** *Fabienne Alvarez, Yves Sarda* ***cast*** *Francis Frappat, Jacques Martial, Joséphine Fresson, Marc Berman, Claire Rigollier, Benoît Régent, Catherine Belkodja, Arnaud Carbonnier, Christophe Galland*
Running time: 80 mins
UK release: Electric, Mar 18, 1988

NORTH SHORE

Surfing picture set in Hawaii. An innocent comes to the island after winning a competition in his native Arizona, then has to get used to waves larger, and people tougher, than he's ever seen before. He makes the grade in the end.
Director *William Phelps* ***producer*** *William Finnegan* ***exec*** *Randal Kleiser* ***script*** *Tim McCanlies, Phelps, Kleiser* ***camera*** *Peter Smokler* ***editor*** *Robert Gordon* ***design*** *Mark Balet* ***music*** *Richard Stone* ***cast*** *Matt Adler, Gregory Harrison, Nia Peeples, John Philbin, Gerry Lopez, Laird Hamilton, Robbie Page, Mark Occhilupo, John Parragon, Cristina Raines, Lord James Blears*
Running time: 96 mins
US release: Universal, Aug 14, 1987

NUTS

In Barbra Streisand's return to films - after a four-year vegetation since *Yentl* - she plays the crowd-pleasing role of a wronged woman wrongly accused of being crazy. She's a cantankerous, possibly certifiable prostitute who has killed a client and insists she's sane enough to stand trial. Her family, hiding a guilty secret, want to put her in a psychiatric hospital for ever. New York's harassed justice system is eager to dispose of her, until public defender Richard Dreyfuss comes on the case. Martin Ritt gives Streisand free rein to play mad and sane, drugged and lucid, violent and sweet, withdrawn and outgoing. Dreyfuss gallantly plays a restrained second banana. **BM**
Director *Martin Ritt* ***producer*** *Barbra Streisand* ***execs*** *Teri Schwartz, Cis Corman* ***script*** *Tom Topor, Darryl Ponicsan, Alvin Sargent, based on the play by Tom Topor* ***camera*** *Andrzej Bartkowiak* ***editors*** *Sidney Levin, Rick Sparr, Jeff Werner* ***design*** *Joel Schiller* ***music*** *Streisand* ***cast*** *Streisand, Richard Dreyfuss, Maureen Stapleton, Karl Malden, Eli Wallach, Robert Webber, James Whitmore, Leslie Nielsen, William Prince*
Running time: 116 mins
US release: Warner, Nov 20, 1987
UK release: Warner, Feb 12, 1988

·0·0·0·0·0·0·0·0·0·0·0·

OFF LIMITS (Saigon in UK)

Back to Nam for *Platoon's* Willem Dafoe, this time as an MP teamed with cool cat Gregory Hines in the harrowing investigation of a prostitute killer who's also a US army officer. The clichéd black/white cop/buddy movie formula and a tepid romantic friendship between Dafoe and Amanda Pays's unshockable nun notwithstanding, this behind-the-lines thriller offers a peculiarly disenchanted appraisal of the American way of doing things in Saigon. With Scott Glenn chilling as the crazed Colonel who leaps out of a chopper, and excellent re-creation of life under fire at the notorious Khe Sanh airstrip, *Off Limits* captures the mayhem and the madness with as much vibrancy, if less style, than the more acclaimed Vietnam combat movies. **GF**
Director *Christopher Crowe* ***producer*** *Alan Barnette* ***script*** *Crowe, Jack Thibeau* ***camera*** *David Gribble* ***editor*** *Douglas Ibold* ***design*** *Dennis Washington* ***music*** *James Newton* ***cast*** *Willem Dafoe, Gregory Hines, Fred Ward, Amanda Pays, Kay Tong Lim, Scott Glenn*
Running time: 102 mins
US release: Fox, Mar 11, 1988
UK release: Fox, Jul 8, 1988

ON THE BLACK HILL

Bruce Chatwin's novel about twin brothers, children of the century, who spend their lives on a hill farm in the Welsh border country has been rendered perhaps too faithfully in an adaptation which rather fails to come to terms with the original's literary subjectivity. As a result, the film tends to be overly episodic and to fall between the stools of psychological study and social history. Fine performances by Bob Peck and Gemma Jones,

as the brothers' parents, though, and several affecting passages, in particular the climactic sequence in which the two 80 year olds gamely allow themselves to be taken on an air flight, and rise - literally and otherwise - above the determinants of their past. **TP**
Director *Andrew Grieve* ***producer*** *Jennifer Howarth* ***exec*** *Colin MacCabe* ***script*** *Grieve, based on the novel by Bruce Chatwin* ***camera*** *Thaddeus O'Sullivan* ***editor*** *Scott Thomas* ***design*** *Jocelyn James* ***music*** *Robert Lockhart* ***cast*** *Mike Gwilym, Robert Gwilym, Bob Peck, Gemma Jones, Jack Walters, Nesta Harris, Rhys Baker, Aled Baker, Huw Toghill, Gareth Toghill, Lynn Gardner, Claire Evans, Eryl Phillips, Lillian Evans, Ceri Morgan, Eric Wynn, Iona Banks, Terry Jackson, Nicola Beddoe, Ronan Vibert, Mark Jones, Lyndon Lewis, Siôn Probert, Jil Richards, Geoffrey Hutchings, Robert Page, James Warrior, Rob Edmunds, Benjamin Whitrow, James Bree, Antonia Pemberton, Patrick Godfrey, Tricia George, Mark Dignam*
Running time: 117 mins
UK release: BFI, May 13, 1988

OPERA DO MALANDRO

Colourful if nothing else, *Opera do Malandro* is a Brazilian song-and-dance exercise in derivativeness. Choosing to copy long-outdated avant-garde ideas about the illusion of narrative and the importance of impulse-following, Ruy Guerra over-directs this slight tale of underworld pursuit into near-unwatchability. Nor does the Latin music bring the film up to listenability. Edson Celulari as a dancing delinquent reaches the pits in a scene in a toilet where he dances himself out of the mirror he thinks he sees himself in. Personally, I didn't think he was dancing that badly, but if you gotta go, you gotta go. **BM**
Director *Ruy Guerra* ***producers*** *Marin Karmitz, Guerra* ***exec*** *Alberto Grana* ***script*** *Chico Buarque, Orlando Senna, Guerra, adapted from a musical by Buarque* ***camera*** *Antonio Luis Mendes* ***editors*** *Mair Tavares, Ide Lacreta, Kenout Peltier* ***music*** *Buarque* ***cast*** *Edson Celulari, Claudia Ohana, Elba Ramalho, Ney Latorraca, Fabio Sabag, J. C. Violla, Wilson Grey, Maria Silvia, Claudia Gimenez, Andreia Dantas, Ilva Niño, Zonaide, Djenane Machado, Katia Bronstein, Luthero Luiz*
Running time: 105 mins
US release: Goldwyn, Jan 30, 1987
UK release: Artificial Eye, Jul 31, 1987

ORION'S BELT

A lethargic Norwegian suspense drama revolving around an amiable trio of petty criminals on a cargo boat who become involved in the transportation of a bulldozer through Soviet-occupied Greenland with the purpose of selling the vehicle, then claiming insurance. Events do not work out, however, and the faintly piratical Tom (we know he is the hero because he has the cleanest anorak) is the only one who survives to face interrogation by the security services. The title refers to an area of land occupied by Americans, Russians and Norwegians. Ola Solum's direction tries too hard to penetrate the labyrinthine ramifications of the plot without taking care to cultivate any action sequences or even evoke much sympathy for Tom's predicament. **MN**
Director *Ola Solum* ***producer*** *Dag Alveberg* ***script*** *Richard Harris, from the novel by Jon Michelet* ***camera*** *Harald Paalgaard* ***editors*** *Bjorn Breigutu, Yogve Refseth* ***music*** *Geir Bohren, Bent Aserud* ***cast*** *Helge Jordal, Sverre Anker Ousdal, Hans Ola Sorile, Kjersti Holmen*
Running time: 101 mins
US release: New World, Oct 9, 1987

ORPHANS

A perfect stage vehicle for Albert Finney, Lyle Kessler's *Orphans* transfers well to the screen despite some residual theatricality. Matthew Modine adds to his gallery of maladjusted young men, playing an abandoned child who supports himself and his seemingly retarded brother (Kevin Anderson) by petty thievery. He brings the well-dressed but drunken Finney into their squalid home, hoping to hold him for ransom. Instead, Finney talks his way out of bondage and takes over, involving the boys in his own nefarious plot. Along the way, he becomes the father they never had. It's been a long time between hits for Alan J. Pakula, but this low-cost drama is as entertaining as anything he's made in years. **BM**
Director/producer *Alan J. Pakula* ***script*** *Lyle Kessler, based on his play* ***camera*** *Donald McAlpine* ***editor*** *Evan Lottman* ***design*** *George Jenkins* ***music*** *Michael Small* ***cast*** *Albert Finney, Matthew Modine, Kevin Anderson, John Kellog, Anthony Heald, Novella Nelson, Elizabeth Parrish, B. Constance Barry, Frank Ferrara, Clifford Fearl*
Running time: 115 mins
US release: Lorimar, Sep 18, 1987
UK release: Fox, Mar 11, 1988

OUTRAGEOUS FORTUNE

A woman-woman buddy picture is a rare chance, seized here with panache by Bette Midler and Shelley Long. Playing would-be actresses who obnox each other from the start and then find they're in love with the same rat, the pair eventually learn to work together for revenge. The long and the short of it is that the squat, foul-tongued Midler and the willowy, butter-wouldn't-melt-in-her mouth Long make a captivating pair, and it's for certain they'll be teamed again by Disney. Old reliable director Arthur Hiller shows a sure touch in channelling Midler's eruptions. **BM**
Director *Arthur Hiller* ***producers*** *Ted Field, Robert W. Cort* ***script*** *Leslie Dixon* ***camera*** *David M. Walsh* ***editor*** *Tom Rolf* ***design*** *James D. Vance* ***music*** *Alan Silvestri* ***cast*** *Shelley Long, Bette Midler, Peter Coyote, Robert Prosky, John Schuck, George Carlin, Anthony Heald, Ji-Tu Cumbuka*
Running time: 100 mins
US release: BV, Jan 30, 1987
UK release: BV, Sep 11, 1987

OVERBOARD

Goldie Hawn makes amends to patriarchal Hollywood for her comedy-feminist fables - *Private Benjamin*, *Protocol*, etc. - with the year's thickest slice of male chauvinism. Hawn plays a rich socialite who falls off a yacht, loses her memory and then falls for macho carpenter Kurt Russell. Soon

Orphans

she's become Little Wifey incarnate, cooking his meals, scrubbing his floors and tending his three kids from a previous marriage. Amnesia's cured in the final reel, but by then the lesson is learnt and the shrew is tamed. The movie's pay-off is dubious, but Hawn has some good two-tone moments as the homely housewife with suppressed socialite urges struggling to get out. **HK**
Director *Garry Marshall* ***producers*** *Anthea Sylbert, Alexandra Rose* ***exec*** *Roddy McDowall* ***script*** *Leslie Dixon* ***camera*** *John A. Alonzo* ***editor*** *Dov Hoenig* ***design*** *James Shanahan, Jim Dultz* ***music*** *Alan Silvestri* ***cast*** *Goldie Hawn, Kurt Russell, Edward Herrmann, Katherine Helmond, Michael Hagerty, Roddy McDowall, Jared Rushton, Jeffrey Wiseman, Brian Price, Jamie Wild, Frank Campanella, Harvey Alan Miller*
Running time: 112 mins
US release: MGM, Dec 16, 1987
UK release: UIP, Jun 10, 1988

·P·P·P·P·P·P·P·P·P·P·P·P·

PALTOQUET (Le Paltoquet)

A curious absurdist whodunit from the style-minded, if not always stylish, Michel Deville, *Paltoquet* brings together a host of eccentric characters who meet nightly in a hangar-like port café and are the principal suspects in a murder investigation led by Jean Yanne. Deville, working from an obscure mystery novel, lards his police procedural with gags, puns and vaudevillesque repartee that undermine the seriousness of the plot and strengthen its theatrical trappings. Despite the all-star casting (including Jeanne Moreau and Michel Piccoli), the film runs out of steam and interest long before the final 'surprise' twist, but Thierry Leproust's studio-bound art direction and André Diot's eerie lighting give it an often hallucinatory aura. **LB**
Director *Michel Deville* ***producer*** *Rosalinde Damamme* ***script*** *Michel Deville, based on the novel* On a tué pendant l'escale *by Franz-Rudolf Falk* ***camera*** *André Diot* ***editor*** *Raymonde Guyot* ***design*** *Thierry Leproust* ***cast*** *Fanny Ardant, Daniel Auteuil, Richard Bohringer, Philippe Léotard, Jeanne Moreau, Michel Piccoli, Claude Piéplu, Jean Yanne, An Luu, Sidy Lamine Diarra, Gérard Essomba, Gérard Dubois, Henri Bensoussan*
Running time: 93 mins
UK release: Artificial Eye, Jul 3, 1987

Paltoquet

PASS THE AMMO

In need of a prayer, David Beaird's assault on the charlatanism of tele-pulpit evangelists was granted one with the Jimmy Swaggart and Jim and Tammy Bakker exposés, although they duly made *Pass the Ammo* seem tame in comparison. Feebly plotted, this creaking comedy concerns an Arkansas backwoods gang (Paxton, Kozlowski) revenging itself on swindling Reverend Ray (Curry) and his Salomé-styled wife (Potts) by hijacking their show at gunpoint during its live broadcast. It all goes nowhere fast, although Anthony Geary is brilliant as a hippy video technician and some of the gags are inspired: notably gang heavy Dennis Burkley's winning over the state cops with his ballad 'Police Man'. **GF**
Director *David Beaird* ***producers*** *Herb Jaffe, Mort Engelberg* ***script*** *Neil Cohen, Joel Cohen* ***camera*** *Mark Irwin* ***editor*** *Bill Yahraus* ***design*** *Dean Tschetter* ***music*** *Carter Burwell* ***cast*** *Bill Paxton, Linda Kozlowski, Tim Curry, Annie Potts, Dennis Burkley, Glenn Withrow, Anthony Geary*
Running time: 97 mins
US release: New Century/Vista, Mar 4, 1988

PATTI ROCKS

One of the funniest and most scatological films of the year, *Patti Rocks* is a sequel of sorts to writer-director David Morris's experimental *Loose Ends* (1975). Two working-class men (Mulkey and Jenkins) drive halfway across Minnesota so Mulkey can give his girlfriend the kiss-off. Along the way, they talk and talk and talk hilariously (and hatefully) about what men do to women because of what women do to men. When they arrive, the outcome isn't what lover-boy planned. As long as films like this get made, the American Empire will not decline. **BM**
Director *David Burton Morris* ***producers*** *Gwen Field, Gregory M. Cummins* ***exec*** *Sam Grogg* ***script*** *Morris, Chris Mulkey, John Jenkins, Karen Landry, based on characters created by Victoria Wozniak in the film* Loose Ends ***camera/editor*** *Cummins* ***design*** *Charlotte Whitaker* ***music*** *Doug Maynard* ***cast*** *Chris Mulkey, John Jenkins, Karen Landry*
Running time: 87 mins
US release: Film Dallas, Jan 15, 1988

PEE-WEE'S BIG ADVENTURE

Although a spin-off from the children's TV series featuring a man in a child's suit, this big screen adventure is inventive enough to paste together its slim narrative with great charm. Pee-wee Herman, all rubbery limbs and made-up face, loses his precious red bicycle and chases it all the way to Hollywood. A familiar route is enlivened by Herman's engaging innocence and energy, as well as the surreal brightly-coloured world created around him, and the result is surprisingly very funny. **DT**
Director *Tim Burton* ***producers*** *Robert Shapiro, Richard Gilbert Abramson* ***script*** *Philip Hartman, Paul Reubens, Michael Varhol* ***camera*** *Victor J. Kemper* ***editor*** *Billy Weber* ***design*** *David L. Snyder*

Pee-wee's Big Adventure

music *Danny Elfman* ***cast*** *Paul Reubens, Elizabeth Daily, Mark Holton, Diane Salinger, Judd Omen, Monte Landis, Damon Martin, Daryl Roach, Starletta DuPois, Ed Herlihy, Lou Cutell, Erica Yohn, Alice Nunn, Jon Harris, Carmen Filpi, Jan Hooks, Jason Hervey, Gilles Savard, James Brolin, Morgan Fairchild, Tony Bill*
Running time: 91 mins
US release: Warner, Aug 9, 1985
UK release: Mainline, Aug 14, 1987

THE PENITENT

Villagers carry on a 200-year-old ritual of re-enacting the crucifixion at spring. When cuckold Julia is up for ritual sacrifice - after which his widow would be compelled to chastity - her rugged lover (Assante) takes his place, in the mistaken belief he can survive the ordeal.
Director/script *Cliff Osmond* ***producer*** *Michael*

Ping Pong

Fitzgerald **camera** *Robin Vidgeon* **editor** *Peter Taylor* **music** *Alex North* **cast** *Raul Julia, Armand Assante, Rona Freed, Julie Carmen, Lucy Reina*
Running time: 94 mins
US release: New Century/Vista, Mar 18, 1988

PENITENTIARY III

Leon Isaac Kennedy stars as a mean mother who inadvertently imbibes a strength-increasing drug before a professional fight, beats his rival to death and is convicted of voluntary manslaughter. Inside the penitentiary two rival factions vie for his pugilistic skills - the warden's team and an unscrupulous dude called Serenghetti. Kennedy agrees to fight and regresses into a killing machine when a friend is almost annihilated by a similarly spaced-out fighter under the influence of the same drug. Rocky buffs who correlate the myth of the noble savage with grinding the rib cage of one's opponent into corn meal mush, in an attempt to prove masculinity, will doubtless enthuse over Kennedy's predicament. **MN**
Director/producer/script *Jamaa Fanaka* **camera** *Marty Ollstein* **editor** *Ed Harker* **design** *Marshall Toomey* **music** *Garry Schyman* **cast** *Leon Isaac Kennedy, Anthony Geary, Steve Antin, Ric Mancini, Kessler Raymond, Jim Bailey, Magic Schwarz, Windsor Taylor Randolph*
Running time: 91 mins
US release: Cannon, Sep 4, 1987

PERMANENT RECORD

America usually confines such family problem dramas as *Permanent Record* to television. Marisa Silver's involving and uplifting film needs only a little of the cinema's greater freedom from censorship to tell its story of teenage suicide. Alan Boyce is a near-perfect kid who jumps from a cliff because near-perfect isn't good enough for him. Keanu Reeves, his far-from-perfect best friend, and the other survivors, feel betrayed, resentful and confused when they discover Boyce didn't die accidentally. Luckily, they're all immersed in performing *HMS Pinafore* at school, so the show does go on. **BM**
Director *Marisa Silver* **producer** *Frank Mancuso Jr.* **exec** *Martin Hornstein* **script** *Jarre Fees, Alice Liddle, Larry Ketron* **camera** *Frederick Elmes* **editor** *Robert Brown* **design** *Michel Levesque* **music** *Joe Strummer* **cast** *Alan Boyce, Keanu Reeves, Michelle Meyrink, Jennifer Rubin, Pamela Gidley, Michael Elgart, Richard Bradford, Dakin Matthews, Barry Corbin, Kathy Baker, Joshua Taylor, Sam Vlahos, David Selberg, Lou Reed*
Running time: 91 mins
US release: Paramount, Apr 22, 1988

P.I. PRIVATE INVESTIGATIONS

For a film so unashamedly stuffed with movie references, it's not surprising that this convoluted Los Angeles thriller about a young Man Who Knows Too Much (and, yes, our hero is watching the Hitchcock film on TV the evening his living nightmare begins) ends up resembling a celluloid clone of the yuppie phantasm genre represented by such pictures as *After Hours* and *Something Wild*. It's the first full-length feature by top British video-promo director Nigel Dick, and the film has all the flash and dash of MTV with about a proportionate degree of substance. **QF**
Director *Nigel Dick* **producers** *Steven Golin, Sigurjon Sighvatsson* **execs** *Michael Kuhn, David Hockman* **script** *John Dahl, David Warfield* **camera** *David Bridges* **editor** *Scott Chestnut* **design** *Piers Plowden* **music** *Murray Munro* **cast** *Clayton Rohner, Ray Sharkey, Paul LeMat, Talia Balsam, Phil Morris, Martin Balsam, Anthony Zerbe, Robert Ito, Vernon Wells, Anthony Geary, Justin Lord, Richard Cummings Jr., Desiree Boschetti, Andy Romano, Sydney Walsh, Jon St. Elwood, Rex Ryon, Richard Herkert, Frank Gargani, Big Yank*
Running time: 91 mins
UK release: Blue Dolphin, Oct 16, 1987

THE PICK-UP ARTIST

Teenage ladykiller Robert Downey meets pretty museum guide Molly Ringwald. He says to her, 'You have the face of a Botticelli and the body of a Degas.' She says to him, 'What's your profession, cupcake?' ('I'm a romantic' he answers.) And the consequence is they fall in love. But slowly: for this is a James Toback movie and first they have to prove themselves by battling against a stacked destiny. This includes her drunken dad Dennis Hopper and gangland nasty Harvey Keitel, who's pursuing Hopper for gambling debts. Feisty and fast-talking, and weaving a neat parallel fable about forms of gambling (for sex, money, love), this is Toback's best film since *Fingers*. **HK**
Director/script *James Toback* **producer** *David L. MacLeod* **camera** *Gordon Willis* **editor** *David Bretherton, Angelo Corrao* **design** *Paul Sylbert* **music** *Georges Delerue* **cast** *Molly Ringwald, Robert Downey, Dennis Hopper, Danny Aiello, Mildred Dunnock, Harvey Keitel*
Running time: 81 mins
US release: Fox, Sep 18, 1987

PING PONG

Opening with a spectacular crane shot that swoops from on high to discover a dead body stuffed in a Soho telephone kiosk, Po Chih Leong's ninth feature turns out to be not so much a Chandleresque thriller of London's Chinatown as a gently wise and witty comedy drama of culture clash. Stereotypes which have so dogged previous portraits of the Asian community are neatly turned on their head as a Macao-born (but long-time British resident) law student is asked to execute the will of a Chinese restaurateur who wants his body returned to the fatherland and his eaterie restored to its former glory. **QF**
Director *Po Chih Leong* **producers** *Malcolm Craddock, Michael Guest* **script** *Jerry Liu, based on an idea by Po Chih Leong* **camera** *Nick Knowland* **editor** *David Spiers* **design** *Colin Pigott* **music** *Richard Harvey* **cast** *David Yip, Lucy Sheen, Robert Lee, Lam Fung, Victor Kan, Barbara Yu Ling, Ric Young, Victoria Wicks, Stephen Kuk, Rex Wei, Hi Ching, Won Hun Tse, Chad Lee, K. C. Leong, David Lyon, Karen Seacombe*
Running time: 100 mins
US release: Goldwyn, Jul 17, 1987
UK release: Electric, Aug 21, 1987

PINOCCHIO AND THE EMPEROR OF THE NIGHT

Atypical of Filmation's prolonged attempt to rival the quality product of Disney and Hanna Barbera, this version of Carlo Collodi's children's tale is a facile, pseudo-moral parable about how Pinocchio is lured towards life's self-indulgent pleasures. A collusion of impoverished animation and fatuous paeans to good citizenship have coagulated into a sickly, alarmingly nice, wholesome piece of dross which will prompt even the most ardent members of the Teddy Ruspin Fan Club to reach for their insulin injections. **MN**
Director *Hal Sutherland* **producer** *Lou Scheimer* **script** *Robby London, Barry O'Brien, Dennis O'Flaherty* **camera** *Ervin L. Kaplan* **editor** *Jeffrey Patrick Gehr* **design** *John Grusd* **music** *Anthony Marinelli, Brian Banks* **voices** *Edward Asner, Tom Bosley, Lana Beeson, Scott Grimes, Linda Gary, Jonathan Harris, James Earl Jones, Rickie Lee Jones, Don Knotts, Frank Welker, William Windom*
Running time: 87 mins
US release: New World, Dec 25, 1987
UK release: Palace, Aug 7, 1987

PLAIN CLOTHES

This year, America ran out of teenagers - or at least American teenagers stopped going mindlessly to every movie about their kind. Martha Coolidge's comedy thus fell by the same wayside as the lookalike *Hiding Out*. Both were slight stories about adult men who feel compelled to pose as high schoolers. In this variation, newcomer Arliss Howard is a suspended cop who drops in at the hellish school where his brother has been accused of killing a teacher. Alexandra Powers as a student and Suzy Amis as a teacher are Howard's love-objects and Robert Stack plays the bumbling principal. **BM**
Director *Martha Coolidge* **producer** *Richard Wechsler, Michael Manheim* **exec** *Steven-Charles Jaffe* **script** *A. Scott Frank, Dan Vining* **camera** *Daniel Hainey* **editor** *Pat Kennedy* **design** *William Apperson* **music** *Scott Wilk* **cast** *Arliss Howard, Suzy Amis, George Wendt, Diane Ladd, Seymour Cassel, Jackie Gayle, Robert Stack, Abe Vigoda, Harry Shearer, Peter Dobson, Alexandra Powers, Loren Dean*
Running time: 98 mins
US release: Paramount, Apr 15, 1988

PLANES, TRAINS & AUTOMOBILES

Film of the Year

Director/producer/script *John Hughes* ***execs*** *Michael Chinich, Neil Machlis* ***camera*** *Donald Peterman* ***editor*** *Paul Hirsch* ***design*** *John W. Corso* ***music*** *Ira Newborn* ***cast*** *Steve Martin, John Candy, Laila Baker, Carol Bruce, Olivia Burnette, Diana Douglas, Martin Ferrero, Larry Hankin, Richard Herd, Susan Kellerman, Matthew Lawrence*
Running time: 92 mins
US release: Paramount, Nov 25, 1987
UK release: UIP, May 27, 1988

PLAYING AWAY

Horace Ové's film about Britain's race problem plays like fringe theatre: half-baked sincerity is no substitute for an involving story and fully realized characters. Norman Beaton's mixed band of Brixton cricketers somehow fix a match with a true-blue suburban village XI. The villagers' stark prejudice or tepid tolerance clash with the Londoners' belligerence or fecklessness. The only glimmer of communication comes when Beaton encounters a half-dotty retiree who acts as if colour were no problem. Scene after scene of this painful botch ends in disarray, the actors left up a tree by the half-baked script. **BM**
Director *Horace Ové* ***producers*** *Brian Skilton, Vijay Amarnani* ***script*** *Caryl Phillips* ***camera*** *Nic Knowland* ***editor*** *Graham Whitlock* ***design*** *Pip Gardner* ***music*** *Simon Webb* ***cast*** *Norman Beaton, Robert Urquhart, Helen Lindsay, Nicholas Farrell, Brian Bovell, Gary Beadle, Suzette Llewellyn, Trevor Thomas, Stefan Kalipha, Bruce Purchase, Joseph Marcell, Sheila Ruskin, Mark Barratt, Valerie Buchanan*
Running time: 102 mins
US release: Alive, Mar 18, 1988
UK release: Electric, Nov 6, 1987

POLICE ACADEMY 4: CITIZENS ON PATROL

The fourth outing of Paul Maslansky's on-going pension plan concerns the belligerent Commandant Lassard's plans to initiate community participation with the help of an infrequently glimpsed Mahoney (Guttenberg) and the regular cast of multi-racial deviants. The law of diminishing returns applies to this morass of slapstick and crotch-level humour. Warner obviously felt it was more viable to contaminate a new young generation rather than sustain existing audiences for the sequels. **MN**
Director *Jim Drake* ***producer*** *Paul Maslansky* ***script*** *Gene Quintano, based on characters created by Neal Israel, Pat Proft* ***camera*** *Robert Saad* ***editor*** *David Rawlins* ***design*** *Trevor Williams* ***music*** *Robert Folk* ***cast*** *Steve Guttenberg, Bubba Smith, Michael Winslow, David Graf, Tim Kazurinsky, Sharon Stone, Leslie Easterbrook, Marion Ramsey, Lance Kinsey, G.W. Bailey, Bobcat Goldthwait, George Gaynes, Billie Bird*
Running time: 87 mins
US release: Warner, Apr 3, 1987
UK release: CCW, Jul 10, 1987

POLICE ACADEMY 5: ASSIGNMENT MIAMI BEACH

Lassard, who's threatened with mandatory retirement, is to address a Miami police convention. His graduates follow him there for some surfing. At the airport, Lassard switches luggage with some crooks and ends up in possession of stolen diamonds. Cue trouble. Steven Guttenberg and Bobcat Goldthwait are absent from the cast this time around.
Director *Alan Myerson* ***producer*** *Paul Maslansky* ***script*** *Stephen J. Kurwick, based on characters created by Neal Israel and Pat Proft* ***camera*** *Jim Pergola* ***editor*** *Hubert De La Bouillerie* ***design*** *Trevor Williams* ***music*** *Robert Folk* ***cast*** *Matt McCoy, Janet Jones, George Gaynes, G.W. Bailey, René Auberjonois, Bubba Smith, David Graf, Michael Winslow, Leslie Easterbrook, Marion Ramsey, Lance Kinsey, Tab Thacker*
Running time: 90 mins
US release: Warner, Mar 18, 1988
UK release: Warner, Jul 15, 1988

POLTERGEIST 3

Paranormal service is resumed: this time in Chicago's skyscraping Hancock Building. Tom Skerritt is maintenance manager there, Nancy Allen is his wife and their visiting niece is - guess who - Heather O'Rourke, the child who vanished into a TV in the original *Poltergeist*. Heather is now grown older, plumper and dismayingly more charmless. Skerritt and Allen provide a TV to tempt her, but she prefers to stick around, causing cracked mirrors, mysterious fires and the return of the ghoulish Kane (see *Poltergeist 2*). The visual FX, alas, are poor and tend to pop up with no discernible narrative logic. Writer-director Gary Sherman once made the memorable *Death Line*, but this is an end-of-the-line movie he and we may prefer to forget. **HK**
Director/exec *Gary Sherman* ***producer*** *Barry Bernardi* ***script*** *Sherman, Brian Taggert* ***camera*** *Alex Nepomniaschy* ***editor*** *Ross Albert* ***design*** *Paul Erads* ***music*** *Joe Renzetti* ***cast*** *Tom Skerritt, Nancy Allen, Heather O'Rourke, Zelda Rubinstein, Lara Flynn Boyle, Richard Fire, Kip Wentz, Nathan Davis*
Running time: 97 mins
US release: MGM, Jun 10, 1988

POUND PUPPIES AND THE LEGEND OF BIG PAW

Based on a Saturday morning TV series and co-produced by toy manufacturers, Tonka Corp., the story centres around attempts to restore the broken Bone of Scone which enables kids and dogs to speak to each other.
Director/design *Pierre DeCelles* ***producers*** *Donald Kushner, Peter Locke* ***execs*** *Ed Griles, Ray Volpe* ***script*** *Jim Carlson, Terrence McDonnell* ***editor*** *John Blizek* ***music*** *Steve Tyrell* ***voices*** *George Rose, B. J. Ward, Ruth Buzzi, Brennan Howard, Cathy Cadavini, Nancy Cartwright*
Running time: 76 mins
US release: Tri-Star, Mar 18, 1988

Police Academy 4

PLANES, TRAINS AND AUTOMOBILES

John Hughes is probably the most underrated phenomenon in the movie business today. Underrated because his clever, touching comedies, until recently nearly always dealing with the joys and torments of adolescence, are usually written off as slick and sentimental; a phenomenon because nearly everything he has written, produced or directed (often he takes all three jobs) has turned into a modest hit at the very least, most of them much more than that.

The simple comparison is to see Hughes as a kind of domestic Spielberg, and both men share a ferocious energy, relative youth, and an instinct for the tastes of their youthful audience which takes little account of critical taste or fashion. Hughes is the more cynical of the two and that quality makes it unlikely he'll ever come up with an *E.T.* But he would never be guilty of the mawkishness of some of *Empire of the Sun* or the gross self-indulgence of *1941*. Sure, his films carry a broad streak of sentiment, but it's usually based on a gift for characterization, a genuine affection for his ugly-duckling heroes, and carefully plotted storylines which are models of economy and structure. *Planes, Trains and Automobiles* shows these virtues at their sleekest and most roadworthy.

A glance at the Hughes biography is a humbling experience for any would-be film tycoon; his output is awesome. Beginning in 1982 with the script of the execrable *National Lampoon's Class Reunion* (which he reportedly disowns), in a space of six years he has been crucially involved - as writer, producer or director - with no less than 14 films; by the time you read this there'll probably be a couple more to add to the list. Of those at least nine have been major box-office hits (in the States at least; the rest of the world has been slow catching up with his very American vision) while the others have been near misses.

The break came with the Michael Keaton vehicle *Mr Mom*, a role-reversal comedy which boosted Keaton to stardom, albeit briefly, and gave its young writer the chance to direct his first feature, *16 Candles*, starring a gawky and unlikely actress in Molly Ringwald. It was a partnership made in heaven, and the first evidence of Hughes' tremendous eye for new or unexpected talent. This solid hit was trumped by *The Breakfast Club*, in retrospect a rather whining and self-regarding piece, but the blueprint for most of his successes in the next few years. Coincidentally it introduced a repertory company of young actors - Judd Nelson, Ringwald, Ally Sheedy, Emilio Estevez - who have been associated with Hughes ever since, although apart from Ringwald he hasn't used any of them again.

John Landis tells a story of how, after his success with *Animal House*, the Hollywood cry went up 'Get Landis - he knows what the kids want!' That cry, with Hughes' name for Landis, must have been echoing around the Hollywood hills after *Breakfast Club*, and, by and large, he did seem to know what the kids wanted. A string of teen-oriented hits followed, the best of them (*Pretty in Pink*, *Ferris Bueller's Day Off*) clever, beautifully written tales of teenage *angst*, prom-night rejection, first love and fast cars.

But Hughes is clearly fed up with the Teenage Shakespeare label; the formula began to look stretched and thin with *She's Having a Baby* (still unreleased in the UK). It was time for a change, and *Planes* is the result.

In almost every way this is a new kind of Hughes film. On the debit side is the cost (a reported $30 million, which seems almost incredible), but everything else is good news, and the best news of all is the superb casting of Steve Martin, fresh from the success of his new 'mature' *Roxanne* image, and John Candy, reliable second-string funny man (*Splash*) who blossoms under Hughes' direction into a comic actor of convincing range.

Martin plays a put-upon businessman determined to make it home for Thanksgiving, but hampered at every turn by a combination of vile weather, broken-down trains, cancelled planes, disappearing hire cars and most of all by Candy's cheerful dork, a kind of saloon-bar Cassandra whose prophecies invariably turn out to be accurate. Hughes' intricately plotted screenplay loads the dice carefully against Candy at the outset and we share Martin's sense of horror and intrusion at his enforced intimacy with this ungracious slob. But Hughes undercuts this simple point of view with cunning characterization and a grandstand scene in which Martin explodes at his room-mate after being forced to sleep in the same bed, covered in beer and then kept awake by Candy's truly revolting sinus clearances (shades of *The Odd Couple*, which is

clearly one of this film's inspirations). We start entirely on Martin's side but end up favouring the dignified Candy, whose looks of hurt goodwill are masterpieces of comic playing and writing. This wonderful scene sets the pattern for the rest of the film; a careful blend of slapstick, more sophisticated humour, and unexpectedly tender observations.

Hughes isn't afraid to slow the pace towards the end, and he never makes the mistake of treating his characters as merely mechanical servants of the plot. He knows the danger built into his idea and is determined to keep it on a human scale; he is helped brilliantly by Martin and Candy who keep the farce (largely) under control, and contrive to establish a natural and warm relationship, which makes the plot twist in the last five minutes all the more touching and affecting.

A comparison with Michael Frayn's *Clockwise* is instructive, and shows just how differently British and American writers view similar material. There is a relationship between the plot-lines for the two films, but there the comparison ends. Frayn's is an admittedly well-choreographed but somehow brutally cold script which (even allowing for its much smaller budget) loses interest after the first half-hour; it's simply a question of what new indignity will befall John Cleese's pompous clock-watcher, and the laughter becomes increasingly forced. We simply don't care about the characters; they lose their humanity, and ultimately the film fails despite its richness of incident and frenzied pace. *Planes, Trains and Automobiles* never makes this mistake, and just when the action might become exhausting (and it nearly does, even in a very short film) Hughes switches gears for a genuinely touching conclusion, which shows Martin's fastidious and inhibited character finding a new humanity from his experience.

In between though there are plenty of straight-ahead laughs; Hughes still has a fondness for physical slapstick and Martin and Candy handle it with ease; a manic chase the wrong way up a motorway; the demolition of a motel frontage, Martin's verbal pyrotechnics with an infuriatingly bland car-hire girl, all set-pieces that stay in the mind. Even better though are the verbal exchanges between Martin and Candy, a double act that owes something to Laurel and Hardy. Martin, in a straighter role than usual, is as good as we've come to expect (let's not discuss *The Three Amigos*), although it would be a shame if his wilder side has gone for ever. But Candy is the film's joy, mining real pathos from his role, suggesting the deeply lonely life of the travelling salesman, while presenting an unremittingly cheerful face to the world. He's playing years older than his actual age in this film and it suits him.

Planes, Trains and Automobiles is no masterpiece. There are too many loose ends for that, particularly a plot involving Martin's faithful wife waiting tearfully at home, an intense performance which suggests something was lost in the cutting-room. But it is a supremely well-crafted film from a director who, on this evidence, will go on to make even better pictures. Teenage America may have lost its most avid chronicler, but the growing maturity of *Planes, Trains and Automobiles* suggests that Hughes is about to strike out for even higher ground.
ADRIAN HODGES

POWER

Richard Gere, now ageing somewhat uncomfortably out of his matinée-idol status, plays a high-flying image consultant who stages campaigns for an assortment of electoral candidates in various parts of the US. Gene Hackman, his ex-mentor, chides him for abandoning his moral principles by supporting clients whose policies he does not believe in. After much wheeling and dealing and revelations in the dirty tricks department, Gere's conscience re-awakens in time for him to ditch a corrupt client and offer crucial advice to the idealistic opposition. Gere does rather too much jet-setting between clients for the different strands of the story to come together, and those that finally do seem both naïve and confused, but this remains a fascinating if flawed account of media manipulation and political expediency. **AB**
Director *Sidney Lumet* ***producers*** *Reene Schisgal, Mark Tarlov* ***script*** *David Himmelstein* ***camera*** *Andrzej Bartkowiak* ***editor*** *Andrew Mondshein* ***design*** *Peter Larkin* ***music*** *Cy Coleman* ***cast*** *Richard Gere, Julie Christie, Gene Hackman, Denzel Washington, E. G. Marshall, Beatrice Straight, Fritz Weaver, Michael Learned, J. T. Walsh, Polly Rowles, Matt Salinger, Tom Mardirosian, Omar Torres, Ricardo Gallarzo, Jessica James, Glenn Kezer, Douglas Newell, Scott Harlan, Nick Flynn, Ed Van Nuys, Noel Harrison*
Running time: 111 mins
US release: Lorimar, Jan 31, 1986
UK release: UKFD, Aug 28, 1987

A PRAYER FOR THE DYING

Turkey of the Year

Director *Mike Hodges* ***producer*** *Peter Snell* ***script*** *Edmund Ward, Martin Lynch, based on the novel by Jack Higgins* ***camera*** *Mike Garfath* ***editor*** *Peter Boyle* ***design*** *Evan Hercules* ***music*** *Bill Conti* ***cast*** *Mickey Rourke, Bob Hoskins, Alan Bates, Sammi Davis, Christopher Fulford, Liam Neeson, Leonard Termo, Camille Coduri, Maurice O'Connell, Alison Doddy, Karl Johnson, Ian Bartholomew, Peggy Aitchison, Cliff Burnett, Anthony Head*
Running time: 108 mins
US release: Goldwyn, Sep 11, 1987
UK release: Guild, May 13, 1988

PREDATOR

Desperate for an opponent capable of giving Schwarzenegger a decent fight (since all earthly opposition has failed to date), the producers have come up with the inevitable match – Arnold vs. Alien. The thing, a chameleon-like big meat eater, is prowling a Latin American jungle, 'which makes Cambodia look like Kansas', when Arnie and the boys burst in to rescue some hostages held by local terrorists. Soon the boys are shredded, leaving the hunk alone to party with predator. Dazzling to look at, but distasteful to contemplate too deeply. **QF**
Director *John McTiernan* ***producers*** *Lawrence Gordon, Joel Silver, John Davis* ***execs*** *Laurence P. Pereira, Jim Thomas* ***script*** *Jim Thomas, John Thomas* ***camera*** *Donald McAlpine, Leon Sanchez* ***editors*** *John F. Link, Mark Helfrich* ***design*** *John Vallone* ***music*** *Alan Silvestri* ***cast*** *Arnold Schwarzenegger, Carl Weathers, Elpidia Carrillo, Bill Duke, Jesse Ventura, Sonny Landham, Richard Chaves, R. G. Armstrong, Shane Black*
Running time: 107 mins
US release: Fox, Jun 12, 1987
UK release: UKFD, Jan 1, 1988

A PRAYER FOR THE DYING

'Northern Ireland,' runs the caption which opens *A Prayer for the Dying*, ushering us into what has largely been a no-go area for mainstream British cinema. In the event, though, we don't stay in the Province for long, just for a single establishing sequence wherein an IRA detachment, including Martin Fallon (Mickey Rourke), blunderingly blows up not the troop transports which are its intended targets but a crowded school bus. The contrivance of this sequence hardly throws any direct light, however melodramatic, on the Ulster situation, but this - it turns out - is not really the picture's prime concern.

Immediately afterwards the action shifts to London, where Fallon, now a deserter to the 'cause', is seeking freedom (in more ways than one) by way of a passage to America. It doesn't come that easy, however, for the IRA are after him, and his contacts in the London underworld drive a hard bargain: to qualify for a passport he must first act as a hit man for them in eliminating an unwanted character in the vice rackets.

The source of *A Prayer for the Dying* is a novel by the best-selling thriller writer Jack Higgins, which may hardly imply a high level of seriousness. Nonetheless, it would be unfair to suggest that the resulting film is conceived as simple exploitation, with Ulster and the IRA as a spurious 'angle'. The patterning of the drama has some ostensible depth, with Fallon being impelled toward redemption, almost in spite of himself, as a result of his friendship with the priest (Bob Hoskins) who witnessed the gangland murder and whom Fallon seeks to silence (distant echoes of *I Confess*) by way of identifying himself in the secrecy of the confessional.

But the film's intermediate - and best - style is in fact that of hyped-up crime melodrama, as Rourke (sporting, it must be said, a very credible Ulster accent) finds himself the pawn of Mr Big, Meehan (Alan Bates). There are stray reminders here that the director, Mike Hodges, was responsible for one of the best British gangster movies, *Get Carter*, and some more immediate echoes (the trademark use of a meat market as the front for chicanery; even the casting, albeit strenuously against type, of Hoskins) of what might be termed the HandMade school of British crime pictures, of which *The Long Good Friday* is probably the best remembered. Bates's monstrous Meehan, operating behind the façade of an undertaking business (and dallying over the more attractive female corpses with an attentiveness bordering on the necrophiliac), is the satanic bridge between this generic terrain and the film's higher ambitions: there is a specific use of anti-religious imagery in the *guignol* episode of Meehan's having a minion 'crucified' in retribution for the attempt to cheat him.

Unfortunately, it is on the other side of the spiritual coin that *A Prayer for the Dying* tends to go adrift; in particular with the characterizations of the priest and - an invention that even D. W. Griffith might have paused over - his blind niece, an embodiment of innocence who falls in

love with Fallon even as she perceives his striving for a better way. Nor is the priest any ordinary priest: he has a background (though it remains unexplained) of service in the SAS, and seems obscurely to be himself wrestling with a past legacy of violence. This background can at least be said to provide a practical explanation for the all but obligatory scene in which Father Hoskins turns into a Pat O'Brien-style two-fisted padre in sorting out a group of Meehan's bully boys.

Some reviewers have suggested Hoskins would have been better off playing Bates's role. This seems to imply an unfairly limiting notion of his capacities; it is the script which renders his efforts, not to mention those of Sammi Davis as the niece, largely null and void. If there is a whiff of the sententious about the discourses between Fallon and the priest on belief and conscience, there is a decided tastelessness to the tryst between Fallon and the girl, and the subsequent attempted rape of the latter by Meehan's psychotic brother, a character with a rather shaky function in the narrative, which is by this stage anyway proceeding in a succession of fits and starts.

There is, though, a nicely sardonic touch to the sequence of Fallon's disposal of the brother's body (Davis's efforts at self-defence having rendered her attacker defunct) by incinerating it at Meehan's crematorium, casually tapping his cigarette ash into the *ad hoc* funeral pyre as he does so. The 'hellfire' overtones here, set off later by the flames of the climactic explosion at the church where both Meehan and the self-martyred Fallon meet their doom, and by the prosaically secular image of the fire brigade putting them out, hint at the potential that the picture has failed to realize.

And the sad thing is that the degree to which the film fails in this respect has been appreciably heightened by the alterations wrought upon it by its American production company. Most obviously, this blunting process resides in the wrap-around score that now booms out at every opportunity: the overlay of bombastic music in the opening massacre, which in the director's cut was achieved in silence, affords a particularly crass instance of the damage done. But small details of editing contrive throughout to shift the balance in the wrong direction. What in Hodges's original version represents a perhaps half successful exercise in high-pitched blood-and-incense melodrama has been converted into a three-quarters unsuccessful demonstration of crash-and-bang banality.

Whatever *A Prayer for the Dying* may have sought to do in the way of illuminating the Irish problem, it has assuredly done nothing to brighten up the traditionally tarnished image of the 'front office'.

TIM PULLEINE

The Princess Bride

PRESIDIO

A string of strong scenes doesn't necessarily make a good film. Peter Hyams' connect-the-dots movie has a car chase (on San Francisco hills), a running chase (in Chinatown), a shoot-out in a cute location (a bottling plant), a drunken reminiscence on a roof-top, a punch-out in a bar, and a declaration of love under a suspension bridge. The picture that's not quite drawn involves the reconciliation of old enemies, army cop Sean Connery and city cop Mark Harmon, and their fluctuating feelings for Connery's flighty daredevil of a daughter, Meg Ryan. The perfunctory plot is a mere McGuffin: some suave conglomerate chiefs also smuggle diamonds. **BM**

Director/camera *Peter Hyams* ***producer*** *D. Constantine Conte* ***exec*** *Jonathan A. Zimbert* ***script*** *Larry Ferguson* ***editor*** *James Mitchell* ***design*** *Albert Brenner* ***music*** *Bruce Boughton* ***cast*** *Sean Connery, Mark Harmon, Meg Ryan, Jack Warden, Mark Blum, Dana Gladstone, Jenette Goldstein*

Running time: 97 mins

US release: Paramount, Jun 10, 1988

PRINCE OF DARKNESS

A crew of scientists are convened by Fr. Donald Pleasance to stave off the threat posed by a canister which is not merely seven million years old but supposedly contains the spirit of Satan himself ... and, believe it or not, as the film progresses, matters contrive to become yet more extraordinary, as well as more and more difficult to make any sense of. A passable diversion for those with a weakness for this sort of stuff; but in sounding echoes of both *Halloween* and *Assault on Precinct 13*, Carpenter makes us only too aware of this film's concomitant lack of vitality. **TP**

Director *John Carpenter* ***producer*** *Larry Franco* ***execs*** *Shep Gordon, André Blay* ***script*** *Martin Quatermass (Carpenter)* ***camera*** *Gary B. Kibbe* ***editor*** *Steve Mirkovich* ***design*** *Daniel Lomino* ***music*** *Carpenter, with Alan Howarth* ***cast*** *Donald Pleasance, Jameson Parker, Victor Wong, Lisa Blount, Dennis Dun, Susan Blanchard, Anne Howard, Ann Yen, Ken Wright, Dirk Blocker, Jessie Lawrence Ferguson, Peter Jason, Robert Grasmere, Thom Bray, Joanna Merlin, Alice Cooper, Betty Ramey, Jessie Ferguson*

Running time: 101 mins

US release: Universal, Oct 23 1987

UK release: Guild, May 13, 1988

THE PRINCESS BRIDE

One of the surprise delights of the past cinema-going year was Goldman's own adaptation of his spoof fairytale, perfectly realized by director Reiner with just the right amount of tongue-in-cheek buckle and swash. Perfectly cast, with pretty leads (Robin Wright, Cary Elwes) playing to a genuine giant, via Wallace Shawn as Brooklynesque villain and Billy Crystal in heavy latex as a Jewish sorcerer. One of those rare films with enough levels to satisfy fully both adult and child. **QF**

Director *Rob Reiner* ***producers*** *Andrew Scheinman, Reiner* ***exec*** *Norman Lear* ***script*** *William Goldman, based on his novel* ***camera*** *Adrian Biddle* ***editor*** *Robert Leighton* ***design*** *Norman Garwood* ***music*** *Mark Knopfler* ***cast*** *Cary Elwes, Mandy Patinkin, Chris Sarandon, Christopher Guest, Wallace Shawn, André the Giant, Robin Wright, Peter Falk, Fred Savage, Billy Crystal, Carol Kane, Peter Cook, Mel Smith, Willoughby Gray, Malcolm Storry, Margery Mason, Betsy Brantley, Anne Dyson, Paul Badger*

Running time: 98 mins

US release: Fox, Sep 25, 1987

UK release: Vestron, Mar 25, 1988

THE PRINCIPAL

What does it mean when films set in high school start to have teachers for heroes? That America is starting to believe again that the system works? In *The Principal* the bad guys are the classroom punks, and the heroes are the title character (Belushi) and his gun-toting security guard sidekick (Gossett). Belushi rides into town, disgraced in his previous job, demoted to the worst sink school in the system. Somehow, inspired by the love of a

beautiful history teacher (Chong) this reject bludgeons the retards into self-respect and academic accomplishment. **BM**
Director *Christopher Cain* ***producer*** *Thomas H. Brodek* ***script*** *Frank Deese* ***camera*** *Arthur Helbert* ***editor*** *Jack Hofstra* ***design*** *Mark Billerman* ***music*** *Jay Gruska* ***cast*** *James Belushi, Louis Gossett Jr., Rae Dawn Chong, Michael Wright, J. J. Cohen, Esai Morales, Troy Winbush, Jacob Vargas, Thomas Ryan, Reggie Johnson, Kelly Minter*
Running time: 109 mins
US release: Tri-Star, Sep 18, 1987

PRISON

This horror picture set in penitentiary environs is the most consistently entertaining movie to emerge from Empire since *Re-Animator*. Its tenuous storyline centres upon the re-opening of an archaic Wyoming prison with a new brutish warden (Smith) possessed of a dark secret. Pivotal to the ensuing viscera and pyrotechnics is a long-dead prisoner, allegedly buried in the basement chair. Director Renny Harlin evokes a suitably cryptic air more derivative of Hammer or Argento than recent, more contrived, fare. The script's imprecisions do not, however, detract from a finale which has the entire cast locked in adversarial combat - replete with such riotous necessities as machine-gun towers, sullen car thieves and, of course, the odd enraged spectre. **MN**
Director *Renny Harlin* ***producer*** *Irwin Yablans* ***exec*** *Charles Band* ***script*** *C. Courtney Joyner* ***camera*** *Mac Ahlberg* ***editor*** *Andy Horvitch* ***design*** *Philip Duffin* ***music*** *Richard Band, Christopher L. Stone* ***cast*** *Viggo Mortensen, Chelsea Field, Lane Smith, Lincoln Kilpatrick, Tom Everett, Ivan Kane, Andre De Shields, Tom 'Tiny' Lister Jr., Steven E. Little, Mickey Yablans, Larry Flash Jenkins, Arlen Dean Snyder, Hal Landon Jr.*
Running time: 103 mins
US release: Empire, Mar 4, 1988
UK release: Entertainment, Jun 17, 1988

PROMISED LAND

The best true-crime stories come from repressed straight-arrow places like Utah, the 'promised land' in the title of this film fostered by Robert Redford's Utah-based Sundance Institute. Jason Gedrick is a high-school basketball star whose hopes didn't pan out. Kiefer Sutherland is the class joke who had no hopes to begin with. Two years on, Sutherland returns to town in thrall to weirdo beauty Meg Ryan. The three meet outside a convenience store that Ryan and Sutherland have robbed. Gedrick, now a cop whose touch no longer thrills ex-cheerleader Tracy Pollan, draws his gun and takes aim. Clips and voiceovers of our cowboy president aim to give the film a political dimension, but it's best when it simply tells the sordid tale. **BM**
Director/script *Michael Hoffman* ***producer*** *Rick Stevenson* ***execs*** *Robert Redford, Andrew Meyer* ***camera*** *Ueli Steiger, Alexander Gruszynski* ***editor*** *David Spiers* ***design*** *Eugenio Zanetti* ***music*** *James Newton* ***cast*** *Jason Gedrick, Tracy Pollan, Kiefer Sutherland, Meg Ryan, Googy Gress, Deborah Richter, Oscar Rowland, Sandra Seacat, Jay Underwood, Herta Ware, Walt Logan Field, Kelly Ausland, Todd Anderson, Dave Valenza, Theron Read, Richard Matthews, Cindy Clark, Charles Black, Tony Kruletz*
Running time: 102 mins
US release: Vestron, Jan 22, 1988
UK release: Vestron, Apr 29, 1988

Prison

·R·R·R·R·R·R·R·R·R·R·R·R·

RAISING ARIZONA

Joel and Ethan Coen forsake the deterministic neo-*noir* world of *Blood Simple* for a determinedly bizarre comedy with Cage and Hunter as a contented no-hoper couple who seek to solve the problem of childlessness by kidnapping one of the sundry offspring of a local tycoon. The fast and furious surface yields plenty of funny effects, but after a while starts to cancel out the gestures towards comic pathos, as well as failing to conceal all of the holes in the plot. **TP**
Director *Joel Coen* ***producer*** *Ethan Coen* ***exec*** *James Jacks* ***script*** *Ethan & Joel Coen* ***camera*** *Barry Sonnenfeld* ***editor*** *Michael R. Miller* ***design*** *Jane Musky* ***music*** *Carter Burwell* ***cast*** *Nicolas Cage, Holly Hunter, Trey Wilson, John Goodman, William Forsythe, Sam McMurray, Frances McDormand, Randall 'Tex' Cobb, T. J. Kuhn, Lynne Dumin Kitei, Peter Benedek*
Running time: 94 mins
US release: Fox, Mar 11, 1987
UK release: UKFD, Jul 3, 1987

RAMBO III

Sylvester Stallone's chest keeps getting bigger and bigger, and John Rambo keeps killing more and more in *Rambo III*, a true comic book for our times. Rambo is a roofer for some monks in Thailand, financing temple repairs with a sideline in stick-fighting, when his old mentor Richard Crenna seeks to recruit him for a mission in Afghanistan. Crenna is caught and Rambo must rescue him, amid enough explosions to account for the recent rise in the price of petrol. Again, Stallone has master-muscled a movie that you can't tell his fans isn't good. Their favourite scene will be the one in which Rambo cures himself of an impaling wound by exploding gunpowder inside it. Ouch! **BM**
Director *Peter Macdonald* ***producer*** *Buzz Feitshans* ***execs*** *Mario Kassar, Andrew Vajna* ***script*** *Sylvester Stallone, Sheldon Lettich* ***camera*** *John Stanier* ***editors*** *James Symons, Andrew London, O. Nicholas Brown, Edward A. Warschilka* ***design*** *Billy Kenney* ***music*** *Jerry Goldsmith* ***cast*** *Sylvester Stallone, Richard Crenna, Marc de Jonge, Kurtwood Smith, Spiros Focas, Sasson Gabai, Doudi Shoua, Randy Raney*
Running time: 101 mins
US release: Tri-Star, May 25, 1988

RAMPAGE

William Friedkin uses a semi-documentary style in this effective drama about a psycho killer's crime and punishment. If he's psycho, vicious as his crime was, should he be punished? Michael Biehn is the assistant district attorney prosecuting multiple murderer Alex McArthur. Biehn agrees to overcome his scruples against capital punishment and seek a judgement that McArthur wasn't insane and is thus eligible for the death penalty. Friedkin trots out the imponderables of the legal definition of insanity in courtroom exchanges considerably more intelligent than the norm. The film loses focus slightly when it lingers on Biehn's unhappy home life and the psychiatrists' illegal manoeuvres. **BM**
Director *William Friedkin* ***producer*** *David Salven* ***script*** *Friedkin, based on the novel by William P. Wood* ***camera*** *Robert D. Yeoman* ***editor*** *Jere*

Huggins **design** *Buddy Cone* **music** *Ennio Morricone* **cast** *Michael Biehn, Alex McArthur, Nicholas Campbell, Deborah Van Valkenburgh, John Harkins, Art Lafleur, Billy Greenbush, Royce D. Applegate, Grace Zabriskie, Roy London, Donald Hotton, Andy Romano*
Running time: 97 mins
US release: DEG, Feb 26, 1988

REAL MEN

Jim Belushi and John Ritter address the question, 'What is a real man?' in a story that must have read better than it plays. Belushi is a Mr Macho type, a bullet-proof CIA agent who could hold his own against 007. Ritter is Mr Wimp, the kind of sissy who cries when he gets shot. Belushi kidnaps the mild-mannered Ritter and drives him to Washington to help unravel a super-human plot. En route, predictably, the pair realize that being

Real Men

a real man means more than acting tough. Writer/director Dennis Feldman was fresh from penning *The Golden Child*. **BM**
Director/script *Dennis Feldman* **producer** *Martin Bregman* **exec** *Louis A. Stroller* **camera** *John A. Alonzo* **design** *William J. Cassidy, James Allen* **cast** *James Belushi, John Ritter, Barbara Barrie, Bill Morey, Iva Andersen, Gail Berle, Mark Herrier, Matthew Brooks*
Running time: 96 mins
US release: UA, Sep 25, 1987

RED HEAT

Walter Hill, the master of destructive drollery, returns to form in this down-market revision of *Gorky Park* that should have been called *Moscow Vice*. Arnold Schwarzenegger is a cop seeking to crack a cocaine ring in the shadow of the Kremlin. In a typically jokey touch, the drug kingpin is cast to resemble John Milius, with whom Hill is currently on the outs. This villain escapes to Chicago, where squared-away Schwarzenegger teams with sloppy local cop Jim Belushi. Between shots and punches, Schwarzenegger demonstrates iron control over his facial muscles, making his occasional utterances, such as 'Who is Dirty Harry?' all the funnier. **BM**
Director *Walter Hill* **producers** *Hill, Gordon Carroll* **execs** *Mario Kassar, Andrew Vajna* **script** *Harry Kleiner, Hill, Troy Kennedy Martin* **camera** *Matthew F. Leonetti* **editor** *Freeman Davies, Carmel Davies, Donn Aron* **design** *John Vallone* **music** *James Horner* **cast** *Arnold Schwarzenegger, James Belushi, Peter Boyle, Ed O'Ross, Larry Fishburne, Gina Gershon, Richard Bright, Brent Jennings, Savely Kramarov, Gene Scherer, Pruitt Taylor Vince, J. W. Smith, Gretchen Palmer*
Running time: 103 mins
US release: Tri-Star, Jun 24, 1988

RED KISS (Rouge baiser)

Growing up Red and romantic in fifties Paris - producer-director Véra Belmont's partly autobiographical period chronicle is often heartfelt and affecting, though weakened by a desire to cram in too many narrative points and characters, and a tendency towards the conventional. Belmont succeeds best in her direction of teen newcomer Charlotte Valandrey as a 15-year-old Parisian who's commitment to a local Stalinist youth cell diminishes as interest in apolitical photo-journalist Lambert Wilson grows. Period-feel is well-managed. Marthe Keller and Laurent Terzieff lend sensitive support as the girl's Polish immigrant parents. **LB**
Director/producer *Véra Belmont* **script** *Belmont, Guy Konopnicki, David Milhaud* **camera** *Ramon Suarez* **editor** *Martine Giordano* **music** *Jean-Marie Senia* **cast** *Charlotte Valandrey, Lambert Wilson, Marthe Keller, Laurent Terzieff, Günter Lamprecht, Laurent Amal, Audrey Lazzini*
Running time: 111 mins
US release: Circle, Nov 2, 1986
UK release: The Other Cinema, Jun 3, 1988

RENT-A-COP

The fact must be faced: Burt Reynolds may never make another good movie, but there's no reason he'll ever stop making movies in which he plays an ex-cop involved with a prostitute. This movie, which followed his similar *Heat* into the toilet, casts the bewigged one as a tainted drug-buster reduced to wearing a Santa suit to foil shoplifters. Higher duties call, however, when hooker Liza Minnelli seeks Reynolds' aid against their common enemy, psycho killer James Remar. The Reynolds-Minnelli pairing is no more inspired than it was in *Lucky Lady*, and director Jerry London might have been wiser to stay in TV. **BM**
Director *Jerry London* **producer** *Raymond Wagner* **script** *Dennis Shryack, Michael Blodgett* **camera** *Guiseppe Rotunno* **editor** *Robert Lawrence* **design** *Tony Masters* **music** *Jerry Goldsmith* **cast** *Burt Reynolds, Liza Minnelli, James Remar, Richard Masur, Dionne Warwick, Bernie Casey, Robby Benson, John Stanton, John P. Ryan*
Running time: 95 mins
US release: Kings Road, Jan 15, 1988

Repentance

REPENTANCE (Monanieba)

Unavoidably difficult, if avoidably overlong, *Repentance* represents a bold attempt (sufficiently bold to have stayed on the Soviet shelf for several years) to confront - albeit allegorically - the legacy of Stalinism. Utilizing black farce and surreal fantasy in the story of a tyrant whose body won't stay buried, the film casts the same actor as both the dictator and his blandly bureaucratic son. The melodramatic exaggeration of the ending, in which the latter finally confronts the reality of his inheritance, perhaps serves to imply the virtual impossibility of truly evaluating the toll of Russia's recent history. **TP**
Director *Tengiz Abuladze* **producer** *Leomer Gugushvili* **script** *Nana Janelidze, Tengiz Abuladze, Rezo Kveselava* **camera** *Mikhail Agranovich* **editor** *Guliko Omadze* **design** *Georgi Mikeladze* **music** *Nana Janelidze* **cast** *Avtandil*

Mikharadze, Iya Ninidze, Merab Ninidze, Zewynab Botsvadze, Ketevan Abuladze, Edisher Giorgobiani, Kakhi Kavsadze, Nino Zakariadze, Nato Otzhigava, Dato Kemkhadze
Running time: 150 mins
UK release: Cannon, Feb 19, 1988

RETRIBUTION

A timid artist survives a suicide attempt, only to find himself possessed by the avenging spirit of a murdered mobster. Through his dreams, he tracks down and kills the murderers in spectacular *grand guignol* fashion. Every time the artist feels a kill coming on, his eyes glow green, the camerawork goes crazy and the sets explode into a riot of backlighting and telekinetic fury. These scenes, in fact, provide the movie with its *raison d'être* and overshadow all the unconvincing characterizations and psychological banter which plug the gaps in between. This would seem to be tailor-made for video, where gore-hounds will be able to fast-forward to people having their heads squashed by fork-lift trucks, being trapped in pigs' carcasses which are then passed through buzz-saws, etc. **AB**
Director/producer *Guy Magar* ***execs*** *Scott Lavin, Brian Christian* ***script*** *Magar, Lee Wasserman* ***camera*** *Gary Thieltges* ***editor*** *Magar, Alan Shefland* ***design*** *Robb Wilson King* ***music*** *Alan Howarth* ***cast*** *Dennis Lipscomb, Leslie Wing, Suzanne Snyder, Jeff Pomerantz, George Murdock, Pamela Dunlap, Susan Peretz, Clare Peck, Chris Caputo, Hoyt Axton, Ralph Manza*
Running time: 109 mins
US release: Taurus, Apr 15, 1988
UK release: Premier/Medusa, Apr 29, 1989

RETURN OF THE LIVING DEAD PART II

Business as usual, as a gang of decaying corpses pursues some kids through the streets of a small town.
Director/script *Ken Wiederhorn* ***producer*** *Tom Fox* ***exec*** *Eugene C. Cashman* ***camera*** *Robert Elswit* ***editor*** *Charles Bornstein* ***music*** *J. Peter Robinson* ***cast*** *James Karen, Thom Mathews, Michael Kenworthy, Marsha Dietlein, Dana Ashbrook, Philip Bruns, Suzanne Snyder*
Running time: 89 mins
US release: Lorimar, Jan 15, 1988

A RETURN TO SALEM'S LOT

Only the title and setting owe anything to Stephen King: the rest is all Larry Cohen, presenting another one of his re-workings of the well-worn horror myths. Michael Moriarty plays an anthropologist who arrives with his bratty young son in the small Maine town of Jerusalem's Lot. The local vampire population promptly railroads him into setting down their long and honourable history for posterity. The vampires turn out to be, in some ways, more civilized than human beings (they extract their daily pintas, painlessly, from cattle), but they are on dodgier moral ground in their breeding of humans as daylight-tolerant underlings, and Moriarty finds himself up against something of a dilemma when he is coerced into making one of the vampires pregnant. As ever, Cohen's incisive imagination compensates for his rather slipshod technique and shoestring production values, and there are splendid bonuses in Sam Fuller as a Nazi-hunter-turned-Van-Helsing-vigilante, a number of Hollywood veterans cast as pillars of the bloodsucking community and a local primary school production of 'Dracula: Our Version'. **AB**
Director/exec *Larry Cohen* ***producer*** *Paul Kurta* ***script*** *Cohen, James Dixon* ***camera*** *Daniel Pearl* ***editor*** *Armond Leibowitz* ***design*** *Richard Frisch* ***music*** *Michael Minard* ***cast*** *Michael Moriarty, Richard Addison Reed, Andrew Duggan, Sam Fuller, June Havoc, Evelyn Keyes*
Running time: 95 mins
US release: Warner, Oct 11, 1987

RETURN TO SNOWY RIVER

The hills of Victoria haven't changed since *The Man from Snowy River* came out in 1982. Kirk Douglas is now Brian Dennehy, but that's a minor detail in the landscape. Rancher Dennehy still has little love for horseman Tom Burlinson, who must battle the power structure, headed by banker Rhys McConnochie and his son Nicholas Eadie, to secure his rightful place in this picture postcard hideaway. What's worse, Burlinson also renews his ardour for the rancher's headstrong daughter, Sigrid Thornton, somehow preferring her over his faithful equine companion Regret. This time, producer/writer Geoff Burrowes directs too, but he fails to strike the same sparks that George Miller did. **BM**
Director/producer *Geoff Burrowes* ***execs*** *Dennis Wright, John Kearney* ***script*** *Burrowes, John Dixon* ***camera*** *Keith Wagstaff* ***editor*** *Gary Woodyard* ***design*** *Leslie Binns* ***music*** *Bruce Rowland* ***cast*** *Tom Burlinson, Sigrid Thornton, Brian Dennehy, Nicholas Eadie, Bryan Marshall, Rhys McConnochie, Mark Hembrow, Peter Cummins, Cornelia Francis, Tony Barry*
Running time: 97 mins
US release: BV, Apr 13, 1988

River's Edge

REVENGE OF THE NERDS II: NERDS IN PARADISE

At a national fraternity conference set in Fort Lauderdale, the Nerds struggle for individual identity amidst conformist pressures and against ostracism by the unlikeable Greeks.
Director/exec *Joe Roth* ***producers*** *Ted Field, Robert Cort, Peter Bart* ***script*** *Dan Guntzelman, Steve Marshall, based on characters created by Tim Metcalfe, Miguel Tejada-Flores, Steve Zacharias, Jeff Buhai* ***camera*** *Charles Correll* ***editor*** *Richard Chew* ***design*** *Trevor Williams* ***music*** *Mark Mothersbaugh, Gerald V. Casale* ***cast*** *Robert Carradine, Curtis Armstrong, Larry B. Scott, Timothy Busfield, Courtney Thorne-Smith, Andrew Cassese, Donald Gibb, Bradley Whitford, Ed Lauter, Barry Sobel*
Running time: 92 mins
US release: Fox, Jul 10, 1987

RIDERS OF THE STORM

Formerly *The American Way*, this 1986 comedy, shot in Britain, was revamped prior to its US release so as to include references to the war in Nicaragua, but neither spurious topicality nor the presence of Dennis Hopper could inject any adrenalin into this dated comic-strip satire. The idea's not bad - Hopper's the captain of a crew of crazy Nam vets who have turned their B52 bomber, circling endlessly over America, into a cult pirate radio station broadcasting pop sedition that is provoked into taking on a Thatcher-like demagogue - actually a drag queen - who's standing for the White House. It's funny in patches, but self-consciously eccentric and ultimately grounded by a lack of any real understanding of what an audience might think smart in the 1988 election year. **GF**
Director *Maurice Phillips* ***producers*** *Laurie Keller, Paul Cowan* ***execs*** *Maqbool Hameed, Jean Ubaud* ***script*** *Scott Roberts* ***camera*** *John Metcalfe* ***editor*** *Tony Lawson* ***design*** *Evan Hercules* ***music*** *Brian Bennett* ***cast*** *Dennis Hopper, Michael J. Pollard, Eugene Lipinski, James Aubrey, Al Matthews, William Armstrong, Nigel Pegram*
Running time: 105 mins
US release: Miramax, Dec 11, 1987

RITA, SUE AND BOB TOO

A study of stunted teenage lives, uncompromisingly set in the ruined landscape of a dead-end Bradford housing estate, *Rita, Sue and Bob Too* nonetheless manages to be abrasively funny. The screenplay, which elevates inarticulacy and banality to near-operatic heights, and the direction, utilizing complex long takes to communicate energy as well as authenticity, mesh together to create an almost Brueghel-like impression of British working-class life that is as untainted by the clichés of left-wing pamphleteering as by any inhibitions about vulgarity and offensiveness. The 'happy' ending may risk seeming a cop-out, but the naturalistic conviction of the performances manages to override even this obstacle. **TP**

Director *Alan Clarke* **producer** *Sandy Lieberson* **exec** *Oscar Lowenstein* **script** *Andrea Dunbar, based on her plays* The Arbour *and* Rita, Sue and Bob Too **camera** *Ivan Strasburg* **editor** *Stephen Singleton* **design** *Len Huntingford* **music** *Michael Kamen* **cast** *Siobhan Finneran, Michelle Holmes, George Costigan, Lesley Sharp, Willie Ross, Patti Nicholls, Kulvinder Ghir, Dany O'Dea, David Britton, Mark Crompton, Stuart Goodwin, Max Jackman, Andrew Krauz, Simon Waring, Maureen Long*
Running time: 93 mins
US release: Orion Classics, Jul 17, 1987
UK release: Mainline, Sep 4, 1987

Rita, Sue and Bob Too

RIVER'S EDGE

From the producers of *Desperately Seeking Susan* comes the flip-side to that bright-eyed urban adventure, set in suburban California where the kids are fast changing into zombies. When a young boy murders his girlfriend, his classmates fail to believe him until they see the body. One (the ever loopy Crispin Glover) wants to cover up the incident, another feels the police should be told. Tim Hunter orchestrates this dissolute group with an unflinching directness, the only excessive note hit by the now obligatory Dennis Hopper cameo, here as an old acid-head obsessed with a life-size doll. **DT**

Director *Tim Hunter* **producers** *Sarah Pillsbury, Midge Sanford* **execs** *John Daly, Derek Gibson* **script** *Neal Jimenez* **camera** *Frederick Elmes* **editors** *Howard Smith, Sonya Sones* **design** *John Muto* **music** *Jürgen Knieper* **cast** *Crispin Glover, Keanu Reaves, Ione Skye Leitch, David Roebuck, Dennis Hopper, Joshua Miller, Roxana Zal, Josh Richman, Phil Brock, Tom Bower, Constance Forslund, Leo Rossi, Jim Metzler, Tammy Smith*
Running time: 99 mins
US release: Island, May 8, 1987
UK release: Palace, Oct 9, 1987

ROBOCOP

Film of the Year

Director *Paul Verhoeven* **producer** *Arne Schmidt* **exec** *Jon Davison* **script** *Edward Neumeier, Michael Miner* **camera** *Jost Vacano* **editor** *Frank J. Urioste* **design** *William Sandell* **music** *Basil Poledouris* **cast** *Peter Weller, Nancy Allen, Daniel O'Herlihy, Ronny Cox, Kurtwood Smith, Miguel Ferrer, Robert DoQui, Ray Wise, Felton Perry, Paul McCrane, Jesse Goins, Del Zamora, Calvin Jung, Rick Lieberman, Lee DeBroux, Mark Carlton, Edward Edwards, Michael Gregory*
Running time: 102 mins
US release: Orion, Jul 17, 1987
UK release: Rank, Feb 5, 1988

THE ROSARY MURDERS

Donald Sutherland can play anything, from dim to brilliant, from passive to swaggering. If asked, he could probably even play short. In Fred Walton's *The Rosary Murders* he plays the Montgomery Clift part from Hitchcock's *I Confess.* Someone is murdering the priests and nuns of Detroit and Sutherland knows who he is. But he can't tell because he learned the killer's identity in the confessional. Sutherland is a tolerant, understanding cleric, in contrast to Charles Durning, his closed-minded superior. The film's plodding pace is set by Sutherland's choice to play his character as too stunned by events to think or speak without long pauses. **BM**

Director *Fred Walton* **execs** *Robert G. Laurel, Michael Mihalich* **script** *Elmore Leonard, Walton* **camera** *David Golia* **editor** *Sam Vitale* **music** *Bobby Laurel, Don Sebesky* **cast** *Donald Sutherland, Charles Durning, Josef Sommer, Belinda Bauer*
Running time: 105 mins
US release: New Line, Aug 28, 1987

ROBOCOP

It has been a curious decade for celluloid fantasy. After the Cold War paranoia of the fifties came the much vaunted return of serious, challenging material in the sixties. But the late seventies and early eighties yielded scant proof that the genre had matured or progressed from an exhortation to keep watching the skies.

Nevertheless, directors like Ridley Scott and James Cameron eschewed juvenilia, attempting to resurrect the infinite possibilities of the sci-fi thriller with such hardcore material as *Aliens*, *Blade Runner* and *The Terminator*. Despite the differences between these three movies, their makers had understood that *film noir* was a style more than a genre. With reverence for its mannerisms, they sought to re-appropriate its elements of despondency and betrayal for fantasy.

It could be said of eighties science fiction that it remains speculative, celebrating the theme of individuality in a restrictive, conformist society. The solipsistic odyssey theme has taken different forms: Terry Gilliam's *Brazil* was a black, Hogarthian romp, while Ridley Scott's *Blade Runner* remained ostensibly a detective piece. A vacancy existed for a hardcore science fiction thriller that was confrontational rather than escapist.

Paul Verhoeven's *Robocop* is the groundbreaker. Its title character is policeman Murphy, played by the relatively unknown Peter Weller. He's a family man who, when he's relegated to crime-ridden Detroit, is instantly dismembered at the hands of a savage gang, then transformed by corporate callousness or expediency into the prototype of a defence unit intended to surpass and usurp existing law enforcement, now privatized and entrusted to the sinister Delta Industries. The creature belies this mutation by pursuing those ultimately responsible for his predicament, with the sporadic assistance of a tough female police officer (Nancy Allen) who becomes his ally following Robocop's metamorphosis along the road back to humanity.

Paul Verhoeven, the Dutch film-maker known primarily for his minor cult successes with *Turkish Delight* and *The Fourth Man*, exploits this first Hollywood excursion (*Flesh and Blood*, although financed by Orion, was made in Spain), to consolidate his skills with the application of religious imagery to reflect political and social mores.

Verhoeven's America is represented by The Old Man (Dan O'Herlihy) and his company, Delta Industries, which promulgates a fraudulent Utopia of consumer durables, where even social stalwarts like policing and medicine have been handed over to Dick Jones (Ronny Cox), a senior executive whose abortive police robot, the clumsily murderous ED-209, precipitates the Robocop project to resurrect Murphy.

Instead of making a portentous statement on the dangers of entrepreneurial exuberance, the director employs acerbic, frequently hilarious, black comedy to substantiate and embroider the main theme, a genre prerequisite, about a subjugated individual dwarfed by a technology-obsessed society and somehow emerging triumphant.

Murphy is, in his son's eyes, secondary to a fictitious TV character, T. J. Laser. The narrative uses this blurring of fantasy and reality to alter our perhaps limited expectations of what a sci-fi thriller called *Robocop* should fulfil. Without detracting from Robocop's efforts to revenge himself upon the gang responsible for his predicament (perhaps aided and abetted by somebody at Delta Industries who intends the destruction of Robocop himself), the obligatory vigilante ethics and actions of the law enforcer become peripheral to the cyborg's flashbacks.

Robocop's memories reveal a domestic landscape wherein Murphy can only recollect a coffee-mug emblazoned 'world-class husband', and a wife and child who bade him farewell as they, like the civilization reflected, peer out from a sanitized vacuum.

As the title character, Peter Weller acquits himself admirably within Rob Bottin's splendidly designed, albeit claustrophobic, costume. He invests Murphy with an empathic edge without recourse to overt pathos or sentiment, and his performance stands above the barbarity of the set pieces.

The grotesque execution of Murphy at the beginning is Verhoeven's inevitable apology for the lack of screen time afforded his primary figure. This systematic dismemberment (instigated by the supremely reptilian king-pin, Clarence Boddiker), emphasizes Robocop's ephemerality when compared to the sadism in which his attackers revel. The role is tailor-made for Verhoeven, given his penchant for crucifixion/resurrection iconography; Boddiker's final bullet through Murphy's head is as metaphoric as a crown of thorns.

The style and visuals of *Robocop* complement the engaging disparity of incessant, over-amplified violence, social comment and comedy.

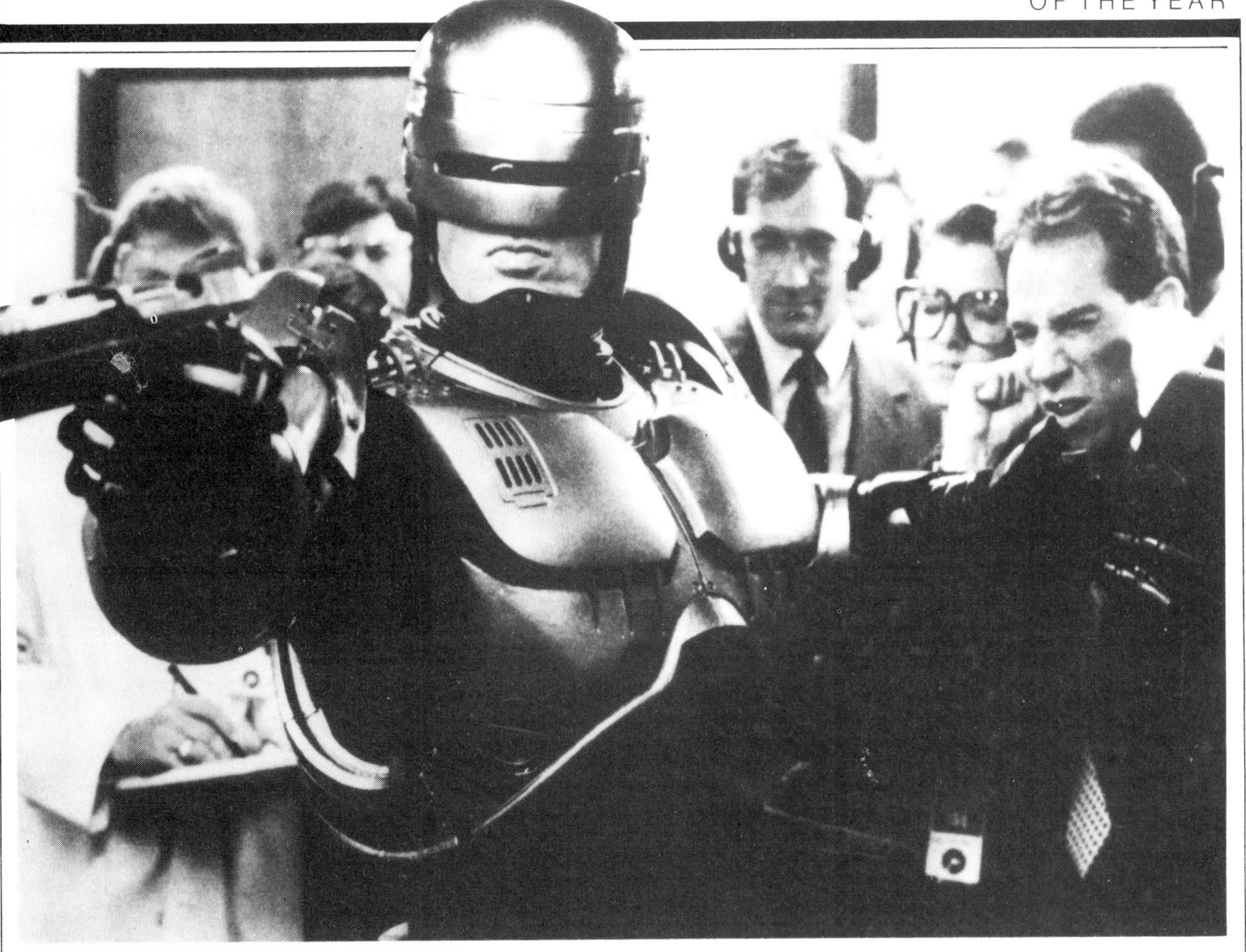

Highlights include the carefully choreographed execution of a gang member driving through a vat of toxic waste, ED-209's prolonged accidental execution of a Delta executive (which provokes hilarity rather than revulsion due to the satirical presentation of the protagonist's reactions in the seqence), and the overall *mise-en-scène*. A flippant, yet abrasive, montage of jokes levelled at the heartlessness of humanity, and its representation in culture, reaches its zenith (or perhaps nadir) with a succession of news breaks which provide a thoroughgoing look at Omni Consumer Products, the division of Delta which initiated the Robocop project, and they incisively furnish the viewer with a cynical approximation of how the trivialization of culture ultimately homogenizes and corrodes society's moral status.

The news readers relate in fatuous tones such tragedies as South Africa's acquisition of the nuclear bomb, and the accidental death of two ex-presidents (cue footage of convulsing bodies) in Acapulco. Crass materialism is the main target of the vitriol in *Robocop*. The commercialism endorsed by 'Nuke Em', a board game advertised on television, is overshadowed by a commercial where an obsequious actor-surgeon promotes designer plastic hearts.

Perhaps only a generation away from the nihilistic teenagers of today, the subsidiary villains in *Robocop* are somehow justifiable delinquents, indifferent to world domination and dreams of longevity, who delight in the amoral simplicity of murder and carnage for momentary fulfilment. Cocaine, money and hardware are the gratifications available also to the yuppie initiator of the Robocop project. Without resorting to moral parables or social indictment, Verhoeven accepts that drugs are both a leisure activity and a billion dollar cottage industry.

The enduring value of *Robocop* is that it addresses and exemplifies the issues it raises, where other genre movies with aspirations to greatness just evade them. Like the new format comic books, particularly Frank Miller's *The Dark Knight Returns*, *Robocop* describes an incomprehensible world in which heroes, whilst possessed of Olympian attributes, are at best undervalued, or worse, destroyed by a hostile society oblivious to their motives.

A cliché persists that 'the bigger the villain, the better the movie.' But Kurtwood Smith as Boddiker, Robocop's nemesis and the generic offspring of Ming The Merciless and The Joker, and Dan O'Herlihy as The Old Man, arguably the *real* adversary, transcend the camp pomposity otherwise expected of this genre. Both these characters express true evil: gluttonous avarice masquerading as corporate enterprise, a subtext validated by the movie's climax wherein Robocop's final declaration of his identity as Murphy is a re-affirmation of life.

It is evident throughout that Verhoeven is a man possessed of a rabidly inventive imagination, who finds beauty amid concrete and the grotesque. *Robocop* is exhilarating in its correlation of levity and gravity, re-vivifying our awareness of each man's ephemeral status. Verhoeven's next project, *Total Recall*, is derived, like *Blade Runner*, from a Philip K. Dick novella and features similar themes to *Robocop*. Accept no imitations from here on since anything else would be just scratches on the chrome. The queue forms here for *Robocop II: This Cyborg For Hire*. Any takers? Well, I'll buy that for a dollar.

MARCUS NATTEN

ROXANNE

An unabashed Steve Martin vehicle and his best to date, scripted by the wild and crazy guy himself from the old Rostand play *Cyrano de Bergerac*. This time the witty but amorously shy man with the long hooter is a small-town fire chief, his love object a visiting astronomer in the shape of Daryl Hannah. Employing Fred Schepisi as director has ensured Martin's fellow actors are given sufficient space to make this more than a one-nose show. **DT**
Director *Fred Schepisi* ***producers*** *Michael Rachmil, Daniel Melnick* ***exec*** *Steve Martin* ***script*** *Martin, from the play* Cyrano de Bergerac *by Edmond Rostand* ***camera*** *Ian Baker* ***editor*** *John Scott* ***design*** *Jack DeGovia* ***music*** *Bruce Smeaton* ***cast*** *Steve Martin, Daryl Hannah, Rick Rossovich, Shelley Duvall, John Kapelos, Fred Willard, Max Alexander, Michael J. Pollard*
Running time: 107 mins
US release: Columbia, Jun 19, 1987
UK release: CCW, Nov 6, 1987

THE RUNNING MAN

Arnold Schwarzenegger's admirers must have been wondering when he would make a gladiator movie. In the near future, the TV ratings battle is for life or death. The current smash is *The Running Man*, in which a convict tries to escape from a maze while hunted by a variety of comic book-style assassins. Arnold is framed and finds himself in the maze. Guess who wins? Maria Conchita Alonso runs along with him in a largely thankless role. Contest host Richard Dawson has the movie's best moments. Paul Michael Glaser, who took over directing in mid-stream, was unhappily stuck with too many shots of contestants zooming down the same tunnel in the hunt for freedom. **BM**
Director *Paul Michael Glaser* ***producers*** *Tim Zinnemann, George Linder* ***execs*** *Keith Barish, Rob Cohen* ***script*** *Stephen E. de Souza, based on the*

Roxanne

novel by Richard Bachman (Stephen King) ***camera*** *Tom Del Ruth* ***editor*** *Mark Roy Warner* ***design*** *Jack T. Collis* ***music*** *Harold Faltermeyer* ***cast*** *Arnold Schwarzenegger, Maria Conchita Alonso, Richard Dawson, Yaphet Kotto, Jim Brown, Jesse Ventura, Erland Van Lidth, Marvin J. McIntyre, Gus Rethwisch, Prof. Toru Tanaka, Mick Fleetwood, Dweezil Zappa, Karen Leigh Hopkins*
Running time: 101 mins
US release: Tri-Star, Nov 13, 1987

RUSSKIES

It's mean to kick a little movie with its heart in the right place, but *Russkies* just won't bear adult scrutiny. Whip Hubley, a Soviet seaman, is separated from two comrades meeting up with an American traitor off Key West. Three boys fond of military games find him and subdue him but all are soon coexisting peacefully. It's the Fourth of July, by the way. The boys' parents eventually miss them, the Marines pursue them, and the nefarious missing pair of *apparatchiks* threaten them. It all comes to a standoff at gunpoint when, lo and behold, everyone agrees to put down their guns and nobody gets hurt. **BM**
Director *Rick Rosenthal* ***producers*** *Mark Levinson, Scott Rosenfelt* ***execs*** *Mort Engelberg, Stephen Deutsch* ***script*** *Alan Jay Glueckman, Sheldon Lettich, Michael Nankin* ***camera*** *Reed Smoot* ***editor*** *Antony Gibbs* ***design*** *Linda Pearl* ***music*** *James Newton Howard* ***cast*** *Whip Hubley, Leaf Phoenix, Peter Billingsley, Stefan DeSalle, Susan Walters, Patrick Kilpatrick, Vic Polizos, Charles Frank, Susan Blanchard, Benjamin Hendrickson, Carole King, Vojo Goric, Al White, Patrick Mickler, Summer Phoenix, Leo Rossi, Gene Scherer*
Running time: 99 mins
US release: New Century/Vista, Nov 6, 1988

·S·S·S·S·S·S·S·S·S·S·S·

SAIGON (See Off Limits)

SALOME'S LAST DANCE

By setting Oscar Wilde's scandalous play in a London brothel in 1892, where Wilde himself attends a performance arranged by Lord Alfred Douglas, Russell once again gives us a demonstration that art is created through the sexual obsessions of its makers. Where that was a limiting, rather puerile view of the great composers, Russell seems spot on with Wilde's camp extravaganza. A brilliant parade of performers, including the weirdly boyish Millais-Scott as Salomé, are deployed with great relish while the single set is never made a limitation. A small triumph. **DT**
Director *Ken Russell* ***producer*** *Penny Corke* ***execs*** *William J. Quigley, Dan Ireland* ***script*** *Russell, based on the play by Oscar Wilde* ***camera*** *Harvey Harrison* ***editor*** *Timothy Gee* ***design*** *Michael Buchanan* ***cast*** *Glenda Jackson, Stratford Johns, Nickolas Grace, Douglas Hodge, Imogen Millais-Scott, Denis Ull, Russell Le Nash, Alfred Russell, Ken Russell*
Running time: 89 mins
US release: Vestron, May 6, 1988
UK release: Vestron, Jul 1, 1988

SALVATION: HAVE YOU SAID YOUR PRAYERS TODAY? (Salvation! in UK)

Underground movie doyenne Beth B. comes part of the way above ground with this maladroit fantasy of heavy metal, sex and TV revivalism, the latter being in its topical reality a subject a good deal more provocative than this film manages to suggest. Stephen McHattie's performance as the dissembling 'Reverend' seems worthy of a better showcase, but while, in its flailing fashion, some of the satire is not without impact, the movie proves to have nowhere to go but into what seems like an interminably extended version of the less interesting sort of pop promo. **TP**
Director *Beth B* ***producers*** *Beth B, Michael H. Shamberg* ***execs*** *Ned Richardson, Michel Duval, Irving Ong* ***script*** *Beth B, Tom Robinson* ***camera*** *Francis Kenny* ***editor*** *Elizabeth Kling* ***design*** *Lester Cohen* ***music*** *New Order, The Hood, Cabaret Voltaire* ***cast*** *Stephen McHattie, Dominique Davalos, Exene Cervenka, Viggo Mortensen, Rockets Redglare, Billy Bastiani*
Running time: 85 mins (80 mins in UK)
US release: Circle, May 31, 1987
UK release: Recorded Releasing, Aug 7, 1987

SAMMY AND ROSIE GET LAID

Turkey of the Year

Director *Stephen Frears* ***producers*** *Tim Bevan, Sarah Radclyffe* ***script*** *Hanif Kureishi* ***camera*** *Oliver Stapleton* ***editor*** *Mick Audsley* ***design*** *Hugo Luczyc Wyhowski* ***music*** *Stanley Myers* ***cast*** *Shashi Kapoor, Frances Barber, Claire Bloom, Ayub Khan Dim, Roland Gift, Wendy Gazelle, Badi Uzzman, Suzetta Llewellyn, Meera Syal, Tessa Wojtczak, Emer Gillespie, Lesley Manville, Mark Sproston, Cynthia Powell, Dennis Colon, Megumi Shimanuki, Buster Bloodvessle, Peter Kelly*
Running time: 101 mins
US release: Cinecom, Oct 30, 1987
UK release: Palace, Jan 22, 1988

SAMMY AND ROSIE GET LAID

My Beautiful Laundrette lavished sarcasm and sensitivity impartially on working-class racism, gay true love, Pakistani family spirit, and a launderette which, being a business enterprise with soul, epitomized Mrs Thatcher's philosophy. The film's very charm subverted practically every ideological position. But this grander follow-up, also by writer Hanif Kureishi and director Stephen Frears, only reminds us how movies resemble pancakes. Just one twist of the wrist makes a masterpiece a soggy mess on the floor.

This is a conflict-fraught cross-section of inner city folk. Rafi Rahman (Shashi Kapoor), deposed premier of a Third World nation, comes to England, expecting it to be all cricket and cucumber sandwiches. He walks bang into a blood-and-fire race riot. His nephew Sammy is a cynical, cocaine-sniffing accountant; Sammy's English wife Rosie is off sex and into feminist bodybuilding and sisterhood with lesbians. Uncle Rafi reveals his patriarchal-capitalist tendencies by offering Sammy and Rosie financial help if they'll give him grandchildren. They discover worse yet: this erstwhile freedom fighter tortured his political opponents once in power. However, he chums up with young Danny, a genial giant of a man who lives with a sort of Peace Squatters' Convoy while wondering whether the sufferings of the common people under Mrs Thatcher don't require violent resistance. Capitalism's cruel bulldozers dispossess the squatters, thus rekindling Rafi's Maoism, though a ghost wearing an electro-torture helmet gets him to do the decent thing and hang himself instead. Meanwhile, our spirit of resistance to Mrs T. has been cheered by the film's sexual climax, a split-screen juxtaposition of three interracial fucks - Rosie with Danny, Sammy with Anna, a gracefully ageing hippy, and Rafi with Alice (Claire Bloom), an erstwhile Memsahib nearly but not quite withered into an English spinster. Finally, Sammy and Rosie sob together over their old uncle; a fresh start, perhaps?

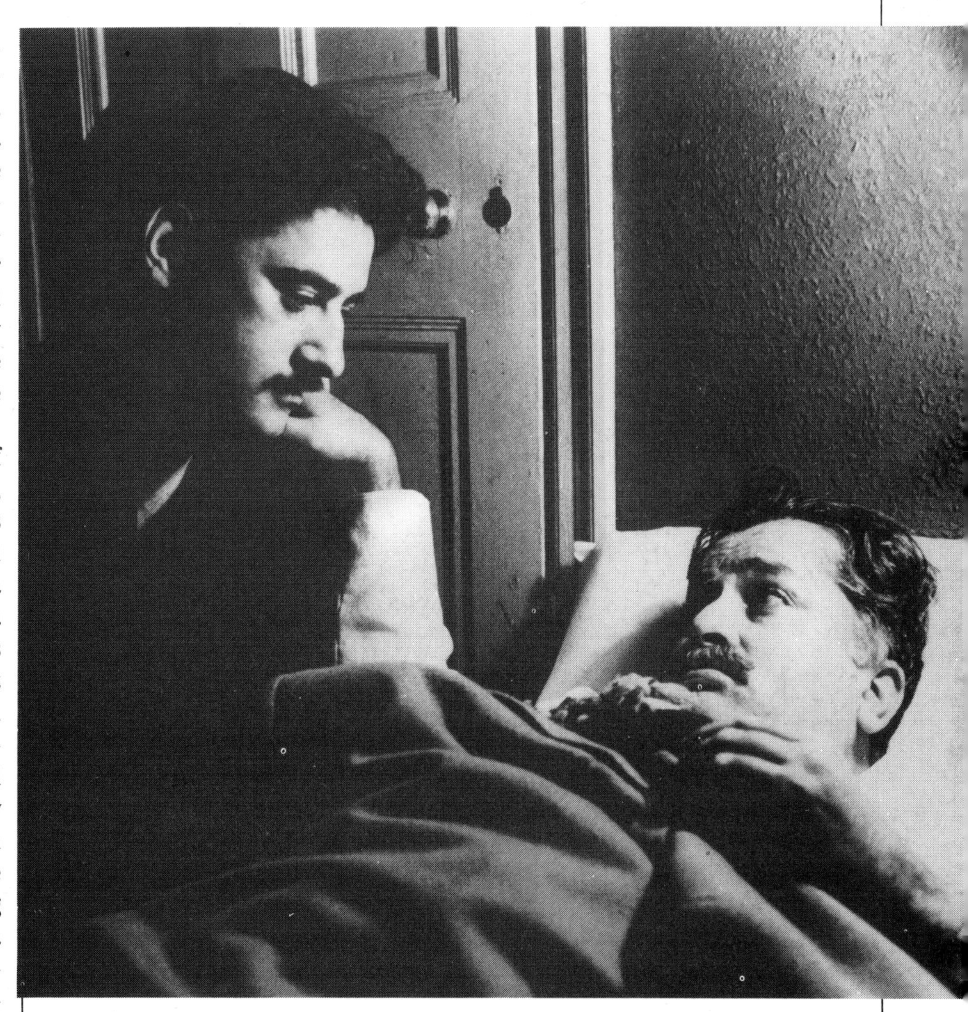

Here's material enough for several months of radical soap operatics, and some of it promises good strong stuff. Rafi's rich past (revolutionary tyrant, capitalist) involves crucial problems in Third World politics. What with money (for Sammy and Rosie), and politics (for Danny), he's got something to test everybody's politics and character. Sammy and Rosie's marriage is practically The State of England: a love-hate stalemate between two halves of the middle class. Sammy is the capitalist half: he's an accountant, a yuppie, a playboy. Rosie is the socialist half: she's into ideology like the Women's Page of *The Guardian*, but robustly proletarian too. The political and personal merge perfectly, like sex and business in *My Beautiful Laundrette*. Having set up a great story, that could wonderfully anatomize the Anguished Eighties, all Kureishi and Frears had to do was tell it.

But no. They're so psyched up with anti-Thatcherite ire that they hurl great chunks of political indignation at us instead. They're anti-police and pro-riot, anti-Sammy and pro-Rosie, anti-Rafi and pro-Danny. Their vehement one-sidedness rules out the give-and-take of drama and politics alike. This leaves the story nothing to work out, so the characters just meander in bewilderment. Sammy is purposeless, Danny dim though nice, Rafi a forever discomfited old

Blimp, Anna an enthusiastic lay, Alice lives in suburbia (symbolizing suspended animation?). A young feminist tears into her ideals: 'You only lived through men. The penis was your lifeline.'

Zilch sensitivity like that doesn't promote reflection, it prevents it. The characters talk like spray-cans gushing graffiti. Desperate for just one non-party-line idea, I actually found myself wishing Rafi would confound these self-righteous lefties with a reasoned justification for torture. After all, it's current or recent practice amidst practically every race, creed, colour, country and ideology in the world today, so it must have some moral rationale going for it. But Kureishi and Frears wouldn't dare be so unconventional. That's confirmed by Kureishi's (frank and sensitive) diary of the film, published with the script. To him and Frears, even everyday English conservatism looks like some evil fungus from outer space. They're not fanatics. It's a more innocent prejudice, but it explains the film's hysteric instability.

And crashing failures of tact. Nasty white cops storm a happy black home to arrest a musician, his brave mother throws boiling fat in their faces, they shoot her. Having set all those emotions going, the film cuts straight to a near-fuck scene; the woman has a 'W' tattooed on each buttock, so that when she's heels over head in love her spreadeagled anatomy will spell 'WOW'. It's cheap, it's contorted, and coming straight after the preceding brutality it's - words fail me. I saw the film with a Saturday-night audience, mostly working-class teens, in Walthamstow (outer edge of inner city, racially mixed). The intended belly laugh provoked icy silence, and the young audience stayed frosty for nearly an hour, until the film's accumulation of small virtues and sex frolics outweighed its crassnesses and reassured them it had a heart.

But, between the knee-jerk politics and sex-joke shock, the human texture goes to pot. Rafi, arriving in London, talks to a stranger about hot buttered toast resembling 'cunty fingers'; yet he's supposedly expecting to find England extremely refined! Against writing like that, and direction as subtle as a jack hammer, the actors haven't a chance. Sammy is an ageing spoilt brat. Rosie is a Julie Walters clone but hard and mean. Even Claire Bloom gets hustled into phoney histrionics. Rafi's mellow cynicism and guilt make him more human than the rest of them.

No doubt there's a dotty audacity about trying to combine *EastEnders* with *Carry on Rainbow Coalition* and a Third World political tragedy. But when Kureishi returns to writing wonderfully about people he knows, he'll look back on this and wonder what on earth came over him.
RAYMOND DURGNAT

SARRAOUNIA

Sarraounia is a splendid, tall warrior woman who enters African mythology when she leads her villagers in a triumphant campaign against an invading tribe. Then the French colonists attempt to stamp out her influence. Seven years in the making, this is a visually exciting epic, only diffused by its indecision whether to be about its eponymous heroine or the obsessive French officers, who carry on with more than an echo of *Aguirre, Wrath of God*. **DT**

Director/producer *Med Hondo* ***script*** *Hondo, based on the novel by Abdoulaye Mamani* ***camera*** *Guy Famechon* ***editor*** *Marie-Thérèse Boiché* ***design*** *Jacques d'Ovidio* ***music*** *Pierre Akendengué, Abdoulaye Cissé, Issouf Compaore* ***cast*** *Aï Keïta, Jean-Roger Milo, Féodor Atkine, Didier Suavegrain, Roger Mirmont, Luc-Antoine Diquero, Jean-Pierre Castaldi, Tidjani Ouedraogo, Wladimir Ivanosky, Didier Agostini, Jean Edmond, Philippe Bellay, Tagara Yacouba Traore, Aboubacar Traore, Abdoulaye Cissé, Jean-François Ouedraogo, Florence Bewendé, Hama Gourounga, Baba Traore, Djibril Sidibe, Sekou Tall, Rajoun Tapsirou, Jacob Sou, Temeddit Ag Hoye, Bed Idriss Traore*
Running time: 121 mins
UK release: ICA Projects, Jan 1, 1988

SATISFACTION

Let's face it - rock 'n' roll is just too boring a subject for a full-length movie. The people who do it for a living are constantly trying to escape into the movies, and movie/TV people always look like they're slumming when they essay rock styles. In Joan Freeman's humdrum film, Justine Bateman fronts a four-girl-one-guy oldies band that can do no better than play a summer-time gig at a beach resort. Is this the life for her, Bateman wonders with a pout and a scowl, or should she go to college? She sings the title tune, a long way after Mick Jagger. Steve Cropper provides the guitar licks she mimes. **BM**

Director *Joan Freeman* ***producers*** *Aaron Spelling, Alan Greisman* ***execs*** *Rob Alden, Armyan Bernstein* ***script*** *Charles Purpura* ***camera*** *Thomas Del Ruth* ***editor*** *Joel Goodman* ***design*** *Lynda Paradise* ***music*** *Michel Colombier* ***cast*** *Justine Bateman, Liam Neeson, Trini Alvarado, Scott Coffey, Britta Phillips, Julia Roberts, Debbie Harry*
Running time: 92 mins
US release: Fox, Feb 12, 1988

SCHOOL DAZE

Spike Lee's dispiritingly unfunny follow-up to *She's Gotta Have It* makes (for better or worse) absolutely no concessions to white audiences or to the demands of movie storytelling in its stop-start saga of life on a Southern black university campus. Glued together by musical numbers, *School Daze* pitches militant activists (led by Larry Fishburne's Dap) against the élitist Gamma Phi Gamma fraternity (led by Giancarlo Esposito's Big Brother Almighty), with pledging freshman Half-Pint (Lee) caught in the middle, and the light-skinned Wannabees fighting it out with the darker Jigaboos among the women. If the film has a message, it's a call to black consciousness, but the most telling scene has Dap's boys confronting some working-class brothers out in the city. There's no resolution as such and very little fun, except a delicious dance duel between the female gangs on a hair-salon set. Not short of ideas, Lee has crammed them all in

without bothering to impose a structure. **GF**
Director/producer/script *Spike Lee* ***exec*** *Grace Blake* ***camera*** *Ernest Dickerson* ***editor*** *Barry Alexander* ***design*** *Wynn Thomas* ***music*** *Bill Lee* ***cast*** *Larry Fishburne, Giancarlo Esposito, Tisha Campbell, Kyme, Joe Seneca, Ellen Holly, Art Evans, Ossie Davis, Spike Lee*
Running time: 120 mins
US release: Columbia, Feb 12, 1988
UK release: Columbia, Jul 29, 1988

SEPTEMBER

Turkey of the Year

Director/script *Woody Allen* ***producer*** *Robert Greenhut* ***execs*** *Jack Rollins, Charles H. Joffe* ***camera*** *Carlo Di Palma* ***editor*** *Susan E. Morse* ***design*** *Santo Loquasto* ***cast*** *Denholm Elliott, Dianne Wiest, Mia Farrow, Elaine Stritch, Sam Waterston, Jack Warden, Ira Wheeler, Jane Cecil, Rosemary Murphy*
Running time: 82 mins
US release: Orion, Dec 18, 1987
UK release: Rank, Jul 1, 1988

THE SERPENT AND THE RAINBOW

Wes Craven brings a genuinely creepy exoticism to this voodoo adventure which, towards the end, loses its way in a surfeit of ghoulish effects. No Indiana Jones, Bill Pullman is wooden as the Harvard anthropologist in search of a zombifying powder wanted by a US drug corporation, and a dull match for Cathy Tyson's feisty, sensual psychiatrist, who takes him to bed. This sometimes confused chiller really belongs, however, to Zakes Mokae, hammily terrifying as the grinning, supernaturally-endowed black police chief - and to the brooding Haiti settings. Not always in control of the material, Craven still directs with panache, revealing he has few peers in his chosen genre. **GF**
Director *Wes Craven* ***producers*** *David Ladd, Doug Clayborne* ***execs*** *Rob Cohen, Keith Barish* ***script*** *Richard Maxwell, A. R. Simoun* ***camera*** *John Lindley* ***editor*** *Glenn Farr* ***design*** *David Nichols* ***music*** *Brad Fiedel* ***cast*** *Bill Pullman, Cathy Tyson, Zakes Mokae, Paul Winfield, Brent Jennings, Conrad Roberts, Badja Djola, Theresa Merritt, Michael Gough, Paul Guilfoyle, Dey Young*
Running time: 98 mins
US release: Universal, Feb 5, 1988

THE SEVENTH SIGN

Life on Earth is about to end. So says Jürgen Prochnow, who's God's messenger. These are the signs. Demi Moore's baby will be born without a soul. Meanwhile, her husband tries to secure a reprieve for the last martyr, about to go into the gas chamber. Not to worry. The apocalypse never arrives.
Director *Carl Schultz* ***producer*** *Ted Field, Robert Cort* ***exec*** *Paul R. Gurian* ***script*** *W. W. Wicket, George Kaplan (Clifford Green, Ellen Green)* ***camera*** *Juan Ruiz-Anchia* ***editor*** *Caroline Biggerstaff* ***design*** *Steven Marsh* ***music*** *Jack Nitzsche* ***cast*** *Demi Moore, Michael Biehm, Jürgen Prochnow, Manny Jacobs, Peter Friedman, John Heard, Akosua Busia*
Running time: 97 mins
US release: Tri-Star, Apr 1, 1988

SHAKEDOWN

Strictly for fans of dirtier-than-thou urban action flicks, James Glickenhaus's film stars Peter Weller as a public defender and Sam Elliott as an uncorrupted cop. Weller turns down a cushy Wall Street job when one of his clients turns out to be innocent, and the murdered cop and his buddies are the guilty parties. The prosecutor in the case is Weller's old girlfriend Patricia Charbonneau, and they can't resist clinching on their lunch hour, between clashes in court. Weller sucks in his cheeks a lot. Elliott looks lost, especially when called on to ride the landing gear of a jet. **BM**
Director/script *James Glickenhaus* ***producer*** *J. Boyce Harman Jr.* ***execs*** *Leonard Shapiro, Alan Solomon* ***camera*** *John Lindley* ***editor*** *Paul Fried* ***design*** *Charles Bennett* ***music*** *Jonathan Elias* ***cast*** *Peter Weller, Sam Elliott, Patricia Charbonneau, Blanche Baker, Antonio Fargas, Richard Brooks*
Running time: 90 mins
US release: UA, May 6, 1988

SHE'S HAVING A BABY

In this autobiographical prequel to his *Mr. Mom*, John Hughes casts Kevin Bacon as a young man who settles uncomfortably into marriage and finally understands why it was the right move only after he becomes a father. Bacon is endearing and often funny as a Chicago advertising copywriter, and Elizabeth McGovern does more than just flash her kewpie-doll beauty as Hughes' ideal of womanhood. Hughes cuts loose with some fantasy sequences that occasionally regress into high school hi-jinks, but overall the film is the closest this overgrown kid has yet come to real life. **BM**
Director/producer/script *John Hughes* ***exec*** *Ronald Colby* ***camera*** *Don Peterman* ***editor*** *Alan Heim* ***design*** *John W. Corso* ***music*** *Stewart Copeland* ***cast*** *Kevin Bacon, Elizabeth McGovern, Alec Baldwin, Isabel Lorca, William Windom, Cathryn Damon, Holland Taylor, James Ray*
Running time: 106 mins
US release: Paramount, Feb 5, 1988

SHOOT TO KILL

(Deadly Pursuit in UK)

Variable thriller from director Roger Spottiswoode of *Under Fire*. Beginning with a superbly staged hostage rescue bid, it then settles for a sub-*Defiant Ones* plot in a *High Sierra* setting. Citified black cop Sidney Poitier and white mountain guide Tom Berenger resolve their differences while pursuing a psychotic killer into Canada. Up ahead, the psycho's busy knocking off everyone in his party except his guide, Berenger's girlfriend (Alley). Can Sid and Tom save her? Lovely scenery and a fine cameo appearance from a moose. But the suspense is modest, and the racial-entente message platitudinous. **HK**
Director *Roger Spottiswoode* ***producers*** *Ron Silverman, Daniel Petrie Jr.* ***script*** *Harv Zimmel, Michael Burton, Petrie* ***camera*** *Michael Chapman* ***editor*** *Garth Craven* ***design*** *Richard Sylbert* ***music*** *John Scott* ***cast*** *Sidney Poitier, Tom Berenger, Kirstie Alley, Clancy Brown, Richard Masur, Andrew Robinson, Kevin Scannell, Frederick Coffin, Michael MacRae, Robert Lesser*
Running time: 110 mins
US release: BV, Feb 12, 1988

SHY PEOPLE

Konchalovsky's fourth film for Cannon describes a New York sophisticate travelling with her degenerate daughter into the dark and mysterious bayous of Louisiana to write about her long lost great uncle. What they find is his dogged young widow (a commendably dignified Barbara Hershey) and her trio of weird sons. The culture clash is deafening, the tedium of this estranged world all too palpable. **DT**
Director *Andrei Konchalovsky* ***producers*** *Menahem Golan, Yoram Globus* ***script*** *Gérard Brach, Konchalovsky* ***camera*** *Chris Menges* ***editor*** *Alain Jakubowicz* ***design*** *Stephen Marsh* ***music*** *Tangerine Dream* ***cast*** *Jill Clayburgh, Barbara Hershey, Martha Plimpton, Merritt Butrick, John Philbin, Don Swayze, Pruitt Taylor Vince, Mare Winningham, Michael Audley, Brad Leland, Tony Epper, Paul Landry*
Running time: 119 mins
US release: Cannon, Dec 4, 1988
UK release: Cannon, Jun 17, 1988

Shy People

SEPTEMBER

Would someone please come to the rescue of Woody Allen? It looks as if he's been at the complete works of Chekhov again. He has ink all over his fingers and autumnal Russian gentility all over his brain.

The plot and characters may come out of Woody's head, but *September* takes one step further the Chekhovian stylistics of *Interiors* and *A Midsummer Night's Sex Comedy*. From the first he has taken the fraught family relationships simmering in a dacha-like mansion. From the second comes a rondo of romantic longing, with six characters in search of the heart's fulfilment.

But this time round all vestiges of the self-aware subversive Allen have been drowned in solemnity. Here is the sempiternal country house, a picturesque wood-frame pile somewhere in Vermont: painted in beige and yellow colours, like the last curling autumn leaves. And here are gathered six of the most archly miserable characters ever to spend 80 minutes stoking each other's *weltschmertz*. There is mousy spinster Mia Farrow, her domineering mom Elaine Stritch, her depressed stepfather Jack Warden and a crew of lovelorn country weekend hangers-on: crusty neighbour Denholm Elliott (who loves Mia), sensitive novelist Sam Waterston (who's loved by Mia) and neurasthenic friend Dianne Wiest (who loves Sam).

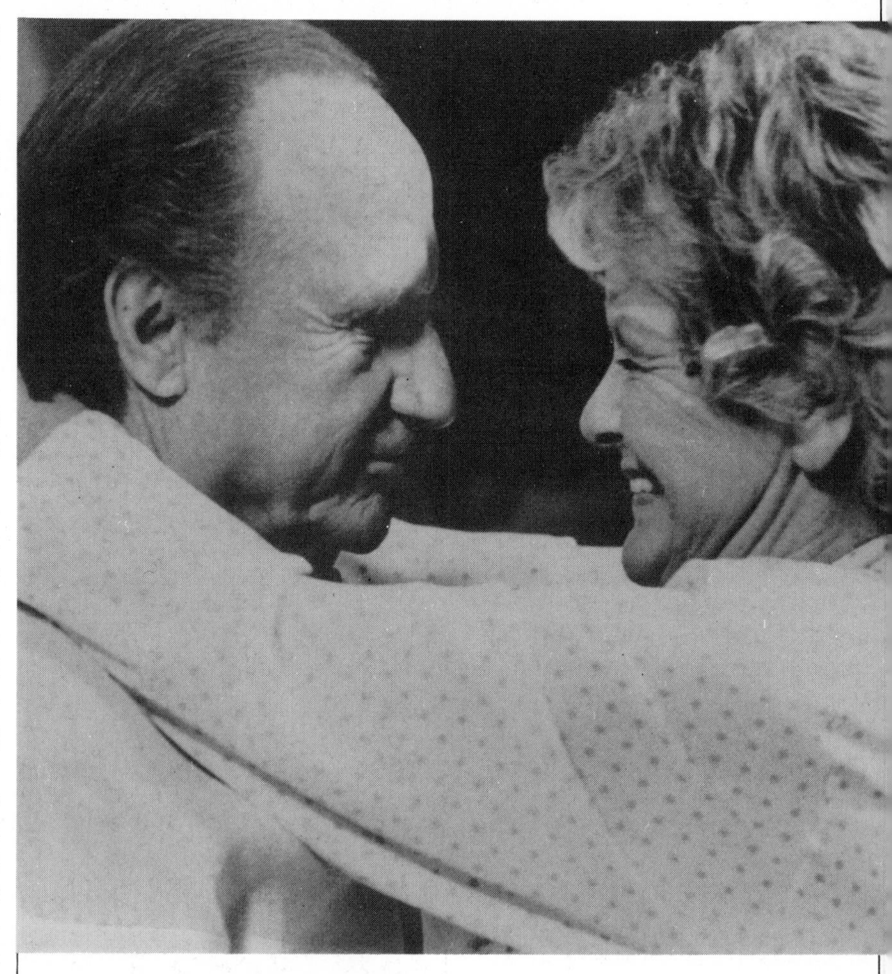

Like his Russian masters, and his Swedish master Bergman, Allen sees the isolated group as a chance to show the human condition in microcosm. But where Chekhov or Bergman deploy their limbo settings to trigger credible crises in credible characters, Allen's *dramatis personae* and catalyzing plot-line smack of nought but tragic posturing. Using bleak colours, crabbed camera movements and maudlin jazz music on a piano, the director moves his characters around the lemony shadowland as if on a miniature railway of human suffering. Forever circling through their stations of despair, they sometimes briefly couple with a gloomy clank and a steamy hiss of self-analysis.

Farrow, done up with granny glasses and tight, mousy hair, looks like Liv Ullman in a Bergman film, and her scenes with Waterston have a trite and doomy preciosity that resembles *Autumn Sonata* adapted for novelette-readers. These two are at the putative heart of a movie that doesn't have one. Allen, as in his comedies, is out to show how human emotions are always sidetracked, disappointed and frustrated; and how - improbably - they can grow rather than shrink in the process. In his comedies Allen is the hilarious embodiment of this paradox: a midget bursting at the seams with querulous vitality, as if possessed by demons punching away inside his frail envelope.

What makes *September* depressing, in its approach to the same themes, is not that Allen is trying to be serious but that he's determined to be humourless. If failure - in love, work, sex or grappling for the meaning of life - is the stuff of his comedies, it triumphs in movies like *Annie Hall* or *Zelig* because the humour parodies or redefines the self-pity. But take out the humour in his films and all that's left is that self-pity.

A self-pity, what's more, depressingly generic and hand-me-down. The film's first twenty minutes are like a bad night at an Ibsen play: everything in the dialogue is plot exposition or threatening preludes to it. 'You have to put the past behind you,' says someone. 'Peter, what's happening to us?' asks someone else. And 'You're wrong if you think your mother didn't suffer terribly over that affair' is the first line Jack Warden has to wrap his tongue around, referring to Mia's childhood shooting of her actress mum's brutal lover.

This Lana Turner-Johnny Stompanato dimension, and the revelations it has in store for *September*'s final reel, make up the only 'story' in the film. Elsewhere we merely move from one agonized *tête-à-tête* to the next, as characters blurt, bleat or just silently suffer through their love.

While Farrow and Waterston bravely tackle impossible roles, Denholm Elliott comes on like the sum of his Dennis Potter teledramas: a walking male menopause with a wry, pained grin. And Dianne Wiest, brilliant in Allen's comedies, is condemned to whine out *sotto-voce* love agonies like a psychodrama version of her maiden aunt in *Radio Days*.

The only characters who spill out of their packaging a little are the oldies. Elaine Stritch is given a cliché role - the devouring ex-actress mum - but fights to untidy it a little. She's savagely sarcastic one moment, tousled and vulnerable the next: the puffy, age-worn face caught in a moment's lamp-lit sadness or dreamy remembrance over the Ouija board. And Jack Warden as her husband, a former Los Alamos physicist who rails against the universe as 'haphazard, morally neutral and unimaginably violent,' invests his unimaginably pompous lines with a gruff, jagged conviction.

But even these actors can't triumph over the movie's unwieldy symbolism. (Best example: Dianne Wiest's memory of her radiologist husband. She never let him take X-rays of her, she says, because 'if he looked inside he'd see things he wouldn't understand and he'd be terribly hurt.') Allen's determination to be Artistic stands like a bell-jar over the whole enterprise. The film is airless and unreal: from the neatly permutated tragic partnerings - which we know will remain neat and tragic, otherwise they'll spoil the high-toned, *maestoso* mood - to the thunderstorm gathering outside, beyond the lemony shadows.

The work's tortured genesis testifies to the difficulty Allen had in getting it right, and his baffling devotion to doing so. The entire film was re-shot after the first go, with a changed cast. What this working-over achieved, in comparison to the first version, we can only guess. But it seems consistent with the sense of a movie that has been refined to death. Allen's answer to a universe 'haphazard, morally neutral and unimaginably violent' used to be to make films that answered back with their own brand of cosmic anarchy. But *September* just lies down under the unbearable weightiness of being. It makes noises that sound like great art but are just great ersatz, resonating with all the right influences and none of the real feelings.

HARLAN KENNEDY

THE SICILIAN

Comparisons may be invidious but, in telling the story of Salvatore Giuliano, Cimino is not within shouting distance of Rosi's classic. In this romanticized version of the life of the Sicilian bandit who became a pawn of the Mafia, Cimino makes a major mistake by casting the effete Lambert in the leading role, but the supporting players are equally dreadful (Joss Ackland a noble exception). Add to this some uninspired visuals and lacklustre action scenes and the result is a fat turkey which saw a lot of emptying seats. **DT**

***Director** Michael Cimino **producers** Cimino, Joann Carelli **script** Steve Shagan, based on the novel by Mario Puzo **camera** Alex Thomson **editor** Françoise Bonnot **design** Wolf Kroeger **music** David Mansfield **cast** Christopher Lambert, Terence Stamp, Joss Ackland, John Turturro, Richard Bauer, Barbara Sukowa, Giulia Boschi, Ray McAnally, Barry Miller, Andreas Katsulas, Michael Wincott, Derrick Branche, Richard Venture*

Running time: 115 mins

US release: Fox, Oct 23, 1987

Siesta

SIESTA

Might have been a brilliant parody of the erotic thriller if one didn't know the makers were actually attempting the real thing. Saddled with a script of numbing banality and a posturing cast, all delivering their worst-ever performances under débutante Lambert's totally unhelpful direction, the result is predictably a stinker. Even the sex can't help when all else has failed. The nookie's as tasty as a wet kipper. **QF**

***Director** Mary Lambert **producer** Gary Kurfirst **execs** Nik Powell, Zalman King, Julio Caro, Anthony Rufus-Isaacs **script** Patricia Louisianna Knop, based on the novel by Patrice Chaplin **camera** Bryan Loftus **editor** Glenn A. Morgan **design** John Beard **music** Marcus Miller, Miles Davis **cast** Ellen Barkin, Jodie Foster, Gabriel Byrne, Julian Sands, Isabella Rossellini, Alexei Sayle, Martin Sheen, Grace Jones, Anastasia Stakis, Gary Cady, Graham Fletcher Cook, Santiago Alvarez, Daniel Martin, Fabian Conde*

Running time: 97 mins

US release: Lorimar, Nov 11, 1987

SILENT VOICE

(Amazing Grace and Chuck in US)

It would take a good deal more than an opening title saying 'Once upon a time ...' to lend any fairytale conviction to this doubtless well intentioned whimsy about a Montana youngster whose horror of nuclear annihilation impels him to a self-denying ordinance in the matter of playing baseball, and how this eventually leads to nothing less than a worldwide ban on nuclear weapons. Joshua Zuehlke is likeably natural in the leading role, but the surrounding narrative is creaky beyond belief, incorporating an extraordinary summit meeting between President Gregory Peck and his Soviet counterpart at which the latter proves amenable to bumbling along in fractured English rather than have the proceedings slowed down by interpreters. **TP**

***Director** Mike Newell **producer/script** David Field **exec** Roger M. Rothstein **camera** Robert Elswit **editor** Peter Hollywood **design** Dena Roth **music** Elmer Bernstein **cast** Jamie Lee Curtis, Alex English, Gregory Peck, William L. Petersen, Joshua Zuehlke, Dennis Lipscomb, Lee Richardson*

Running time: 115 mins

US release: Tri-Star, May 22, 1987

UK release: Col, Feb 19, 1988

SISTER, SISTER

A formula Gothic that somehow attracted excellent actors, *Sister, Sister* is watchable, but only just. There's bad blood in the bayou as Eric Stoltz puts up for the night in an antebellum mansion, run as a guest house by sisters Judith Ivey and Jennifer Jason Leigh. Ivey is the sister who copes, Leigh the one who mopes. All three stars wear red hair, a clue to the demonic thoughts snaking around just below the roots. There is a possibly murderous hired hand and a mysterious death far in the past. Past and present menaces stalk through the gloomy corridors and along the dark waters. **BM**

***Director** Bill Condon **producer** Walter Coblenz **script** Condon, Joel Cohen, Ginny Cerrella **camera** Stephen M. Katz **editor** Marion Rothman **design** Richard Sherman **music** Richard Einhorn **cast** Eric Stoltz, Jennifer Jason Leigh, Judith Ivey, Dennis Lipscomb, Anne Pitoniak, Benjamin Mouton*

Running time: 91 mins

US release: New World, Feb 5, 1988

SITTING IN LIMBO

Latest from the National Film Board of Canada's alternative drama programme features non-professional actors from Montreal acting out a story of immature teenagers trying to cope with the realities of adult life, and babies. Reggae soundtrack has contributions from Jimmy Cliff and others.

***Director** John N. Smith **producers/script** David Wilson, Smith **camera** Barry Perles, Andreas Poulsson **editor** Wilson **cast** Pat Dillon, Fabian Gibbs, Sylvie Clarke, Debbie Grant, Compton McLean, Millicent Dillon*

Running time: 95 mins

UK release: Other Cinema, Dec 11, 1987

SLAM DANCE

An unexpected change of pace for the director of *Dim Sum*, a brightly lit and loudly scored askance look at an old-fashioned thriller plot set on the West Coast. Tom Hulce plays a cult cartoonist who becomes embroiled in a conspiracy while his emotional life is in turmoil. A bizarrely mixed supporting cast, including screenwriter Don Opper, make watchable a movie that frequently goes off the tracks (partly due to production interference). A very likeable oddity. **DT**
Director *Wayne Wang* ***producers*** *Rupert Harvey, Barry Opper* ***exec*** *Cary Brokaw* ***script*** *Don Opper* ***camera*** *Amir Mokri* ***editor*** *Lee Percy* ***design*** *Eugenio Zanetti* ***music*** *Mitchell Froom* ***cast*** *Tom Hulce, Mary Elizabeth Mastrantonio, Adam Ant, Don Opper, John Doe, Harry Dean Stanton, Robert Beltran, Virginia Madsen, Millie Perkins, Judith Barsi, Rosalind Chao, Sasha Delgado, Joshua Caceras, Marty Levy*
Running time: 101 mins
US release: Island, Oct 2, 1987
UK release: Palace, Nov 13, 1987

SLATE, WYN AND ME

Vietnam veteran Slate (Sacks) and his oafish brother Wyn (Burke) are small-town Australian thugs whose attempted robbery of the local bank turns sour when Wyn impetuously murders a policeman. They abduct a witness to the homicide (Thornton), an attractive girl that Wyn cannot bring himself to kill. The ensuing escapades hang uncomfortably around the narrative chestnut of a half-hearted emotional triangle with predictable consequences. It is not merely the blue-collar Americano wardrobe nor the uninspired rock soundtrack that provokes such forced allusiveness to the American road movie drama genre but the obsequious deference to *The Hit*, *Butch Cassidy* and, of course, *Bonnie and Clyde*, the seminal picture in this genre, which *Slate, Wyn and Me* never has a hope of surpassing. **MN**
Director *Don McLennan* ***producer*** *Tom Burstall* ***execs*** *Anthony I. Ginnane, William Fayman* ***script*** *McLennan, based on the novel* Slate and Me and Blanche McBride *by George Savage* ***camera*** *David Connell* ***editor*** *Peter Friedrich* ***design*** *Paddy Reardon* ***music*** *Peter Sullivan* ***cast*** *Sigrid Thornton, Simon Burke, Martin Sacks, Tommy Lewis, Lesley Baker, Harold Baigent, Michelle Torres, Murray Fahey, Taya Straton, Julia MacDougall, Peter Cummins, Reg Gorman, Warren Owens, Eric McPhan, Simon Westaway, Kurt von Schneider*
Running time: 91 mins
US release: Hemdale, Nov 25, 1987
UK release: Palace, Jul 17, 1987

SOMEONE TO LOVE

Another psychiatrist's couch impromptu from American cinema's favourite neurotic *manqué*, Henry Jaglom. This time he has taken over an abandoned theatre in Santa Monica, filled it with real-life weirdos and celebs (Monte Hellman, Andrea Marcovicci, Orson Welles in his last film) and set about conducting a talk-in on love and loneliness. Sounds like the worst idea since sliced bread. But the talk is good and the film is full of funny, transforming moments: as when Michael Emil tries to chat up a magisterially *distrait* Sally Kellerman, or when Welles opens his mouth late-on to spout a stream of resonant aphorisms. **HK**
Director/script/director *Henry Jaglom* ***producer*** *M. H. Simonsons* ***camera*** *Hanania Baer* ***cast*** *Orson Welles, Henry Jaglom, Andrea Marcovicci, Michael Emil, Sally Kellerman, Monte Hellman, Oja Kodar, Stephen Bishop, Dave Frishberg*
Running time: 109 mins
US release: Castle Hill, Apr 21, 1988

Slam Dance

SOMEONE TO WATCH OVER ME

Film of the Year

Director/exec *Ridley Scott* ***producers*** *Thierry de Ganay, Harold Schneider* ***script*** *Howard Franklin* ***camera*** *Steven Poster* ***editor*** *Claire Simpson* ***design*** *Jim Bissell* ***music*** *Michael Kamen* ***cast*** *Tom Berenger, Mimi Rogers, Lorraine Bracco, Jerry Orbach, John Rubinstein, Andreas Katsulas, Tony DiBenedetto, James Moriarty, Mark Moses, Daniel Hugh Kelly, Harley Cross*
Running time: 106 mins
US release: Columbia, Oct 9, 1987
UK release: Columbia, Mar 11, 1988

SOMETHING WILD

Demme delivered the proof (if anyone needed convincing) that he is one of the most talented American directors around with this exuberant mix of yuppie nightmare and road movie. Griffith (in her best performance to date) appears as Lulu, an anarchic free spirit who teases straight tax-advisor Charlie (the excellent Daniels) into living the wild life. Then it turns out she is really someone else with a volatile ex-hubbie just out of jail. With its snappy soundtrack and improvisatory quality, it is a winner all the way. **DT**
Director *Jonathan Demme* ***producers*** *Demme, Kenneth Utt* ***exec*** *Edward Saxon* ***script*** *E. Max Frye* ***camera*** *Tak Fujimoto* ***editor*** *Craig McKay* ***design*** *Norma Moriceau* ***music*** *John Cale, Laurie Anderson, David Byrne* ***cast*** *Jeff Daniels, Melanie Griffith, Ray Liotta, Margaret Colin, Tracey Walter, Dana Preu, Jack Gilpin, Charles Napier, Robert Ridgely, Su Tissue, Kristin Olsen*
Running time: 114 mins
US release: Orion, Nov 7, 1986
UK release: Rank, Jul 3, 1987

SOMEONE TO WATCH OVER ME

Can Ridley Scott make a movie in the present tense? The world's leading exponent of designer cinema - his films resemble visions of Valhalla whether set in next century LA or Napoleonic France, alien-infested Space or unicorn-infested Utopia - has his first contemporary outing with *Someone to Watch Over Me*. Scott enthusiasts nervously awaiting the result wondered: how on earth will a visionary who feeds on far-flung times cope with a humble tale of crime and adultery set in modern New York? As soon commission Aeschylus to script an episode of *Hill Street Blues*.

But Scott has used the film to prove what his previous movies already proclaim: that all the world can be a crucible for myth-making, and so can all times. Indeed, late eighties Manhattan is a mere 30 years adrift of 2017 LA (time and setting of *Blade Runner*): and, in early scenes of *Someone to Watch Over Me*, the Big Apple looks like a city in training to host *Blade Runner II*. Outside, the Scott *sfumato* is at work - steam and smoke wreathing the rain-sleek streets and furling across the raking spotlights - while inside, in the death-destined niterie, strobe lights duel with photographers' flashbulbs through the Scott-ish clouds of incense smoke.

It's wonderful, it's intoxicating, but how long, we wonder, can the director keep it up? Answer: in varying degrees for most of the movie. Scott now knows how to ring changes on the visual temperature. But it never descends to the luke-warm. The movie as scripted, by Howard Franklin, is a modest morality tale of love and crime: lowly cop from Queens (Tom Berenger) falls for the murder-witness millionairess he's assigned to protect (Mimi Rogers) and nearly sacrifices his wife (Lorraine Bracco) and child to his ill-starred love.

The story's pitfalls are clear: much moralizing, much contrivance and much surging-violin pathos in prospect. The first temptation might be to play the whole thing for street realism: use the gritty *verismo* of modern cop dramas to sandpaper away the sentimentalities. Scott does the opposite. Instead of smoothing down the sentimentalities, he builds on them and transforms them: he turns the movie into a fairy tale in *film noir*. The penurious cop falling for the beautiful millionairess is the lowly swain setting his cap at the royal princess. And the millionairess's apartment is the incarcerating tower, embodying the age-old fairy tale wisdom

that palaces can be prisons in disguise.

But this being the nervous, sexually-disenchanted eighties, our swain cannot simply be a straw-in-the-mouth innocent. In the age of AIDS, when Aphrodite is interchangeable with Armageddon, there are few of those around any more. So our hero is a happily married hick-from-the-sticks (or hick from Queens, the New York equivalent), to whom sophistication is a five-syllable word he's never heard of. He lives in a shanty bungalow with a tumbledown yard. On surveillance duty, he tunes out the millionairess's classical music by listening to baseball games on his personal stereo. And he even has to have a tie bought him by her when they go to a Guggenheim party: she can't bear to be seen with him wearing that strip of imitation flock wallpaper he arrived in.

This would all be fairly loony stuff if handled the wrong way. But Scott grooms the movie for hyperbole from the start. In a fairy tale, heroes, heroines and villains are allowed an extra yard of expressive implausibility. So, when the gargoyle-faced villain gives early chase to Miss Rogers, who's just seen him knife the niterie owner, he only *just* can't separate the lift doors as they close behind him. And when the villain's henchman infiltrates Miss Rogers' apartment, where Mr Berenger is sleeping on the job (with Miss Rogers), the henchman is defeated by that old standby, the maze of mirrors. Our hero is allowed time to wake up, track the intruder down, find his own bearings in the mirror maze and then shoot him dead. Some people have all the unfair advantages.

The nod to *Lady From Shanghai* is appropriate. Scott's hero, like Orson Welles's, is a romantic fall guy, pushed around by the multiplying faces of a *trompe l'oeil* destiny. Whenever he thinks he has a hold on reality, he doesn't. Safety is a mirage: the villain isn't in the bag when he's arrested, he's re-released on a technicality. Romance is a mirage: Miss Rogers won't give up all for love, or at least not for love of him. And even his grand break with the past is a mirage: his wife and kid go as far as her sister's and virtually wait for him to come back.

Fate's tendency to rebound like a ball on elastic is a Scott *leitmotif. The Duellists* had a duel that kept repeating itself over decades. *Alien* was about a man-eating monster that couldn't be killed and had a nasty habit of changing for dinner (never the same outfit twice). *Blade Runner* had a homicidal, never-say-die android. And *Legend*, with its stubborn Demon King finally defeated by an onslaught of light, proclaimed that the only way to outwit evil destiny was to scatter the oneiric darkness in which it thrives: just like cinema itself.

The rebounding destiny in *Someone to Watch Over Me* is plainer and purer than in any previous Scott film. The movie says: however much human beings flirt with change, or romance with the ideal of self-transformation, they end by returning to where they've planted their roots: such roots as they have. The film's charge and poignancy come from the cycle of vain heartbreaks and lost emotional ventures that result. Nobody wins. The girl doesn't get the man. The man doesn't get the girl. The wife keeps her husband (we suppose), but has lost her unquestioned faith in his feelings.

But the story also has a surprise consolation prize, one that's implied in the title. In the whirligig of changing relationships, the 'someone to watch over me' takes on a touching interchangeability. It starts here as the policeman guarding the murder-witness. It modulates into the murder-witness caring for the policeman. ('Let me watch over you tonight' says Miss Rogers when Berenger returns from his bruising bust-up with his wife.) And it is even crowned by the child taking on the protector role in the last-scene hostage crisis, when he finds and seizes the hidden gun under the table.

In this light the film's insistent little rituals of clothes-swapping - Berenger drapes his coat over Rogers during a cold walk in the streets, later she and a cop exchange clothes to fool the villain at the shoot-out - hint at the fluidity of the watcher-protector role. Though love may not be the great leveller, survival certainly is. Indeed the one thing that draws and keeps the lovers together is the threat from the killer-on-the-loose. When the threat ends, so does the romance.

No wonder the film pictures Miss Rogers' apartment as a delirium-for-the-senses under siege from a hostile outside world. Scott makes it a place as heightened and artificial as the love affair it incubates. A Daedalus maze in marble, glass and gold, its air is literally opaque with mystery (Scott has been at the incense canister again) and its airwaves spin an unceasing thread of operatic arias. This is the kind of music the Sirens must have played for Odysseus, except that Tom Berenger, unlike the wily Greek, omits to put wax in his ears.

Some foolish critics have suggested these scenes evince an obsession with class, and show Scott's weak-kneed worship of the wealthy and their gilt-edged lifestyle. But the film's counterpoint between the gorgeous East Side and tumbledown Queens is no more than an emblem for the emotional counterpoint in the hero's head: between a tousled terrestrial reality he already has (namely his family) and an unattainable dream he wants to reach out for (Miss Rogers). To attack the movie as concerned with class or wealth *per se* is as pertinent as attacking the Hansel and Gretel story for its classist approval of marzipan mansions over humble peasant cottages.

Someone to Watch Over Me is a dream of passion spun out of the smoke and mystery of modern New York. It's a tragic fable that puts its hero through the higher cycles of hope and loss, dream and delusion, and then returns him sadder, wiser and spun-dried to the habitable realities he and we came from.
HARLAN KENNEDY

The Last Emperor: After being evicted by a warlord's troops, John Lone, The Last Emperor, leaves the Forbidden City and gets to see the outside world for the first time since early childhood. He launches himself into a playboy lifestyle, but the splintering of his marriage gives him much to think about apart from nostalgia for the days of ceremonial spectacle.

War Panic: She married someone else because he was out of a job. It was some while ago but, as the train travels back from the seaside, Sarah Miles reveals to Derrick O'Connor that her heart still throbs for him. Such emotional revelations are par for the course in the Blitz London explored by John Boorman's ***Hope and Glory*** *(above and right)*. But if it's too late for the oldies to find happiness, the kids can still have a whale of a time. That's more than can be said for the British schoolboy played by Christian Bale in ***Empire of the Sun*** *(bottom right)*. He gets separated from his parents when the Japanese invade Shanghai, and has to survive on his own. Russian tanks notwithstanding, the repressed English passions of Miles and O'Connor are a far cry from the freewheeling Czech attitude to sex expressed by Daniel Day-Lewis and Lena Olin in ***The Unbearable Lightness of Being*** *(far right)*.

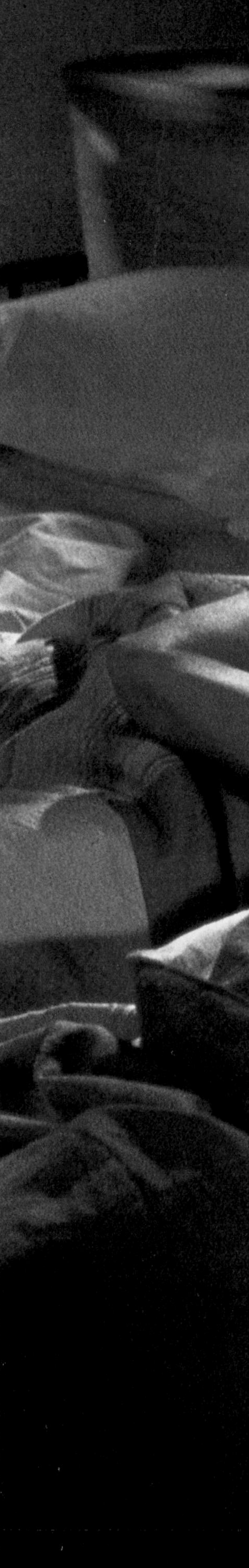

The Trouble With Living: Michael Douglas tries to console Glenn Close, a ***Fatal Attraction*** *(far left)* who threatens to break apart his nice little family. But the thought of all those who have passed on fills Anjelica Huston with melancholy as she recalls an innocent love from her girlhood in John Huston's swan-song ***The Dead*** *(left)*. From the moment they first catch sight of each other in a Paris café, John Lone and Keith Carradine are enemies. They take their battle of wits into the boxing-ring, but that's by no means the end of the affair in ***The Moderns*** *(below)*. Lindsay Crouse gets taken for a ride by Joe Mantegna in ***The House of Games*** *(bottom left)* and mistakenly thinks she is pulling the strings. Danny DeVito is an also-ran in the aluminium-siding business and there's a lot of frustration driving him to smash up his rival's Cadillac in ***Tin Men*** *(bottom right)*.

Guns and Cops: Lorraine Bracco's skill with a pistol ensures her family survives and gets back together after overcoming the threats that present themselves at the end of ***Someone to Watch Over Me*** *(above)*. That particular nightmare might never have started had not the killer nabbed by gun-wielding cop Tom Berenger *(right)*, Bracco's delinquent husband, been liberated by the court.

It was a corpse *(far left)* that started the drama rolling in ***The Big Easy*** but the apparently honest policeman Ned Beatty *(left)* knew more than he was letting on about the drugs-dealing that lay behind the wave of killings. It was all part of his pension plan. And it was drug barons that would have turned Paul Weller into maggot-food if he had not been transmogrified into man-of-steel ***Robocop*** *(above)*. If this law enforcement machine was on the market, every police force in the country would have to have one.

Foodie Films: Nobuko Miyamoto receives much-needed instruction in noodle-making from a motley gang of tutors in *Tampopo* while a *yakuza* and his moll are getting up to naughty business with prawns, nipples and egg yolks in their hotel bedroom *(top and above)*. This Japan is a sensuous paradise compared to the desolate coast of Jutland in the 1870s where Isabelle Audran brings the skills acquired in Parisian restaurants to bickering islanders more accustomed to a diet of gruel and religion in *Babette's Feast* *(right)*.

SOUTH OF RENO

In the desert south of Reno little moves. Even TV - just one snowy channel available here - provides little to make the eyeballs flicker. So railroad switchman and roadside visionary Jeffrey Osterhage is reduced to throwing glass on the highway in hopes someone will get a flat tyre and have to stop and talk to him. His wife, Lisa Blount, is quite rightly bored with this and prefers the company of a greasy mechanic, Lewis Van Bergen. Somewhere in amongst all Mark Rezyka's long shots of the immobile desert, there's a revenge plot trying and failing to surface. **BM**

Director *Mark Rezyka* ***producer*** *Robert Tinnell* ***execs*** *Victor Markowicz, Joanna Stainton* ***script*** *Rezyka, T. L. Lankford* ***camera*** *Bernard Auroux* ***editor*** *Marc Auroux* ***design*** *Phillip Duffin* ***music*** *Nigel Holton, Clive Wright* ***cast*** *Jeffrey Osterhage, Lisa Blount, Joe Phelan, Lewis Van Bergen, Julia Montgomery, Brandis Kemp, Danitza Kingsley, Mary Grace Canfield, Bert Remsen*

Running time: 94 mins

US release: Castle Hill, Apr 22, 1988

SPACEBALLS

Mel Brooks has always stood foursquare for low comedy. He calls his movies 'parodies', but this time he ventures further than before into outright joke-stealing. *Spaceballs* uses the plot and characters of *Star Wars* as a framework for grabs from, and digs at, as many films as Brooks could squeeze in, including his own. There's the let's-see-how-this-movie-ends gag from *Blazing Saddles*, John Hurt's upset stomach from *Alien*, a page or so of dialogue straight from the end of *It Happened One Night*, the wrecked Statue of Liberty from *Planet of the Apes*, the laboured long-range communication with people in the next room from *Airplane II* and countless others. Of the actors, Rick Moranis gets the most mileage from his character, Dark Helmet. **BM**

Director/producer *Mel Brooks* ***script*** *Brooks, Thomas Meehan, Ronny Graham* ***camera*** *Nick McLean* ***editor*** *Conrad Buff IV* ***design*** *Terence Marsh* ***music*** *John Morris* ***cast*** *Mel Brooks, John Candy, Rick Moranis, Bill Pullman, Daphne Zuniga, Dick Van Patten, George Wyner, Michael Winslow, Joan Rivers, Lorene Yarnell, John Hurt*

Running time: 96 mins

US release: MGM/UA, Jun 24, 1987

UK release: UIP, Dec 11, 1987

SQUARE DANCE

It's a tough life down on the farm, especially when your only companion is a grumpy grandpa (Robards). So Winona Ryder packs up to rejoin her flighty mother (Alexander) in the city. Life isn't much better there, but at least there's life. Daniel Petrie's slight coming-of-age drama depicts a neglected class, the former farmers of America, clustering near but not necessarily in the city. Teen fave Rob Lowe, wearing a bad haircut and a puzzled look, contributes an affecting portrait of a marginally retarded boy. Jane Alexander co-produced to get a crack at a role in which she isn't noble. **BM**

Director/producer *Daniel Petrie* ***execs*** *Charles Haid, Jane Alexander* ***script*** *Alan Hines, based on his novel* ***camera*** *Jacek Laskus* ***editor*** *Bruce Green* ***design*** *Jan Scott* ***music*** *Bruce Broughton* ***cast*** *Jason Robards, Jane Alexander, Winona Ryder, Rob Lowe, Deborah Richter, Guich Koock, Elbert Lewis, Charlotte Stanton, J. David Moeller, Dixie Taylor, Irma P. Hall, Barbara Britt, Brad Leland, Dee Pyland*

Running time: 112 mins

US release: Island, Feb 20, 1987

UK release: Enterprise, Nov 13, 1987

THE SQUEEZE

This is a film in the tradition of *Turk 182!* - a busy, barely watchable, forgettable action picture about little people who expose a corrupt system in New York. The variable Michael Keaton gets few laughs here as a deadbeat pursued by aspiring private eye Rae Dawn Chong. Behind in his alimony payments, hard at work on his dinosaur sculpture composed of dozens of TV sets, Keaton discovers a plot to fix the local lottery. Talking fast - originally Keaton's ticket to stardom, this time, directed by Roger Young, tedious to endure - our hero at length lines up all the plot strands in a rush-rush finale. **BM**

Director *Roger Young* ***producers*** *Rupert Hitzig, Michael Tannen* ***execs*** *Harry Colomby, David Shamroy Hamburger* ***script*** *Daniel Taplitz* ***camera*** *Arthur Albert* ***editor*** *Harry Keramidas* ***design*** *Simon Waters* ***music*** *Miles Goodman* ***cast*** *Michael Keaton, Rae Dawn Chong, Joe Pantoliano, Danny Aiello III, Leslie Bevis, Lou Criscoulo, John Davidson, George Gerdes, Ronald Guttman, Paul Herman, John Dennis Johnston, Jeffrey Josephson, Liane Langland, Meat Loaf, Pat MacNamara, Richard Portnow, Gerald J. Quimby*

Running time: 102 mins

US release: Tri-Star, Jul 10, 1987

UK release: Columbia, Feb 5, 1988

STACKING

Languorously directed by Martin Rosen (screen animator of the Richard Adams animal novels) *Stacking* is an unassuming rites-of-passage story set in the Montana hayfields in 1954. When her father (Baker) is injured fixing the stacker at harvest time and dissolves into boozy self-pity, and her dreaming mother (Lahti) deserts, it's up to slight, 14-year-old Anna Mae (Follows) to save the diminished family farm with the help of unreliable old hand Buster (Forrest). Rosen's little film belongs to his young star: Follows is a smart, pensive, loyal proto-feminist in an aggressively male world who's already seen through her mother's nail varnish and the sexual intent of the local youths. The mother's flight is disturbing, but you just know things are going to be okay down on the farm with Anna Mae. **GF**

Director/producer *Martin Rosen* ***exec*** *Lindsay Law* ***script*** *Victoria Jenkins* ***camera*** *Richard Bowen* ***editor*** *Patrick Dodd* ***design*** *David Wasco* ***music*** *Patrick Gleeson* ***cast*** *Christine Lahti, Frederick Forrest, Megan Follows, Jason Gedrick, Ray Baker, Peter Coyote, James Gammon, Kaiulani Lee, Jacqueline Brookes, Irene Dailey, Pat Coggins*

Running time: 109 mins

US release: Spectrafilm, Oct 9, 1987

Stacking *(left)*
Square Dance *(below)*

STAKEOUT

John Badham, adept at action movies with a difference (*WarGames, Short Circuit*) here yokes thrills and romantic comedy more skilfully than it's been done in a long time. Richard Dreyfuss and Emilio Estevez play cops assigned to watch Madeleine Stowe's house in case her escaped con boyfriend, Aidan Quinn, comes home. Dreyfuss insinuates himself into Stowe's life while the exasperated Estevez can only watch through binoculars from across the street. Just as the romance has come to a boil, Quinn does come home, resulting in a chase with a conventional outcome. Dreyfuss is as charming as he was in *Tin Men*, and Estevez repeats his callow turn from *St. Elmo's Fire.* **BM**

***Director/exec** John Badham **producers** Jim Kouf, Cathleen Summers **script** Kouf **camera** John Seale **editors** Tom Rolf, Michael Ripps **design** Philip Harrison **music** Arthur B. Rubinstein **cast** Richard Dreyfuss, Emilio Estevez, Madeleine Stowe, Aidan Quinn, Dan Lauria, Forest Whitaker, Ian Tracey, Earl Billings, Jackson Davies, J. J. Makaro, Scott Andersen, Tony Pantages, Beatrice Boepple, Kytle Woida, Jan Speck, Kim Kondrashoff*

Running time: 117 mins

US release: BV, Aug 5, 1987

UK release: Warner, Feb 26, 1988

STAND AND DELIVER

The story of a Hispanic mathematics teacher who coaxes outstanding calculus exam results from his initially reluctant and defiant class makes surprisingly engrossing cinema. Based on true events at Garfield High School in East LA in the eighties, it features Edward James Olmos as unglamorous Jaime Escalante who speaks to his kids in their own street vernacular and, challenging and cajoling cool hoodlums like Lou Diamond Phillips (*La Bamba*), demolishes the theory that school is for sissies, eventually instilling them with pride. Social deprivation, racism, crime and negative family attitudes are alluded to in passing, but collective and individual endeavour win out as Olmos's high-scorers baffle the authorities with their newly developed skills. Ramon Menendez directs tightly and engagingly throughout. **GF**

***Director** Ramon Menendez **producer** Tom Musca **exec** Lindsay Law **script** Menendez, Musca **camera** Tom Richmond **editor** Nancy Richmond **design** Milo **music** Craig Safan **cast** Edward James Olmos, Lou Diamond Phillips, Rosana De Soto, Andy Garcia*

Running time: 102 mins

US release: Warner, Mar 11, 1988

STARS AND BARS

This is *not* one of those wonderful movies Europeans sometimes make about the United States. William Boyd's script follows the misadventures of a British art dealer despatched to the American South on the trail of a rediscovered Renoir. The film's vision of America has the authenticity of something cooked up in an Oxford study, and filmed at Bray Studios. Working with a played-out plot device - the one about a valuable picture - the film's central character is mostly without interest, forcing Day-Lewis to draw on an off-the-shelf repertoire of 'embarrassed Englishman' gesticulations in order to keep the thing going. Half-hearted attempts to build in a romantic angle fall very flat. One wishes Boyd would stick to what he does best, writing novels. **JP**

***Director** Pat O'Connor **producer** Sandy Lieberson **exec** Sheldon Schrager **script** William Boyd, based on his novel **camera** Jerzy Zielinski **editor** Michael Bradsell **design** Leslie Dilley, Stuart Craig **music** Stanley Myers **cast** Daniel Day-Lewis, Harry Dean Stanton, Martha Plimpton, Matthew Cowles, Joan Cusack, Maury Chaykin, Deirdre O'Connell, Will Patton, Steven Wright, Keith David, Lauri Metcalf, Lenne Headly, Kent Broadhurst, Rockets Redglare, Spalding Gray, Celia Weston, Beatrice Winde, Bill Moore*

Running time: 94 mins

US release: Columbia, Mar 18, 1988

UK release: Columbia, Sep 16, 1988

THE STEPFATHER

With its story of a serial monogamist who wipes out his existing family whenever the children threaten to move on and break up the nuclear unit, *The Stepfather* was welcomed by some British critics as the perfect antidote to the cloying ideals of *Fatal Attraction*. Although well acted and tightly written, this low-budget thriller is undermined by some of the same flaws as the James Dearden-scripted hit: a willingness to sacrifice psychology to plot construction, *and* to ignore narrative coherence in favour of thrills. Proceedings are not helped by some clumsy symbolism and (anti-) Hitchcock allusions. **JP**

***Director** Joseph Ruben **producer** Jay Benson **script** Donald E. Westlake **camera** John Lindley **editor** George Bowers **design** James William Newport **music** Patrick Moraz **cast** Terry O'Quinn, Jill Schoelen, Shelley Hack, Charles Lanyer, Stephen Shellen, Stephen E. Miller, Robyn Stevan, Jeff Schultz, Lindsay Bourne, Anna Hagan, Gillian Barber, Blu Mankuma, Jackson Davies, Sandra Head, Gabrielle Rose, Richard Sargent, Margot Pinvidic, Rochelle Greenwood, Don S. Williams, Don MacKay, Dale Wilson, Gary Hetherington, Andrew Snider, Marie Stillin. Paul Batten, Sheila Paterson*

Running time: 98 mins

US release: New Century/Vista, Jan 21, 1987

UK release: Virgin, Jan 8, 1988

Sticky Fingers

STICKY FINGERS

Shop Till You Drop could have been the alternative title of Catlin Adams' fantasy about what happens when two women have too much money. Helen Slater and Melanie Mayron (who co-wrote with Adams) play poor musicians who can't pay the rent - until a drug-dealing friend asks them to keep a package for her. The package turns out to contain almost $1 million. They swear they won't touch it, but before you can say Bergdorf Goodman, Slater and Mayron are off on a series of gigantic shopping sprees. Carol Kane and Eileen Brennan abet their debauch and a vast cast of male baddies pursue them. If a man had made this movie, women would object. **BM**

***Director** Catlin Adams **producers/script** Adams, Melanie Mayron **camera** Gary Thieltges **editor** Bob Reitano **design** Jessica Scott-Justice **music** Gary Chang **cast** Helen Slater, Melanie Mayron, Danitra Vance, Eileen Brennan, Carol Kane, Loretta Devinephen McHattie, Christopher Guest, Gwen Welles, Shirley Stoler*

Running time: 97 mins

US release: Spectrafilm, May 6, 1988

STORMY MONDAY

Wrong day of the week for this atmospheric but implausible *Long Good Friday* wannabe, set in T. Dan Smith's Newcastle. Visiting developer Tommy Lee Jones plays another heavy in his *Big Town* mould, and Melanie Griffith is his moll. The tough but tender hero is Sean Bean, while the club owner, usually a cameo, is the more prominently displayed Sting, wielding a double bass and hosting some visiting Polish jazz artistes. The town is dolled up with Reagan posters, American flags and a giant Pepsi bottle, but Mike Figgis didn't give as much thought to the movie's plot as to its set design. **BM**

***Director/script/music** Mike Figgis **producer** Nigel Stafford-Clark **camera** Roger Deakins **editor** David Martin **design** Andrew McAlpine **cast** Melanie Griffith, Tommy Lee Jones, Sting, Sean Bean, James Cosmo, Mark Long, Brian Lewis, Derek Hoxby, Heathcote Williams, Prunella Gee, Guy Manning, Alison Steadman, Al Matthews, Caroline Hutchison, Fiona Sloman*

Running time: 93 mins

US release: Atlantic, Apr 22, 1988

SUMMER SCHOOL
'I ain't no English teacher,' says Mark Harmon as he's dragooned into supervising a classroom of remedial learners, and this comedy ain't got no jokes. Carl Reiner's film is an endless montage of classroom skits with an uplifting ending tacked on. Harmon's little charges come out of a scriptwriting exercise book: a big mean-looking black kid who turns out to get the highest grade, two twerps obsessed with *The Texas Chainsaw Massacre*, a girl whose baby starts to arrive during the exam, a sleepyhead who turns out to moonlight as a male stripper, etc. Kirstie Alley plays the obligatory part of the nice history teacher. **BM**
Director *Carl Reiner* ***producers*** *George Shapiro, Howard West* ***exec*** *Marc Trabulus* ***script*** *Jeff Franklin* ***camera*** *David M. Walsh* ***editor*** *Bud Molin* ***design*** *David L. Snyder* ***music*** *Danny Elfman* ***cast*** *Mark Harmon, Kirstie Alley, Robin Thomas, Patrick Laborteaux, Courtney Thorne-Smith, Dean Cameron, Gary Riley, Kelly Minter*
Running time: 98 mins
US release: Paramount, Jul 22, 1987

SUNSET
There's no gunfighter like an old gunfighter, and James Garner as Wyatt Earp in decline is as good as any creaky actor could be in this misbegotten 'exposé' of old Hollywood. Blake Edwards twists the facts cruelly to create a story around Tom Mix (Willis) and Earp, his expert adviser, who unravel a *Chinatown*-ish scandal together in the dawn of the talkies. 'It's all true, give or take a lie or two' is the script's genial excuse for multiple anachronisms and solecisms. Malcolm McDowell does a villainous turn as the Happy Hobo, a Chaplinesque clown-turned-mogul. Some of this may have been meant to be funny. **BM**
Director/script *Blake Edwards* ***producer*** *Tony Adams* ***camera*** *Anthony B. Richmond* ***editor*** *Robert Pergament* ***design*** *Rodger Maus* ***music*** *Henry Mancini* ***cast*** *Bruce Willis, James Garner, Malcolm McDowell, Mariel Hemingway, Kathleen Quinlan, Jennifer Edwards, Patricia Hodge, Richard Bradford, M. Emmet Walsh, Joe Dallesandro, Andreas Katsulas, Dermot Mulroney*
Running time: 107 mins
US release: Tri-Star, Apr 29, 1988

Surrender

SUPERMAN IV: THE QUEST FOR PEACE
The Metropolis Daily Planet (star reporter, Clark Kent) has a new proprietor in no two minds about how to arrest its declining fortunes: go down-market and aim for some cheap sensationalism. Could this be a coded allusion to the situation of the Cannon organization, new proprietors of the celluloid Superman? At any rate, this instalment of the saga is well below par on production values and special effects; worse, the script is a tedious ragbag of stray sub-plots, with some smug platitudes about nuclear disarmament (apparently the message-mongering price of Christopher Reeve's renewed involvement) thrown in for bad measure. **TP**
Director *Sidney J. Furie* ***producers*** *Menahem Golan, Yoram Globus* ***exec*** *Michael Kagan* ***script*** *Lawrence Kohner, Mark Rosenthal* ***camera*** *Ernest Day* ***editor*** *John Shirley* ***design*** *John Graysmark* ***music*** *John Williams* ***cast*** *Christopher Reeve, Gene Hackman, Jackie Cooper, Marc McClure, Jon Cryer, Sam Wanamaker, Mark Pillow, Mariel Hemingway, Margot Kidder, Clive Mantle, Damian McLawhorn, William Hootkins, Jim Broadbent, Stanley Lebor, Don Fellows*
Running time: 89 mins
US release: Warner, Jul 24, 1987
UK release: CCW, Jul 24, 1988

SURRENDER
The best of Michael Caine's five films this year, *Surrender* is a splendid bit of piffle about how money can subvert love. Successful novelist Caine, a two-time loser in the divorce wars, is fearful of losing the rest of his shirt to another woman. Sally Field, who works in a factory producing motel paintings, is about to leave Steve Guttenberg, an egotistical lawyer. Caine and Field, concealing their circumstances, fall for each other, but when she finds out he's well off ... Field's zaniness is sometimes a bit studied, but Caine is at the top of his form as an incurable romantic. **BM**
Director/script *Jerry Belson* ***producers*** *Aaron Spelling, Alan Greisman* ***execs*** *Menahem Golan, Yoram Globus* ***camera*** *Juan Ruiz Anchia* ***editor*** *Wendy Green Bricmont* ***design*** *Lilly Kilvert* ***music*** *Michel Colombier* ***cast*** *Sally Field, Michael Caine, Steve Guttenberg, Peter Boyle, Jackie Cooper, Iman, Julie Kavner, Louise Lasser, Michael Andrews, Jerry Lazarus, Tony Borgia*
Running time: 95 mins
US release: Warner, Oct 9, 1987
UK release: CCW, Nov 13, 1987

Suspect

SUSPECT
Objection, your honour. The defence counsel is presenting herself as a harassed, hard-working public defender and she looks suspiciously like the glamorous film star Cher. Objection sustained. Credibility is the first casualty in this Washington-set conspiracy romp, in which the murder of a Justice Department clerk and the suicide of a judge lead to revelations of corruption in high places. It all tastes like Watergate warmed-over and Peter Yates' direction amplifies rather than moderates the creakings of the plot. But Cher and Dennis Quaid do their best, and their best is quite a bit: she as the *ersatz* Ms Perry Mason, he as a truant juror helping out with the sleuthing. **HK**

***Director** Peter Yates **producer** Daniel A. Sherkow **exec** John Veitch **script** Eric Roth **camera** Billy Williams **editor** Ray Lovejoy **design** Stuart Wurtzel **music** Michael Kamen **cast** Cher, Dennis Quaid, Liam Neeson, John Mahoney, Joe Mantegna, Philip Bosco, E. Katherine Kerr, Fred Melamed, Michael Beach*
Running time: 121 mins
US release: Tri-Star, Oct 23, 1987
UK release: Columbia, Jun 3, 1988

SWAN SONG

The story of a Cantonese composer whose work is denounced during the Cultural Revolution and is after his death 'rehabilitated' by being transformed into western pop idiom, *Swan Song* is a work of evident sincerity as well as bravery. Yet, for all the intrinsic interest and good intentions, the eyelids droop at the manner of the story's telling, which remains vague and rambling in a way that seems only partly ascribable to the difficulty for a western viewer in adjusting to a different set of behavioural codes. **TP**
***Director** Zhang Zeming **producer** Hu Jiaqiang **script** Zeming, based on the short story by Kong Jiesheng **camera** Meng Qingpeng, Zheng Kangzhen **editor** Qiu Keping, Yan Xiuying **design** Zhang Jingwen, Pen Jun **music** Zhou Xiaoyuan **cast** Kong Xianzhu, Chen Rui, Mo Shaoying, Liang Yujin, Lui Qianyi, Wang Xuan, Luo Ling, Feng Diquing, Li Jianjun, Liang Shaosheng, Ouyang Fenren, Wang Weibo*
Running time: 100 mins
UK release: ICA Projects, May 20, 1988

SWIMMING TO CAMBODIA

On that thorny ground of filmed theatre, Jonathan Demme's concise record of Spalding Gray's one-man show triumphs by its director's sure touch. Gray speaks with marvellous passion and wit about his experiences working on *The Killing Fields* (clips are obligingly provided for some hilarious illustration) as well as delivering reflections on politics at home and in South East Asia. Demme supplies subtle camera movements and lighting as well as an inventive soundtrack by Laurie Anderson. **DT**
***Director** Jonathan Demme **producer** R. A. Shafransky **execs** Lewis Allen, Peter Newman **script** Spalding Gray **camera** John Bailey **editor** Carol Littleton **design** Sandy McLeod **music** Laurie Anderson **cast** Spalding Gray, Sam Waterston, Ira Wheeler*
Running time: 87 mins
US release: Cinecom, Mar 13, 1987
UK release: Mainline, Aug 21, 1987

SWITCHING CHANNELS

The Front Page was remade just 14 years ago. Here Ted Kotcheff takes another run at *His Girl Friday.* The old Hecht-MacArthur vehicle still draws laughs, but Burt Reynolds and Kathleen Turner are no Cary Grant and Rosalind Russell. The setting this time is a TV news network, which adds some razzle-dazzle video but subtracts plausibility. A Xerox machine supplants the old roll-top desk, and the condemned man's girlfriend is now his lawyer. As the wily editor who will do anything to keep his top reporter, Reynolds is less comatose than in other recent roles. Turner, believable as a reporter, lacks Russell's sassiness. Christopher Reeve is a bright spot as the blond bombshell Turner wants to marry. **BM**
***Director** Ted Kotcheff **producer** Martin Ransohoff **exec** Don Carmody **script** Jonathan Reynolds, based on the play* The Front Page *by Ben Hecht, Charles MacArthur **camera** François Protat **editor** Thom Noble **design** Anne Pritchard **music** Michel Legrand **cast** Kathleen Turner, Burt Reynolds, Christopher Reeve, Ned Beatty, Henry Gibson, George Newbern, Al Waxman, Ken James, Barry Flatman, Ted Simonett, Anthony Sherwood, Joe Silver, Charles Kimbrough*
Running time: 105 mins
US release: Tri-Star, Mar 4, 1988

Swimming to Cambodia

·T·T·T·T·T·T·T·T·T·T·T·T·

TAFFIN

Brosnan plays a freelance debt collector who pits himself against property developers determined to construct a chemical plant on the local athletic field.

Director *Francis Megahy* ***producer*** *Peter Shaw* ***exec*** *Allan Scott* ***script*** *David Ambrose, based on Lyndon Mallet's book* ***camera*** *Paul Beeson* ***editor*** *Peter Tanner* ***design*** *William Alexander* ***music*** *Stanley Myers, Hans Zimmer* ***cast*** *Pierce Brosnan, Ray McAnally, Alison Doody, Jeremy Child, Dearbhla Molloy, Jim Bartley, Alan Stanford, Gerald McSorley, Patrick Bergin, Britta Smith*
Running time: 96 mins
US release: MGM, Feb 26, 1988

TAKE IT EASY

(American Anthem in US)

Ex-Olympic medallist Mitch Gaylord débuts in this youth-oriented story of one man's struggle against personal conflicts. Mitch finds consolation and encouragement in prospective girlfriend Janet Jones, a beautiful and talented gymnast who wonders whether she can ever love a boy with a different hair colour. This testament to how endurance and hard work can triumph over adversity culminates in a series of impeccably choreographed gymnastics scenes. The set-pieces suggest that director Albert Magnoli (*Purple Rain*) is just yearning to become Adrian Lyne when he grows up. **MN**

Director *Albert Magnoli* ***producers*** *Robert Schaffel, Doug Chapin* ***exec*** *Freddie Fields* ***script*** *Evan Archerd, Jeff Benhamin* ***camera*** *Donald E. Thorin* ***editor*** *James Oliver* ***design*** *Ward Preston* ***music*** *Alan Silvestri* ***cast*** *Mitch Gaylord, Janet Jones, Michell Phillips, John Aprea, Michael Pataki, Stacy Maloney, Maria Anz, R. J. Williams, Peter Tramm, Patrice Donnelly, Jenny Ester, Megan Marsden, Tiny Wells, Dick McGarvin, Andrew White*
Running time: 101 mins
US release: Columbia, Jun 25, 1986
UK release: UKFD, Jul 17, 1987

TAMPOPO

Film of the Year

Director/script *Juzo Itami* ***producers*** *Itami, Yasushi Tamaoki, Seigo Hosogoe* ***camera*** *Masaki Tamura* ***editor*** *Akira Suzuki* ***design*** *Takeo Kimura* ***music*** *Kunihiko Murai* ***cast*** *Tsutomu Yamazaki, Nobuko Miyamoto, Koji Yakusho, Ken Watanabe, Rikiya Yasuoka, Kinzo Sakura, Manpei Ikeuchi, Yoshi Kato, Shuji Otaki, Fukumi Kuroda, Setsuko Shinoi, Yoriko Doguchi, Masahiko Tsugawa*
Running time: 114 mins
US release: New Yorker, May 27, 1987
UK release: Electric, May 6, 1988

TEEN WOLF TOO

A lame exercise lacking even the dubious appeal of Michael J. Fox as the aspirant lupine of the title. In a retelling of the original storyline, Jason Bateman indulges in the usual morass of comic collegiate situations of sub-*Porkies* banality. Christopher Leitch replaces the light pacing he brought to TV's *Moonlighting* with one-dimensional sitcom-style humour. **MN**

Director *Christopher Leitch* ***producer*** *Kent Bateman* ***execs*** *Thomas Coleman, Michael Rosenblatt* ***script*** *R. Timothy Kring from story by Joseph Loeb III, Matthew Weisman* ***camera*** *Jules Brenner* ***editors*** *Steven Polivka, Kim Secrist, Harvey Rosenstock, Raja Gosnell* ***design*** *Peg McClellan* ***music*** *Mark Goldenberg* ***cast*** *Jason Bateman, Kim Darby, John Astin, Paul Sand, James Hampton, Mark Holton, Estee Chandler, Robert Neary, Stuart Fratkin, Beth Ann Miller, Rachel Sharp, David Burton, William H. Burton, Kathleen Freeman, Eric Matthew*
Running time: 94 mins
US release: Atlantic, Nov 20, 1987
UK release: Entertainment, Feb 12, 1988

THE TELEPHONE

Whoopi Goldberg's (virtually) one-woman show is a mirthless rehearsal of all the bad dirty jokes that writers Harry Nilsson and Terry Southern could think up on an off day. Goldberg plays a principled but impecunious actress who holes up in her flat with an owl and a goldfish. Threatened with disconnection by a phone company that doesn't recognize the purity of her art, she over-uses the telephone to schmooze with her friends and hector random victims in badly assumed accents. When *is* this woman going to make a good film? **BM**

Director *Rip Torn* ***producers*** *Robert Katz, Moctesuma Esparza* ***script*** *Harry Nilsson, Terry Southern* ***camera*** *David Claessen* ***editor*** *Sanda Adair* ***design*** *David Myers* ***music*** *Christopher Young* ***cast*** *Whoopi Goldberg, Severn Darden, Amy Wright, Elliott Gould, John Heard*
Running time: 82 mins
US release: New World, Jan 22, 1988

Terminus

TERMINUS

Directed by one of France's top cinematographers, this sci-fi road pic with a glitzy cast was not well received. Plot centres on a futuristic international sport, described by one reviewer as 'somewhere between American football and European motor rallying', which is controlled by a mad scientist involved in illegal foetus traffic. Film was cut for UK release, in a seemingly misguided attempt to add pace by subtracting philosophical musings and some exposition.

Director *Pierre-William Glenn* ***prod/exec*** *Anne François* ***script*** *Glenn, Patrice Duvic, based on an original idea by Alain Gillot* ***camera*** *Jean-Claude Vicquery* ***editor*** *Thierry Derocles* ***music*** *David Cunningham* ***cast*** *Johnny Hallyday, Karen Allen, Jürgen Prochnow, Gabriel Damon, Julie Glenn, Dieter Schidor, Janos Kulka, Dominique Valera, Jean-Luc Montama, Ray Montama, Bruno Ciarrochi, David Jalil, André Nocquet*
Running time: 83 mins
(110 mins in original version)
US release: Hemdale, Dec 25, 1987
UK release: Fox, Feb 5, 1988

TAMPOPO

The idea for *Tampopo* first came to Juzo Itami while he was sitting at the counter of a Tokyo noodle joint. In front of him the chef was cutting small onions into slices. 'It was so exciting; this small knife sinking into the soft, white scallion and making little tapping sounds against the Chinese chopping-board. I though, ah, we can make a very good movie out of that.' And so they did. A *pièce de résistance*, if you like.

Food gets a raw deal on the big screen compared to such cinematic staples as the Sex Scene and the Car Chase. Yet it is a vital constituent of our everyday lives: *everyone* eats, while not everybody has an active libido or a driving licence. Great Foodie Films of Our Time are conspicuous by their absence. Everyone remembers the finger-lickin' chicken-legs in *Tom Jones*, or the mammary-shaped blancmange moulds in *La Grande bouffe*, or the haunch of meat which is so lovingly carved by *Le Boucher*. But these are exceptions. In most movies, food is merely a fact of life to be mentioned in passing: a throwaway custard-pie gag, or a plateful of spaghetti to set the scene for another Mafia hit.

And yet food is such photogenic stuff it might almost have been invented with cinema in mind. Think of it up there, projected larger than life in mouth-watering Technicolor and with an accompanying Dolby soundtrack of sizzles and slurps. The Scratch 'n' Sniff card is redundant here. The imagination can easily tease the olfactories into filling the gaps left by sight and sound. Food in all its forms, from cultivation and preparation to final table presentation, offers a full menu of possibilities to the film-maker. But, time and again, Film Foodies are left with a food-free spectacle. Dining, you suspect, is a dirty word in the cinema, something in which the characters may indulge once they're safely out of frame.

The recent popular success of *Tampopo* and *Babette's Feast* suggests the possibility of an upsurge of interest in the gastronomic genre. But, while opportunistic Manhattan eateries did a roaring trade in offering Babette's *cordon bleu* recipes to the post-cinema crowd, one has yet to learn of enterprising oriental restaurateurs capitalizing on Itami's film to plug their noodle soups. It is the quest for the perfect *ramen* - Chinese noodles in pork broth - which provides *Tampopo* with its basic story. For the Japanese, *ramen* is very much a fast food, to be served up from the hip and guzzled on the run, but it is also one of those deceptively simple dishes which are tricky to get just right.

Tampopo (Japanese for 'dandelion') is the name of the youngish widow who runs a third-rate noodle joint in one of Tokyo's downtown areas. She is sweet-natured, attractive, but not impossibly so, and she is played by the director's wife and favourite leading lady, Nobuko Miyamoto. Into her life comes Goro, a cowboy-hatted truck-driver. He compliments her on her pickles, but is forced to admit that her noodles, though they have sincerity, lack guts. To put it bluntly, her noodles *suck*.

With no discernible motive other than that arising from a sense of detached aestheticism, he sets out to transform her into the best *ramen* chef in town. With his trusty sidekick Gun, he enlists the help of various other fellow travellers on the byways of life: a gourmet vagrant, a chauffeur who doubles as a chef, and a belligerent admirer of Tampopo who fisticuffs his way into Goro's friendship before agreeing to rejig the noodle shop's interior décor. Itami has called his film a '*ramen* Western', and the central storyline does indeed seem to be a curious combination of *Shane*, *Rio Bravo* and *The Seven Samurai*: cowboy hero rides into town, licks local problems and rides off again into the sunset.

But that's not all. Around this *entrée* Itami has woven a series of tasty little appetizers and snacks: incidental anecdotes and digressionary mini-fables which punctuate the film by illustrating the foibles of a food-obsessed society. The set-up is reminiscent of Buñuel's *Le Fantôme de la liberté*, or maybe of certain episodes of *Monty Python's Flying Circus*. At intervals, the camera simply drifts away from the main characters to follow a man running down the street, or a waiter trundling a food-laden trolley along a hotel corridor, or a group of businessmen preparing to enter a restaurant.

There is, it is said, an American company which has developed rustle-free packaging, but, if so, this marvellous invention has yet to filter through to our fleapits. Itami, like all right-minded cinephiles, says he *hates* people who make a lot of noise during films. The dandified *yakuza*, a recurring character in *Tampopo*, enters with a direct address to the audience, warning them not to rustle candy wrappings (he also throws in a timely threat to the owners of digital watches which bleep).

Later, the same gangster can be seen holed up in a hotel suite with his moll. The couple proceeds to demonstrate one of Itami's central theses, that sex and food are inextricably linked. He seasons her nipples with salt and lemon, and traps wriggling shrimps on her torso. Ensconced in a private world of gourmet sex, the mess-mates liven up a private bout of French kissing by slipping an unbroken egg yolk from mouth to mouth: a sort of X-rated variation on that old pass-the-orange party game. When she reaches orgasm, the yolk breaks and trickles down her chin: a viable Safe Sex alternative, perhaps, to more conventional love-making processes utilizing ovum and orifice. This is not just erotic: it is funny. Film-makers in the West tend to forget that sex is not necessarily a serious business.

The film ends with a shot of a mother suckling her baby. 'Food and sex are very related,' Itami has affirmed in an interview. 'By suckling the breast of his mother, the baby is taking nourishment and, at the same time, love. We start life like that, and afterwards the two things are separated, but still there are deep connections. When boy meets girl, they go to dine in a restaurant before making love.' One should also note that Goro doesn't just drive any old truck. He drives a *milk* truck.

Tampopo may be a very sexy film, but Rude Food is only one of Itami's ingredients. The art and practice of eating, as an integral part of the human experience, offer the opportunity for poking fun at every sort of attitude and affectation. Social differences are magnified at the meal-table. The preparation of a plate of chow can reflect and affect the balance of a relationship. There is foodie pretentiousness in the segment where an elderly *sensei* urges a young acolyte to take a slice of pork in his chopsticks, tap it on the side of the bowl and 'appreciate its *gestalt*.' There is accomplished snobbism, when an overdressed matron instructs her young female charges in the art of eating spaghetti without a sound, only to be shown a nearby *gaijin* who hoovers up his pasta with noisy relish. (Incidentally, though *Tampopo*'s appeal is far from being parochial, occidental audiences should be reminded that, in Japan, it is considered *polite* to eat *ramen* with a lot of slurping sound effects.)

There is foodie delinquency when an old lady sneaks into a supermarket to squeeze the peaches and prod the soft cheeses. There is loss of face, as a table of businessmen is shamed by the gauche underling who proves himself the only one able to find his way around the French menu. There is social conditioning: a dying woman clings to life just long enough to cook a last meal for her husband and children. The *yakuza* is finally gunned down in the street, and in his fading breath tells his moll of one last culinary treat they will now never be able to share: the intestines of a freshly-slaughtered wild boar, stuffed with yam. It is somehow apt that the dying man appears to be covered, not in blood, but with tomato ketchup.

There is also a feast of film references for movie buffs, with a touch of *Death in Venice*, drummed home by the Mahler soundtrack, when the white-suited gangster reminisces about his seashore encounter with the oysters of a sensual fisher-girl. There is a nod towards silent comedy when a Chaplinesque tramp leads Tampopo's young son into a restaurant kitchen and, with consummate cheeky timing, whips up a rice omelette under the very nose of the prowling night-watchman. Then there are echoes of the training sessions from kung-fu movies: Tampopo is put through her paces in kitchen management, lifting vats and ladling broth, while task-master Goro stands by with a stop-watch.

In the long run, however, all foodstuffs boil down to their lowest common denominator: the fulfilment of a physical need. The sights, the sounds, the smells are all calculated to get the gastric juices flowing, to set the alimentary system in action and thus to ensure survival of the human animal. *Tampopo*, for all its philosophical playfulness, its satire and its entertainment value, ends up making you very, *very* hungry. After repeated shots of glistening lumps of pork nestling in big close-up against crisp slices of steaming leek, the film-goer can only run salivating into the night, panting desperately for a Japanese restaurant. The tastebuds have been tickled: now the needs must be fulfilled. *Itadakimasu*, as they say at the Japanese dinner-table.

ANNE BILLSON

Testimony

TESTIMONY

Everything you always wanted to know about Shostakovich and were afraid you'd end up learning from Ken Russell. Not that director Tony Palmer doesn't come on like our Ken. This epic dances through history in wide screen and black-and-white, with only a nude Glenda Jackson missing from the tale of persecuted musical genius (Kingsley) vs. the bastards-in-power (Terence Rigby as Stalin). Homages are rife (Wellesian *chiaroscuro*, bits of Eisenstein); and David Rudkin's script fluctuates between bio-pic banality ('It's the music that matters, not me') and quotes from the unauthenticated Shostakovich diaries. But it all goes at a fair lick, and Kingsley as Shostakovitch is at least preferable to Cornel Wilde as Chopin. **HK**

Director/producer/editor/design *Tony Palmer* ***execs*** *Grahame Jennings, Michael Hendry, Michael Kustow* ***script*** *David Rudkin, Palmer, based on* Memoirs of Dmitri Shostakovich *as edited by Soloman Volkov* ***camera*** *Nic Knowland* ***cast*** *Ben Kingsley, Magdalen Asquith, Mark Asquith, Terence Rigby, Ronald Pickup, John Shrapnel, Robert Reynolds*

Running time: 157 mins

UK release: Enterprise, May 13, 1988

THREE MEN AND A BABY

Turkey of the Year

Director *Leonard Nimoy* ***producers*** *Ted Field, Robert W. Cort* ***exec*** *Jean François Lepetit* ***script*** *James Orr, Jim Cruickshank, based on* Trois hommes et un couffin *by Coline Serreau* ***camera*** *Adam Greenberg* ***editor*** *Michael A. Stevenson* ***design*** *Peter Larkin* ***music*** *Marvin Hamlisch* ***cast*** *Tom Selleck, Steve Guttenberg, Ted Danson, Nancy Travis, Margaret Colin, Celeste Holm, Philip Bosco, Paul Guilfoyle, Derek de Lint*

Running time: 102 mins

US release: BV, Nov 25, 1987

UK release: Warner, Apr 1, 1988

THREE MEN AND A BABY

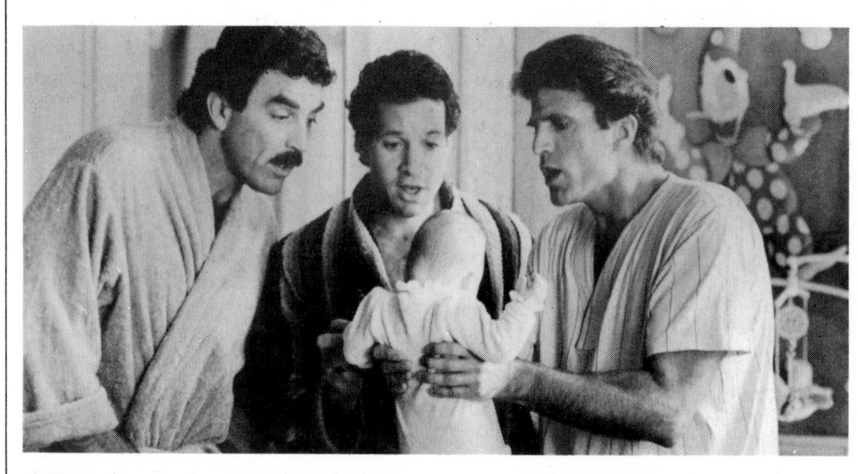

The two-page ad in *Variety* was as impressive as its numbers were questionable. *Three Men and a Baby* was scoring big around the world. Early days yet, but adding to the $160 million US take, the re-mould had earned a total of $17 million in Australia, Italy, Spain, Sweden, Britain, Norway, New Zealand, Finland and Denmark.

Not, you notice, a word about France. Well, of course not. Despite a poster and TV blitz (with six broadcast channels available, all films suffer overkill in France these days), the version according to Disney greedily opened too soon after the French original had smashed every TV ratings record at Christmas. Welcome, then, to a first. A turkey in nappies.

Part of Disney's colossal financial turnaround since Michael Eisner, The Jolly Greenback Giant, took over Uncle Walt's paint shop, has been its success in re-treading French hits. As Hollywood tries to invest in proven success (hence, all those sequels) instead of originality, all the studios have tried making Big Macs out of *steak frites*. Only the Disney chef has succeeded.

While Gene Wilder floundered by turning the ensemble comedy, *Pardon mon affaire*, into a one-man-show about *The Lady in Red*, Disney, or rather its feisty adolescent son Touchstone quietly set up a winner with *Down and Out in Beverly Hills* - neatly modernizing Jean Renoir.

Re-treads apart, the French industry has a love-hate relationship with Hollywood. The row over cultural imperialism fires annually during the all-American festival at Deauville (as if Hollywood needed a festival to launch its movies). Yet French films continue to flop as the public prefers to queue for the latest US blockbuster and French directors (I'd say producers but that's an almost non-existent species in France) keep promising French films *à l'americain*. They don't work, either. And, although curious, nobody bothers much with Hollywooden remakes. Certainly not this one.

As my French is no better than that of British film critic Philip French, I too was confused about the original title, *Trois hommes et un couffin*. We weren't alone in thinking: coffin. Only difference, we got our genres crossed. He expected a *policier*. I avoided the press screenings of ... not another French horror film!

It opened quietly, hype was nil, reviews were good - '*drôle et attendrissante*.' Within a day, *la bouche à l'oreille* had spread around Paris. Reminiscent of the rapid word of mouth about *Bonnie and Clyde* in London, circa 1968 (when I heard two women praising it on the bus home from the press show. That's fast!). The queues agreed with *Paris Match* - there *was* champagne in this baby's bottle. The fizz made it the movie of 1985 - 135,614 tickets sold in the first week, a million in a month, final total: 14,000,000!

I could see why. With her fourth feature, actress-writer Coline Serreau created a wholly sensitive comedy of immense charm, humour, observation and *beaucoup de tendresse*. Three *mecs* who share a rambling Paris apartment find a baby in a cradle (oh, that's a *couffin!*) at their front door and do their best to cope with it, learning much about themselves, life, love and all that jazz. Simple plot. Beautifully played, shot, timed and mounted.

Coline Serreau also had impeccable timing off-screen. She turned up at the César awards, direct from a play she was appearing in, at the precise moment she won Best Film. She also collected Best Script, and much Hollywood interest from studios studying the French returns.

Before it opened Stateside in April 1986, Michael Eisner secured remake rights by agreeing *l'auteur* could direct. Weeks before shooting, Serreau showed her timing again. She quit - remaining on the credits as original author and the 'production consultant' no one seemed to have conferred with. She's refused to explain her departure, although it must be close to the 'never-again' experience with movie moguls and money-machos of that previous Oscar-nominated French director, Diane Kurys.

Officially, Serreau left due to ill health. If so, it must have been brought on by reading the final script from James Orr and Jim Cruickshank (who previously wrote *Tough Guys*). They had thrown the baby out and kept the bath water. Plus jokes about 'doodling' - a polite term for what their script was full of. Oddly, for a father of three lads, Eisner then muddled his Spocks and invited Leonard Nimoy to direct the baby trek. A company choice; financial not artistic. Nimoy is to comedy what Ingmar Bergman is to Westerns.

Serreau selected her *trois hommes* from the lower divisions of French screen actors. André Dussollier is best known as one of the Alain Resnais repertory quartet for three successive features. Michel Boujenah was the latest comedy smash on stage, whose flirtation with movies secured him a César. Roland Giraud, who stole the movie with his rapid-fire indignation - particularly at the strident nanny he booted out - only made the final cut when Jean-Claude Brialy was deemed too old to be living with the other two!

Disney also cast cheaply, as usual; more from TV than (as Robin Williams says) the exit door of the Betty Ford Clinic. Tom Selleck needed a hit if he ever hoped to leave *Magnum*'s islands. Since too few saw his great Joe Wambaugh movie, *The Onion Field*, Ted Danson was known only from *Cheers*. (As the baby's father, he was made an actor instead of an airline steward, in a botched switch inspired by AIDS.) And although he has made more films than his *Diner* cohorts, Steve Guttenberg has been confined by his *Police Academy* role. Three men in search of a cinema image.

The Frenchmen were credible: the American guys are unbelievable. Hollywood did more than anglicize Pierre, Michel and Jacques. It turned them into types. Up-market, rich, plastic. They seemed to live in a disco and mentioned money in almost every other breath. No way they'd rest egos (or libidos) to tend a leaking baby. They'd simply hire the fleet of nurses they'd obviously screwed their way through.

Four minutes shorter, the new film is no potty-by-potty remake. Some of the best scenes have been axed (no strident nanny) or shortened. What's left is lazily acted, dimly directed as, to quote the Disnoid's publicists, Nimoy brought 'integrity and freshness to the material.' The tiny McGuffin about the guys' expected package - not the baby as they presume but drugs - is blown up into a car chase. Schubert is replaced by Marvin Hamlisch. The baby is younger - for reasons unknown. Except, if kids can drive cars to school in America, I suppose a baby on the verge of walking - she did in the final scene of the original - is considered almost a teenager.

One scene that still worked - slightly yuckier in Hollywood - had the trio crooning the kid to sleep. Still not enough feeling to save the film. Out for big bucks, the cultural imperialists dived into surgery, removed the film's heart, replacing adroit comedy with leaden farce.

And Coline Serreau? She's been biding her time before her next movie, doing commercials. One had two women discussing kitchen furniture. French headline about that shot was, of course: *Trois femmes et un coup fin.*

TONY CRAWLEY

THREE O'CLOCK HIGH

Life at an all-American southern California high school is disrupted by arrival of a legendary bully. He picks a fight with the film's hero (Siemaszko), who's recently been appointed student store manager. The imminence of their combat drives Siemaszko into paroxysms of terror.

Director *Phil Joanou* ***producer*** *David E. Vogel* ***execs*** *Aaron Spelling, Alan Greisman* ***script*** *Richard Christian Matheson, Thomas Szollosi* ***camera*** *Barry Sonnenfeld* ***editor*** *Joe Ann Fogle* ***design*** *Bill Matthews, Tom Bugenhaven* ***music*** *Tangerine Dream* ***cast*** *Casey Siemaszko, Anne Ryan, Stacey Glick, Jonathan Wise, Richard Tyson, Jeffrey Tambor, Liza Morrow, Phillip Baker Hall, John P. Ryan*

Running time: 97 mins

US release: Universal, Oct 9, 1987

THROW MOMMA FROM THE TRAIN

Danny DeVito's directing début is a mock-Hitchcock comedy that proves surprisingly thoughtful. Billy Crystal is a blocked writer who supports himself teaching cretins like DeVito. DeVito mistakes Crystal's pedagogy for incitement to a crime: he'll kill Crystal's hated wife if Crystal will kill DeVito's domineering mother. But DeVito doesn't tell Crystal this until after Crystal's wife goes missing and the cops move in. Then the question of obeying the title's imperative arises. Director DeVito lampoons such Hitchcockian mannerisms as the spinning overhead shot and the audible heartbeat, and writer Stu Silver engages in a lot of wordplay. **BM**

Director *Danny DeVito* ***producer*** *Larry Brezner* ***exec*** *Arne L. Schmidt* ***script*** *Stu Silver* ***camera*** *Barry Sonnenfeld* ***editor*** *Michael Jablow* ***design*** *Ida Random* ***music*** *David Newman* ***cast*** *DeVito, Billy Crystal, Kim Greist, Anne Ramsey, Kate Mulgrew, Branford Marsalis, Rob Reiner, Bruce Kirby, Oprah Winfrey, Olivia Brown, Philip Perlman, Stu Silver, J. Alan Thomas, Randall Miller, Tony Ciccone*

Running time: 88 mins

US release: Orion, Dec 11, 1987

UK release: Rank, Jun 24, 1988

Throw Momma From the Train

A TIGER'S TALE

Another implausible older-woman-goes-for-cute-teen-guy film, *A Tiger's Tale* is a botch from start to finish. Writer Peter Douglas should blame director Douglas for being hired by producer Douglas. C. Thomas Howell, a Texas vet's son who keeps a tiger yearling in a cage in the front yard, gets into Kelly Preston's blouse but finds he prefers the earthier charms of the girl's mother, Ann-Margret. Preston retaliates by pin-pricking mom's diaphragm. After an aborted visit to an abortionist, A-M is off to California, but will she take the boy along? The film isn't funny where it's supposed to be and is where it isn't. **BM**

Director/producer *Peter Douglas* ***script*** *Douglas, based on the novel* Love and Other Natural Disasters *by Allen Hannay 3d* ***camera*** *Tony Pierce-Roberts* ***editor*** *David Campling* ***design*** *Shay Austin* ***music*** *Lee Holdridge* ***cast*** *Ann-Margret, C. Thomas Howell, Charles Durning, Kelly Preston, Ann Wedgeworth, William Zabka, Tim Thomerson, Steven Kampmann, Traci Lin, Angel Tompkins, James Noble, Linda Rae Favila, Steve Farrell, David Denney, Jo Perkins*

Running time: 97 mins

US release: Atlantic, Feb 12, 1988

UK release: Entertainment, May 27, 1988

A TIME OF DESTINY

William Hurt's over-the-top performance causes the unwanted titters that ruin Gregory Nava's attempt at an old-fashioned revenge drama. Hurt is the half-psycho son of an unforgiving father. When the father dies in an accident while trying to keep his daughter from running off with Timothy Hutton, Hurt resolves to get Hutton. It's 1943 and Hutton is en route to lick Hitler, so Hurt contrives to join Hutton's unit at the front. Hutton thinks Hurt is his best buddy, but remains clueless despite the cocked-head, eyeball-rolling tip-offs that bring howls from the audience. The climax atop a bell tower is cacophonous if nothing else. **BM**

Director *Gregory Nava* ***producer/script*** *Anna Thomas* ***execs*** *Carolyn Pfeiffer, Shep Gordon* ***camera*** *James Glennon* ***editor*** *Betsy Blankett* ***design*** *Henry Bumstead* ***music*** *Ennio Morricone* ***cast*** *William Hurt, Timothy Hutton, Melissa Leo, Stockard Channing, Megan Follows, Francisco Rabal*

Running time: 118 mins

US release: Columbia, Apr 22, 1988

THE TIME TO DIE (Tiempo de Morir)

Gabriel García Marquez does not seem to adapt well to the cinema. Rosi and Guerra both failed, and, here with an original screenplay by the great author, this Columbia-Cuban co-production never takes wing. A man released from jail - for a killing he was forced into 18 years before - attempts to lead a quiet life. But he is pursued by one of the dead man's sons and forced to fight a duel all over again. While the drama echoes any number of revenge Westerns, the dull performances and variable direction never generate sufficient tension to overcome the inherent risibility of the situation. **DT**

Director *Jorge Alí Triana* ***producer/script*** *Gabriel García Marquez* ***exec*** *Gloria Zea* ***camera*** *Mario García Joya* ***editor*** *Nelson Rodríquez* ***design*** *Patricia Bonilla* ***music*** *Leo Brower, Nafer Durán* ***cast*** *Gustavo Angarita, Sebastian Ospina, Jorge Emilio Salazar, Maria Eugenia Davila, Lina Botero, Enrique Almirante, Carlos Barbosa,*

Monica Silva, Hector Rivas, Luis Chiape, Rodolfo Miravalles, Lucy Martinez, Edgardo Roman, Nelly Moreno, Patricia Bonilla, Alicia De Rojas
Running time: 98 mins
UK release: Artificial Eye, Feb 19, 1988

THE TIME TO LIVE AND THE TIME TO DIE (Tongnian Wangshi)

Majestic autobiographical film from Taiwan's Hou Xiaoxian. After the breezy calling-card of *A Summer at Grandpa's* this movie is more like an invitation to a funeral, sombrely printed and edged in black. But its matter-of-factness is stunning, and so is its stoical, unflinching eye for human detail. Mother is dying of cancer, dotty grandma wants to go back to the China of her youth, and our hero struggles with the dreams and nightmares of adolescence: sexual stirrings, school exams, gang warfare. The film's length is justified in the accumulation of observation and revelation, and in the sense of an epic compassion. **HK**
Director *Hou Xiaoxian* **producer** *Zhang Huakun, Yue Wanli* **execs** *Lin Dengfei, Xu Guoliang, Zhao Qibin* **script** *Zhu Tianwen, Xiaoxian* **camera** *Li Pingbin* **editor** *Wang Qiyang* **design** *Lin Chongwen* **music** *Wu Chuchu* **cast** *You Anshun, Tian Feng, Mei Fang, Tan Ruyun, Xiao Ai, Yan Shenghua, hou Donghong, Xin Shufen*
Running time: 137 mins
UK release: ICA Projects, Apr 8, 1988

Tough Guys Don't Dance

TIN MEN
Film of the Year

Director/script *Barry Levinson* **producer** *Mark Johnson* **camera** *Peter Sova* **editor** *Stu Linder* **design** *Peter Jamison* **music** *Fine Young Cannibals, David Steele, Andy Cox* **cast** *Richard Dreyfuss, Danny DeVito, Barbara Hershey, John Mahoney, Jackie Gayle, Stanley Brock, Seymour Cassel, Bruno Kirby, J. T. Walsh, Richard Portnow, Matt Craven, Alan Blumenfeld, Brad Sullivan, Michael Tucker*
Running time: 112 mins
US release: BV, Mar 6, 1987
UK release: UKFD, Jul 31, 1987

TOKYO POP

Carol Burnett's daughter Carrie Hamilton exhibits a winning comic sense in Fran Rubel Kuzui's romantic musical about an American singer who becomes top of the Tokyo pops. Bleach-blonded and black-jacketed, Hamilton mugs and stomps her way through her role as a stranger in a very strange land, where a rocked-up version of 'Home on the Range' can turn the fans delirious. Hamilton's love interest and musical collaborator is Yutaka Tadokoro, an actual rock star we are told. 'Sure!' seems to be the extent of Tadokoro's vocabulary, which is fine with Hamilton, who thereby finds him 'really easy to talk to'. **BM**
Director *Fran Rubel Kuzui* **producers** *Kaz Kuzui, Joel Tuber* **script** *Fran Rubel Kuzui, Lynn Grossman* **camera** *James Hayman* **editor** *Camilla Toniolo* **design** *Terumi Hosoishi* **music** *Alan Brewer* **cast** *Carrie Hamilton, Yutaka Tadokoro, Taiji Tonoyoma, Tetsuro Tamba, Masumi Harukawa, Toki Shiozawa, Hiroshi Mikami, Mike Cerveris, Gina Belafonte, Daisuke Oyama, Hiroshi Kobayashi, Hiroshi Sugita, Satoshi Kanai*
Running time: 99 mins
US release: Spectrafilm, Apr 15, 1988

TOUGH GUYS DON'T DANCE

Some storytellers need the electric hum of their own prose. Norman Mailer turns his enjoyably convoluted Cape Cod murder novel into a feebly re-imagined creation for the movies. Ryan O'Neal of the Ivy League curls is our hardboiled ex-con hero (miscasting coup of the year?) and around him the screen fills up with dames, dicks and dead bodies. Only the movie's ending achieves an air of crafted black comedy worthy of the novel: 'Land of Hope and Glory' plays on the soundtrack while O'Neal dumps the film's entire consignment of corpses, one by one, over the side of his boat. **HK**
Director *Norman Mailer* **producers** *Menahem Golan, Yoram Globus* **execs** *Francis Coppola, Tom Luddy* **script** *Norman Mailer, based on his novel* **camera** *Michael Moyer, Danny Dukovny* **editor** *Debra McDermott* **design** *Armin Ganz* **music** *Paula Erickson* **cast** *Ryan O'Neal, Isabella Rossellini, Debra Sandlund, Wings Hauser, John Bedford Lloyd, Lawrence Tierney, Penn Jillette, Frances Fisher, R. Patrick Sullivan, John Snyder, Stephan Morrow, Clarence Williams III, Kathryn Sanders, Ira Lewis, Ed Setrakian, Faith Cahn, Edward Bonetti, Joel Meyerowitz, Greg Hodal, Katrina Marshall*
Running time: 109 mins
US release: Cannon, Sep 18, 1987
UK release: Cannon, Jan 15, 1988

TIN MEN

One of the pleasures of writing about a film, book, or whatever, is what might be termed the 'jigsaw element'. This involves sorting through the text, reassembling it this way, that way, discovering how it fits together by unscrambling it and in the process finding new things in it. The better the film, the more the fun (which accounts for the fact that more words have been spilled over the likes of Renoir and Hawks than Michael Winner). And then there's the delicious problem of where to begin: the edges, the sky, the central figures ...?

I'm an edges man myself. But since *Tin Men* is such a wonderful mosaic of a film, it's probably best to touch briefly on the plot and central characters before collecting together all the edging pieces.

Richard Dreyfuss and Danny DeVito are the tin men of the title - aluminium-siding salesmen (the American equivalent of double-glazing hustlers). Dreyfuss is a big success, DeVito an also-ran. They cross paths, literally, when DeVito crashes into Dreyfuss's Cadillac. In his quest for revenge, Dreyfuss 'steals' DeVito's wife (Barbara Hershey) only to discover that the betrayed husband doesn't care. As Dreyfuss and Hershey grow together, DeVito's life falls apart. Finally, he loses his licence to sell aluminium siding when he is 'shopped' to a committee investigating home improvement scams. At the same time, Dreyfuss, now happily settled with Hershey, quits the aluminium business because he sees no future in it.

Tin Men is a 'little' film, without any of the usual hooks that support Hollywood movies. It is not a genre film with a supporting structure of suspense and anticipation. It is not an issue film, making statements about nuclear power, the war in Nicaragua or marital infidelity. Nor is it an 'adventure film' with regular set-pieces, an exercise in special effects or a youth movie with a soundtrack to sell.

Set in Baltimore in 1963, when the sixties hadn't quite begun - hence one of the great jokes of the film, a character obsessively teaching the words of Ritchie Valens' 1959 hit 'La Bamba' to anyone foolish enough to listen - one of *Tin Men*'s great strengths is its sense of time and place. Whether Baltimore in 1963 was actually like that I don't know, but it feels right (unlike the tele-series *Bonanza*, about which one of the characters, in a marvellously conceived running gag, repeatedly speculates as to whether the show offers a 'realistic depiction of the West', because no one at the ranch ever admits to being horny). The point here is not realism, but a feel for period. On one level at least, as with Levinson's *Diner*, the film is a homage to memory. But *Tin Men* is more ambitious than

the earlier film, which settled on the simple delights of presenting for our entertainment a group of characters unconsciously crossing the divide between adolescence and manhood.

One clear aim of the film is to show the camaraderie that comes from people working, talking and drinking together. Thus not only are Richard Dreyfuss and Danny DeVito given equal screen space but neither dominates the ensemble scenes in which they appear. The result is a slew of magic moments: a brief and inconsequential, but lovingly crafted, conversation about Dreyfuss's ability to dance the merengue; a waitress's bitter put-down of DeVito; another character's sudden observation at the salad counter of an eaterie that 'there must be a God,' because green things come up from the soil.

But the magic moments aren't only that, they move the narrative forward and inform it. Thus the opening, in which, after the camera has lovingly prowled over a Cadillac, the car is bought by Dreyfuss and promptly rammed into by DeVito just outside the car showroom. This not only leads to the line 'My car's got a sixteenth of a mile on the clock and it's already been hit,' but points to the end where Dreyfuss, now an ex-tin man, contemplates a future selling VW Beetles.

Similarly complex is the comic sequence in which Dreyfuss and the laconic Jack Mahoney pose as photographers from *Time* magazine taking pictures of houses 'before' and 'after' they have been improved with aluminium siding. Only too quickly the woman of the house emerges, imploring to become an 'after' rather than a 'before'. The scene serves to illustrate the kind of scams the tin men are being investigated for, and to show just how much Dreyfuss is a role player - later we will see him play a distressed widower as part of his plan to seduce Hershey.

DeVito too is a role player, but he has no control over his imagination, and no luck. His best scam is to give away so much in a deal, then leave and have his partner return to the house and say DeVito has just had a heart attack and his job is on the line - which it is - unless a new deal can be arranged; the plan works but it turns out the man is massively in debt already! DeVito is not only amoral and unlucky, he has no sense of self. He lives only for the moment. He hugely enjoys throwing his wife's clothes on the street (breaking a window in his excitement) and delights in further humiliating Dreyfuss, when, with egg still literally on Dreyfuss's face after an altercation that has led to their both being in police custody, he elaborates on how he likes his eggs done. DeVito's constant complaint, as his job slides away and his house and belongings are impounded for non-payment of tax, is 'Why are all these things happening to me?'

In contrast to DeVito, Dreyfuss not only is successful but he has a capacity for change. Thus, Hershey's presence, at first reluctantly accepted, brings about a shift in his attitude. Similarly, Mahoney's heart attack brings with it the realization that selling aluminium siding isn't the only thing in the world. Finally he's even willing to ditch the holy of holies, his Cadillac, for a future with Volkswagen.

These transformations, though they stem from the character Dreyfuss plays, are articulated through conventional Hollywood plot devices (Dreyfuss at one point even 'losing' Hershey back to DeVito in a game of pool, only to cheerfully admit, 'I'm not that honourable a guy'). Thus, the change in Hershey from bespectacled clerk to object of desire and Dreyfuss's winning of her back (after discovering she'd been a pawn in a revenge scenario, Hershey leaves Dreyfuss) require the suspension of belief that is Hollywood. But if *Tin Men* is a Hollywood film, it still reaches out in unexpected ways to engage us.

And despite being a 'little' film, a film to enjoy for itself, *Tin Men* does have a bizarre topicality. Tom Wolfe recently wrote that most contemporary politicians have the morals of aluminium siding salesmen. Imagine DeVito translated to government and the 'sleaze factor' that has bedevilled the Reagan administration is explained in one fell swoop. On screen DeVito is an amoral but amiable rogue, but ...

Levinson doesn't ram his points down our throats. Instead he does that most subtle of things, creates a convincing and minutely observed world and then invites us to judge the characters as they try to dance their way out of their problems, and to laugh at their antics at the same time.

PHIL HARDY

Under Satan's Sun

TRAVELLING NORTH

Sydney-born Leo McKern is on splendidly cantankerous form as an ex-communist civil engineer who takes his lovely 50-year-old bride (Blake) to an idyllic retirement home in North Queensland, despite the disapproval of her carping daughters. Paradise is interrupted, though, by McKern's worsening heart condition and his selfish obsession with it which threatens to wreck the marriage. Carl Schultz's faultless direction of David Williamson's adaptation from his own play gently explores the problems of late middle-age, and, alongside McKern and Blake's mature performances, Henri Szeps and Graham Kennedy excel as respectively their concerned doctor and the friendly neighbour with whom the old tyrant loves a political argument. **GF**

Director *Carl Schultz* ***producer*** *Ben Gannon* ***script*** *David Williamson* ***camera*** *Julian Penney* ***editor*** *Henry Dangar* ***design*** *Owen Paterson* ***music*** *Alan John* ***cast*** *Leo McKern, Julia Blake, Graham Kennedy, Henri Szeps, Michel Fawdon, Diane Craig, Andrea Moor, Drew Forsythe, John Gregg, Rob Steele, John Black, Roger Oakley*

Running time: 97 mins

US release: Cineplex, Feb 12, 1988

UK release: Recorded Releasing, May 13, 1988

TWO MOON JUNCTION

Replay of *Last Tango in Paris* with blonde beauty (Fenn) giving her virginity to a hunk (Tyson) instead of her fiancé (Hewitt).

Director *Zalman King* ***producer*** *Donald P. Borchers* ***execs*** *Mel Pearl, Don Levin* ***script*** *King, MacGregor Douglas* ***camera*** *Mark Plummer* ***editor*** *Marc Grossman* ***design*** *Michelle Minch* ***music*** *Jonathan Elias* ***cast*** *Sherilyn Fenn, Richard Tyson, Louise Fletcher, Kristy McNichol, Martin Hewitt, Burl Ives*

Running time: 104 mins

US release: Lorimar, Apr 29, 1988

·U·U·U·U·U·U·U·U·U·U·U·U

THE UNBEARABLE LIGHTNESS OF BEING

Film of the Year

Director *Philip Kaufman* ***producer*** *Saul Zaentz* ***exec*** *Bertil Ohlsson* ***script*** *Jean Claude Carrière, Kaufman, based on the novel by Milan Kundera* ***camera*** *Sven Nykvist* ***editors*** *Walter Murch, B. J. Sears, Vivien Hillgrove Gilliam, Stephen A. Rotter* ***design*** *Pierre Guffroy* ***music*** *Mark Adler, Ernie Fosselius* ***cast*** *Daniel Day-Lewis, Juliette Binoche, Lena Olin, Derek de Lint, Erland Josephson, Pavel Landovsky, Donald Moffat, Daniel Olbrychski, Stellan Skarsgard, Tomek Bork, Bruce Myers, Pavel Slaby, Pascale Kalensky, Jacques Ciron, Anne Lonnberg, Laszlo Szabo, Vladimir Valenta, Clovis Cornillac, Leon Lissek, Consuelo de Havilland*

Running time: 172 mins

US release: Orion, Feb 5, 1988

UK release: UIP, Apr 15, 1988

UNDER SATAN'S SUN

(Sous le soleil de Satan)

A determinedly solemn film lacking the realist vigour characteristic of other recent Pialat pictures, *Under Satan's Sun* nevertheless exerts a hypnotic power in its fractured telling of a country priest's confrontation with evil. Sandrine Bonnaire and Gérard Depardieu are convincing as lost souls struggling with inner torment. He is a cleric obsessed with the idea of holiness who meets Satan, she is woman lost on her path of evil and remorse. **JP**

Director *Maurice Pialat* ***exec*** *Claude Abeille* ***script*** *Sylvie Danton, based on the novel by Georges Bernanos* ***camera*** *Willy Kurant* ***editor*** *Yann Dedet* ***design*** *Katia Vischkof* ***music*** *Henri Dutilleux* ***cast*** *Gérard Depardieu, Sandrine Bonnaire, Maurice Pialat, Alain Artur, Yann Dedet, Brigitte Legendre, Jean-Claude Bourlat, Jean-Christophe Bouvet, Philippe Pallut, Marcel Anselin, Yvette Lavogez, Pierre D'Hoffelize*

Running time: 103 mins (98 mins in UK)

UK release: Cannon, May 6, 1988

Travelling North

THE UNBEARABLE LIGHTNESS OF BEING

'In Prague, in 1968, there lived a young doctor called Tomas.' Kicking off with an adult game of doctors and nurses, this three-hour adaptation of Milan Kundera's acclaimed novel immediately establishes the promiscuous hero of this complex saga of sex, love, fidelity and tanks. Another caption introduces the artist Sabina, a free spirit in suspenders and bowler hat who is the leading player in Tomas's *ronde* of sexual adventures. Next, the film casually shifts to the provincial spa town where Tomas meets the spiritually frustrated Tereza, a waif-like figure clutching a book, from whom he begins to learn that love and sex may mix after all, and that it is possible for him to live with a woman.

Kundera opened very differently, with his narrator reflecting on Nietzsche and the idea of eternal return. Not exactly the stuff of even middle-brow art cinema, one might think. Indeed, many deemed his tragi-comic novel, with its juggling of sex and politics, philosophy and kitsch, completely unfilmable.

After all, didn't all this obsession with lightness - independence, sexual freedom, political wariness - seem as old hat as Sabina's fetish object? But with Milos Forman unwilling to touch a Czech subject, producer Saul Zaentz turned to a director who has never made anything bound by fashion - Philip Kaufman.

Kaufman's roots lie somewhat parallel to those of the young hero's in his Kundera 'variation' (to use his own phrase), having been himself engaged in radical activities. Following his Cannes prize-winner of the early sixties, *Goldstein*, his first big studio-backed movie was a de-mythologized, literally weather-beaten look at the Jesse James legend, *The Great Northfield Minnesota Raid*, in 1972. Participation in the scripts of *The Outlaw Josey Wales* and *Raiders of the Lost Ark* followed, and then another three-hour movie, *The Right Stuff*, in 1983. The latter was promoted as a patriotic hymn to the first US astronauts, but what appeared on the screen was an often wickedly ironic demonstration of how human these media puppets were, with far more heroic presence given to their unsung progenitor Chuck Yeager. The result was a commercial disappointment.

Kaufman hardly made things easy for himself when he chose to adapt Kundera. As with *The Right Stuff*, what mattered to him was capturing an *essence* on screen. And he sensed that a cinema audience would respond most directly to the central love story. Out went any idea of Resnais-like fragmentation, multiple flashbacks or an interpretative voice-over. As he told Kundera himself, 'We're going to lose the most interesting character - the narrator.' With his chosen co-scenarist Jean-Claude Carrière, veteran of those final Buñuel narratives that trailed off in all directions, they transformed an elliptical novel into a direct, chronological sequence of scenes that were virtually all about *love*, its expression and its repression. When they sought the blessing of the Paris-based émigré author, a former teacher of screen-writing, he told them firmly to 'eliminate'.

Aside from removing Tomas's family, so making him a younger and more obviously sympathetic philanderer, the only character substantially reduced in the process of adaptation is the Swiss academic Franz. When the Russian tanks arrive in Prague, the first of the threesome to leave for Geneva is Sabina. There she meets Franz. Being a married man, the impossibility of any commitment on his part allows Sabina to sustain the 'lightness' of her life. Franz, in Kaufman's film, only really exists as a foil to Sabina, and as a screenwriter's convenient parallel to the embattled fidelity between Tereza and Tomas. And this is a film replete with mirror images, the splintered glassworks of Sabina's Swiss period being the most direct metaphor around.

On first viewing, I felt like some other critics

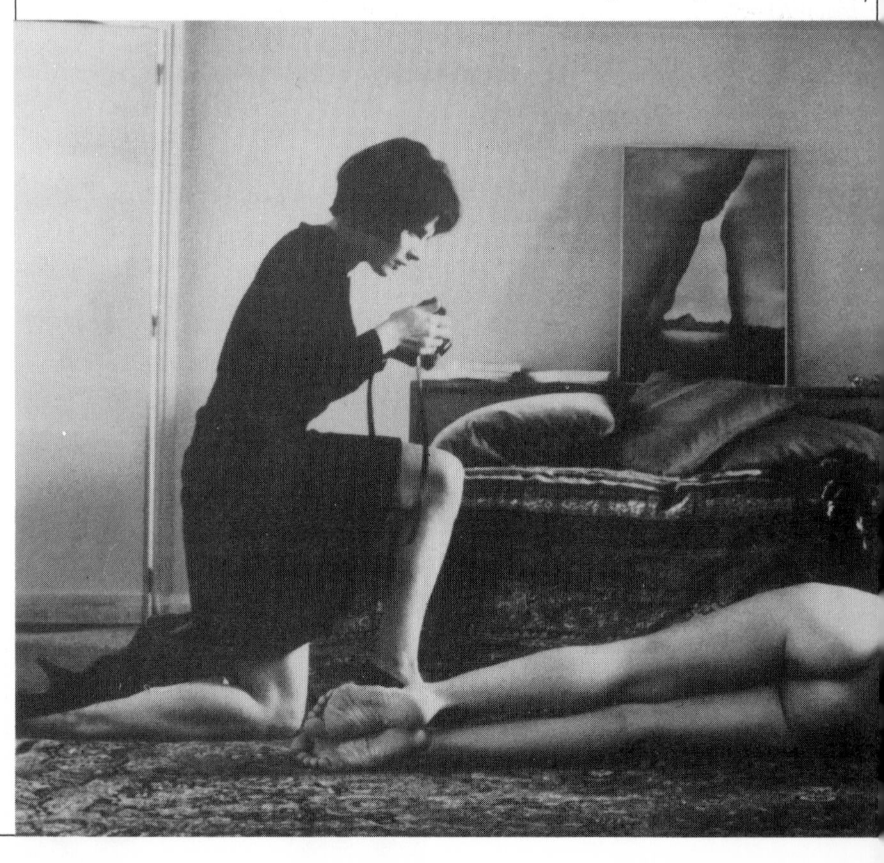

that, for all the persuasively choreographed erotic scenes and the breathtaking staging of the Russian invasion (a chilling assembly of newsreel and reconstruction, and the only truly *obscene* act on view), it was all something of a pale shadow of Kundera. But a second look revealed Kaufman's achievement in secure pacing, assured wit and a telling placing of characters adrift in an absurd political machinery. Kaufman clearly adores his central trio and the contradictions they inhabit. By his own confession, 'I fight for lightness, but I sometimes find myself pursuing heaviness.'

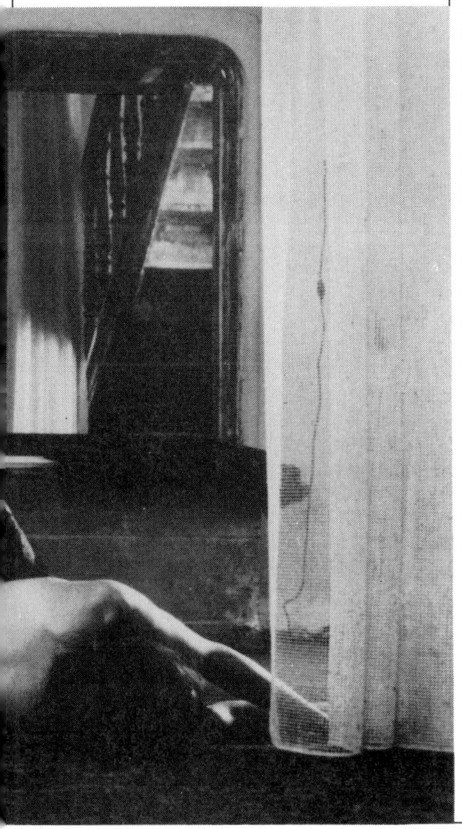

As for those erotic scenes, Kaufman has made them for once really tell us about the characters and their relationships. The first encounter between Tomas and Tereza - a childlike, naughty doctor-patient game - is shown as a moment of high sexual abandon. When Tomas returns to Tereza in Prague, after life together in Geneva fails, they let fly at each other with an even greater intensity. Tereza's shrieks of joy tell us that this is more than habitual sex, that they are deeply in love. When Sabina, who becomes close to Tereza at Tomas's instigation, participates in a nude photography session with her, the women's attitudes to their bodies show us the tensions between them and prepare their eventual complicity.

Of course much credit is due to Kaufman's shrewd casting (and his habitual avoidance of star names). Daniel Day Lewis's fox-like demeanour, confidence and sense of inner vulnerability fulfil the promise shown in his diverse supporting roles. Both the women are strong presences. Lena Olin, a Bergman protégée, has exactly the ripe physicality that makes Sabina seductive and strong, while her open, vibrant face quickly reveals a deep emotional core. Juliette Binoche, previously a hysterial ingénue in André Téchiné's *Rendezvous* and an object of sustained adoration in Leos Carax's *Mauvais Sang*, here at last is given the space to reveal herself as a wonderfully spontaneous actress, her gamine features never exploited for obvious sentimentality.

There is also a gallery of fine cameos from the likes of Erland Josephson and, in particular, Daniel Olbrychski, who's superbly lubricious as the man from the Ministry of the Interior trying to win a retraction from Tomas of a critical article he penned on Oedipus, guilt and the Stalinists. To solve the problem of having so many nationals in one film, Kaufman coached his cast into a soft East European accent, which is pleasing on the ear and ultimately comes to seem the obvious choice.

Shot on well-chosen locations in France, the film owes much to some wonderful photography by Sven Nykvist. Significantly, Kaufman screened Bergman's *The Silence* (shot by Nykvist) during preparations for the film. The great Swedish cameraman captures the dark hues of Prague just as well as he creates a luxuriant idyll for the couple's final retreat to the country.

Is the closing section of the film a touch sentimental? After Tomas has been reduced to window-cleaning for a living while Tereza works in a tawdry bar, they decide to seek a life outside the city. There is certainly a difficulty in making Tereza's love for her dog something other than cutesy, given the absence of the novel's accompaniment of thoughts on happiness, mankind and animals. If it is a weakness, then in Kaufman's scheme of things this final bucolic fantasy is a necessary release from the urban nightmare that has gone before.

Throughout, Kaufman steers his narrative with an unhurried sense of lives unfolding, matched by a sober camera style and the sometimes fervent, sometimes melancholic music of Janacek, which was a Kundera suggestion - he has always championed the composer, and even advised on the best performers to use on the soundtrack. While audiences may have been initially drawn to the film by its palatable eroticism (and Adrian Lyne could certainly learn a thing or two here), it is ultimately emotions that take over as Tomas and Tereza go on their final, fateful journey down a roadway of strangely aching beauty. It gives us hope, as Sabina puts it in another context, against the 'uglification' of the world, that 'where the persecutors have overlooked it' one can find beauty.

DAVID THOMPSON

THE UNHOLY

'Somebody around here just hates priests,' says police detective Ned Beatty to Ben Cross, 'you could be number three.' Certainly looks like it. Unlucky Father Ben has hit one of those American parishes big on death, demonology and special effects. The local nightclub has a line in Satanic sacrifice and, back in the rectory, blind priest Trevor Howard keeps saying things like 'You are the one!' or 'At last, Desiderius!' No one knows what he means, least of all the audience, who, when not puzzling over the plot, have to hold on to their stomachs as one emetic effect succeeds another. **HK**

Director *Camilio Vila* ***producer*** *Matthew Hayden* ***execs*** *Frank D. Olin, Wanda S. Rayle, Duke Siotkas* ***script*** *Philip Yordan, Fernando Fonseca* ***camera*** *Henry Vargas* ***editor*** *Mark Melnick* ***design*** *Fonseca* ***music*** *Roger Bellon* ***cast*** *Ben Cross, Hal Holbrook, Jill Caroll, William Russ, Trevor Howard, Claudia Robinson, Ned Beatty, Nicole Fortier*

Running time: 100 mins

US release: Vestron, Apr 22, 1988

THE UNTOUCHABLES

After several excursions which touched on self-parody, De Palma regains his cinematic stride in this bold and brassy retelling of the story of Elliot Ness and his team pitched against the twenties Chicago gangland led by Al Capone. Scrupulously styled with a taut script by David Mamet, an epic score by Morricone and great costumes by Armani, the film's leads are a formidable bunch, with Connery and De Niro both in cracking form and Costner proving himself to be a Gary Cooper for the eighties. De Palma even throws in a great set-piece, his rail station shoot-out, and the whole is irresistible entertainment in the manner of a bygone Hollywood era. **DT**

The Untouchables

Director *Brian De Palma* ***producer*** *Art Linson* ***script*** *David Mamet* ***camera*** *Stephen H. Burum* ***editors*** *Jerry Greenberg, Bill Pankow* ***design*** *William A. Elliott* ***music*** *Ennio Morricone* ***cast*** *Kevin Costner, Sean Connery, Charles Martin Smith, Andy Garcia, Robert De Niro, Richard Bradford, Jack Kehoe, Brad Sullivan, Billy Drago, Patricia Clarkson*

Running time: 119 mins

US release: Paramount, Jun 5, 1987

UK release: UIP, Sep 18, 1987

·V·V·V·V·V·V·V·V·V·V·V·V

VICE VERSA

This entertaining remake of Peter Ustinov's 1948 film encourages Judge Reinhold to give free rein to his rubbery, apt-to-blubber features. He plays a self-centred yuppie who, through a supernatural coincidence, exchanges consciousnesses with his bratty 11-year-old son. The newly miniaturized yuppie learns responsibility by caring for his suddenly over-sized offspring. Reinhold's antics as the man with an 11-year-old brain, reminiscent of Steve Martin's portrayal of a dual personality in *All of Me*, add up to a classic of physical comedy. **BM**

Director *Brian Gilbert* ***producers/script*** *Dick Clement, Ian LaFrenais* ***exec*** *Alan Ladd Jr.* ***camera*** *King Baggot* ***editor*** *David Garfield* ***design*** *Jim Schoppe* ***music*** *David Shire* ***cast*** *Judge Reinhold, Fred Savage, Corinne Bohrer, Swoosie Kurtz, David Proval, Jane Kaczmerek*

Running time: 98 mins

US release: Columbia, Mar 11, 1988

VINCENT - THE LIFE AND DEATH OF VINCENT VAN GOGH

John Hurt's impassioned reading of Van Gogh's letters to his brother Theo - tracing his abandonment of the seminary, years of penury as an obsessive painter, and the gloom that enveloped him prior to suicide - is the only text for Australian-based film-maker Paul Cox's unique, empathic tribute to his Dutch countryman. Using few actors (as peasants and the odd bawd), Cox visualizes the world of trees, fields, skies and sunflowers as he imagines Van Gogh saw it - evoking simultaneously his ecstatic inspiration and emotional turmoil. Shot in a grainy, impressionistic style, far removed from Minnelli's *Lust for Life* Van Gogh biopic, neither documentary nor melodrama yet containing elements of both, this is a visionary work which reinforces Cox's own emergent status as a great, driven artist. **GF**

Director/camera/editor *Paul Cox* ***producer*** *Tony Llewellyn-Jones* ***script*** *Cox, based on the letters of Vincent Van Gogh* ***design*** *Neil Angwin* ***music*** *Norman Kaye* ***voice*** *John Hurt*

Running time: 103 mins

US release: Illumination, Mar 16, 1988

Vincent

·W·W·W·W·W·W·W·W·W·

WALKER

Alex Cox's agitprop allegory of Reagan's intervention in Central America re-creates the imperial degradations of Colonel William Walker (Harris), a deluded disciple of Manifest Destiny who invaded Nicaragua with a small band of mercenaries in 1855 and proclaimed himself president of a brutal 'democracy'. Featuring Cox's travelling stock company of actors and rock stars (plus Marlee Matlin as the Colonel's fiery deaf and dumb fiancée) and shot on Nicaraguan locations, *Walker* betrays Rudy Wurlitzer's slick satirical screenplay and emerges as a wayward, half-indulgent mess from a director unable to relinquish the half-baked spaghetti Western theatrics he tested out in the awful *Straight to Hell*. **GF**

Director *Alex Cox* ***producer*** *Lorenzo O'Brien* ***script*** *Rudy Wurlitzer* ***camera*** *David Bridges* ***editors*** *Carlos Puente Ortega, Cox* ***design*** *Bruno Rubeo* ***music*** *Joe Strummer* ***cast*** *Ed Harris, Richard Masur, Rene Auberjonois, Keith Szarabajka, Sy Richardson, Xander Berkeley, John Diehl, Peter Boyle, Marlee Matlin, Alfonso Arau, Pedro Armendariz, Roberto Lopez Espinoza, Gerrit Graham, William O'Leary, Blanca Guerra, Alan Bolt, Miguel Sandoval*

Running time: 95 mins

US release: Universal, Dec 4, 1987

WALL STREET

Oliver Stone transposes his favourite Faustian plot-line from Vietnam to New York in another lesson in old-fashioned morality, wrapped up in the *nouveau chic* world of high finance. Charlie Sheen's ambitious young broker comes under the wing of ace insider dealer Gecko, a coruscating performance by Michael Douglas that steals the movie. But Gecko's ruthless ways impinge on Charlie's solid union-man father (played by Sheen Sr.), and what begins as a dynamic and exhilarating movie becomes bogged down in a tearful hospital bed scene and some horrendous dialogue, causing the film to crash faster than the real thing. **DT**
Director *Oliver Stone* ***producer*** *Edward R. Pressman* ***script*** *Stanley Weiser, Stone* ***camera*** *Robert Richardson* ***editor*** *Claire Simpson* ***design*** *Stephen Hendrickson* ***music*** *Stewart Copeland* ***cast*** *Michael Douglas, Charlie Sheen, Daryl Hannah, Martin Sheen, Terence Stamp, Hal Holbrook, Sean Young, Sylvia Miles, Richard Dysart, Saul Rubinek, Annie McEnroe, James Spader, Tamara Tunie, Franklin Cover, Chuck Pfeiffer*
Running time: 124 mins
US release: Fox, Dec 11, 1987
UK release: Fox, Apr 29, 1988

WEEDS

Worthy but humdrum comedy of ex-cons rehabilitating themselves, with Nick Nolte as the paroled lifer who turns playwright. Summoning his ex-mates from the slammer, he forms the penal system's answer to the Group Theatre. Heavily influenced by Odets and Genet (obviously top of the reading list in the prison library), they go from strength to strength and take Off-Broadway by storm. The movie audience, though, feels less stormed than sedated: lulled by the sound of liberal preaching and the made-for-TV images and ideas of writer-director John Hancock. **HK**
Director *John Hancock* ***producer*** *Bill Badalato* ***execs*** *Mel Pearl, Billy Cross* ***script*** *Dorothy Tristan, Hancock* ***camera*** *Jan Weincke* ***editor*** *Dennis O'Connor, David Handman, Jon Poll, Chris Lebenzon* ***design*** *Joseph T. Garrity* ***music*** *Angelo Badalamenti* ***cast*** *Nick Nolte, Lane Smith, William Forsythe, John Toles-Bey, Joe Mantegna, Ernie Hudson, Mark Rolston, J. J. Johnson, Rita Taggart, Orville Stoeber, Essex Smith, Anne Ramsey, Ray Reinhardt, Amanda Gronich, Felton Perry*
Running time: 115 mins
US release: DEG, Oct 16, 1987

WELCOME IN VIENNA

Axel Corti returns to the Vienna of *The Third Man* vintage, embroiling Americans in an intrigue of divided loyalties amid the post-war rubble. There is a scene involving stolen medicine but no ferris-wheel. Gabriel Barylli and Nicolas Brieger are Viennese Jews who escaped to America before the war and return as conquerors. The army assigns them to the cultural detail. The idealistic one falls in love with an actress (Messner), whose Nazi father has bought his freedom by telling Washington all he knows about the Reds. The corruptible one schemes to steal the girl. Corti's black-and-white film expertly evokes the tumult of that period when Austria cast itself as Germany's victim instead of its co-conspirator. **BM**
Director *Axel Corti* ***script*** *Georg Stefan Troller, Corti* ***camera*** *Gernot Roll* ***editor*** *Ulrike Pahl, Claudia Rieneck* ***design*** *Fritz Hollgersch-Wandtner* ***music*** *Hans Georg Koch* ***cast*** *Gabriel Barylli, Nicolas Brieger, Claudia Messner, Hubert Mann, Karlheinz Hackl, Liliana Nelska, Kurt Sowintz, Joachim Kemmer, Heinz Trixner*
Running time: 126 mins
US release: Roxie, Jan 22, 1988

The Whales of August

THE WHALES OF AUGUST

Playwright David Berry's Chekhovian chamber piece about two elderly sisters - gentle but firm Sarah (Gish) and blind, cantankerous Libby (Davis) - living out their lives on an island off Maine in the early fifties has been extended by Lindsay Anderson into a lyrical cinematic meditation on old age and impending death. Gish and Davis, the sweet and sour of American movies, harmonize perfectly as they argue about installing a picture window over the now whale-less bay, with Libby rising wraith-like in the night to try and lure Sarah towards the grave. No less important to the film's celebratory harnessing of Hollywood iconography are Ann Sothern as the still skittish old neighbour, Vincent Price as a gentlemanly but cadging Russian émigré, and Harry Carey Jr. as the clattering handyman. **GF**
Director *Lindsay Anderson* ***producers*** *Carolyn Pfeiffer, Mike Kaplan* ***exec*** *Shep Gordon* ***script*** *David Berry, based on his play* ***camera*** *Mike Fash* ***editor*** *Nicolas Gaster* ***design*** *Jocelyn Herbert* ***music*** *Alan Price* ***cast*** *Bette Davis, Lillian Gish, Vincent Price, Ann Sothern, Harry Carey Jr., Frank Grimes, Frank Pitkin, Margaret Ladd, Tisha Sterling, Mary Steenburgen*
Running time: 91 mins
US release: Alive, Oct 16, 1987
UK release: Curzon, May 27, 1988

THE WHISTLEBLOWER

As a counterweight to the right-wing fantasies of the James Bond film, *The Whistleblower* dramatizes a favourite left-wing paranoid nightmare: that no one in Britain is safe from its security services. Nigel Havers is a GCHQ Russian linguist whose revulsion at his country's spying leads him to contemplate going public, but he falls to his death. His father, Michael Caine, knows enough to doubt that Havers' death was accidental. Others die, a Blunt-type (Gielgud) is discovered living comfortably, and Caine has it all explained to him in the fancy country home where the ruling class plot against us ordinary people. It seems Britain is so desperate for American's early warning against Russian nuclear attack that no one and nothing can stand in the way of maintaining the 'special relationship'. **BM**
Director *Simon Langton* ***producer*** *Geoffrey Reeve* ***execs*** *Philip Nugus, John Kelleher, James Reeve* ***script*** *Julian Bond, based on the novel by John Hale* ***camera*** *Fred Tammes* ***editors*** *Robert Morgan* ***design*** *Morley Smith* ***music*** *John Scott* ***cast*** *Michael*

Caine, James Fox, Nigel Havers, John Gielgud, Felicity Dean, Barry Foster, Gordon Jackson, Kenneth Colley, David Langton, Dinah Stabb, James Simmons
Running time: 104 mins
US release: Hemdale, Jul 7, 1987
UK release: Rank, May 29, 1987

WHITE MISCHIEF
Turkey of the Year
Director *Michael Radford* ***producer*** *Simon Perry* ***script*** *Radford, Jonathan Gems, based on the book by James Fox* ***camera*** *Roger Deakins* ***editor*** *Tom Priestley* ***design*** *Roger Hall* ***music*** *George Fenton* ***cast*** *Charles Dance, Greta Scacchi, Joss Ackland, Sarah Miles, John Hurt, Geraldine Chaplin, Ray McAnally, Trevor Howard, Susan Fleetwood, Alan Dobie, Hugh Grant, Jacqueline Pearce, Catherine Neilson, Murray Head, Gregor Fisher, Edwin Mahinda*
Running time: 107 mins
US release: Columbia, Apr 22, 1988
UK release: Columbia, Feb 5, 1988

WHO FRAMED ROGER RABBIT?
A brilliantly bone-headed concoction of gags, both sight and sound, Robert Zemeckis's film goes all the way in combining live action with animation (by Richard Williams). It's the first feature-length cartoon that dares to offer what short cartoons uniquely deliver: painless socko violence. It's 1947 and private eye Bob Hoskins is hired to look into the death of an animation czar in Toontown, where cartoon characters live. Hoskins encounters Donald Duck, Betty Boop, Dumbo and all the stars while he tries to clear the title Toon from being framed-up by crooked judge Christopher Lloyd. The film is so much fun it'll surely be banned in Sweden. **BM**
Director *Robert Zemeckis* ***producers*** *Robert Watts, Frank Marshall* ***execs*** *Steven Spielberg, Kathleen Kennedy* ***script*** *Jeffrey Price, Peter S. Seaman, from Gary K. Wolf's book* Who Censored Roger Rabbit? ***camera*** *Dean Cundey* ***editor*** *Arthur Schmidt* ***design*** *Elliot Scott, Roger Cain* ***music*** *Alan Silvestri* ***cast*** *Bob Hoskins, Christopher Lloyd, Joanna Cassidy, Stubby Kaye, Alan Tilvern, Richard Le Parmentier, Joel Silver, Betsy Brantley* ***voices*** *Charles Fleischer, Kathleen Turner, Amy Irving, Lou Hirsch, Mel Blanc, Morgan Deare, Mae Questel, Tony Anselmo, Joe Alakey, June Foray, Richard Williams, Wayne Allwine, Russi Taylor, Tony Pope, Cherry Davis, Peter Westy, Frank Sinatra*
Running time: 103 mins
US release: BV, Jun 24, 1988

WHO'S THAT GIRL
Turkey of the Year
Director *James Foley* ***producers*** *Rosilyn Heller, Bernard Williams* ***execs*** *Peter Guber, Jon Peters, Roger Birnbaum* ***script*** *Andrew Smith, Ken Finkleman* ***camera*** *Jan De Bont* ***editor*** *Pembroke Herring* ***design*** *Ida Random* ***music*** *Stephen Bray* ***cast*** *Madonna, Griffin Dunne, Haviland Morris, John McMartin, Bibi Besch, John Mills, Robert Swan, Drew Pillsbury, Coati Mundi, Dennis Burkley, Jim Dietz, Cecile Callan, Karen Baldwin, Kimberlin Brown, Crystal Carson, Elaine Wilkes*
Running time: 94 mins (92 mins in UK)
US release: Warner, Aug 7, 1987
UK release: CCW, Oct 23, 1987

WHITE MISCHIEF

Lacking the glossily romantic opulence of an *Out of Africa* or the quiet intelligence of *The Kitchen Toto, White Mischief* comes a very poor third in recent Dark Continent stakes. But perhaps it was always destined to be an also-ran. However fascinating James Fox's original book about Kenya's Happy Valley set and the sensational murder of the dissolute Lord Errol in 1941, there just wasn't the material for a feature film.

The book was readable enough thanks to its surface mixture of gossip, speculation and, albeit guarded, revelation, all set against a backcloth of colonial decadence. But it had no substance and provided no real solution to the mystery behind Lord Errol's murder.

Michael Radford admits he encountered two fundamental problems when he started writing the screenplay for *White Mischief*. The first was that Fox's book was 'very diffuse, a meticulous investigation of a crime rather than a drama.' The second was that the people who lived in the Happy Valley 'were morally reprehensible and therefore unlikeable.' It was only when Radford felt he could make a connection between their hopes and fears and his own that he felt able to give them 'the depth they needed to come alive on the screen.'

This necessary connection turned out to be the Swinging Sixties, for which the film was to be a 'requiem'. 'In those days,' says Radford, 'we believed in freedom, but we never achieved it. Twenty years later, we're still hanging on to the idea of it by our fingernails. The Happy Valley set were children of their age too. They were the people Scott Fitzgerald wrote about, people who thought they had everything, but actually had nothing.'

It all sounds a bit like reports of early-morning Beverly Hills breakfast meetings where an earnest film-maker tries to convince the 'money' he has an immensely bankable project. Stress the decadence and dissolution of the past but with a modern 'hook' (to remind the baby-boom financier of his own pleasantly misspent adolescence).

It turned out that the original money, Cineplex Odeon, were less than enthused by the script which Radford and his co-writer Jonathan Gems presented. Cineplex were 'all for clarity' and 'rattled by ambiguity.' One of the company bosses is said to have told Radford,

'you are subtling me to death.'

Cineplex withdrew from the production while it was shooting on location in Kenya. To the rescue rode David Puttnam, then head honcho of Columbia Pictures, Barry Spikings' Nelson Entertainment and even Jake Eberts, late of Goldcrest. A seemingly formidable trio.

The result was perhaps the longest production credit in film history: Columbia Pictures, Nelson Entertainment and Goldcrest present a Michael White/Umbrella Films Production in association with Power Tower Investments (Kenya) and the BBC with the participation of Curzon Film Distributors, British Screen and Jake Eberts.

Nevertheless, the finished film seemed to contain everything that must have been the cause for concern in the first place. It's a thoroughly silly, muddled screenplay without any kind of real coherence. At times it's melodrama, at others it resembles a comic strip in its failure to give any real substance to the characters. A potentially fine cast of British actors respond by pouting and posturing. And Radford's direction is go-slow in its pacing.

For those who don't know, *White Mischief* tells a squalid tale of love, adultery, drugs and dottiness among the wealthy British expatriate community in the first years of the Second World War. Newcomers to this notorious settlement are the 57-year-old Sir 'Jock' Delves Broughton and his gorgeous young bride Diana (Greta Scacchi).

Within minutes (it seems) Diana is between the sheets with Josslyn Lord Hay (Charles Dance), who's devilishly good-looking and the most shameless adulterer of them all. Errol and Diana openly flout their affair before an increasingly bitter Broughton.

When Errol is shot, Broughton is arrested, tried and acquitted. Diana, desperate to find out who killed her lover, is soon painfully confronted with the truth (which we thought she knew all the time anyway), as Broughton blows his own brains out all over his distraught wife (historically, he committed suicide a year later at the Adelphi Hotel in Liverpool).

Never was such a bunch of unlikeable characters gathered together in such unsympathetic profusion, in a setting which, for all its exotic potential, could have been Scarborough to the extent it is shown to impinge on this ghastly ensemble. It's Africa itself that just may be the vital missing ingredient.

QUENTIN FALK

WHO'S THAT GIRL

Watching *Who's That Girl* tends to leave you speechless. It's Madonna's third big-screen outing and the studio bosses may well be wondering why the pop idol's many millions of fans don't buy as many cinema tickets as they do records, and why producers can't seem to find the right part for her talents.

At least with this attempt Madonna has contributed four songs to the soundtrack, including the catchy title piece. And her co-star Griffin Dunne (hubby Sean Penn didn't get involved this time) encourages a few smiles. But that's about it.

Who's That Girl was promoted as a romantic comedy in the screwball tradition of *Bringing Up Baby* (from which it borrows more than a few ideas and jokes), but whoever sketched out Madonna's character seriously misjudged the sort of person she could play.

The production notes set the scene: 'Fresh from the slammer and a four-year sentence for a crime she didn't commit, Nikki Finn is hopping mad. Detectives are hounding her, and a whole bunch of thugs want her dead. Nikki on the other hand wants nothing more than to find the dude who put her away on a bum rap.'

Well, there you have this thrilling tale in a nutshell. The film starts excellently with an animated credit sequence that explains the background, showing Madonna getting framed for the murder of her boyfriend but retaining a key to the safe-deposit box which contains documents proving her innocence.

Then the animation blends into an opening scene that introduces Nikki Finn in front of her parole board. She doesn't look attractive, has an unbearably squeaky voice (presumably thought to be amusing) and skips about like some demented peroxide Barbie doll. At this juncture the discerning movie-goer would slurp his/her Coke, abandon the popcorn and exit stage right. The professional film reviewer must just grimace, clutch the arm rests even harder, and prepare for the worst.

It seems to be prerequisite for characters in Madonna films to have silly names in an attempt at humour - *Shanghai Surprise* offered a few gems, but *Who's That Girl* matches Nikki Finn with Loudon Trott - the Dunne character.

Despite his ponderous moniker, Dunne gives the film all he's got. His charm and subtle comedy skills are such that at some junctures he almost looks like saving the day, but these qualities are swallowed up in the script's hunt for conventional comic material.

Like Grant in *Bringing Up Baby*, and with a similar bumbling suavity, Dunne spends a lot of time in evening dress trying to track down a snarling wild cat (actually a rare Patagonian Felis Concolour we are told). But, instead of the witty and elegant Katharine Hepburn, he gets a street-credible Madonna trying to be a madcap Marilyn Monroe.

Who's That Girl runs the whole gamut of staged comedy devices - from car chase and hospital scene to climactic duel and gun fights. Along their fun-packed odyssey to prove Nikki's innocence the couple wreck a beautiful Rolls-Royce (the production notes claim they used four Rolls-Royces - even more sacrilegious than ruining the movie!) and get involved with a couple of hoods.

While all this is going on, Loudon Trott tries to prepare for his wedding on the following day to the boss's daughter (the boss is - surprise, surprise - the villain of the piece). Hollywood producers seem overly fond of ruining weddings on celluloid, perhaps reflecting some deep-rooted fear of marriage. Loudon also has to deliver the wild cat to millionaire Montgomery Bell, played by Sir John Mills who must have wondered what on earth he had got himself into.

Unsurprisingly, Dunne leaves his vacuous fiancée at the altar and despatches the villain, choosing to abandon his job as a well-paid attorney and head off with Madonna to open an animal clinic - smart move Griffin!

As with *Shanghai Surprise*, the elements which looked good on paper - Madonna the hot performer, Griffin Dunne in demand after the success of *After Hours*, and director James Foley a seasoned maker of Madonna pop videos - produced a fiasco. Producers and directors just don't seem to know how best to use Madonna's talents on the screen. Maybe her ego, or some perception of how her fans see her, got in the way, but there's some serious re-thinking to be done.

MARK ADAMS

WHOOPS APOCALYPSE

Slapdash farce with aspirations to 'alternative' status in its attempts to lampoon power politics. The degree of (non-) topicality can be gauged from the fact that the British PM, barmy of course, is presented in the guise of Peter Cook offering what seems to be a vocal caricature of Harold Macmillan, and its (lack of) satirical invention from such notions as having this character sponsor a drive to reduce unemployment by enlisting volunteers to jump off Beachy Head. For the rest, the 'humour' seems substantially to reside in a resort to undeleted expletives. **TP**

Director *Tom Bussman* ***producer*** *Brian Eastman* ***script*** *Andrew Marshall, David Renwick* ***camera*** *Ron Robson* ***editor*** *Peter Boyle* ***design*** *Tony Noble* ***music*** *Patrick Gowers* ***cast*** *Loretta Swit, Peter Cook, Michael Richards, Rik Mayall, Ian Richardson, Alexei Sayle, Herbert Lom, Joanna Pearce, Christopher Malcolm, Ian McNeice, Daniel Benzali, Shane Rimmer*

Running time: 91 mins

US release: MGM, Feb 12, 1988

UK release: Miracle, Mar 6, 1987

WILLOW

If George Lucas hadn't made the three *Star Wars* movies, his medievalesque *Willow* might seem stunningly original instead of enjoyably derivative. This tale of a band of outsiders vanquishing Evil incarnate (Marsh) has predictable proportions of swashbuckling, monster-mongering, romance, scenery and humour. Val Kilmer plays the Han Solo figure, little person Warwick Davis is Skywalkerish, a pair of brownies function like comic robots, and Joanne Whalley is a somewhat sympathetic princess. There is even a villain with a skull-like helmet. As for plot, Davis as Willow accepts the mission of protecting a full-sized infant from the bare-fanged Marsh, and you can guess the rest. **BM**

Director *Ron Howard* ***producer*** *Nigel Wooll* ***exec*** *George Lucas* ***script*** *Bob Dolman* ***camera*** *Adrian Biddle* ***editors*** *David Hanley, Michael Hill, Richard Hiscott* ***design*** *Allan Cameron* ***music*** *James Horner* ***cast*** *Val Kilmer, Joanne Whalley, Warwick Davis, Jean Marsh, Patricia Hayes, Billy Barty, Pat Roach, Gavan O'Herlihy, David Steinberg, Phil Fondacaro, Mark Northover, Kevin Pollak, Rick Overgon, Marie Holvöe, Julie Peters*

Running time: 125 mins

US release: MGM, May 20,1988

WINGS OF DESIRE

Having thrown off his obsession with all things American, Wenders finds fresh fields in the divided city of Berlin and creates a love story for our time. The characters are split between the angels who watch over us and Berlin's mortals who flounder about in spiritual dissatisfaction. One angel - the benign Bruno Ganz - falls for a trapeze artist and becomes flesh to express his desire for her. With remarkable photography by veteran Henri Alékan (silky monochrome predominating as the angels' point of view), the film nearly grinds down under the weight of Peter Handke's abstruse dialogue. Fortunately Wenders is the fleeter talent, and a rich cameo by Peter Falk brightens the introspective tone. **DT**

Director *Wim Wenders* ***producers*** *Wenders, Anatole Dauman* ***exec*** *Ingrid Windisch* ***script*** *Wenders, Peter Handke* ***camera*** *Henri Alékan* ***editor*** *Peter Przygodda* ***design*** *Heidi Ludi* ***music*** *Jürgen Knieper* ***cast*** *Bruno Ganz, Solveig Dommartin, Otto Sander, Curt Bois, Peter Falk*

Running time: 130 mins

US release: Orion Classics, Apr 29, 1988

UK release: Recorded Releasing, Jun 24, 1988

WISH YOU WERE HERE

David Leland's uneven directorial début tackles Britain in the past again, this time the dismal fifties, with the exit from austerity still some distance away. This subject is the unsentimental education of teenage Lynda (a gustily confident début by Emily Lloyd) in a dismal coastal town. While shocking everyone by screaming about naughty bits, her real sexual encounters are depressingly uneventful. Despite much humour and an awkwardly upbeat ending, British melancholia and repression win the day, and it seems eroticism still begins at Calais. **DT**

Director/script *David Leland* ***producer*** *Sarah Radclyffe* ***camera*** *Ian Wilson* ***editor*** *George Akers* ***design*** *Caroline Amies* ***music*** *Stanley Myers* ***cast*** *Emily Lloyd, Clare Clifford, Barbara Durkin, Geoffrey Hutchings, Charlotte Barker, Tom Bell, Chloe Leland, Charlotte Ball, Pat Heywood*

Running time: 92 mins

US release: Atlantic, Jul 24, 1987

UK release: Palace, Dec 4, 1987

Wish You Were Here

waiting for opening time, avoiding Withnail's randy uncle, seeking nourishment by shotgunning fish in a stream, cooking by stuffing a chicken in a tea kettle, this pair is always entertainingly idiotic. **BM**
Director/script *Bruce Robinson* ***producer*** *Paul Heller* ***execs*** *George Harrison, Denis O'Brien* ***camera*** *Peter Hannan* ***editor*** *Alan Strachan* ***design*** *Michael Pickwood* ***music*** *David Dundas, Rick Wentworth* ***cast*** *Richard E. Grant, Paul McGann, Richard Griffiths, Ralph Brown, Michael Elphick, Daragh O'Mallery, Michael Wardle, Una Brandon-Jones, Noel Johnson, Irene Sutcliffe*
Running time: 107 mins
US release: Cineplex Odeon, Jun 19, 1987
UK release: Recorded Releasing, Feb 12, 1988

WOLF AT THE DOOR

Donald Sutherland, the most consciously artistic of actors, plays Paul Gauguin as the artist saw himself: a god among pygmies. Henning Carlsen's worthy but slow chronicle covers the least interesting period of Gauguin's life, the years between his two sojourns in Tahiti. His supreme confidence about everything doesn't help Gauguin manage the details of his life: he's dumbfounded when he can't sell his anti-naturalistic pictures, hurts himself in a brawl, is deserted by his friends, provokes his mistress into robbing him and eventually finances his return to the South Seas by selling his Van Goghs. Smoking a long-stemmed

Witches of Eastwick *(left)*
Withnail and I *(below)*

WITCHES OF EASTWICK

'Just your average horny little devil,' Jack Nicholson plays this fiendish comedy role to the hilt, ensuring enjoyment even for those who miss the measured cadences of John Updike's source novel. Cher, Susan Sarandon and Michelle Pfeiffer, manless in New England, find their wish for masculine solace comes truer than they dreamed. Nicholson takes a house in their town and seduces all three, who subsequently discover strange powers. Eventually they're compelled to use them on this charming vulgarian, who proves too diabolical to be vanquished completely. George (*Road Warrior*) Miller directs with an eye to excess. **BM**
Director *George Miller* ***producers*** *Neil Canton, Peter Guber, Jon Peters* ***execs*** *Rob Cohen, Don Devlin* ***script*** *Michael Cristofer, based on the novel by John Updike* ***camera*** *Vilmos Zsigmond* ***editors*** *Richard Francis-Bruce, Hubert C. De La Boiuillerie, Howard Stein* ***design*** *Polly Platt* ***music*** *John Williams* ***cast*** *Jack Nicholson, Cher, Susan Sarandon, Michelle Pfeiffer, Veronica Cartwright, Richard Jenkins, Keith Jochim, Carel Struycken*
Running time: 118 mins
US release: Warner, Jun 12, 1987
UK release: CCW, Oct 23, 1988

WITHNAIL AND I

Two out-of-work actors in late sixties London seek respite from boredom and the cold in a cottage deep in the countryside. There they encounter more of the same. It seems an unlikely scenario for rollicking comedy, but, in writer-director Bruce Robinson's hands, the laughs are frequent. Richard E. Grant is Withnail, an outspokenly egotistical brooder who is beginning to realize that he will 'never play the Dane.' Paul McGann is 'I', a shy but slightly luckier thespian who plays wet to Withnail's wind. Spending their hours either drinking or

A World Apart

pipe, resplendently draped in bohemian garb, Sutherland strides magnificently through the film and provides the chief reason for sitting through it. **BM**
Director *Henning Carlsen* ***script*** *Christopher Hampton, based on a script by Carlsen, Jean-Claude Carrière* ***camera*** *Mikael Salomon* ***editor*** *Janus Billeskor Janson* ***design*** *André Guerin* ***music*** *Ole Schmidt* ***cast*** *Conald Sutherland, Valerie Glandut, Max von Sydow, Sofi Graböl, Merete Voldstedlund, Jürgen Reenberg*
Running time: 140 mins
US release: International Film Marketing, Jul 31, 1987

THE WOO WOO KID

(See In The Mood)

A WORLD APART

Anti-apartheid activist Diana Roth (Hershey) is imprisoned by the South African security forces – and the privileged childhood of Molly (Jodhi May), eldest of her three daughters, is brutally terminated. The autobiographical first screenplay by Shawn Slovo (whose activist mother Ruth First was jailed for 117 days, psychologically tortured, and eventually assassinated in 1982) provides a bruised, claustrophobic female perspective for cinematographer Chris Menges' powerful directorial début. *A World Apart*'s angle on apartheid is barely less white/middle-class than *Cry Freedom*'s but it is a considerably better film, benefiting especially from Hershey's clipped and implacable Roth, May's confused Molly, and Linda Mvusi's anguished black maid. **GF**
Director *Chris Menges* ***script*** *Shawn Slovo* ***camera*** *Peter Biziou* ***editor*** *Nicolas Gaster* ***design*** *Brian Morris* ***music*** *Hans Zimmer* ***cast*** *Barbara Hershey, Jodhi May, David Suchet, Jeroen Krabbé, Paul Freeman, Tim Roth, Linda Mvusi, Yvonne Bryceland, Albee Lesotho, Nadine Chalmers, Carolyn Clayton-Cragg, Merav Gruer*
Running time: 113 mins
US release: Atlantic, Jun 17, 1988

·Y·Y·Y·Y·Y·Y·Y·Y·Y·Y·Y·

YOU CAN'T HURRY LOVE

Love is all David Packer wants when he arrives in Los Angeles, but love is the one thing LA is too corrupt and kinky to provide in writer-director Richard Martini's mirthless satire. Packer experiments with various girl-getting personalities, conveyed through a video dating service. But the falser his front, the worse his results: an exhibitionist who can only make it in shop windows (Van Kamp), a performance artist who likes S&M (McNichol), among others. Charles Grodin appears dispensing condoms, and Bridget Fonda helps Packer find the kind of love he really wants. **BM**
Director/script *Richard Martini* ***producer*** *Jonathan D. Krane* ***camera*** *Peter Lyons Collister, John Schwartzman* ***editor*** *Richard Candib* ***design*** *Douglas A. Mowat* ***music*** *Bob Esty* ***cast*** *David Packer, Scott McGinnis, Bridget Fonda, David Leisure, Anthony Geary, Frank Bonner, Lu Leonard, Merete Van Kamp, Sally Kellerman, Charles Grodin, Kristy McNichol, Judy Balduzzi, Danitza Kingsley*
Running time: 92 mins
US release: Vestron, Jan 29, 1988

YOU TALKIN' TO ME

Two actors - one a black man (Williamson), the other fixated on Robert De Niro's performance as Travis Bickle in *Taxi Driver* (Youngs) - visit Hollywood in search of fame and fortune. After abandoning his New York style for surf-god looks, and doing his Bickle act for real, Youngs falls in with a psycho right-wing TV producer and becomes a spokesman for 'the pure truth, the white truth', and loses his self-respect in the process.
Director/script *Charles Winkler* ***producer*** *Michael Polaire* ***camera*** *Paul Ryan* ***editor*** *David Handman* ***music*** *Joel McNeely* ***cast*** *Jim Youngs, James Noble, Mykel T. Williamson, Faith Ford, Bess Motta, Rex Ryon, Brian Thompson, Alan King*
Running time: 97 mins
US release: UA, Sep 25, 1987

·Z·Z·Z·Z·Z·Z·Z·Z·Z·Z·Z·

ZELLY AND ME

In Tina Rathbone's first feature, Zelly (Rossellini) is the loving French nanny of orphaned little Phoebe (Jones), whom her guardian/grandmother (Johns) indulges with elaborate treats one moment and sadistically punishes the next. Joan of Arc (a nod, surely, to Rossellini's own cinematic lineage) is the role model for this martyred child, but when Zelly tries to abduct her the scheme falls flat because her beau (*Blue Velvet* director David Lynch) has been deceiving her with a fantasy of his own. This small psychological piece, set in Virginia in 1958, is at times suffocatingly coy, but Rossellini, Johns and Jones comprise the most bizarre of female trios, while Lynch's cameo is a hoot. **GF**
Director/script *Tina Rathbone* ***producers*** *Sue Jett, Tony Mark* ***execs*** *Elliott Dewitt, Rathbone* ***camera*** *Mikael Salomon* ***editor*** *Cindy Kaplan Rooney* ***design*** *David Morong* ***music*** *Pino Donaggio* ***cast*** *Isabella Rossellini, Glynis Johns, Alexandra Jones, Kaiulani Lee, David Lynch, Joe Morton*
Running time: 87 mins
US release: Columbia, Apr 15, 1988

BABYTALES FOR GROWN-UPS

Babies to the left of us, babies to the right. Into the valley of birth rode the 1987-8 movie audiences. If it wasn't *Baby Boom* it was *Three Men and a Baby*. If it wasn't *Raising Arizona* it was *She's Having a Baby*. Shame on you if by the time you read this you don't know how to change a nappy, warm a bottle or hold a baby upside down and slap it lightly to cure the colic.

Many of us wanted to hold these movies upside down and slap them. We strongly suspected we were being led down a diaper-strewn path towards the cinema's latest notion of an Age of Innocence. And when not being confronted with squalling infants, the alternative looked suspiciously similar. This was the Child's Eye View of War. It included Boorman's *Hope and Glory*, Spielberg's *Empire of the Sun* and - stretching 'war' to encompass larger historical upheavals - Bertolucci's *The Last Emperor*.

As any baby can tell you, movies move in mysterious ways. Much of the time they arrive in shapeless droves, week by week, to baffle any critic or cinephile looking to make a grand statement about trends. Then all of a sudden, like a convoy of double-deckers, a whole lot of semi-identical films arrive at once. The philosophy-prone critic seizes his pen and charges deliriously into deep thoughts.

But the trouble is that the critic, trained to review individual trees, often loses the ability to see the whole wood. As a result, even when he feels set free to generalize, he still doesn't see the whole wood, he sees copses at best.

The baby and boy's-eye-war movies are each such a copse. The wood they belong to - identifiable for simplicity's sake as 'Hollywood' but taking in the whole forest of Anglo-American popular film-making today - also incorporates other important and related copses. The Yuppie Punishment comedy (*After Hours*, *Something Wild*) and the Dangerous Adultery thriller (*Fatal Attraction*, *Someone to Watch Over Me*), to name two, are each a vital part of the same cultural ecology that has produced 1987's Cinema of the Child.

That ecology is all about the changing politics of human relationships: whether with equilibrium between the sexes (in Yuppie Punishment) or with family structures (in Babies and Boy's War) or with both in the same movie (in Dangerous Adultery). The film-making forest today has been formed by a decade of eruptions political (feminism) and medical-apocalyptic (AIDS), that between them seem designed to question or re-cast our whole perspective on the nuclear family and the male-female relationship.

The first thing that's clear about the Baby Movies is that they aren't about babies at all. They're about the grown-ups who rear them and the way they react to them. The small, alien creatures in these films who crawl around the floor, make goo-goo faces and do unspeakable things in their nappies, are a catalyst to grown-up lives, thoughts and emotions. They come into unstructured homes and say 'Structure yourself.' They deal with the climate of panic anarchy evident in the Yuppie Punishment and Deadly Adultery films by saying, 'Let's return to family values, domestic solidarity and the nesting instinct.'

Babies can be a major influence for conservatism, and that's how they're mostly being

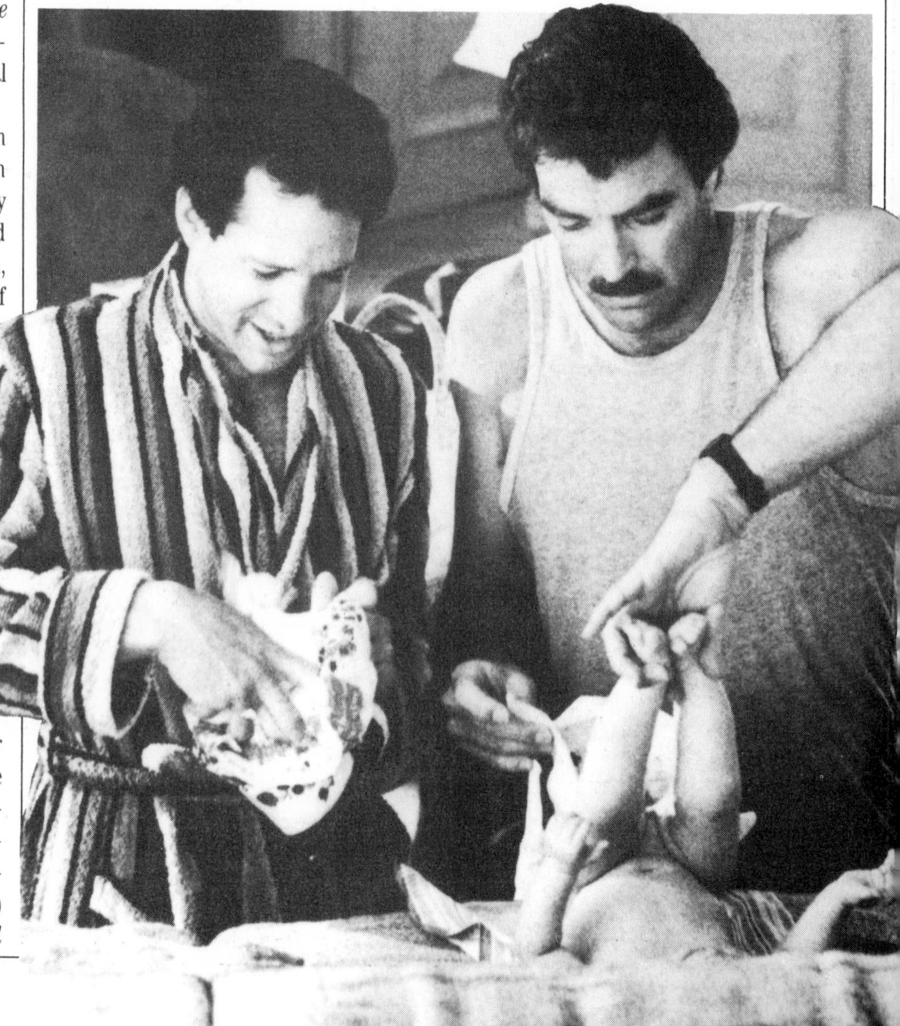

bequeathed by a never-heard-of-relative (*Baby Boom*) or is just plain kidnapped (*Raising Arizona*). The ruse is Hollywood's answer to virgin birth. It's high-concept immaculacy.

The ruse has another importance too in today's climate of moral evangelism. It's part of the films' proselytizing strategy to show that the 'family' is an ideal to which all groups can aspire, not just *bona fide* parents. A 'family' can be three reformed girl-chasing bachelors living together in New York; it can be a single mother-cum-reformed careerist living in the country; it can even be the brownstone-dwellers of *Batteries Not Included*, raising their adopted brood of cutey-pie flying saucers. A family in today's cinema is almost any group that rears little ones while keeping firmly at bay the outside world.

So what happens when the world impinges? John Boorman's *Hope and Glory* and Steven Spielberg's *Empire of the Sun* - both child's-eye-views of war - each give us the flip side to the 'Fortress Family' movie.

Or at least each appears to. Both in Boorman's brilliant portrait of the artist as a young Blitz kid and in Spielberg's film of Ballard's autobiographical tale of life under the Japs, the family drawbridge is let down and the vulnerable child is exposed to the world outside. In *Empire* the child is literally separated from his parents, torn away on the tide of history. In *Hope* the boy grows away emotionally: countering the conventional horror of the grown-up view of war with his own subversive discovery of its possibilities for adventure and renewal.

In the current Baby Movie climate this affirmative view of the 'orphaning' effect of war is almost heresy. And it takes a non-Hollywood individualist like Boorman to perpetrate it. Compared to *Hope and Glory*, *Empire of the Sun* - subtly betraying Ballard at every turn - rubs home family values with a sickly emphasis and never lets us forget the hero's search, amid the sanitized ordeals of Spielberg's POW camp, for surrogate parents. The grown-ups towards whom the boy gravitates - Nigel Havers' doctor, Miranda Richardson's British wife - are nothing like their physically or emotionally disfigured originals in the book. Kindly, attractive, long-suffering, they could have come straight out of a Computer Adoption Service. And when the boy is finally united with his real parents - an event almost thrown away in the book - Spielberg lays on the full inspirational works, John Williams music and all.

For all the film-maker's loudly telegraphed

Batteries Not Included *(above)*
Raising Arizona *(right)*
Three Men and a Baby *(below)*

deployed in the cinema today. The irony of the baby movies is that they come on like Anarchy Incorporated - their sales pitch to film-goers is essentially 'Come and see Diane Keaton lose her cool by having spaghetti thrown at her or Tom Selleck by having his shirt wee'd on' - and under cover of mayhem and hilarity they slip us the Family Values message.

It's a message born of fear, in an age when the family is under siege as seldom before. In whatever shape that institution moves into the next millennium, it's unlikely to be the same shape we've got used to in this one. Feminism has drawn a red line through the old family model of the hunter-achiever husband and the stay-at-home housekeeper wife. And over the last ten years the cinema has saluted that fact: see movies in which dad does mum's job from *Kramer vs. Kramer* to *Author, Author!* to *Table for Five*. (And *Three Men and a Baby* is the same story with three surrogate dads replacing one real one.)

The family is also under siege, or increasingly will be, from a well-known virus. No one was really joking when they said Glenn Close played the AIDS virus in *Fatal Attraction*. Of course she did. And the deadly threat was not just to Michael Douglas but to his family too.

Feminism proposes, AIDS disposes. Between the upheavals of sexual-political reformation and the new improved wages-of-sin on offer from today's microbes, no wonder the hidden command in much of today's cinema is 'Pull up the drawbridge.' Survival lies in domestic togetherness. The family that stays together has a prayer together.

And the Baby Movies show us the wonderful things that can happen in the process. Most of the films have been a resounding hit at the box-office, and no wonder. Their fairy tale simplicity can be swallowed at one viewing. Their message is loud, clear and primary. Baby Can Save The World. The objects of Baby's redemptive powers include: Robin Hood criminality (*Raising Arizona*), selfish careerism (*Baby Boom*), compulsive philandering (*Three Men and a Baby*) and self-interest in general. In short, all the ills that audiences see the late eighties as heir to - from rampant yuppyism to disease-spreading promiscuity - can be cured by going back to the family unit and bringing a new bundle of innocence into the world.

Newness, optimism and moral hygiene are the bywords. Heaven forbid in these films that we should hint at the procreative processes that go into producing babies. Or even at the messy business of actually giving birth. In most of these movies, as in fairy tales, the toddler appears on the doorstep (*Three Men and a Baby*) or is

The Lost Boys

career move into 'adult' themes and prestige literature, *Empire of the Sun* looks like the same Spielbergian mixture as before. The work of a potential genius of the movie image suffering from chronic Babyvision.

Babyvision, even more disconcertingly, is what Bertolucci's *The Last Emperor* suffers from. Here again, at least in part, is a child's-eye-view of historical turmoil. But the 'innocent eye' of Pu Yi, as he's bundled from power at age six and then from his home, the Forbidden City, at age 21, is hyperbolized and then politically exploited by the film-maker. The hero's naïveté shades imperceptibly into the movie's disingenuousness. Pu Yi is an orphan of history searching for a political 'family'. He finds it - Hallelujah and praise the Little Red Book - in the China of Mao.

Just like Spielberg, Bertolucci uses the theme of orphanhood to lower the existential drawbridge and send his hero into the strife-ridden outside world. But just like Spielberg (and unlike Boorman), he ducks out of letting his hero actually find himself. Pu Yi's ultimate destiny, his ultimate 'family', is predetermined: not by history (we have no evidence that Pu Yi became a convinced Communist nor even that he wrote his 'own' confessional prison diaries) but by the director's politics. Bertolucci, like other film-makers in the Babyvision age, ends by bringing his hero 'home' and pulling up the drawbridge. It may be a different kind of drawbridge and a different kind of home, but the basic message is the same. We have found our own truth: intruders and corrupters, keep out.

The sense of moral evangelism in *The Last Emperor* is dismayingly close to the climate, further West, of the TV hot gospellers and the Moral Majority. Here too, innocence is a flower easily bruised and blasted by contact with the world. But here too, salvation means not what is good and self-fulfilling for the individual but what fits in with the vested-interest creeds and doctrines of the sanctified 'majority'. The Moral Majority has never, of course, been counted, and the phrase has no force beyond the alliterative. But it has come to possess an almost religious inviolability.

The era of moral rearmament and Reaganite conservatism has created the climate in which Babyvision thrives. Babyvision movies tell us two things. Firstly, grown-ups are in danger unless they heed the innocence of the very young. Secondly, the very young are in danger unless they are succoured and protected, in a siege-like home, by the grown-ups. The era of Reach-Out-And-Touch has been scrapped.

Indeed it's hard to find an American movie featuring young characters today in which, if they're exposed to the outside world at all, they're not caught up in an apocalyptic tug-of-war between Good and Evil. In John Schlesinger's *The Believers* Martin Sheen's son is at risk from a coven of voodooists who believe in the sacrifice of the first-born. In Marek Kanievska's *Less Than Zero* the soul of teenager Robert Downey - confused, vulnerable, lovable - is at risk in a world of drugs, crime and male prostitution: a world whose hell-fire lighting seems borrowed from a production of *Dr Faustus*. And in the recent bunch of teen-vampire pics - like *Near Dark* and *The Lost Boys* - young souls and lives are bartered and battled for as if there were no tomorrow: which in these AIDS-subtext films is probably peddled as the underlying fear.

Apocalyptic overstatement is widely on offer. Indeed a major component of Babyvision movies is that their 'innocent' eyes, peering up from the playpen floor, see anything unfriendly in blown-up, giant, Fee Fi Fo Fum terms. A film like *Fatal Attraction* qualifies as Babyvision for grown-ups. Glenn Close begins as a feisty career woman whose worst sin is that she knows her own mind. Then, before our very eyes, she's transformed by the movie's frightened (male) perspective into a homicidal witch. (Just like 'mummy' whenever she gets angry with us or spanks or punishes us.)

And even a director like Oliver Stone has made his own idiosyncratic contract with today's Fortress Family era. In both *Platoon* and *Wall Street*, the underlying quest of the hero (Charlie Sheen) is for the ideal father figure: a quest whose nursery-story simplicity - the choice in both films is between Shining Good (Willem Dafoe, Martin Sheen) and Snarling Evil (Tom Berenger, Michael Douglas) - suggests that Babyvision can be at work even in the jungles of South-East Asia or South-East Manhattan.

No doubt America owes some of the daddy-worship to the presence of that doddering old man in the White House: a man who seldom does a wicked thing and never remembers it even when he does. Babyvision is in part the tribute paid by Hollywood to its very own President. With this 80-year-old Super-Pop in charge, who would want to do anything other than lie down on a fluffy hearth-rug and have his tummy rubbed or his bottom powdered?

Next year, though - 1989 - Americans won't have Reagan to baby them around any more. Nor will Reaganism be on hand to cheer on the Moral Majority with its own brand of hate-and-brimstone aw-shucks Christianity. America and Hollywood will have to face the awesome task of growing up. The nurseries and playrooms will have to be closed off or converted. (Into, heaven forbid, studies or libraries?) And dialogue will have to come not out of the mouths of babes and sucklings, nor of heroes and heroines who share their simple vision, but out of grown-up people steeling themselves to enter the 1990s with a new President. It's time to throw away the rattles.

HARLAN KENNEDY

AWARDS

FILM	EVENT	CATEGORY	WINNERS
Agent trouble	César	*Best Supporting Actress*	Dominique Lavanant
Anna	Golden Globe	*Best Actress – Drama*	Sally Kirkland
Au revoir, les enfants	Venice César César César César César César	*Golden Lion* *Best Film* *Best Screenplay* *Best Editing* *Best Director* *Best Cinematography* *Best Decor*	Louis Malle Louis Malle Louis Malle Emanuelle Castro Louis Malle Renato Berta Willy Holt
Babette's Feast	Oscar	*Best Foreign Language Film*	Gabriel Axel
Bear Ye One Another's Burdens	Berlin	*Silver Bear (Best Actor)*	Jörg Pose, Manfred Möck
Bird	Cannes	*Best Actor*	Forest Whitaker
Broadcast News	Berlin	*Silver Bear (Best Actress)*	Holly Hunter
Champ d'honneur	César	*Best Music*	Michel Portal
Commissar	Berlin	*Silver Bear (Special Jury Prize)*	Alexander Askoldov
Contract Mother	Venice	*Best Actress*	Kang Soo-Yeon
Le Cri de hibou	César	*Best Female Hopeful*	Mathilde May
Cry Freedom	BAFTA	*Best Sound*	Jonathan Bates, Simon Kaye, Gerry Humphreys

Babette's Feast

Cry Freedom

FILM	EVENT	CATEGORY	WINNERS
The Debt	Berlin	*Silver Bear*	Miguel Pereira
Drowning by Numbers	Cannes	*Best Artistic Contribution*	Peter Greenaway
84 Charing Cross Road	BAFTA	*Best Actress*	Ann Bancroft
Gold-Rimmed Glasses	Venice Venice	*Best Art Direction* *Best Costumes*	Luciano Ricceri Nanà Cecchi
Good Morning, Vietnam	Golden Globe	*Best Actor – Comedy/Musical*	Robin Williams
Le Grand chemin	César César	*Best Actress* *Best Actor*	Anémone Richard Bohringer
Harry and the Hendersons	Oscar	*Best Make-up*	Rick Baker
Hip, Hip, Hurrah	Venice Venice	*Best Cinematography* *Special Jury Award*	Sten Holmberg Kjell Grede

FILM	EVENT	CATEGORY	WINNERS
Hope and Glory	Golden Globe	*Best Motion Picture – Musical/Comedy*	John Boorman
	BAFTA	*Best Supporting Actress*	Susan Wooldridge
House of Games	Venice	*Best Screenplay*	David Mamet
I've Heard the Mermaids Singing	Genie	*Best Actress*	Sheila McCarthy
	Genie	*Best Supporting Actress*	Paule Baillargeon

Hope and Glory

Jean de Florette

FILM	EVENT	CATEGORY	WINNERS
Innerspace	Oscar	*Best Visual Effects*	Denis Muren, William George, Harley Jessup, Kenneth Smith
Les Innocents	César	*Best Supporting Actor*	Jean-Claude Brialy
Jean de Florette	BAFTA	*Best Supporting Actor*	Daniel Auteuil
	BAFTA	*Best Cinematography*	Bruno Nuytten
	BAFTA	*Best Film*	Claude Berri
	BAFTA	*Best Adapted Screenplay*	Claude Berri, Gerard Brach
The Last Emperor	Oscar	*Best Picture*	Jeremy Thomas
	Golden Globe	*Best Motion Picture – Drama*	Bernardo Bertolucci
	Oscar	*Best Director*	Bernardo Bertolucci
	DGA	*Best Director*	Bernardo Bertolucci
	Golden Globe	*Best Director*	Bernardo Bertolucci
	César	*Best Foreign Film*	Bernardo Bertolucci
	Golden Globe	*Best Screenplay*	Bernardo Bertolucci, Mark Peploe
	Oscar	*Best Adapted Screenplay*	Mark Peploe, Bernardo Bertolucci
	Oscar	*Best Costume Design*	James Acheson
	Oscar	*Best Cinematography*	Vittorio Storaro
	Oscar	*Best Art Direction*	Ferdinando Scarfiotti, Bruno Cesari
	Oscar	*Best Editing*	Gabriella Cristiani
	Golden Globe	*Best Original Score*	Ryuichi Sakamoto, David Byrne, Cong Su
	Oscar	*Best Original Score*	Ryuichi Sakamoto, David Byrne, Cong Su
	Oscar	*Best Sound*	Bill Rowe, Ivan Sharrock
Lunga Vita alla Signora!	Venice	*Silver Lion (shared)*	Ermanno Olmi
Maurice	Venice	*Best Actor*	James Wilby/Hugh Grant
	Venice	*Best Music*	Richard Robbins
	Venice	*Silver Lion (shared)*	James Ivory
Moonstruck	Berlin	*Silver Bear (Best Director)*	Norman Jewison
	Oscar	*Best Original Screenplay*	John Patrick Shanley
	WGA	*Best Original Screenplay*	John Patrick Shanley
	Oscar	*Best Actress*	Cher
	Golden Globe	*Best Actress – Comedy*	Cher
	Golden Globe	*Best Supporting Actress*	Olympia Dukakis
	Oscar	*Best Supporting Actress*	Olympia Dukakis

FILM	EVENT	CATEGORY	WINNERS
Mother of Kings	Berlin	*Silver Bear (Outstanding Achievement)*	Janus Zaorski
My Life as a Dog	Golden Globe	*Best Foreign Language Film*	Lasse Hallström
The Name of the Rose	BAFTA BAFTA	*Best Make-up* *Best Actor*	Hasso Von Hugo Sean Connery
La Passion Béatrice	César	*Best Costumes*	Jacqueline Moreau
Pelle the Conqueror	Cannes	*Golden Palm*	Bille Agust
Platoon	BAFTA BAFTA	*Best Director* *Best Editing*	Oliver Stone Claire Simpson
Radio Days	BAFTA BAFTA	*Best Costume Design* *Best Production Design*	Jeffrey Kurland Santo Loquasto
Red Sorghum	Berlin	*Golden Bear (Grand Prix)*	Zhang Yimou
Roxanne	WGA	*Best Adapted Screenplay*	Steve Martin
The Sacrifice	BAFTA	*Best Foreign Film*	Anna-Lena Wibom, Andrei Tarkovsky
Salaam Bombay	Cannes	*Camera d'Or*	Mira Nair
The South	Cannes	*Best Director*	Fernando Solanas
Thou Shalt Not Kill	Cannes	*Jury Prize*	Krzysztof Kieslowski
Travelling avant	César	*Best Male Hopeful*	Thierry Fremont
The Untouchables	Golden Globe BAFTA	*Best Supporting Actor* *Best Score*	Sean Connery Ennio Morricone

Wall Street

The Witches of Eastwick

FILM	EVENT	CATEGORY	WINNERS
Wall Street	Oscar	*Best Actor*	Michael Douglas
Golden Globe	Best Actor - Drama	*Michael Douglas*	
Wish You Were Here	BAFTA	*Best Screenplay*	David Leland
Witches of Eastwick	BAFTA	*Best Special Visual Effects*	Mike Lanteri, Mike Owens, Edward Jones, Bruce Walters
A World Apart	Cannes	*Best Actress*	Barbara Hershey, Jodhi May, Linda Mvusi
	Cannes	*Special Grand Prize of the Jury*	Chris Menges
Zoo ... La Nuit	Genie	*Best Picture*	Roger Frappier, Pierre Gendron
	Genie	*Best Director*	Jean-Claude Lauzon
	Genie	*Best Original Screenplay*	Jean-Claude Lauzon
	Genie	*Best Cinematography*	Guy Dufaux
	Genie	*Best Actor*	Roger Le Bel
	Genie	*Best Supporting Actor*	Germain Houde
	Genie	*Best Film Editing*	Michel Arcand
	Genie	*Best Art Direction*	Jean-Baptiste Tard
	Genie	*Best Costume Design*	Andrée Morin
	Genie	*Best Score*	Jean Corriveau
	Genie	*Best Sound*	Yvon Benoît, Hans-Peter Strobl, Adrian Croll
	Genie	*Best Sound Editing*	Marcel Pothier, Dianne Boucher, Viateur Paiement

THE US YEAR

Two Hollywood studios tried essentially the same approach this year to managing a film-making business. Both were responding to the way profitability has suffered despite record box-office takings, largely due to a rise in the average price for a studio-produced movie to just under $20 million. Both shuddered to learn that Sylvester Stallone received around $20 million for *Rambo III* and that other costs on the movie exceeded $40 million. Something had to be done, and forcing the Writers Guild into a strike over residuals wasn't the only answer.

One studio reduced costs by using second-line stars in carefully plotted TV-style comedies, the other by using little known actors in dramas aimed at international audiences. Both studios declined to deal with big-ticket producers and packagers, opting to keep control in-house. Both studios had clear visions of how Hollywood must change to preserve its current prosperity.

The two studios are Disney and Columbia. Disney prospered from its policy, rising to second place behind Paramount at the box-office, and first place in terms of profitability. Columbia lost hundreds of millions of dollars after giving up on its new approach before it had even been tested in cinemas.

The reason for the different outcomes lies in the two companies' boardrooms. After rescuing a moribund film-making operation four years ago, Disney's management team is solidly entrenched, never more so than this year, when hit after hit rolled out from Mickey Avenue. But Columbia's chief, David Puttnam, was never central to the plans of the studio's owners, Coca-Cola. Coke was mainly concerned with executing a lucrative financial manoeuvre that incidentally happened to take away Puttnam's authority.

SHAKE-UPS

Puttnam's resignation in September immediately after Coca-Cola merged Columbia into its other film-making subsidiary Tri-Star provided American newspaper readers with their best 'what happened?' story. The year's other major disasters, the decline and near-fall of Cannon and Dino De Laurentiis's DEG, had too strong an air of inevitability to rival the saga of Puttnam's departure. Lorimar's purchase by Warner, Orion's purchase by former TV mogul John W. Kluge, Universal parent MCA's moves to fend off a threatened takeover by real estate baron Donald Trump, MGM/UA's possible sale by canny asset-trader Kirk Kerkorian - these shifts paled into insignificance beside the question of whether David Puttnam had been too good for Hollywood.

Lindsay Anderson directs Lillian Gish in *The Whales of August* (*above*). Martin Rosen in the Montana hayfields for *Stacking* (*right*).

FALL OF PUTTNAM

The irony in the Columbia débâcle was that Puttnam left after 13 months in office for the most traditional of reasons: his authority was undermined. Conspiracy theorists reasoned that he couldn't have gone if powerful enemies like producer Ray Stark, Coke spokesman Bill Cosby, super-agent Michael Ovitz and even stars Bill Murray and Warren Beatty hadn't pulled some strings. Commentators struck by Puttnam's inability not to say nasty things about people he dislikes sought to portray his fall as a morality play: the man who wanted to reform Hollywood was knifed by the Old Guard. Much was made of chit-chat like Ray Stark's gibe about 'British Columbia', referring to Puttnam's preference for British directors.

All of that made great copy, but the fact is that Puttnam wasn't fired, he resigned. He left with a

Norman Mailer brings *Tough Guys Don't Dance* to the screen (*above*). Brian De Palma guides Kevin Costner through *The Untouchables* (*left*).

multi-million dollar buy-out of the remainder of his contract. He got out three weeks after Coke announced it was adding several hundred million dollars to its own balance sheet by consolidating Columbia and Tri-Star, and that it was naming Tri-Star chairman Victor Kaufman to head the combined studios. In the deal, Coke retained 49 per cent of Tri-Star and left the impression that, if Kaufman could make the new venture a success, it might sell out the rest. Coke seemed indifferent to Puttnam's reaction.

DIFFERENT APPROACHES

It was a foregone conclusion that Puttnam would not work under Kaufman, even if Puttnam's contract hadn't specified autonomy in putting pictures into production. Kaufman is a deal-maker with an affinity for hiring stars and paying them top dollar. Kaufman's Tri-Star bought in *Ironweed*, which paired Jack Nicholson and Meryl Streep at a cost of over $20 million, but grossed negligibly. He was willing to pay $5 million to sign TV star Bruce Willis for the flop *Sunset*. Despite Kaufman's statement that he intended to run Columbia and Tri-Star as separate entities, Puttnam couldn't have felt comfortable yoked to a partner running in the opposite direction. Indeed, Kaufman's promise of autonomy for Columbia sounded hollow only six weeks after Puttnam left, when the studio underwent a staff cut to reduce its operating budget by 30-40 per cent.

In the furore surrounding Puttnam's departure, the most constant note was gloating over his fall by Hollywood's movers and shakers. From one end of town to the other they pronounced Puttnam an impractical dreamer for having been so outspoken over what he called 'the abuses of the system'. Little attention was paid to the possibility that Puttnam might have been able to make Coke some money despite putting box-office considerations second after social relevance. In fact, the Kaufman regime immediately acted to reduce the possibility that any of Puttnam's films might become hits. Many Christmas playdates for *The Last Emperor* were cancelled, and *Hope and Glory* was given a muted semi-arthouse release. Kaufman announced a $105 million writedown of Columbia's unreleased inventory of pictures, a sharp and perhaps premature slap at Puttnam's judgement in choosing them. 'They are strangling my smaller pictures at birth,' Puttnam lamented. In a repudiation of Puttnam's vehement dislike of signing producers to lucrative multi-film deals, Kaufman signed Old Guardsman (and one-time Columbia chairman) Frank Price to a lucrative multi-film deal. Paramount's head of production Dawn Steel was brought in as Columbia Pictures' new president. Lacking Puttnam's title and his responsibilities, Steel's choice of pictures will be subject to Kaufman's approval. 'She has good commercial taste,' said Kaufman, writing *finis* to the Puttnam era.

DISNEY HITS HOME

What a difference a mile east of Columbia Plaza, where Disney was proving that its new, carefully costed emphasis on happy movies for happy people was a sustainable success story. There was a direct contrast at Christmas-time, when Disney triumphed with TV actors Ted Danson and Tom Selleck in *Three Men and a Baby* while Columbia flopped with Bill Cosby in *Leonard Part 6*.

Disney corporate chairman Michael Eisner backed studio chairman Jeffrey Katzenberg's clever alignments of seemingly past-their-best actors like Richard Dreyfuss and Bette Midler. For the privilege of being in a Disney-crafted hit, stars accepted less than top dollar. The studio dazzled competitors with its ability to sign talent to exclusive long-term deals. 'They're like Moonies over there,' was one complaint. 'It's almost a cult.'

Every Disney film was made for a price, for an audience. The studio's films appealed to audiences because they seemed to have thought behind them, not just prayers. Disney was the first studio with the wit to give Robin Williams a role that exploited his talent for manic free-association comedy, in *Good Morning Vietnam*. When the studio spent big money, as in *Who Framed Roger Rabbit*, it was all on the screen.

Andrei Konchalovsky in the bayous for *Shy People* (*above*). Alan Rudolph does *The Moderns* (*right*).

While other major studios were giving up on the teen genre, Disney did modestly well with *Can't Buy Me Love*. Disney even made big money backing a very cheap comedy, *Ernest Goes to Camp*, that starred a character famous only for being obnoxious in TV adverts.

OLDER AUDIENCES

Disney and all of Hollywood benefited from the adult (over-25s) return to movie-going. Though no one could call Disney's largely white-bread movies highbrow, they were clearly aimed at grown-ups. Part of the reason for Disney's preference for using TV stars like Shelley Long was to attract older TV viewers back into cinemas. The margin by which video sales and rentals exceeded box-office receipts widened, but exhibitors sought comfort in the thought that the pleasure of seeing good movies on tape may be leading adults to seek out newer good movies in the cinemas.

Making movies for an adult audience requires more than just up-ageing the cast. In the palmiest days of youthpix a few years ago, kids would go see any movie with their favourite stars, provided the TV advert indicated that adulthood and conventionality took pratfalls in the picture. Kids enjoyed movies that looked like messes to adults. The studios that had made money giving free rein to undisciplined talent - Universal, in particular - were in the worst position as the worm turned. The studios in the best position to catch adults' interest were the ones that most effectively disciplined their film-makers to focus on the marketable elements of

Bill Forsyth directs *Housekeeping* (*top*). John Sayles handles *Matewan* (*above*).

their projects. *The Untouchables*, for instance, was Brian De Palma's biggest hit since *Carrie*, because Paramount forced him to restrain his impulses to show off.

THE MOVIE FACTORY

Paramount, the box-office leader, enriched its shareholders by manufacturing products like *Fatal Attraction* and *Beverly Hills Cop II*. No one could have predicted that *Fatal* would be the year's top money-maker, but Paramount was sure at least that it wouldn't lose money, because it tooled and re-tooled the picture from concept to final print.

TUMBLING INDIES

The antithesis of Paramount and Disney were Cannon and DEG, two seats-of-the-pants operations that got kicked around comprehensively.

The three Hustons who made *The Dead*: Tony wrote the script, John directed and Anjelica, his daughter, acted.

Cannon, miraculously, survives, by the grace of an Italian real estate mogul named Giancarlo Parretti who somehow has been led to believe that Menachem Golan's erratic taste can someday make money for him. DEG, Dino De Laurentiis's folly, is now extinct.

Cannon managed to achieve a negative net worth estimated at $200 million when such films as *Superman IV* consistently failed to earn their costs back, let alone provide cash to service the monstrous debt incurred by the incautious buying sprees of previous years. After losses of $60 million in 1986 and $98 million in 1987, the company's stock dropped to below three dollars a share (from a high of $45.50), as asset after high-priced asset was dumped at fire-sale prices to meet crippling interest payments on the 'junk bonds' the company had issued in its expansion. The hardest blow was perhaps the company's settlement of US government charges that it had mis-stated facts about its earnings since 1982, using these mis-statements to raise $339 million from the public. Somehow, though, the company kept making films despite its record of failure and evident inability to understand the US market.

Cannon and DEG had sought to build major American companies but forgot to make major American movies. Both benefited from the bigger-fool atmosphere of the American stock market in 1986. Investors bought $88 million of DEG stock, figuring that there would always be a bigger fool to buy the paper at a higher price. Instead, after the company lost $70 million in 1987-8, the stock plummeted from $19 to less than a dollar.

Cannon and DEG established costly distribution infrastructures that were second-rank setups to begin with and then had the impossible task of selling movies that never should have been made. Golan (and his partner Yoram Globus) and De Laurentiis had done well in the past by pre-selling enough foreign and ancillary rights to their pictures to guarantee profits even if the picture did no business in the US. They could turn out long strings of rubbishy flops and still get finance for more.

Now, though, acting as their own distributors in the US and paying big money to strike prints and buy TV adverts, Cannon and DEG needed good movies. But neither got even one good hit. The closest Cannon came was a couple of pics starring ex-karate champ Chuck Norris. DEG built studio facilities in North Carolina and churned out numerous films in the $6-10 million dollar range with hackneyed plots and unappealing stars. One after another these unpromotable films reached their date of release and dropped off the cliff like lemmings. The final straw for DEG was a movie called *Million Dollar Mystery*. The movie's gimmick was that it contained a clue to the whereabouts of a real million-dollar treasure. So few people went to the movie, however, that the person who spotted the clue and collected the money made more than DEG collected in rentals.

AFTER THE CRASH

Cannon and DEG are merely the largest failures among the many companies that floated stock issues in recent years. The market crash of 19 October hit Hollywood in general harder than the rest of American industry. But after most of the market recovered, many new and marginal entertainment stocks stayed down, reflecting investor scepticism that any newcomer can effectively storm the town. Hits eluded wealthy TV producer Aaron Spelling, whose company used investors' money for flops like *Surrender*. Carolco, despite its *Rambo* franchise, has yet to prove it can produce non-*Rambo* hits. New Century, after a short under-financed attempt to become a sort of mini-Cannon with movies like *Heat* and *Russkies*, merged itself into producer-director Taylor Hackford's company.

WOBBLY LORIMAR

Lorimar Telepictures, so successful when it stuck to TV, over-reached itself buying the MGM lot and trying to compete with the majors. It was said that chairman Merv Adelson was eager to become an old-style movie mogul so he could get off the B-list for Hollywood parties to which mere TV moguls are relegated. But after Adelson's partner Lee Rich left to become chairman of MGM/UA in 1986, Lorimar lost nearly $100 million in the film business. The company's films, commissioned by super-agent Bernie Brillstein wearing his other hat as head of Lorimar's film division, were interesting failures like *Orphans*, but failures nevertheless. After a protracted death-struggle, around which ex-Fox owner Marvin Davis hovered, Warner Bros bought the whole operation.

LION NOISE

MGM/UA, enjoying stability for the first time in years in its new incarnation just across the street from the lot where the lion once roared, turned out a couple of hits. The bi-annual Bond film, *The Living Daylights*, made UA's year. *Moonstruck*, one of the babies Puttnam threw out with the bath water when he arrived at Columbia, turned around to MGM and became a huge hit. Things were going so well, in fact, that owner Kirk Kerkorian let it be known that he might be willing to sell again. The last time he sold the studio, he made hundreds of millions buying it back shortly afterwards from Ted Turner.

ORION SHAPES UP

Orion, the one start-from-scratch success in recent history, was menaced by Sumner M. Redstone, owner of TV giant Viacom and an investor who has profited in the past by threatening movie company takeovers. Redstone accumulated a quarter of Orion's stock before being bought out by former TV mogul John Kluge. Redstone's profit exceeded $20 million. Kluge, a friend of Orion chief Arthur Krim, came in as a 'white knight' and wound up with two-thirds of the company. Orion was otherwise in fine shape after releasing such good performers as *Robocop*, *Throw Momma from the Train*, *No Way Out* and *Colors*.

SMALL HITS BIG

Vestron, which moved with commendable caution into film production from video distribution, was this year's small company with a large hit, *Dirty Dancing*. Last year's, Hemdale, when it wasn't picking up kudos for having backed *The Last Emperor*, was in court arguing with Vestron over the video rights to *Platoon*. Vestron used its eventual $15.7 million settlement from Hemdale to offset its losses from the shake-out in the video rental business.

TOO MANY FILMS

Independent film production rose sharply, spurred in part by an out-of-date perception of video viewers' receptivity to obscure titles. Too many low-cost films were made for cinema distributors to digest - 37 per cent of independent features never reached the cinemas. Video outlets began scaling back their choice of tapes, rejecting films that hadn't benefited from a cinema launch. A year ago, as many as three-fifths of all films made for under $4 million went into the black, but far fewer cheapos made since then look like being profitable.

SPEAKING SPANISH

Several studios found crossover audiences for films oriented towards Hispanic audiences. Columbia sold *La Bamba* in the mainstream as a rock 'n' roll movie but supplemented its gross with over 50 prints in Spanish, marketed as a Hispanic success story. Warner had a modest success when it picked up *Stand and Deliver* from public television. But *The Milagro Beanfield War* failed in both Hispanic and mainstream markets.

FOREIGN SPACE

Imports, seeking the same dollar as American independents, have suffered in recent years. Arthouses have been hard hit by the rise of urban multiplexes, and among the majors only Orion retains any interest in distributing subtitled movies. French movies still draw American cinéastes, but Italian movies are increasingly rare. *Tampopo* broke new ground for Japan, and *Babette's Feast* from Denmark found an audience.

Americans saw fewer British movies than usual in a Bond year, unless *The Last Emperor* qualifies. *Cry Freedom* failed to attract even a *Killing Fields* audience. *The Lonely Passion of Judith Hearne* was a particular disappointment. Among English-speaking nations only Australia succeeded in making a movie that attracted a mass American audience, *Crocodile Dundee II*.

BART MILLS

Wayne Wang takes a break from Chinese themes to film Tom Hulce and Mary Elizabeth Mastrantonio in the thriller *Slam Dance*.

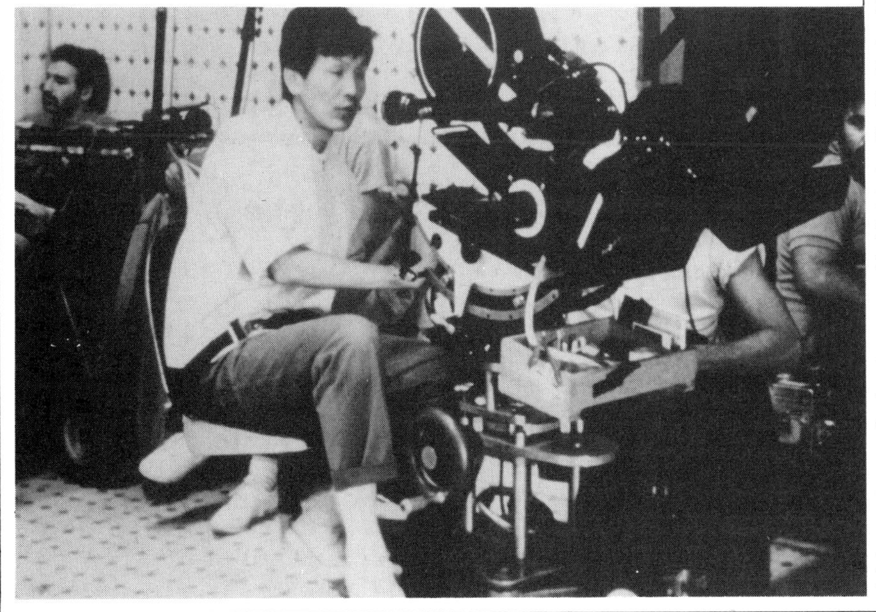

THE UK YEAR

The British love nothing more than a good moan. Cadge a conversation amongst the self-styled film business types in the Groucho Club, L'Escargot, or any of the industry watering-holes in the environs of Soho, and you can listen to any number of whinges about the state of the UK film industry (a.k.a. why my script/concept/treatment keeps getting rejected).

That is not to say film industry folk do not have plenty to moan and groan about. Britain must be one of the few countries in Europe with a government that shows little or no interest in the film industry, almost going out of its way to make financing hard to get and to discourage foreign interest and investment.

To outsiders, the movie business must appear a glamorous and glitzy world filled with pouting starlets, harassed directors and cigar-chomping producers, with only the few being chosen to appear bedecked in all their finery and waltz into the BAFTA awards under an assault from popping flash guns. The British film industry is - and traditionally has been - a small community, especially when it comes to the movers and shakers who still inhabit the Soho meeting places.

TV MUSCLES IN ON MOVIES

Now the British business is being forced - not exactly screaming and shaking - to slightly open its doors. During 1987 and into 1988, practically all the independent television stations, along with the BBC, announced film projects of their own, following the example set by Channel Four some years ago.

The big question, though, is whether in the long-term this step will be a good thing for the film industry (emphasis on *film*); granted a lot of these television executives and commissioning editors are sharp folk, but whether they can fully understand and appreciate the difference between filmic drama as against television drama remains to be seen.

Talking about film primarily in television terms creates a product that doesn't really embrace what cinema has to offer. How many television executives, one wonders, spend much time in cinemas and can comprehend what the elusive 'cinema experience' truly is? It should be remembered that Channel Four wheeled out a lot of films that stood no chance of getting a theatrical release before movies like *My Beautiful Laundrette* and *Letter to Brezhnev* finally clicked at the box-office.

INCOMING TV CASH

The TV companies have three options when setting up film operations; clear theatrical rights when a television film is being made, commission an independent production company to make the feature, or set up a separate division to make films.

The BBC made *Little Sisters* on location in the US, and it seems likely the Beeb will follow the policy of commissioning independent companies to make their films. The Granada Group is operating on two fronts - Granada TV made *The Fruit Machine* and plans more projects while Granada Film Productions, formed early in 1988, has developed its own production programme. The latter has already wrapped *Tree of Hands*, starring Lauren Bacall, and *Joyriders*, set in Ireland.

Other independent stations with film ambitions include Anglia, Scottish TV, Yorkshire, TVS and Central TV. London Weekend TV recently made its first feature, *A Handful of Dust*, working with an independent production company. Thames Television's long-established film arm Euston also has feature projects planned.

OTHER MONEY

Apart from these television stations, the entities most actively involved in local production are Channel Four and the government-backed film investment company British Screen.

Simon Relph, head of British Screen, describes his organization's contribution to the local film industry as 'pretty remarkable'. That claim can't really be argued with, considering British Screen will probably invest in 25 per cent of all British films made in any one year. But he operates on an annual budget of around $6 million, and usually invests no more than $500,000 in each project, which means producers still have to find a hefty chunk of their budgets from other sources.

British Screen and Channel Four are often involved in some of the same films. Recent examples include *Vroom*, *American Roulette*, *Paris by Night*, *The Nature of the Beast*, *We Think the World of You* and *High Hopes*. The two companies share similar viewpoints on what a British film should be - unlikely to be a blockbuster but with high production values and good acting, generally adding up to an 'interesting' production.

Between the two of them they account for rather a lot of typical 'British' films with plenty of worthy social-minded content and not a great deal of pure entertainment value.

MISSING INGREDIENT

'Entertainment' is, of course, what the British public wants. According to industry statistics the UK's cinema attendance rose from 72 million in 1986 to 76 million in 1987, and the film they all wanted to see was Paul Hogan's *Crocodile Dundee*. Of the top 20 grossing films only one could even vaguely be classified as British, the James Bond film *The Living Daylights*, which, though it featured a mainly British cast, was partly filmed at Pinewood Studios and had a British director, was still financed out of the US.

Over the past few years British film-makers have had more than a few problems making entertainment films. Producers and directors are good at packing their productions with rich acting, period detail, eccentric characters and intellectual ideas, but rather bad at coming up with a film that appeals to the masses.

PRODUCTION HOUSES

In 1987 about 50 films were either filmed in the UK or shot overseas with British investment. Of that 50, probably no more than ten were totally British financed and some of those ten may have been partly financed by an early sale to an American distributor, a deal that will give other investors confidence in the project.

The most active film production companies (as compared to the investment houses) are George Harrison's HandMade Films, Zenith, Palace Pictures and Working Title.

HandMade splits its production slate between

acted in *Mona Lisa* and *The Lonely Passion of Judith Hearne* got to direct *The Raggedy Rawney*. Bruce Robinson followed *Withnail and I* for HandMade with *How to Get Ahead in Advertising*, while David Leland, who co-scripted *Mona Lisa*, directed *Checking Out* in the US following his success with *Wish You Were Here*.

The latter was financed by Zenith, which also likes to split its production slate between the UK and the US, especially since it has a multi-picture production deal with US-based distributor Atlantic Releasing.

In the US, Zenith was involved with Paul

Derek Jarman records *The Last of England* (*left*). Jack Clayton does *The Lonely Passion of Judith Hearne* (*below*). Stephen Frears on *Sammy and Rosie Get Laid* (*bottom*).

Britain and the US. In 1987 the company started *The Powwow Highway*, directed by Jonathan Wacks, and Nic Roeg's *Track 29*, both filmed in the US, and Bob Hoskins' directorial début *The Raggedy Rawney*, filmed in Czechoslovakia, and the Hoskins-Maggie Smith starrer *The Lonely Passion of Judith Hearne*.

HandMade is rather unusual as far as the British film industry goes. Unlike most of the other indigenous production companies it is totally self-financing, and tends to shun co-production or even co-financing deals. The company made *Mona Lisa* in association with Palace Pictures and swore 'never again', and unlike most other companies who are still drawn to the Soho area it has attractive offices close to Sloane Square in the plusher part of London.

HandMade also tends to work with the same people time and time again. Bob Hoskins, who

Schrader's *Patty Hearst*, with Natasha Richardson in the lead role, while UK-based films in 1987 included *For Queen and Country*, *Sour Sweet*, *Paris by Night* and *Just Ask for Diamond*.

When *Just Ask for Diamond* lost its original title, it also lost a ready-made publicity campaign. The film, directed by Stephen Bayly, was to have been called *The Falcon's Malteser*, and the publicity plan involved handling out boxes of Malteser sweets. Unfortunately, the estate of Dashiell Hammett got wind of the film and had an injunction brought out against the title.

Palace Pictures has been busy increasing its production slate. In 1986 it made *The Dream Demon*, *The Courier*, *Shag* and, most importantly, *High Spirits*. Writer/director Neil Jordan has been Palace's most successful creative talent with hits like *The Company of Wolves* and *Mona Lisa*, but *High Spirits*, with a cast including Peter O'Toole, Steve Guttenberg and Daryl Hannah, was his and Palace's attempt to crack the US market.

Ditto in 1988 with Palace's film *Scandal*, starring John Hurt, Bridget Fonda and Joanne Whalley. It's about the Profumo scandal of the early sixties, which is generally credited with bringing down the government of the day and still has enough resonance to garner mucho publicity.

Another film that was a publicity bandwagon from start to finish was *Buster*, starring Phil Collins and Julie Walters, about Great Train robber Buster Edwards. A hand-in-hand walk along the beach at Cannes 1987 for Collins and Walters started the ball rolling, and the sheer pleasantness of Collins and Walters meant the tabloids kept their interest until shooting finished.

Though still a relatively young production company, Working Title has established a strong reputation with such critical successes as *My Beautiful Laundrette* and *Wish You Were Here*. Other recent Working Title projects were *Sammy and Rosie Get Laid* and *A World Apart*.

CROSSING THE WATER

As most British producers now recognize, the trick is making a film that can travel well to the US. That means broader subject-matter, larger budgets, and a name actor that the Yanks will recognize; *A World Apart*, with Barbara Hershey in the lead, dealt with South Africa.

Working Title's Tim Bevan believes achieving regular supply to the US is important, rather than UK producers being regarded as 'a distant cousin who should be placated once in a while.'

He added: 'If you can make medium-budget pictures like *A World Apart* that deal with a universal story, not necessarily shot in Britain, you have a fighting chance.'

RUNAWAY PRODUCTION

Along with the admitted problems British producers have with raising the readies, the financial realities of filming in the UK still remain problematic. More and more producers are being asked to make their budgets stretch further and further, and some are finding an answer by switching their location from Britain to an Eastern bloc country.

Producer Mark Forstater took the Zenith film *The Wolves of Willoughby Chase* to studios and locations in Czechoslovakia, despite the fact the film is set in Victorian England. The reason was simple: the film he made for $4 million in Czechoslovakia would have cost twice as much to film in the UK.

So Stephanie Beacham, Mel Smith, Geraldine James and the British crew settled down in Prague to savour the rather different environment of Eastern European film-making – language difficulties and a military presence.

Also in Prague at the same time was producer Norma Heyman (fresh from wrapping *Buster*)

with *The Burning Secret*, starring Faye Dunaway and Klaus Maria Brandauer, while Ed Simons took *Dr Jekyll and Mr Hyde - A Journey into Fear*, toplining Anthony Perkins and Glynis Barber, to Hungary.

MORE AMBITION

Possibly the most interesting film to watch of the 1988 crop will be *Slipstream*, a sci-fi film shot at Pinewood and costing about $13 million which was raised by a British company, Entertainment, without any foreign investment or pre-sales. Entertainment is primarily a film and home-video distributor. But when it decided to get into movie-making it took the high road - a big-budget film with name actors (Mark Hamill, Bob Peck, F. Murray Abraham and Ben Kingsley), an American producer (Gary Kurtz) and an American director (Steven Lisberger).

CLOSING DOORS

British production - and more importantly the confidence of the British film industry - has taken blows over the past few years in relation to the state of local studios. Pinewood went four-wall in May 1987, meaning it decided to purely rent out its stages rather than provide full crewing. Then, in the summer of 1988, Cannon announced it was selling Britain's oldest surviving studio Elstree to a shadowy investment consortium which had plans to use the 28-acre site for property development.

Oddly enough, the Cannon announcement came at a time when Elstree was full - with Steven Spielberg's *Indiana Jones and the Last Crusade* taking up many of the stages - as were Pinewood and Shepperton. The British studios have learned to survive on a mixture of features, TV productions, commercials and pop promos. Pinewood lost the new Bond film *Licence Revoked* to a Mexican studio, but managed to fill its stages with a mixture of other ventures, and was much boosted when Warner Brothers decided to film *Batman* there.

South African stories: Richard Attenborough covers *Biko* (*left*). Chris Menges does *A World Apart* (*below*).

END OF AN AFFAIR?

British film-makers are lucky in that they share a common language with the US, making the American market theoretically somewhat easier to crack. But US interest in British films does seem to go in waves - after *A Room With a View* and *Mona Lisa* they were flavour of the month, but that can so easily change.

As Simon Perry, producer of *White Mischief*, pointed out: 'For British films it is either feast or famine. The Americans' fascination never seems to last very long, but when another *A Room With a View* appears, that will encourage a new wave of romances, and trysts will be made.'

Some of the folk involved with selling British films to overseas markets seem to feel the latest American love-affair with British pictures is ebbing. The appetite amongst the smaller US distributors for the specialized low-budget film that the British usually make seems to be on the wane, and it is up to local producers and directors to come up with some less parochial fare.

In Britain it is always easy for film-makers to find a target - the government is very little use to them, the financial community has no faith in them and the American money men's opinion wavers from one side to another. But despite a limited production output, the admitted plethora of technical skill, acting talent and creative abilities the British do have should keep the films coming.

MARK ADAMS

ELLEN BARKIN

Hollywood's directors, writers and agents seem to divide women's roles into two groups; the first provide an occasion for what press releases like to call 'an emotional *tour-de-force*' - intended to absolve *angst* and induce Oscars. The rest are roles for victims - characters who are derided, beaten, humiliated, rebuked and generally treated like garbage by the lead male.

For the latter category, performers like Barbara Hershey, Kathryn Harrold and Teri Garr come to mind, none of whom, despite their abilities, have procured a part that catapults them into the mainstream. It is regrettable that there exists such an inherent fascination with the testing of women's fortitude. Most fine women's roles, excluding bimbos, man-eaters or vacuous ornamentation, involve the depiction of pain and suffering.

Until *The Big Easy*, Ellen Barkin was the movie world's reluctant Patron Saint of the Walking Wounded. She did it so well, but some knew she was capable of much more. Take *Diner*, a poignant re-creation of male camaraderie, in which Barkin resisted with considerable pain and fortitude the humiliation afforded by her musically-obsessed husband, David Stern. The pivotal scene that encompassed their prematurely-crumbling marriage played around his reproaches when she mis-files part of his record collection. The emphasis shifted from Stern's obvious lack of sympathy/empathy for his wife to her attempt, arms crossed in a gesture of gentle defiance, to retain her dignity, and thus avoid ending up a victim to his misplaced fanaticism.

Later on in the movie, she is utilized by the ubiquitous Small Town Boy With Dreams, and one-time suitor, Boogie (Mickey Rourke), to impersonate some voluptuous denizen of the sock-hops and drive-ins, Carol Heathrow, upon whose deflowering rests a sizeable bet. Smuggled to Rourke's house (where the clandestine adjudicators await), and adorned in a Sandra Dee wig, Boogie cannot bring himself to countenance her part in the deception, and Barkin is just perfect leaning against his car, shrugging off the potential embarrassment of the charade with customary resignation and an

air of quiet despondency.

Despite the critical and monetary success of *Diner*, the big parts continued to elude her. She assiduously beat a path of wounded depressive, but always genuine, characterization through a string of more-or-less unsuccessful movies such as *Tender Mercies*, *Harry and Son* and *Daniel*. Two more significant, though hardly innovative, roles came a little later. First, in W. D. Richter's wildly convoluted camp failure *Buckaroo Banzai*, she flirted with the potential of self-parody as Penny Pretty, the neurotic and suicidal love-interest for the swaggering super-hero of the title, played by Peter Weller. Penny was a Pearl White for the Valium Generation, reviled by bar-room hecklers, tortured with ants, honey and John Lithgow's implausible Italian accent. Despite the film's inconsistencies she was very funny and able to prove her versatility. Broadening her range slightly, she was a vulnerable girl dreaming of love and emotional reciprocation in *Enormous Changes at the Last Minute*.

Barkin is a native of the Bronx and admits to being selective about the inordinate amount of garbage she is offered. Her reticence about appearing in crudely packaged blockbusters and generally abusing her talent derives partly from a long incubation period at drama school.

The Big Easy jubilantly inaugurates a new era for Ellen Barkin. As Annie Osborne, the quietly officious D.A. spearheading an investigation into Louisiana police corruption, she transforms a potentially inhibitive role as repressed love interest into a spunky, assuredly-combative figure who is not humiliated, exploited, nor even discarded by the male lead. Something of a turning-point for the anaemic genre of detective romance, the movie came ensconced with fine music, effervescent Cajun locales, and a deft screenplay by Daniel Petrie which enticed interest in the Quaid/Barkin liaison.

There is a sex scene early on in *The Big Easy* wherein (without recourse to the customary ploy of introducing women's breasts as separate characters complete with close-ups) Barkin's face conveys true ecstasy. Unlike Kim Basinger, Ellen Barkin does not have to equate sexy with emerging half-naked in the middle of a waterfall. Intermittently moaning 'Stop that' in response to Dennis Quaid's caresses from 'neath her skirt, Miss Osborne clings to the bedpost for reassurance. Barkin gets to enjoy herself and get the guy.

In a casting matrix besotted with cosmetic appeal and personality pigeon-holing, it isn't surprising Barkin's fragile, unconventional beauty is somehow anomalous. Like Debra Winger, she continually pursues quality roles which won't compromise her professionalism. This has given Barkin a reputation in certain quarters for being a nuisance, but it does not hurt to care more for the rudiments of a performance than the billing one's dog's hairdresser is going to get.

Her latest movie was *Siesta*, a dreamy fable of a female skydiver's obsession with her mentor, Gabriel Byrne. Under Mary Lambert's direction, Barkin lethargically ambles around Spain as an amnesiac apparition colliding with character-actor cameos placed like 35mm lifebuoys to upholster a drowning script. With customary ease and just a hint of suffering, Barkin exonerates herself from *Siesta*'s debris.

For various reasons Barkin hasn't worked for a while now. In the past, under the direction of Douglas Sirk, George Cukor or even Elia Kazan, the Barkin persona would have flourished. But better parts will come and, until then, Barkin will wait at her apartment in New York with a measure of her customary resilience.

MARKUS NATTEN

JULIETTE BINOCHE

The dark helmet of hair may suggest a homage to Louise Brooks. But the more comprehensive impression strikes a closer chord of memory: her oval face, wide-set eyes, and full, slightly parted lips irresistibly recall Anna Karina, the actress whom a generation ago at least one critic unambiguously dubbed the Galatea of Jean-Luc Godard.

The parallel is, though, evoked, not so much by any direct likeness of Juliette Binoche to Karina as by the context of Léos Carax's *Mauvais sang* (strangely rendered for British consumption as *The Night Is Young*), the film in which she first impelled notice. (She had, in fact, previously played a leading role in André Téchiné's *Rendezvous*, but that movie contrived to make little impact beyond French shores.)

The whole manner and tone of *Mauvais sang* is neo-Godardian to an unmistakable degree; and reminiscent specifically of the Godard movies in which Karina was featured. Most apparently, perhaps, it recalls *Alphaville* and *Pierrot le Fou*, deriving from the former its setting of a 'post-modern' city, from the latter the theme of 'the last romantic couple', a strange doomed idyll amid a fantasized gangster conspiracy; moreover, Binoche's character is actually called Anna and is initially discovered as the mistress of an older man played by Michel Piccoli, himself an actor who found fame in the early Godard era and appeared in *Le Mépris*.

Godard was married to Karina during the time they worked together, and the resulting films could be seen, at one of many levels, as love letters to, and candid camera records of, his wife of that time. And again the comparison tends to hold: Carax and Binoche became partners in life as well as work during the making of *Mauvais sang*. The apparent blurring of art and life is heightened by the way the film's main lead, Denis Lavant, seems to represent the director's *alter ego* to the extent of bearing a more than passing resemblance to him.

The same blurring process could be said to apply to the preparation of the movie: Carax said in an interview that he and Binoche spent two months together, 'talking our way into it, going to movies and looking at paintings,' while Binoche vouchsafed that Carax's way of 'explaining' the character she was to play was (shades of Godard indeed) to show her Dreyer's last film, *Gertrud*. Not only that, but the process of filming was scarcely conventional. The company took over an old warehouse and effectively turned it into a studio, which also provided accommodation for Carax, Binoche and Lavant during shooting. This spread over no less than six months, and Binoche (who says that, coming from a theatre background, she previously found filming strange) maintains that the slow pace allowed her to relax into the role and to achieve more spontaneity. Might her initial nervousness have become part of the characterization? The actress demurred, but Carax was in no doubt that it had.

This might seem to propose Carax in the guise of Pygmalion, but there is more to it than that. For one thing, Binoche has herself voiced an ambition to turn director. And for another, she has in the meantime gone on to achieve much wider celebrity as one of the stars of Philip Kaufman's film version of Milan Kundera's novel *The Unbearable Lightness of Being*, a picture hailed in some quarters as the first 'European' art movie to be directed by an American, and a film which - however exaggerated some of the claims made for it - has justly received widespread attention.

Playing, in English, the role of a Czech, Binoche seems more convincing than some others in the multinational cast, but perhaps this is merely a function of her inhabiting the role so completely. Her Tereza begins as a bookish innocent and progressively - heartrendingly - acquires responsibility and commitment, to the extent of being able to inspire her initially feckless husband with a new sense of seriousness. The gamine-like quality of the earlier scenes is a trickier proposition than the enigmatic half-vulnerability of the woman in *Mauvais sang*, but Binoche makes it uncloyingly persuasive.

And the gradual onset of moral 'weightedness' (the exile's reaction to the evasive 'lightness' of the hedonistic West) is made similarly believable; partly, no doubt, because it is offset by a capacity to conjure the erotic - a trait most strikingly evinced in the photographic session with Sabina (Lena Olin), where provocativeness and a sort of coyness blend together to communicate an authentic and singular sensuality. Again, the rural idyll of the movie's closing sequences depends crucially upon the feeling of Binoche having assumed a sort of 'earth mother' dimension. All in all, this is a performance containing a rare combination of physical and emotional resonance.

Anna Karina, it may be recalled, never properly fulfilled her promise after the break with Godard. But somehow, whether or not Juliette Binoche continues a professional liaison with Carax, one fancies that, given any sort of natural justice, she has far horizons in the international cinema.

TIM PULLEINE

WILLEM DAFOE

Some actors are born to play goodness, some to play evil. And some like Willem Dafoe - the most excitingly ambivalent actor of the late eighties - have the unfair advantage of being born to play both.

Dafoe has a face that can look babyish or skull-like, depending on which way you turn it to the light. In *Streets of Fire* and *To Live and Die in LA* he looks as if he has just emerged from a coffin. The skin of his face is stretched over bony cheekbones, the eyes are sunken, the mouth is a smiling rictus. It would be no surprise to see worms crawl out of him while he stands there delivering his lines.

In a film like *Platoon* the actor can look as if he has one foot still in the cradle. Turn him away from the shadows and the features look unformed rather than dissolute, the eyes child-like rather than sepulchral. And the purring voice registers dreamy innocence as fluently as psychotic menace.

Had he lived in the Roaring Thirties, Dafoe would undoubtedly have been signed up by Warner Brothers to play all their baby-faced gangsters. Cagney and he would have fought it out for the 'You dirty rat' concession, and Dafoe would also have put in for Scarface, Baby Face Nelson and Little Caesar. Instead the actor was born in 1955, in Appleton, Wisconsin, and squeezed into movies by the back door of New York experimental theatre. For ten years he was a lead member of Manhattan's Wooster Group, specializing in 'performance' theatre where, Dafoe once said, 'There's lots of text, but psychology and narrative aren't necessarily important.'

And *voilà*, the perfect credo for his first lead movie role: the gang leader in *The Loveless*. Prodigiously devoid of plot or psychology, the film was an existential theme-and-variations on *The Wild One*. In most of his scenes Dafoe just stood there, or sat there astride his motorbike, glowering. He looked like a baby from Hell dressed in black leather. No one knew - the audience certainly didn't - what went on in that sinister mind behind the face (part James Dean, part Dan Duryea) curtained with diseased innocence.

Likewise in *Streets of Fire*. Walter Hill, who also spits on movies with psychology, cast Dafoe as another gang leader. More smoky-menacing lines delivered astride a Harley-Davidson; and another chance for Dafoe to look as if he was on an away-day ticket from Hades. Hill's sleaze-and-smoke décor for the movie seemed made for this actor. Partying in an eternal *walpurgisnacht*, Dafoe wore an artfully-styled quiff of greasy hair, voluptuously reddened lips and black-leather braces over a bare torso: proving he could look physically androgynous as well as morally ambiguous.

Balzac once called Natty Bumppo, hero of Fenimore Cooper's *Leatherstocking Tales*, a 'moral hermaphrodite'. That hits Dafoe off nicely. Charm and infant sweetness leaven even his scuzziest roles. In Friedkin's *To Live and Die in LA*, Dafoe was the smiling psycho with the gleaming eyes and the cadaverous purr, who always had more charisma - and time for charisma - than William Pederson's busy, macho, robotic cop.

The thing that could unravel Dafoe's current career is an excess of mundane action-man roles. His only slip so far is his latest film, *Off Limits* (*Saigon* in UK). Playing a killer-hunting cop in the US Army's Criminal Investigation Department, Dafoe has a role so B-movie platitudinous it could have been played by Robert Stack. An actor who thrives on the incarnation of mysterious forces rather than the indexing of common human motives has here to do all those things that lesser actors have to do. He has to wax morally indignant (about a series of prostitute murders); he has to have a fast-quipping buddy-buddy relationship (with sidekick Gregory Hines); and he even has - woe of woes! - to fall in love. There is at least a camp glee in seeing an actor of Dafoe's stature and complexity fall into the arms of the French nun he loves, saying 'I'm sorry, sister. The world is so insane!'

The most fascinating tweak in Dafoe's career so far has been *Platoon*. He got to play the good guy. And not your average gallivanting macho-man (for which see *Off Limits*), but some weird pot-smoking semi-saint plucked from Oliver Stone's mythopoeic imagination. Sergeant Elias is the glowing image of compassionate man, and Stone had the insight to see that Dafoe's eerie, flayed 'blankness' as an actor could evoke goodness as well as evil. Half-stripped, as he is more than once in the film, Dafoe looks like a crucified Christ out of a German painting: racked, sinewy, forgiving, a figure straight from the concentration-camp school of radiant martyrdom.

Next stop for Dafoe - hardly surprising - is Scorsese's *The Last Temptation of Christ*: with Dafoe taking on the Messianic mantle. The mind boggles at the prospect of a hell-driving Scorsese behind the camera and a heaven-representing Dafoe in front. Whatever kind of film it turns out to be, it is clearly Dafoe's big break. After that, one hopes, the deluge.

HARLAN KENNEDY

CRISPIN GLOVER

Crispin Glover is a deeply weird actor. Sometime around 1985, after he had spent half a decade being weird in the background of high school and youth gang movies - *My Tutor*, *Teachers*, *Racing With the Moon*, *At Close Range* - Hollywood obviously decided it had to do something with him. He was not fitting in with the general teen mêlée: in fact he stuck out like a sore thumb. You could not fail to notice this bizarre bean pole with the hooked nose, protruding cheekbones, gangling gait, unruly hair (he could have made a career out of playing the 'before' picture in Brylcreem ads) and general air of someone who has just escaped from Bellevue.

In addition, Glover does not 'deliver' his lines in a movie so much as torture the truth out of them. He hisses, croons, whispers, strangulates his dialogue. These sounds are usually accompanied by gestures suggestive of someone trying to throttle a large snake.

Early example: in *At Close Range* Glover is standing guard on a dark street for his pals who are robbing a warehouse. Then he has to spot a car and shout the simple line, 'Ah, come on, guys, there's a car!' Glover's enactment is as follows. Clasping his stomach with one hand and embracing his hair with the other, he squirmingly rotates his body, as if in imitation of the late Salomé, and delivers the following sound: 'Aaaggh, c'maarghhhn, garrrs, thesss a cahaurghhh!'

This is wonderful stuff. Confronted with such acting, Hollywood had only two alternatives. Either get rid of the guy or start giving him major roles. Sanity prevailed. Glover's first promotion was to playing Michael J. Fox's dad in *Back to the Future*: one of those dual parts (old dad and young dad) that many actors find so challenging.

Glover's answer to the challenge was, as usual, to go picturesquely bananas. As old dad he looked for once like the 'after' picture in a Brylcreem ad. He wore specs, a slight stoop and a slicked-down short back and sides. But appearances did not deceive hardened Glover fans. This was, they quickly discerned, the loony as before. The threshing-machine gestures began to accompany the lemon-squeezer voice:

and when dad went young in the movie, it was back to our beloved Glover, a young man overboard in the Ocean of Life, the sinking man's Jerry Lewis.

With *River's Edge* the apotheosis is complete. Glover took the lead role and practically hijacked the movie. Not surprisingly, any critic who thought this film was meant as a serious, doom-and-gloom statement about youth couldn't handle Glover. 'Is he being a contorted James Dean or a contorted early Brando?' bleated the unhappy Pauline Kael. But *River's Edge* is a black comedy, as it virtually spells out in its own casting. (As well as Glover, it boasts Dennis Hopper as a primetime pothead trailing an inflatable doll lover.)

Glover gave a spooked-out, baroque, gesticulating performance - part Marcel Marceau, part Richard III - that made his character at once funny and appalling. Not surprisingly, the eccentric young actor was soon the darling of the TV chat shows. He's hewn out a virtual second career from appearing with the likes of Johnny Carson, David Letterman and Britain's own Jonathan Ross.

What makes Crispin tick? The nervous energy (faked or real) is the prime moving part, and it's wondrous to behold. Witness his first Carson appearance. There was the youthful Glover, fidgeting, clutching his thighs and berserkly caressing the chair arms. An occasional jerky hand harvests his shoulder-length hair, and his feet wear candy-striped brogues designed to blind the unwary. 'Being on the show is a very confusing experience,' he drawls breathlessly. (Carson, by the look of him, clearly agrees.) 'I've lost my voice, I'm nervous,' he adds: and then goes on to recount that he had to post-sync the whole of *Back to the Future* because his voice died on day one of shooting.

Soon, at Carson's prompting, the actor brings out one of the miniature sculptures he makes as a hobby. It is an object of strange terror. It looks like a gnome trapped in a prison and it also operates as a musical box, playing 'Let It Be'.

The question we have to ask is: how does an actor born and raised in laidback LA ever get to be like this? Perhaps it was the traumatic influence of his first professional acting role. At age 14, Glover played the eldest Von Trapp son in *The Sound of Music*, on stage at the Dorothy Chandler Pavilion. Three years later he was making movies and the rest is history. Or at least hysteria.

A movie with Glover in it is a thing apart. Who else could survive acting in two Sean Penn pics (*Racing With the Moon* and *At Close Range*) and emerge with no physical or career damage? Who else could appear as an ordinary suburban dad in a movie featuring a mad scientist (*Back to the Future*) and seem substantially madder than the scientist? Above all, who else in Hollywood today is a major media event whether he appears inside a feature film or outside one? Glover has restored a salutary lunacy to the art of serious acting. He has brought a touch of Wonderland to Tinseltown. After the Mad Hatter - the Mad Glover.

HARLAN KENNEDY

RICHARD E. GRANT, PAUL McGANN

Withnail and I gave Richard E. Grant the chance to do what he does best - overact with hilarious abandon. But it was Paul McGann's restrained acting in what could be considered the supporting role which ensured that the film didn't deteriorate into an over-the-top one-hander.

The comedy in *Withnail and I* is both brutal and clever, but so English that the acting of the two newcomers must take much of the credit for the film's critical success in the US.

Although the film wasn't shown to the British cinema-going public until the spring of 1988, it had been made in 1986 and screened to British film-biz folk as early as January 1987. So word about Grant and McGann's strong performances spread. Both have already consolidated their careers in television, film and in Grant's case in a 'sssh-you-know-who' commercial. Grant is again thesping for writer-director Bruce Robinson in his next pic, *How to Get Ahead in Advertising*.

The two performances in *Withnail and I* are in complete contrast with each other; Grant's is eccentric, manic, slightly dangerous but overall enjoyable. His character is gaunt, acerbic, and constantly on the hunt for the next drink, drug or cigarette. He plays it with battered arrogance and an appealingly childish quality that never allows him to be totally unlikeable.

As in previous roles, McGann seems to possess an innate sense of pride and intelligence, and in *Withnail*, with his hair slicked back and wearing a formal three-piece suit in one scene, he has a British arrogance and elegance. There is an overwhelmingly 'theatrical' quality about his performance and a sense of irony in his use of language which seems to point to comedy or satirical parts being best suited to him.

Both men are good-looking, but in different ways. Grant has a classical appearance and a jaunty confidence in his walk, while McGann, slightly smaller than his co-star, has more contemporary looks and a more gentle, subtle quality.

It is to McGann's credit that, against such opposition, his '... & I' character (called Marwood in earlier versions of the script) did not get lost altogether - even when playing opposite that regular scene-stealer Richard Griffiths, whose performance as the predatory homosexual Uncle Monty was another high-point of the film.

The bulk of the laughs were obviously going to go to the outlandish Withnail, whether he was smearing liniment on his body to keep warm, drinking cigarette lighter fluid, or searching for child urine in a bid to outwit the drink-drive tests. But bedecked in John Lennon-style glasses, and sporting a nervous disposition, McGann instils his role with an inner strength and confidence that Grant's blustering Withnail could never have.

It is towards the end of the film, when the two realize their friendship is coming to end with the closing of the sixties, that they get a chance to show their serious acting skills as well as their comedy attributes. McGann, with his hair shorn for an acting role, seems a taller and stronger character, while Grant is still clinging to his dreams. Both play the final scenes for sadness and pathos, with the camera lingering on a forlorn Withnail, who stands in a park under pouring rain.

It seems certain that both Richard E. Grant and Paul McGann are destined for busy acting careers. Already the two have been involved in a number of film and television projects, and it would appear that they are at the forefront of the younger generation of British actors.

MARK ADAMS

JENNIFER GREY

Of all the pretty young women who could have been Hollywood's latest darling last August, Jennifer Grey, whose nose isn't exactly straight and whose smile just isn't scrumptious enough for a McDonald's ad, was the least likely to be flavour of the month.

First off, August is a bad month in which to try to become a star. The films that reach theatres tend to be downers aiming to get a foothold in the market before the autumn season begins.

Secondly, just when Grey's breakthrough movie was being released her name hit the news in a different and tragic connection. She was a passenger in a car driven by her companion Matthew Broderick that was involved in a collision on a road in Northern Ireland, killing the two occupants of the other car. For a while she shuttled between the injured Broderick's bedside in Belfast and balloon and soda-pop launch parties for her movie in Hollywood.

Nevertheless, *Dirty Dancing* came out of left field to become a huge late-season hit. Set in 1963, it was the first film since *Saturday Night Fever* to exploit the tease and tussle of coupling to music in a crowded room with clothes on. Grey and Patrick Swayze lived up to the title, drawing young and old to a film that was both up-to-date and nostalgic.

Of the film's surprising success Grey says, 'I think we're back in the sixties again: people have slowed down. In the seventies, people were too much in a hurry - to lose their virginity, to be grown up. Promiscuity was promoted as being cool and hip. Maybe this means there's a return to courtship and romance. Dirty dancing can be very satisfying - and you don't have to worry about birth control. It's a form of safe sex.'

Dirty Dancing, a young woman's coming-of-age story, takes place during a family vacation at a Catskills resort. Grey plays the idealistic younger daughter of a doctor with an exemplary life already planned out. But then she falls for Swayze, the resort's dance instructor, who teaches her all about dancing and love.

'It was the end of an innocent era and the beginning of the Sexual Revolution,' Grey says. 'It was before President Kennedy was assassinated, before the Beatles, before people made love on their first date.' Although Grey was a mere three years old in 1963, she remembers the era. 'My big sister from Alabama - she was actually the housekeeper - would pull out her portable record player, put on the Supremes and do this dancing in the living room. To me she looked like Diana Ross.'

Grey, the daughter of *Cabaret* star Joel Grey, grew up thinking what fun it would be to be a dancer on Tom Jones' variety show. Later, she opted for acting and embarked on a career of auditioning, understudying and waitressing. She still bridles when she recalls how people used to tell her she would have no trouble because of her father: 'That used to burn me up. I wanted to be recognized on my own terms.'

But, until *Dirty Dancing* came along, she found it difficult to get work, let alone recognition. She had bit parts in *Reckless*, *Red Dawn* and *American Flyers*. Then *Ferris Bueller's Day Off* offered her a slightly larger bit, as Matthew Broderick's bratty little sister.

It seemed like a break when Francis Coppola got her to read Diane Lane's part in *Cotton Club* at a script read-through. Since Lane was held up shooting *Streets of Fire*, Grey rehearsed with the rest of the cast for three weeks. Later, she was hired to replace the actress playing the part of Nicolas Cage's wife. Grey spent nearly six months filming scenes. Everything seemed promising, except that her part was cut to ribbons.

Even getting cast in *Dirty Dancing* didn't promise much. The film was an independent low-budget production, and there had been many recent movies exploiting the pop tunes of the late fifties and early sixties.

But it was a part in which Grey saw potential. 'Women's parts are usually written so thinly,' she says. 'When I saw this one I said, "There's a whole person here." I was amazed there was a character like this in a movie, and that I'd be able to audition to play her. I couldn't believe how much I related to her.'

Though Grey hadn't danced professionally before, she won the role on her dance skills. 'They wanted someone who was a natural dancer,' she notes. So she went to the audition with her favourite Jackson Five cassettes and jumped around. 'Seven people sat behind a desk watching me. It was wildly frightening.'

Since *Dirty Dancing*, Grey has appeared opposite Madonna and Matt Dillon in *Bloodhounds of Broadway* and in *The Sixth Family* with Kevin Bacon. After seven years as a struggling actress, how does she feel about the perils of success? She dismisses them. 'Work is great but I don't think it's everything. It's important to know who you are and what you want. I'm dying to have a family. Success only ruins people if they don't know who they are to begin with.'

NANCY MILLS

MELANIE GRIFFITH

It was in Jonathan Demme's exuberant and unpredictable *Something Wild* that Melanie Griffith achieved her first starring role. Or perhaps I should say roles; starting as Lulu, who sports a black bob and African jewellery to initiate the yuppie hero into some wild sex ('Are you game?' she wickedly purred, waving manacles in his face) she was transformed into Audrey, the blonde small-town girl who had taken a few wrong turnings in her life, but proved to be just as irrepressibly *vital*.

Not that Griffith hadn't appeared in films before, just that the parts had become a little predictable. Teenage nymphets in *Night Moves* and *The Drowning Pool*, a stripper in *Fear City*, a hardcore porno actress in *Body Double*. *Something Wild* was the breakthrough she must have been hoping for.

Jonathan Demme says that, while reading Max Frye's script for the film, 'it was somewhere around page three that the image of Melanie Griffith came to mind.' Styled like Louise Brooks (though it seems Madonna was more of a role model for Griffith), she gives orders to tax-consultant Charlie in a teasing, big-sister voice that was definitely non-deductible. Then she showed us that the irresistibly anarchic Lulu was merely the fantasy side of her real character, Audrey, and reverted to her blonde self. The high spirits of the film owed a lot to Griffith's excitement in seizing the chance to show her range from daring wild thing to affectionate and supportive companion, albeit one absolutely with a mind of her own.

Now with a baby son and two marriages (Don Johnson and Steven Bauer) behind her, perhaps Griffith feels it's time to stop playing naughty girls. As every interview will tell you, she is the daughter of Tippi Hedren, the one-time commercials model who was elevated to the role of leading lady by Alfred Hitchcock. The tension between Hedren and Hitchcock on the set of *The Birds* resulted in little Melanie being the recipient of a cruel joke - a miniature Barbie doll of mother in a coffin, a gift from the fat man Tippi Hedren rejected.

One of Griffith's early roles was in her mother's much-panned paean to wildlife conservation, *Roar*. Frolicking with big cats - we're talking lions and tigers - at home led to at least one gashing of Griffith's face by an over-zealous claw-carrier. When Griffith says in *Body Double*, 'I don't do animal acts,' it's hard not to read it as an in-joke.

Griffith appeared in a commercial at nine months, but she was first revealed on the big screen in Arthur Penn's 1975 mystery thriller *Night Moves*. Aged 15, her nude appearances caused some gasps (though actually the swimming scenes were done, rather presciently, by a body double), but she was cast by Penn to play one of her generation, a member of the post-hippie I'll-try-anything school. At first spied by a bemused Gene Hackman, she stood naked behind a clothes line. 'When we all get liberated like her, there'll be fighting in the streets,' Hackman is told. The mould was set the following year; she turned up in much the same kind of provocative part alongside Paul Newman in *The Drowning Pool*.

A succession of minor supporting roles followed until the opportunity arose to play Holly Body in Brian De Palma's *Body Double*. She fought hard to get it - De Palma had once turned her down for *Carrie* - and for many the movie came to life with her entrance, even though it was a good hour in. De Palma's erotic thriller mixed elements of *Rear Window* and *Vertigo* in its convoluted story of an out-of-work actor duped into witnessing the murder of a beautiful woman whom he sees performing an 'exotic dance' routine each night alone in her apartment. Only when he spies a nude Griffith in a porno clip doing the same dance does he realize she was a 'body double'. Griffith's no-nonsense playing of Holly, with her squeaky-dirty voice that elides child-like naïveté and adult all-knowingness (remember Judy Holliday), provides the film with its only truly cogent character. Her aplomb in wearing open-assed leather suits, her simple laugh when she is told she has a terrific smile, made her seem sublimely poised above the apparently sordid nature of her profession.

Since *Something Wild*, Griffith has starred as a beautiful adventuress in *Cherry-2000*, set in the year 2017 when men apparently prefer robots to women (she proves them wrong), and opposite Sting in a thriller set in Newcastle, *Stormy Monday*. Even though neither role comes near the promise of *Something Wild*, Melanie Griffith looks set for a longer career than her mother. Not only is she strikingly attractive, with her sharp yet pliant features and those smiling eyes, but she can most definitely act, with or without handcuffs.

DAVID THOMPSON

HOLLY HUNTER

'God was my casting director,' says James L. Brooks. Well, the deity sure earned his percentage when he picked The Girl for *Broadcast News*. She was the pivotal dynamo - and smarter than the guys. 'Has there ever been,' *Newsweek* was to ruminate, 'a more complex, less stereotypical career woman on the screen?'

At first Brooks mused, endearingly, about Debra Winger - it made sense. Then Sigourney Weaver or Dianne Wiest. Elizabeth Perkins had a chance. So did the stage and screen Megs from *Crimes of the Heart* ... Except, well, Mary Beth Hurt was William Hurt's ex-wife - possibly awkward for them. And Jessica Lange would be awkward for Brooks if she insisted he made her last cowboy, Sam Shepard, into an anchorman.

In the end - the very end, the weekend before rehearsals started, 'the last minute of the last minute of the last minute,' says Brooks - he decided to see Holly Hunter. Having spent three years doing little else but honing his script, he could be forgiven for not knowing Holly from Kim Hunter.

Now, though, we all know what Hurt calls the 'ball of fire' from Conyers, Georgia. At 29 and five feet two inches, she's a giant with a steel spine - and fluid funny-bone. And unlike so many of the denizens of the Hollywood she refuses to live in, she takes chances. All the time. Talk to her co-artisans and the same litany crops up - courage, bravery, risks, energy. ('Authority,' adds Albert Brooks.) 'I just enjoy throwin' myself at stuff,' is her version. 'I'd rather have someone say, Tone it down, Hunter!'

Minus any major publicity clouds, Holly Hunter leapt into three fine films in one year. The Georgia accent remained much the same (to British ears). The roles, the performances were different - and all winners. A barren cop whose hubby steals not one baby for her, but quins, in *Raising Arizona*. The spunky Southerner organizing blacks into *A Gathering of Old Men* faced with a lynch mob. And ... 'the most extraordinary thing that ever happened to me.'

Being Chered out of the Oscar was the only bad news about *Broadcast News*. As Brooks admits, 'The picture couldn't have held its ambitions without Holly. Her age, her freshness, her casual bravery - and she's funny!' She also cries enough to be this year's Sissy Spacek. Though it was Jessica Lange, remember, not Sissy, who revamped her raunchy Meg. Which proves the truth about Holly. She does more - much more - than cry well. She's gutsy, earthy, funny, sad, mad, never bad.

Her great friends, the Coen brothers - Joel and Ethan who tried hard to spring her from Broadway for *Blood Simple* - wrote *Raising Arizona* for her. She's a cop (called Ed). Nicolas Cage is a crook (called Hi). She fingerprints him, takes his mugshots. Again and again. After marrying him, she spins the film on its axis, doing what Cher could never do - leaving Nicolas caged at the starting gate.

Then, along came Brooks to do for Holly what he'd done for Debra Winger - only Holly seems to be more aware of it and ready, willing, clearly able to spin the break into future fortune, artistic and otherwise. As the *Broadcast News* producer she shares the wittiest love story since, well, *Terms of Endearment*.

'She's the type of actor - and personality - to convey an unstoppable, brook-no-opposition desire to accomplish something.' That could almost be Jim Brooks talking - except it's Joel Coen. 'She has unlimited range,' adds Ethan. 'When we were writing Ed, we were sort of hearing her voice.'

Holly shone first as an actress when a high-school freshman. Her teacher put her in a play competition and one of the judges invited her into his summer stock company in upstate New York. At 16 she didn't want to quit - acting or New York - and left the family farm in Georgia for drama school. In, of all places, Pittsburgh.

One bio says she got a job three weeks after graduation. It reads well. Until she reminds you it was in *The Burning*, a horror film that never reached cult status. She had a role in *Animal Behavior* and was, so Jonathan Demme reminded me, in his *Swing Shift*. She later joined Mary Steenburgen in *The End of the Line*.

She made her major impact on stage - a rarity in these days of tele-spawned superstardom - starring in four Beth Henley plays and making Hollywood sit up. But her first break was taking over Meg from Mary Beth Hurt in *Crimes of the Heart*.

After *Broadcast News* Holly went on into Henley's *The Wake of Jamey Foster*, *The Lucky Spot* (with her friend Christine Lahti) and the one she's just filmed in good time for the next Oscar night, *The Miss Firecracker Contest*.

One secret of her success could be her four years at that Carnegie-Mellon University, in Pittsburgh. It's a college that teaches acting and ... engineering. 'Yeah, a strange combination,' she laughs, 'but it has a great reputation for both.' Exactly like the finely-tuned Holly Hunter.

TONY CRAWLEY

CHRISTINE LAHTI

As played by Christine Lahti in Bill Forsyth's *Housekeeping*, Sylvie Fisher, an unrepentant transient reluctantly appointed guardian to her two orphaned adolescent nieces, elevates eccentricity into an art form. Building mountains of gleaming tin cans in the kitchen and yellowing newspapers in the parlour, sleeping on a bench in the small-minded Idaho town of Fingerbone in broad daylight, stowing huge fish in her raincoat, riding with the bums in a boxcar, and barely fazed by fire or flood, Sylvie makes an irresponsible mother substitute - but a perfect guide to Forsyth's quietly lyrical world of enchantment, one habitually revealed in the commonplace.

Snubbed by the materialistically-minded Lucille, Sylvie leads Ruth (already showing signs of pixillation) on an illicit expedition through the woods to a tiny deserted house where the trees shield the frost from the sun, and the 'children' who live there from prying eyes. The scene is a sublime evocation of faerie (which only Michael Powell among British directors has hitherto achieved, in *I Know Where I'm Going*) owing greatly to Lahti's unsentimental incarnation of this singular woman - both earthy and unearthy - who was brilliantly transferred to the screen from Marilynne Robinson's 1981 novel of domestic entrapment and female restlessness.

Although the director later wreaths Sylvie in mist as she lays back in a rowing boat, trailing her fingers in the water and summoning the ghost of her drowned father as she sings 'Goodnight Irene', or showers her with bonfire sparks, Lahti somehow manages to keep the character rooted in reality, tenuous though Sylvie's grip on it is. Her ability to convey distraction may yet prove her greatest asset: that she didn't receive her second Oscar nomination for Sylvie - she was given the nod for her ex-dancehall singer Hazel in Jonathan Demme's *Swing Shift* - was a travesty of justice.

Diane Keaton had originally been cast to play Sylvie, but dropped out just before Forsyth began shooting in September 1986, cancelling Cannon's financial support. Lahti was recommended to him independently by David Puttnam, who rescued the project by bringing it to

Columbia, its producer Robert Colesberry, and New York casting director Margery Simkin. Says Forsyth: 'It was tremendously comforting to start work with Christine. What she did - and it's probably something few stars would have done - was to completely embrace Sylvie as a character. Sylvie's got a very appealing, eccentric otherworldliness, but there are other reasons why she's a vagrant and slightly unbalanced. Instead of just concentrating on the kookiness, Christine created the darker side of her in a whole biography that went back to her younger life - through the war and her marriage, beyond the book [set in the early fifties].'

Robinson told Lahti that she 'had brought to life the exact Sylvie I had imagined.' Lahti denies, however, that she knew how to play Lahti intuitively. 'I was really frightened. I didn't know what I was going to do, and it always intrigues me when I get that kind of fear before doing a part. But there were two big traps for Sylvie that I wanted to avoid. First, I couldn't play her without a problem, like an Aunt Mame with magic dust in her pocket - I had to find the side of her that's messed up. She's got as many problems as the little girls, but she covers them up in different ways and is as careful about intimacy as they are because she's been burned as much. Secondly, I didn't want to play her as a one-dimensional, crazy bag-lady. I think I successfully avoided that trap.'

Raised in Michigan where she switched from a language major to drama at Ann Arbor, Lahti excelled at mime, did stints as a singing cocktail waitress, in regional theatre, commercials, off-Broadway (and later on) before her screen début in ... *And Justice for All* in 1979. She did excellent work in *The Executioner's Song* and *Amerika* on TV, and in the Mary Tyler Moore movie *Just Between Friends*.

A curious analogue to *Housekeeping* was her following film, Martin Rosen's low-budget agrarian drama *Stacking*, set in the Montana hayfields in 1954 and starring her as another woman who dreams of leaving. This time she's an unhappy wife and mother, who sits in the window of her cafe and gazes at the highway - until Peter Coyote rides up on a big motorbike. Another off-centre beauty dreaming of her lost girlhood, Lahti's Kathleen starts less sympathetic or independent than Sylvie but busts out in what the actress describes as 'a rather violent way in order to go and realize her potential.' In a year in which it became fashionable for stars to play vagrants and drifters - Meryl Streep in *Ironweed*, Faye Dunaway in *Barfly* - Lahti's instilling of a certain perverse pride in her characters enabled each of them to flee but keep well clear of the gutter. She has since appeared in Sidney Lumet's *Running on Empty*, in which she's an ex-hippy radical who bombed a factory that was researching into napalm and has duly lived underground for 15 years. She admits a personal affection for the hippy sensibility.

Like Sylvie, but unlike Meryl, Faye, Sigourney or Jane, Lahti doesn't swim with the mainstream. 'I have one criteria for choosing a part and that is the quality of the material. If a film happens to be a big commercial Hollywood movie, then that's fine, but more often than not the best projects that come my way are smaller, independent, off-beat films. If I could do films with Bill Forsyth all my life, I'd be happy.'

GRAHAM FULLER

Holly Hunter: **The dynamic TV producer of *Broadcast News* *(above)* was a police booking officer in *Raising Arizona* *(far left)* but she got so bored of taking Nicolas Cage's mug shot that she married him. Childless, they both turned to crime, starting with the kidnap of a wealthy tycoon's child *(left)*, a little bundle that makes them dream of happiness.**

Crazy People: Nobody is going to tell Emily Lloyd she has problems, however many rude words she utters in ***Wish You Were Here*** *(top)*, but Crispin Glover takes the award for weird gestures and perverse line delivery as he contemplates a little problem of corpse-disposal in ***River's Edge*** *(above)*. You know there's going to be an upset somewhere down the line when Sheila McCarthy, an 'organizationally-impaired' temp, takes a job at a chic art gallery in ***I've Heard the Mermaids Singing*** *(right)*. The anarchic Meg Ryan drives through middle America with her new husband, the sensitive Kiefer Sutherland, as if they were travelling to happiness, but things don't turn out that way in ***The Promised Land*** *(top right)*. It's raining when ***Withnail and I*** *(far right)*, Paul McGann and Richard E. Grant, take one of their walks through Regent's Park, and that's pretty much the way things are in Bruce Robinson's elegy for the sixties.

Generally Sane: **Ellen Barkin's dress is not the only thing that's red hot when she comes together with her Spanish trapeze artist lover in *Siesta*** *(above)*. **John Mahoney sits on a bench and ponders another scam with Richard Dreyfuss, his partner in the aluminium-siding business** *(right)*. **Whatever turns a film into a surprise hit, Jennifer Grey brought it to *Dirty***

Dancing *(top)*. **Willem Dafoe wonders why his commanding chief wants to get him away from the streets of** ***Saigon*** *(above)*. **Christine Lahti sets up an eccentric household for her orphaned nieces in** ***Housekeeping*** *(far left)*. **Juliette Binoche tries to live with her husband's philandering in** ***The Unbearable Lightness of Being*** *(left)*.

Cinema's Year of the Baby: The man on the phone is not a willing father but he tries hard to do it right in the year's baby-hit, ***Three Men and a Baby*** *(above)*. The bundle that arrived on Diane Keaton's doorstep is a sweetie but even she threatens the smooth running of her executive lifestyle *(right)*.

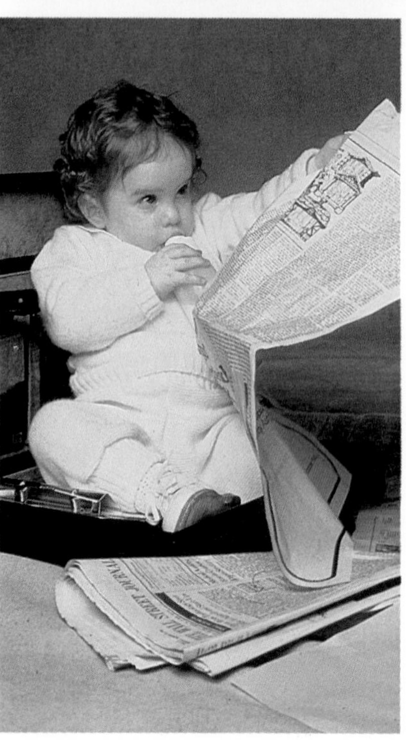

Christian Bale tries to find his parents on the streets of Shanghai in *Empire of the Sun* *(above)* **while the young Pu Yi explores his domain in *The Last Emperor*** *(far left)* **and the kids in *Hope and Glory* have so much fun** *(left)*.

Dennis Quaid has to go through his paces in *Innerspace*. Bared down, he's ready for anything. Miniaturized and injected into the body of a hypochondriac supermarket clerk, Martin Short, he has to give the instructions that he hopes will save his life and get him back to full human proportions. Expelled in a sneeze he gets to marry his journalist girlfriend, Meg Ryan, and there's no hard feelings between him and his former body buddy.

EMILY LLOYD

Let's have that name again. E-mi-ly Lloyd. Loiters in the lingual department, doesn't it? Rather like the name of that other little Lady L, the one by Nabokov. This is not to suggest that Lloyd is a nymphet or anything. She's too old for that now: after all, she celebrated her 16th birthday on the set of *Wish You Were Here*. Lynda, the character she was playing, was 16 too, just old enough to offset any uncharitable notions one might be entertaining about the legal nature of her sex scenes in the garden shed with 55-year-old Tom Bell. Sordid, somewhat, but nothing in the jailbait category.

If an actress has appeared in only one motion picture to date, and if she happens to be so *right* in that role you think she cannot possibly be acting, you may be forgiven, perhaps, for confusing her with the character she is portraying. Lloyd has made another movie since *Wish You Were Here*, but that has yet to be released. For the time being, she *is* Lynda whether she likes it or not.

And Lynda, let's face it, is a saucy so-and-so, a girl who refuses to bow to convention by keeping her sexuality under wraps. She is stuck in a fifties English seaside town (Bognor? Or possibly Worthing? It doesn't matter; they all look the same) with her upright widowed father and her priggish little sister. The most fun that anyone seems to be having is when they do the hokey-cokey down at the local dance-hall. She is, as she says, *bloody* bored, and who can blame her? Lynda resorts to infantile shock tactics. She hoists up her skirts and shows her knickers to the local bus crews. She bends over and flashes her backside at the neighbours. And she uses a lot of rude words. All the time. Very loudly.

It's not much of a movie. Lynda loses her virginity to a bus conductor, takes up with a one-legged older man and gets pregnant. There is a scene where she stands on a chair in a posh tearoom and shouts 'I like willies!' She rejects the options of abortion or adoption and ends up as an unmarried mother. Head held high, she wheels her pram through the local park in front of all the gob-smacked townsfolk. That's it.

The story is apparently based on the early life of Streatham brothel-keeper Cynthia Payne (the Luncheon-Voucher entrepreneur whose later career also inspired the writer-director's script for *Personal Services*). It could almost be an old-fashioned morality tale - watch your language, girls, and keep your legs crossed, or *this* could happen to you - with its downbeat ending perversely disguised as some sort of rebellious triumph. Despite all the defiant willie-espousal, Lynda's sexual adventures are dreary little affairs, devoid of either warmth or exhilaration. *Wish You Were Here* takes no risks in its grim depiction of lower-middle-class values from a long-gone age. It pitches its humour at a determinedly crude level of *coitus interruptus* and condom-eating dogs. It is all depressingly British. Without Lloyd, it would probably be unwatchable.

But, from the moment you see her cycling along the promenade, skirt rucked up around her thighs, her facial features set in a louche, butter-*would*-melt expression, you know this girl has got *it*: that indescribable quality so rare in British film actors. There is nothing remotely stage-crafty about her. She delivers her lines as though they have only just popped into her brain. She is pretty, but not in a bland, dolly-bird sense; she is every dirty old man's dream ticket, a combination of baby-faced innocence and suggestive know-it-all. She is not playing to an audience, it seems: she is just being herself.

She is every Bad Girl you ever knew: the sort who dabbled in below-the-belt petting, who had a cheeky reply to each adult's reproof, who shamelessly ran the gamut of all the rudest four-letter words at an age when you were still thinking 'damn' was pretty strong stuff. La Lloyd is not perfect: one of the few off-key notes in her performance is a crying jag when her sobs sound awkward and forced, but tear-shedding techniques can always be acquired, while pure screen presence cannot. Pedigree doesn't count for much, but, if it did, Lloyd's certainly got the goods: her father is actor Roger Lloyd Pack, while her mother (get this) used to be Harold Pinter's secretary.

The question is: is she a One-Film Wonder? Lynda's a tough act to follow. The instant that *Wish You Were Here* hit Cannes 1987, the film *criterati* started slobbering over the Lloydlet's performance, praising it to the skies. She was compared to all the usual people: hailed as the New Monroe, the New Bardot, the New Julie Christie, the New Madonna. (Can't they think of someone original, for once? How about the New Carroll Baker? Now *there's* a Baby Doll for you.) Hollywood went bananas for her. She guested on *The Johnny Carson Show*. She was showered with scripts. She was signed to a three-picture deal with United Artists. The girl already gets to approve the director on any project she's involved with.

One-Film Wonder or not, it seems Lloyd has already slipped through the fingers of the British Film Industry. This could turn out to be a Good Thing for her, a Bad Thing for the Brits. Wish you were here, indeed. Her next performance is as a street-smart teenager in a film called *Cookie*, directed by Susan Seidelman. For this, she has perfected a Brooklyn accent. The project after that is Norman Jewison's *In Country*, for which she will have to perfect a Southern accent. One wishes her well, but one also hopes, fervently, she is not taking Meryl Streep as her role-model.

ANNE BILLSON

JOHN MAHONEY

A major pleasure of cinema-going is the sudden discovery of new acting talent. Not necessarily raw youth; in fact, more often than not, a seasoned performer who, after years of spit-and-cough, has been thrust into something altogether more substantial and eye-catching.

In truth, John Mahoney doesn't really fit into either of these categories. At the age of 48, his screen surge has been truly spectacular, arriving with juicy roles in no less than three major movies over the past year.

He was Richard Dreyfuss's soft-spoken partner Moe in *Tin Men*, an accident-prone philanderer in *Moonstruck*, and a dangerously ambitious judge in *Suspect*. In a fourth film, as a silky smooth American Embassy official in Polanski's *Frantic*, he made a cameo shine in an otherwise negligible film.

The parts in each film have been substantially different, but a common factor has appeared to be Mahoney's quintessential American-ness.

In fact, the actor was born in Manchester, England, didn't arrive in the States until he was 19 and, after periods in the army and as associate editor of a medical journal, eventually signed on for acting lessons at the age of 35.

Back in England, Mahoney had been a child actor and was, briefly, associated with the Birmingham Repertory Company. But his parents so disapproved of a stage career, instilling in him their fears about job security, that he decided to quit.

Arriving in America, he joined the army in order to secure early eligibility for citizenship. All his spare time at Fort Leonard Wood in Missouri was spent writing down phonetically how his chums spoke, in an eventually successful effort to wipe out all traces of an English accent. After a spell teaching English at Quincy College and Western Illinois University (where he gained a BA and an MA), Mahoney moved to Chicago to become a freelance medical writer. His Americanization seemed complete.

Then, at 35, he had what he describes as a mid-life crisis: 'I decided I just couldn't spend the rest of my life wishing I'd taken a chance on the theatre'. He enrolled in a class at Chicago's St Nicholas Theatre where playwright-director David Mamet was a moving force and in no time had landed his first professional role in the world première of Mamet's *The Water Engine* in 1977.

Appearing with Malkovich in *Ashes* led to membership of the prestigious Steppenwolf Theatre where, after some 30 more plays and a trio of award nominations for shows like Ayckbourn's *Taking Steps* and Miller's *Death of a Salesman*, he eventually landed Off-Broadway in 1985, playing Harold in *Orphans* to prize-winning acclaim. Another clutch of trophies followed when he played opposite Swoosie Kurtz in John Guare's *House of Blue Leaves*.

At which point Hollywood decided to take some notice of this decidedly mature character actor.

It was the Guare play and the actor's 'quiet confidence' that persuaded Barry Levinson to cast Mahoney in *Tin Men*, his raucous sixties-set comedy about Baltimore aluminium siding salesmen and their scams.

Playing a more vulnerable character than the others, who suddenly, and painfully, has intimations of mortality, was clearly a good experience for Mahoney: 'It's a character I truly loved - warts and all. And there were warts; his ethics left much to be desired, and justifying what he did while still loving him required a great deal of understanding of the human condition, not to mention an advanced degree in rationalization.'

In *Moonstruck*, Mahoney provided an oasis of WASP calm and gentle humour amid the Italianate ghetto-blasting. He was the running joke - a womanizing professor who keeps being drenched by his young dinner dates. Later he's a chaste escort giving considerable cheer to Cher's cuckolded mother.

However, with Peter Yates's *Suspect*, he not only enjoyed considerable screen time but also a role, as Judge Matthew Helms, which gave a great deal of scope to his intelligence as a performer. Helms is presiding judge in the Washington trial of an itinerant Vietnam vet accused of killing a pretty young Government secretary.

Public defender Cher has her work cut out dealing not only with what seems a hopeless case, but also in countering a judge determined to give her a hard time. Helms' aggressive, patronizing attitude turns out to have altogether more complex, and sinister, motives.

Mahoney claims to be, first and foremost, a theatre man. 'I'd love to be a character actor who gets billing,' he has said. 'It seems to me all the great film actors really are character actors these days: De Niro, Hackman, Hoffman. But if I could make vaguely the amount of money doing theatre that I can in movies, I'd stick with that.'

QUENTIN FALK

SHEILA McCARTHY

Cast your mind back over the decades and think of dumb female characters. The fifties was their era: Monroe, Mansfield, Mamie Van Doren and - most memorably perhaps - the marvellous Jean Hagen in *Singin' in the Rain*. It was not a good decade for bright, articulate, independent female characters.

The sixties were hardly any better, the permissive ethos being a distinctly one-sided affair, with women generally reduced to bikini-clad bimbos who served merely to symbolize the rampant liberation of male protagonists. Then, after a brief, typically half-hearted flirtation with some of the less provocative ideas arising from the then-fashionable feminism of the early seventies, the backlash was in full swing and women degenerated from being dead brains to, more often than not, dead bodies.

There is in fact nothing intrinsically wrong with playing a female character who isn't exactly the distaff equivalent of Albert Einstein; it's just that so many of the witless women who grace our screens have been robbed of any claims to dignity. You'll probably find that only the late great Judy Holliday managed to invest her on-screen ignorance with a modicum of integrity and the sense that, in a different movie, under more propitious circumstances, she might have been something of a whizz-kid.

Sadly, in the eighties, there are few potential successors to Judy. Unless you're Meryl Streep - and even if you are - the roles offered actresses tend to revolve around the stereotypes promoted by the likes of *Betty Blue*, *9½ Weeks* and *Fatal Attraction*. Sex is back with a vengeance.

That's why Sheila McCarthy's performance in Patricia Rozema's *I've Heard the Mermaids Singing* comes as such a pleasant surprise. A lot of credit, of course, must go to Rozema, who wrote and directed the film. But the film is also McCarthy's: she's on-screen throughout and invests the central character of Polly with warmth and quirky humour.

McCarthy hasn't any film history to speak of. But in her native Canada she established some sort of reputation for herself in both contemporary and classical roles for theatre and TV. She's done Ophelia, Sally Bowles and Audrey in

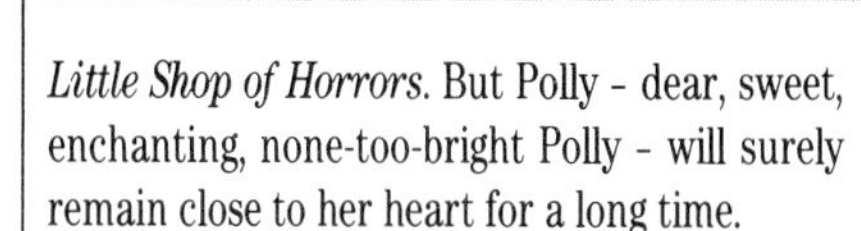

Little Shop of Horrors. But Polly - dear, sweet, enchanting, none-too-bright Polly - will surely remain close to her heart for a long time.

Polly is, by her own admission, an 'organizationally impaired' temp. When she finds herself a job at a chic art-gallery, you just know she's going to make a fool of herself. Things aren't helped by her platonic crush on gallery curator Gabrielle, and Polly's seemingly uneventful life reaches some sort of nadir when the photographs she has taken and sent, anonymously, to Gabrielle are contemptuously and callously dismissed as junk.

Why do we care about Polly? Because McCarthy manages to make her both funny and touching. When her boss takes her to a smart Japanese restaurant, Polly's gauche manners arouse ambivalent emotions in us. On the one hand, as she sits with legs stretched straight and forward under the table, her toes peeking up at the other side; or as she sips her milk - yes, milk! - leaving a thin white moustache on her upper lip; or as she casually orders from the menu, only to be served uncooked octopus; as McCarthy's beautifully understated performance plumbs depths of clumsiness, we are moved to laugh at her genuinely funny predicament. At the same time, however, Polly is a heroine with whom we can identify (she's ordinary, well-meaning, kind of *nice*), and the scene reflects badly not on her but on cool, sophisticated Gabrielle, whose blithe assumption that everyone would know how to eat Japanese smacks of self-obsession and insensitivity - qualities of which Polly is never guilty.

Indeed, if Polly's naïveté is a fount of comedy, it is also a benchmark by which we may measure the duplicities and pretensions of the art world. Even more impressively, Polly is an unusually independent woman, quite content to live alone with her darkroom, her photos and her records of 'Lakme'. Rarely do we see in the movies a character - let alone a female - so happy in solitude, but McCarthy's placid performance suggests, behind the wide, smiling eyes, depths of quiet self-assurance: Polly's faith in herself ultimately acknowledges and transcends the stigma of organizational imperfection.

Look behind Polly's batty façade, in fact, and she's not so dumb after all. Not only is she turned by Rozema into a creditable photographer, but she actually enjoys her own company - a mark, surely, of wisdom in a world where we so often worry over the attention of others. Moreover, intelligence need not always be articulated in the verbal mode: Polly's dignity, clear from the actress's witty but never flippant performance, springs subtly from within. Without sentimentality or self-pity, Polly becomes radiant through her resigned but resourceful acceptance of self.

The danger is that McCarthy - along with her director the creator of one of the most genuinely likeable screen characters in years - will be typecast. Last year, she assured me that she was not at all like Polly in real life ('a real Polly would be far too self-conscious to act the part of Polly convincingly'). Significantly, she recently took the part, in a love-story for television, of a university professor. Which only goes to show: if you're going to play a dumb cluck, you've got to have talent a-plenty to do it well.

GEOFF ANDREW

MEG RYAN

Before the release of *Top Gun* two years ago, Meg Ryan was an unknown - except to fans of a day-time soap opera called *As the World Turns*. Her visibility improved the instant she shouted across to her Navy pilot husband, 'Hey Goose, you big stud! Take me to bed or lose me for ever.'

Since then Ryan has seized a number of opportunities to display her extrovert sexuality. In *Innerspace* she was the feisty journalist whose boyfriend Dennis Quaid is miniaturized in an experiment and injected accidentally into the body of Martin Short. In *Promised Land* she played the hellcat who married Kiefer Sutherland three days after meeting him and proceeded to wreck his life. 'Where the cat?' she says on waking. 'The one that shit in my mouth.'

In *D.O.A.* she was a ditsy college freshman who helped professor Dennis Quaid solve the mystery of who poisoned him. And in *Presidio* she appeared as Lieut. Colonel Sean Connery's vixenish daughter, who gets involved with police inspector Mark Harmon when he comes to investigate a murder in a military compound.

Ryan's career to date has consisted largely of scene-stealing, an illustration of how hard it is for even the most watchable woman to become a star. It took Eddie Murphy one scene (where he subdues a barful of rednecks in *48 Hours*) to get above the title. Sean Penn did it with two or three scenes in *Fast Times* at *Ridgemont-High*. Michael Keaton needed one break: *Night Shift*.

Male ensemble movies still come out of Hollywood in great numbers, giving actors a platform from which to launch a career. Denzel Washington came out of *A Soldier's Story*; Mickey Rourke, Kevin Bacon and Steve Guttenberg can thank *Diner* for their careers. But, apart from Glenn Close and Meg Tilley, who remembers the women from *The Big Chill*? The careers of Mary Kay Place and JoBeth Williams have gone nowhere near as far as those of the men in the cast: William Hurt, Kevin Kline, Tom Berenger and Jeff Goldblum.

Nor does TV seem to propel many young actresses to stardom the way it did Michael J. Fox, Tom Hanks, and most recently Kirk Cameron. To break into films at all, the likes of Lisa Bonet and Justine Bateman must take supporting parts or B-list projects.

'I'm not in the position that men are in,' Ryan says, acknowledging that a man with similar credits might be farther along professionally. 'I haven't carried a movie yet. But I do know now what to look for in a part.

'A lot of women do good work but nine-tenths of it isn't central to the conflicts in the movie. So I've learned to make sure my character's agenda and the story's agenda are the same. Also, I try to protect myself by working with the best people.'

In *D.O.A.*, her character, Syd, becomes integral to the plot when Dennis Quaid's character superglues his hand to her arm and then drags her around the screen looking for clues.

'Oh my God, she's such a little geek!' Ryan shrieks about her character in *D.O.A.* 'She's not a pretty little *ingénue* who floats around. She's just trying to find her way in the world. Physically she's clumsy, but she starts to find the woman she'll become.'

What she'll probably become is a woman much like Ryan herself, who at 26 is friendly and upbeat about life. Ryan started acting in order to help pay her tuition while studying journalism at New York University. The suggestion came from her mother, then a casting director. She made some commercials before winning the tiny role of Candice Bergen's daughter in *Rich and Famous*.

After two years of earn-while-you-learn training on *As the World Turns*, Ryan came to Hollywood, one semester shy of completing university. Initially, she got small roles in films like *Armed and Dangerous* and *Amityville 3-D*, which didn't do much for her career.

Her three scenes in *Top Gun* changed everything. 'It all happened so oddly,' Ryan says. 'I always liked acting, but I never thought of it as a viable way to make a living. I thought I'd do community theatre. I still don't know if I can really make it. I don't trust that I'll be doing this for the rest of my life.' She still thinks about a career in journalism.

As for the film roles she should be playing, she thinks screwball, both comic and tragic. And she'd like to film a script she's co-written about a woman who gets near marriage but escapes every time.

'This past year has been a very intensive course in Hollywood, acting and the business,' she says. 'My roles are all so wildly different from one another. It's not very exciting for me to do the same old thing. The more something scares me, the better time I have.

'I've realized it's necessary to balance it with some intellectual endeavour. I don't mean to sound like a prig, but you have to get away from this environment and not think just about yourself.'

BART MILLS

DENNIS QUAID

Dennis Quaid has perfected the art of the smirk. It is a perpetual, cosmetic affectation that he refined in *Innerspace* and perfected for his role as the seductive Louisiana cop in *The Big Easy*.

Quaid's grin could never be mistaken for Mickey Rourke's semi-indifferent smile nor William Hurt's faintly demonic sneer. As the adage says, 'If you've got it, flaunt it'. When Dennis Quaid smirks, he shines.

Initially emulative of his brother Randy, he encountered the charm of the Great God Serendipity on the set of *The Missouri Breaks* which featured, apart from Randy, such stalwarts of masculinity as Jack Nicholson and Marlon Brando. After a peripheral appearance in the James Dean epitaph *September 30, 1955*, Quaid emerged as the tortured, post-adolescent ex-football hero in Peter Yates's *Breaking Away*.

He then rose to greater prominence in *The Long Riders*. Although Quaid's much-vaunted ability to accommodate prototypical American traditionalism was firmly in evidence in this tale of an outlaw gang, he was getting too old to play dissonant, young Americans.

The time had come to play dissonant older American boys. But as Gene Hackman's son and rival for Barbra Streisand's affections in *All Night Long*, Quaid was out of place. He trod water for a while with a series of sensitive made-for-television movies before emerging in 1983 as the sardonic astronaut Gordon Cooper in *The Right Stuff*.

It was the perfect showcase for what has come to be known as the Quaid persona - acerbic, ebullient, with just the faintest tinge of amorality and indifference. It's a persona that fits both the movies and the nineties: *Innerspace* summarized Quaid as a simple variation of New Man, a sensitive type with uneven quantities of tradition and modernity. As astronaut Tuck Pendleton, Quaid sported hair gel, drank Southern Comfort with embittered gusto, and venerated vintage soul records - a sort of Bruce Willis with academic qualifications. *Innerspace* should have been, as directed by Joe Dante, a chance to maximize Quaid's personality. However, as the miniaturized astronaut injected into the backside of paranoid supermarket

clerk Martin Short, most of his scenes insulated him from a script that became increasingly sidetracked by indulgent in-jokes. Tuck was a distillation of practically every role Quaid had previously portrayed, yet *Innerspace* didn't allow him to resonate.

With its PG parameters, *Innerspace* did endear Quaid to a younger audience, but it sacrificed his fractionally off-centre home-cooked charm to Martin Short's comic metamorphosis. Quaid's two big try-outs for heart-throb territory came in thrillers, the Peter Yates-directed *Suspect* and *The Big Easy* from Jim McBride.

In the former, as Eddie Sanger, a Washington political lobbyist on jury duty, he tried a Gregory Peck impersonation, helping lawyer Cher to defend a deaf-mute Vietnam veteran. It was a noble enough part, deviating somewhat from the realm of astronaut, boxer or country singer, but Cher dominated and Quaid became peripheral, something of a token good guy.

Remy McSwain in *The Big Easy* was much more of a part: a complacent, spasmodically corrupt Louisiana policeman a world apart from the homicidal fascists that congregate in movies set in New York and LA. The incandescent ambience of New Orleans facilitated the character and his obsession with enjoying life. McSwain was simultaneously Bacchanalian celebrant and gentleman predator to Barkin's abstemious civil servant. Quaid's volatile temperament was sweetened by the laissez-faire charm of a man who refused to rush life.

Quaid has wisely avoided tough-guy roles that demand little more than the exertion of one's forehead veins before the mugger/rapist is blasted into oblivion. Like the Kevin Costner part in *The Untouchables* or Harrison Ford in *Witness*, the cop in *The Big Easy* is slow to anger but practical enough to defuse the ambiguity that blurs right from wrong.

Quaid has been working on a second movie with McBride, both singing and acting as Jerry Lee Lewis in *Confessions of a Criminal Mind*. Quaid also returned to Louisiana for *Everybody's All American* in which he played a romanticized crumbling deity of American football for director Taylor Hackford. In *D.O.A.*, a remake of the classic *noir*, he is Frank Bigelow with 24 hours to live and find his executioner. These three movies will vindicate his potential as more than a sensual libertine for the AIDS era.

So far he has been more safe than dangerous. Only *The Big Easy* postulates a surrogate Humphrey Bogart, an actor given the chance to pervert the stereotypical Capraville boy into something fractionally more subversive. Paradoxically, this new Dennis Quaid might find himself out of step with the old one; for *Innerspace* and *The Big Easy* conclude with wedding sequences - in the former to Meg Ryan (his real-life girlfriend) and then, more intimately, to Ellen Barkin. In this season of familial reaffirmation, Hollywood still wants to love happy endings and for Quaid that should work out just fine.

MARKUS NATTEN

TALKING ABOUT FILM BUSINESS

Quotes compiled by Tony Crawley

Being a director is like being pecked to death by a thousand pigeons. Everybody's got questions ... You get out of the car in the morning. All you want is a bacon sandwich and there they are: 'What do you want me to do about this? How are we going to do that?' It even got to the point when I'd go to the loo they'd be banging on the door.

I might direct again ... But there's some brilliant directors around. May as well let 'em do it. I ain't giving up my day job, I'll tell you that.
Bob Hoskins

There's no secret that in the past 18 months Cannon passed a terrible time. And there's no secret that we got offers, even from the majors and private people, who said, 'Let's start a new company.' No! Because Cannon is our baby – we built it from nothing.

We made mistakes. No question about that. But we learn from the mistakes and will do better.
Menahem Golan

I think Columbia should be shot for what they've done with *The Last Emperor*. That's one of the most wonderful films I've ever seen and it should have done triple business in the US.
Denis O'Brien of HandMade Films

There is disillusionment wafting through the heady winds of the American dream.
David Puttnam

How could he say the American dream is dead? He spent one year here and left with millions of dollars. Only in America!
Ray Stark

The test of a free marketplace is fundamental to our economic and political system. If Mr Puttnam wants to escape its 'tyranny', he should make pictures with his own money, not that of trusting and innocent investors.
Bertram Fields

If it's a good film, it can spread the name and memory of Hanna Senesh. If it's a bad film, give it a few years and someone else will try again.
***Menahem Golan on his* Hanna's War**

I've been a director since I was at school and told the teacher how to run the class. I never act anyway. I just am.

It's better directing myself than working with most of the assholes I've made films with. It's much harder to make a picture with an untalented idiot like Herzog.
Klaus Kinski on his directing début, *Paganini*

My one regret in life is that I'm not someone else.
Woody Allen

I could make five failures, five pictures that nobody liked, and I'd still be 'the guy who directed *The Godfather.*'

I probably have genius. But no talent.
Francis Coppola

He goes to that part of the brain that doesn't want to be touched.
Martin Scorsese on David Cronenberg

I forced him to play a piano that is completely out of tune, so he had a good excuse if the music is not good.
Sergio Leone on Ennio Morricone

If I have to explain my movies, the movie is worthless - and if the movie is worthless, no speech that I could give will make any difference.
Walter Hill

At one point, *Esquire* talked to us about publishing it - as the most rejected script in Hollywood. I said: I don't want to end up as a trivial pursuits question. The movie *is* going to be made one day ...
Alan Rudolph on setting up The Moderns

I remember reading how *Drive, He Said* was booed at Cannes and I thought if *that* can happen to a movie that good it can certainly happen to me.
Jonathan Demme

There's a terrible catharsis with a good horror film - facing your fears and surviving is like purging yourself. I'll walk out *exhausted!* For me, it's better than six months with a psychiatrist.
Chuck Russell, director of
Nightmare on Elm Street III

I always make films in America because there's money there. it's a simple case of no money, no film.
Alan Parker

The medium is too powerful and important an influence on the way we live - the way we see ourselves - to be left solely to the tyranny of the box-office or reduced to the sum of the lowest common denominator of public taste.
David Puttnam

I'm not going to be asked any conceptualizing questions, right? It's the thing I hate most. I've always felt trapped and pinned down and harried by those questions. Truth is too multi-faceted to be contained in a five-line summary.

You read books, see films that depict people being corrupted by Hollywood. But it isn't that. It's this tremendous sense of insecurity. A lot of destructive competitiveness. I think it's good to just do the work and insulate yourself from that undercurrent of low-level malevolence.
Stanley Kubrick

Cannes? It's like Butlins on acid.
Frank Clarke, screenwriter of
The Fruit Machine

I adore TV - like everyone else. But I watch very little. Because there's so very little worth watching.
Bernardo Bertolucci

I pitched stories to Columbia years ago. They never read them but liked the sound of *Son of Celluloid.* Fun title, they said - what's it about? When I said, 'About a cancer that does impersonations of movie stars,' their faces hit the floor. Wham! Suddenly, I wasn't so welcome in their offices anymore.

Underworld was my first filmed book. I think there's about seven of my lines left in it ... I didn't think there was any way they could ruin *Rawhead Rex* - set in Kent in mid-summer. Very important to the story to have fields of corn, a brilliant English summer. So I knew it was bad news when they decided to film it in Ireland in February.
Clive Barker

WHAT ACTORS SAY

Quotes compiled by Tony Crawley

I've a script with Bernardo Bertolucci right now and I hope he'd like to do it - the life of Puccini. I'd like to try that!
Sylvester Stallone

My problem is that people get intimidated by someone big and beautiful like me. They hate to think I can be smart as well.
Dolph Lundgren

For years, I spent so much on my girlfriend that eventually I had to marry her - for my money.
Richard Pryor

I lost my virginity as a career move.
Madonna

My job is to make people laugh. The critics' job is to stop me.
Paul Hogan

I don't wanna become a professional politician. I suppose the precedent is there for running for President. But it's not in my astrological forecast.
Clint Eastwood

Love isn't intellectual ... it's visceral.
Kelly McGillis

Warren Beatty doesn't drink, he doesn't smoke, he plays the piano beautifully, he's extremely intelligent, learned, knowledgeable. You look for something to get him on and you can't. They say he's obsessed with women. But he isn't. He's obsessed with power. He likes to dominate men as well as women.

I asked Richard Burton why he made so many films, why he didn't go back to the theatre ... He said: Because I couldn't bear not to have somewhere to go in the mornings.
Gabriel Byrne

We always put on the screen what we don't want to have happen in our lives. We try to make our lives safe, orderly, calm. Think of all the things you don't want to have happen - they make good movies.

As far as I'm concerned, I'm a Zen Buddhist student first - an actor second. If I can't reconcile the two lives I'll stop being an actor. The other is more important - I spend more time off-screen than on.
Peter Coyote

An actor friend introduced me to my agent, Susan Smith. We met and had a couple of drinks and she got shit-faced. Really, really shit-faced! I said to myself: That's the agent for me.
Brian Dennehy

Who cares about the script? I choose my films because of the director. I hate reading scripts. They're not interesting - no photos!
Béatrice Dalle

Oh, I get it. It's simple. PG means the hero gets the girl, 15 means that the villain gets the girl - and 18 means that everybody gets the girl.
Michael Douglas on British censorship ratings

Hey, don't call me an actor, man. Call me something else. Put down animal on my passport - or businessman because I'm in the business of living and surviving. But don't call me an actor ... that's something I don't have a lot of respect for now.

I don't care about sex any more. It's years since I made love. Nowadays I so much prefer motorcycles.
Mickey Rourke

I know little about Orson Welles' childhood and seriously doubt that he ever was a child.
Joseph Cotton

What makes a star? Hmm. Everything! Charisma - what I used to call in drama school: the shine. Internal, emotional, physical energy - it goes beyond the body and you can't control it.

To be in love with your director - that way lies madness. You lose your judgement sometimes in a love affair.
Faye Dunaway

What is a star? Someone you don't mind spending two hours in a cinema with - even if the film is bad.
Claude Lelouch

I don't do these things just to be clever, to shock and outrage for the sake of publicity. My behaviour isn't exactly abnormal by Australian standards.
Pamela Stephenson

You've not made it as a film actress, in my opinion, if you're not called a monster at some time in your career.
Bette Davis

A lotta people say the film makes them want to go home and make love. And I was in an airplane and this woman comes running to me and says: You won't believe this but I just bought my husband a pair of handcuffs - we're gonna use them tonight!
Melanie Griffith on Something Wild

We had such a good time, the public had a good time, too. That's the secret of *Cannonball* and *Smokey and the Bandit* and films like *Police Academy*. They're laughing so much they didn't hear the words. If you listened to the words - you'd throw up!

America loves to make heroes - and then destroy them. Make them real low. Limping is not enough ... If they're destroyed real bad, they can even become heroes again. Most Oscar winners have had a tracheotomy.
Burt Reynolds

I relate much more to medieval times - those small buildings close to the ground, those doors a mere five feet tall. Remember, then most of the people were about my size.
Linda Hunt (four feet, nine inches)

I'm amazed at how fit Timothy Dalton is. His big sport is - fishing!
Maryam d'Abo

I'm still trying to figure out what the fun part of making movies is.

Meryl Streep is an acting machine in the same sense that a shark is a killing machine.
Cher

I have no method. I've a smattering of things learned from different teachers. Nothing I can put in a valise, open up and say: Now which one would you like?
Meryl Streep

I'm not opposed to sheer entertainment but geez, I didn't fit into kids' pictures and what else was there - *Exorcist 7, Airplane 14, Jaws 29!* I just didn't want to take those parts you'd see Orson Welles do, where he'd be hiding behind a pillar or something. So, I decided to just grow up with my kid.
James Caan

I really don't like reading scripts. It's a real effort for me to pick one up and look at it. Which is not very good - I might throw something good out.

Me - a sex symbol? I tell ya, there are ten million women out there that ... don't know who I am!

Yeah, my real name is Coppola. But nobody took me seriously.
Nicolas Cage

As an actor, there's almost no stage when you're not feeling raw - either because you're working and exposing yourself or because you're not working and you're vulnerable because of that.
Gayle Hunnicutt

No that's not me - the actor who's in everything is Gérard Depardieu. I've never seen a French film he wasn't in except *La Cage aux Folles* and he might be in the chorus of that for all I know.
Gene Hackman

I like my crazy name. Even during the times I didn't work people remembered it because it was always cropping up - in crossword puzzles, stuff like that.
Rip Torn

Of course, he's had his problems. One of them is being smart - not a great advantage for an actor.
Writer Terry Southern on Rip Torn

Most of the stuff I'm sent these days is garbage. I wouldn't miss it if I never acted again.
Richard Widmark

I never worry if it's a big production. I don't have any fantasies about Hollywood - that's just more people standing on the set.
Tom Hulce

How did they make me look ugly for the end of *The Last Emperor?* That was the real me.
Joan Chen

Suddenly you start to get these roles as the mother of the *ingénue* you'd have been playing five years ago - it happens in a very swift moment.
Julie Christie

I've always had a big mouth. But if you're reasonably smart about what you're saying and the results improve the quality of your work, then I think it's your job to speak up.

It's not difficult to be successful. But it is difficult to remain human.
Susan Sarandon

It's difficult to be married outside the profession. A lawyer might not understand that going to bed with Gabriel Byrne for three days is work for me.
Ellen Barkin

I'll never marry. I don't want my man saying someday to me:'I have a mistress.' It would be inevitable in marriage and I couldn't survive that.
***Myriam Mézières, star of* A Flame in My Heart**

Where Meryl Streep is an intellectual, Shirley MacLaine follows her gut. I like that better. Shirley's an extraordinary person - a little round the bend.
Charles Dance

When the time comes, I'm gonna have a face-lift, jaw-lift, eye-lift. Everything that's falling *will* be lifted. And the things that can't be lifted *will* be *moved.*
Little Richard

A CRITIC AND SOME PLAYERS

THE LIFE OF KENNETH TYNAN

Kathleen Tynan *(Weidenfeld and Nicolson)*

The man who wrote 'What when drunk one sees in other women, one sees in Garbo sober' can never be said not to have made a significant contribution to the cinema. Almost in the same class is his interview with the 71-year-old Louise Brooks. Yet even now Kenneth Tynan is regarded as primarily a man of the theatre.

His second wife Kathleen chronicles a passion for movies dating back to his school days. How many other people, let alone 14-year-olds, went to see *Citizen Kane* five times in one week in 1942? Serious appreciation of the American mainstream cinema is generally thought to have started with the *Cahiers du cinéma* writers in the late fifties; Tynan was writing in praise of W. C. Fields, James Cagney and the Hepburn-Tracy comedies at the very start of the decade. It was not until 1964 that his film criticism reached a wide readership through his weekly column in the *Observer*. By then his views had altered. He was championing Godard and the Czech cinema (*Courage for Everyday, The Shop on Main Street* and *A Blonde in Love*). In 1966 he resigned from the *Observer*. His wife concludes 'he knew he could have no impact on the outcome of a movie, as he could on a play.'

Tynan's work as a screenwriter went largely unnoticed. Two years as adviser to Michael Balcon resulted in a shared credit on *Nowhere to Go* (one suspects his biographer has not seen the film) but four other projects which started pre-production were called off before shooting started. A second shared credit, on *Macbeth*, led to discussions about a film for Polanski with an erotic subject. This foundered when the director rejected the proposed story-line.

Taken together, all this amounts to very little. The real importance lies rather in the intellectual credit he was able to impart to a despised medium. This may not have been the achievement he sought. It has value, just the same.

TIMEBENDS: A LIFE

Arthur Miller *(Methuen)*

The story of Arthur Miller's involvement with the cinema is also a chequered one. He first went to Hollywood as a writer on what eventually became *The Story of G.I. Joe*; but the film reached the screen with the script credited to three others. So when he returned in 1950 his concern was 'all about power for me, about using the power I had presumably earned with my plays'. He was there with Elia Kazan to try to interest Harry Cohn of Columbia in an original script, *The Hook*, about gangsterism in the New York docks. This leads to a description of the meeting in Cohn's office which deserves a place among the classics of its type. Miller's power was insufficient to reach agreement on terms that were acceptable.

Miller does not simply present Hollywood as the thwarter of talent, although this aspect is not overlooked. He illustrates it through Clifford Odets rather than the more usual Scott Fitzgerald. On the other hand he recalls dinner parties attended by powerful studio executives where 'the conversation was by no means always vapid.' No doubt marriage to Marilyn Monroe provided him with the power necessary to get *The Misfits* made on terms he considered satisfactory. Delays to the start of shooting meant that the marriage was in a perilous condition by the time the cameras started rolling. Miller's own account does not suggest, as other writers have done, that it was only a commitment to the film that kept the marriage alive. But it was over by the time shooting was completed.

The first film of *Death of a Salesman* offended him on accounts of its distortion of Willy Loman; his opinion of the Schlöndorff version is not recorded, but he does imply approval of Dustin Hoffman's performance on stage. This is a book whose importance extends beyond either the theatre or the cinema. It is also a record of one of the most thoughtful, observant and judicious minds of our time.

THIS 'N THAT

Bette Davis *(Sidgwick & Jackson)*

Bette Davis obviously considers that her professional life has been adequately covered in previous books. She deals with a variety of topics in *This 'n That*, an oddly appealing, if rather unorthodox, book.

She writes first of all about herself as a woman who has undergone a mastectomy, followed by a stroke, and made a complete recovery. Those who shrink from accounts of hospitalization should not be put off.

The later part of her career occupies the central chapters and then she tells of running the Hollywood Canteen during the war. This includes a cherishable account of her confrontation with the Victory Committee under the chairmanship of James Cagney.

The book was completed but not delivered to the publishers when her daughter's 'not too nice' book, *My Mother's Keeper*, appeared. Miss Davis writes in her Foreword: 'She wrote a letter to me in her book. I decided to write a letter to her in my book.'

COMING ATTRACTIONS

Terence Stamp *(Bloomsbury)*

Covering the period from Stamp's discovery that he wanted to become an actor to his audition for his first film role, as Billy Budd, this second volume of autobiography reflects the excitement of an East Ender starting his career who sensed the coming of a new age, the Sixties.

Containing hardly any mention of the hardships, setbacks and self-doubt that one has learned to consider a part of any actor's early life, the book shows Stamp slowly learning about his profession, via a would-be Lee Strasberg, Jos Tregoningo, and the films of James Dean to a period spent touring the country in rep. Some responsibility for the seeming smoothness of Stamp's early career must be ascribed to his luck in the choice of flat-mates. Asked whether he had been (improperly) coached for his scholarship application to the Webber Douglas Academy of Dramatic Art, Stamp is able to deflect their anxieties by ascribing his (thorough) tuition to 'a packer from Liberty's.' And it was Michael Caine who taught him how to find his marks on the night before he went up to screen-test for *Billy Budd*. Stamp gives a warm account of the way Caine took over his education: providing him with books, guiding him as to what perfumes to give the girls, and how to turn a cheerful face to life.

DETOUR: A HOLLYWOOD TRAGEDY

Cheryl Crane *(Michael Joseph)*

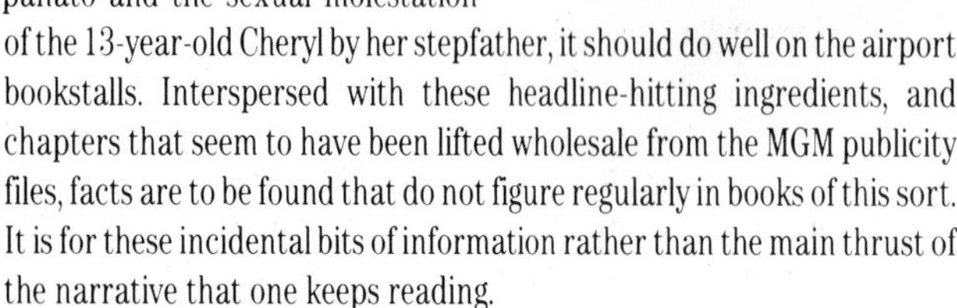

It may be an indication of the age of the movie business that two other recent books are concerned largely with parent/children issues. *Detour* is an account by Cheryl Crane of life with mother, who in her case was Lana Turner.

This is a book to be marketed on its sensational elements. As these include the murder of Johnny Stompanato and the sexual molestation of the 13-year-old Cheryl by her stepfather, it should do well on the airport bookstalls. Interspersed with these headline-hitting ingredients, and chapters that seem to have been lifted wholesale from the MGM publicity files, facts are to be found that do not figure regularly in books of this sort. It is for these incidental bits of information rather than the main thrust of the narrative that one keeps reading.

THE SALAD DAYS

Douglas Fairbanks Jr. *(Collins)*

The father/son relationship at the centre of *The Salad Days* seems to belong to an entirely different world. It was not without its tensions. These mainly concerned money, of which Fairbanks Snr. (known to his son as Pete) had a plentiful supply, and Jr. very little, as well as an inherent pride in not drawing his father's attention to the fact. The name alone amounted to aristocracy in Hollywood, but father and son both appear to have shared a weakness for the company of the European, and particularly the British, nobility.

The circles to which the author had access by virtue of being his father's son are part of film legend. The four original partners in United Artists make occasional appearances. Decorum dictates that the World shall not be allowed to know that its Sweetheart got a bit tiddly now and again. Charlie Chaplin sits in the gutter to discuss with the 17-year-old actor his stage success in *Young Woodley*. Other famous names, particularly female ones, come and go. He marries Joan Crawford. There are liaisons with, among others, Gertrude Lawrence and Marlene Dietrich. As war approaches, he is sent as an unofficial agent of the US government to South America. The anecdotes keep flowing, names continue to be dropped. Cumulatively the effect is bland. From an author - he makes a point of having previously published short stories - in such a privileged position, this naïve and breathless record of adventures in several glamorous worlds falls well below expectations.

This volume concludes in 1941. A further instalment is promised. It is to be hoped that the publishers will have found a more reliable indexer when that comes out.

SPENCER TRACY: TRAGIC IDOL

Bill Davidson *(Sidgwick & Jackson)*

The flow of star biographies continues almost unabated. A curious convention of the genre is that there is almost invariably a sub-title. In the case of *Spencer Tracy: Tragic Idol*, it is hard to feel that the subject merits such a resounding epithet.

The book is founded on the proposition that in the days of the major studios, with stars under long-term contract, only carefully sanitized accounts of their lives were allowed to appear in print. The publicity departments took care of that. This book adopts a 'now it can be told' approach. Sadly, the two main revelations - that Tracy lived with Katharine Hepburn although, as a Roman Catholic, he refused to divorce his wife Louise, and that he had a drink problem ('Hell, I used to take two-week lunch hours') - have long been public knowledge. The real interest is the book's account of the mechanism by which Louis B. Mayer sustained his despotism over MGM. The studio security staff exercised surveillance over major stars, barmen were paid to call the studio at the first sign of trouble, and an in-house ambulance service was maintained so that roistering drunks could be picked up before the police arrived. In fact, Tracy appears to have been a solitary drinker.

As far as his career is concerned, there is little fresh to add. Tracy was one of the greats. That is there to be seen in every performance he gave. His secret died with him. Bill Davidson has found an occasional revealing quotation but there are no surprises.

BRANDO: THE UNAUTHORIZED BIOGRAPHY

Charles Higham *(Sidgwick & Jackson)*

In the best American tradition, Charles Higham has done a monumental research and interview job for his biography of Brando. The result is a well-ordered, factual account of the actor's career and his private life. Brando became a theatrical star in the first production of *A Streetcar Named Desire* but, although he continued to return to New York between films, he has never appeared on Broadway again. Yet he is on record as saying he went to Hollywood 'in a state of extreme anxiety and discomfort.' The stresses and contradictions of the actor's life are judiciously laid out but the author scrupulously refrains from making comments of his own. One rumour, at least, is contradicted. Brando did not want Carol Reed fired from *Mutiny on the Bounty*, and he did not work well with Reed's replacement, Lewis Milestone. The only failing of the book's approach is that it gives equal weight to the means Brando employed to obtain his effects as Stanley in *Streetcar* and his partiality for Mrs Cooper's lemon meringue pie.

YUL BRYNNER: THE INSCRUTABLE KING

Jhan Robbins *(W. H. Allen)*

On Yul Brynner I can write with some limited personal experience, having been on location with him on *Return of the Seven* and *The Long Duel*. The character summoned up by Jhan Robbins is immediately recognizable. He carried egotism and omniscience to the point of parody and seemed to be humorously challenging you to credit the enormity of his claims.

With so much mystery deliberately created about Brynner's origins, Robbins does well to print the myth as myth and leave it at that. It is on the career that he falls down. The claim that Brynner wanted to play Richard III, Ahab, King Lear and Shaw's Caesar, and studio executives would not let him do so, is recorded in the text. Of course, there is no means of knowing whether these roles were genuinely long-standing ambitions or merely chosen to anger the executives to whom he was speaking. On the other hand, Fox did give him top billing over Joanne Woodward in the film version of Faulkner's *The Sound and the Fury* just as MGM had done above Maria Schell and Claire Bloom in *The Brothers Karamazov*. Neither was a great success, either at the box-office or with the critics. Both were opportunities for Brynner to substantiate his acting claims.

THE MARILYN SCANDAL: HER TRUE LIFE REVEALED BY THOSE WHO KNEW HER

Sandra Shevey *(Sidgwick & Jackson)*

MARILYN MONROE: A LIFE OF THE ACTRESS

Carl E. Rollyson Jr. *(Souvenir Press)*

Sandra Shevey's book takes the award for the longest sub-title. Whether it scores on any other grounds depends largely on one's point of view. This is a feminist interpretation. The author also asserts that the star was murdered and that Robert Kennedy was deeply involved. Those who are persuaded by both these propositions will no doubt find much to agree with in the book. Others may find it sloppily written and repetitive. Most of the revelations from Those Who Knew Her come from publicity and make-up men, who were hardly in a position to know her well.

For a more objective account it would be better to turn to *Marilyn Monroe: A Life of the Actress*. This is not without its quirks. It reads as though it started out as a doctoral thesis and has been expanded to its present form. Some original research is claimed but a good deal of reference is made to published material. The author writes that none of these earlier books 'treats movies as events in the biography of a working actress, events that might fill in the gaps in her identity.' Whether this somewhat gnomic proposition actually means anything of any significance is open to question. It does inspire a good chapter on *Bus Stop*. The summary of the early years and the early movies is pleasantly straightforward but, on reaching the later stages, things change. The thesis comes to the fore. Stanislavsky is invoked. 'To marry Miller must have seemed nothing less than an organic imperative.' This version is no threat to *Timebends*.

JANE FONDA

Michael Freedland *(Weidenfeld and Nicolson)*

At least there is no sub-title to Michael Freedland's *Jane Fonda*. The actress's life and career appears to be retold entirely from the clippings file but the author repeatedly puts his own interpretation on these reports. He is presumably so convinced of the seminal importance of Jane Fonda's comment 'Barbarella has no sense of guilt about her body. The film wants to make something beautiful out of eroticism' that he quotes the remark again verbatim six pages later. He also appears to be under the impression that Lee Remick appeared in *The Exorcist*. These instances of careless writing and inaccuracy do nothing to inspire confidence.

PAST FORGETTING

Peter Cushing
(Weidenfeld and Nicolson)

Like Bette Davis, Peter Cushing has been moved to fill in some of the gaps in his 'Autobiography'. Like its predecessor, the new volume is written in a tone of mild surprise that anyone should be interested in what he has to say. It is indeed a slim volume, and even then rather lacking in substance, but the illustrations have been chosen with care and they are beautifully captioned. They say more than the words about the care with which this actor creates a new face for each part he plays. As a bonus he reproduces some of the trifles with which Peter Ustinov whiled away idle moments on the set of *The Moment of Truth*. Unlike much of this sort of thing, these have not staled with the passing of time.

MICKEY ROURKE

Bart Mills *(Sidgwick & Jackson)*

The paperback format allows a generous ratio of stills to text and when, as in Bart Mills' *Mickey Rourke*, they are also well reproduced, the result is a useful work of easy reference. The text is a model of its kind. It provides a succinct account of the early years and then devotes a chapter to each of the major films. There are extensive quotations from the actor and these are supplemented by extracts from the critical receptions to his performances.

HOGAN: THE STORY OF A SON OF OZ

James Oram *(Columbus Books)*

In marked contrast is this book on Paul Hogan which goes into great detail about the history of 'larrikin' comedians, the Sydney Harbour bridge and the eating habits of the Australian crocodile. The avowed subject of the book tends to get lost among all these digressions. There is a generous ration of colour in the illustrations but too many merely feature Hogan with the same unfailing on-camera smile. But no doubt to express such sentiments is to risk being thrown into the crocodile-infested waters of Walkabout Creek.

TIMOTHY GEE

HURRAY FOR HOLLYWOOD?

As the years pass by and Hollywood becomes little more than a place where deals are made, it's noticeable that Hollywood's past has become increasingly attractive to both deal-makers (who dream of dealing with Harry Cohn rather than faceless lawyers), audiences (tired of being offered endless models of the same film) and critics. This year has been no exception.

CITY OF NETS

Otto Friedrich *(Headline)*

A panorama of Hollywood in the forties, *City of Nets* first establishes how isolated were the various communities that collectively comprised Hollywood (to the extent that \$500-a-week writers didn't socialize with \$1,500-a-week writers) and then carefully makes connections between the inhabitants of these independent villages. The thread Otto Friedrich uses is not yet another round of interviews with survivors (see Barry Norman below), but a synthesis of existing studies, biographies and autobiographies by people from the period. The resulting exercise in collective memory, with all the myth-making and contradictions laid bare, is a marvellous mosaic. It contains some of the best Hollywood stories - Groucho Marx conducting 100 members of the Los Angeles Symphony Orchestra into screenwriter Ben Hecht's living room (Hecht's house was palatial but not that grand) in response to the decision by Hecht and fellow members of the Ben Hecht Symphonietta that Groucho and his mandolin were not distinguished enough to join - pours the cold water of research on some of the more fanciful ones (Faulkner's working from home, the conditions under which Chandler wrote the script for *The Blue Dahlia*) and introduces a few apocryphal ones (Otto Preminger coming across a group of fellow expatriates talking together in Hungarian and protesting 'Come on, we're all in America now, so talk German').

The picture of Hollywood that emerges is a more complex one than usual, in which the studio politics, union problems (an issue surprisingly rarely covered in histories of Hollywood considering how vulnerable studios were to strikes), egos, ideologies and fanciful ideas rubbed together uneasily. *City of Nets* is also a useful book, an instant reference source, something to turn to for a check on more partial accounts of events.

TALKING PICTURES

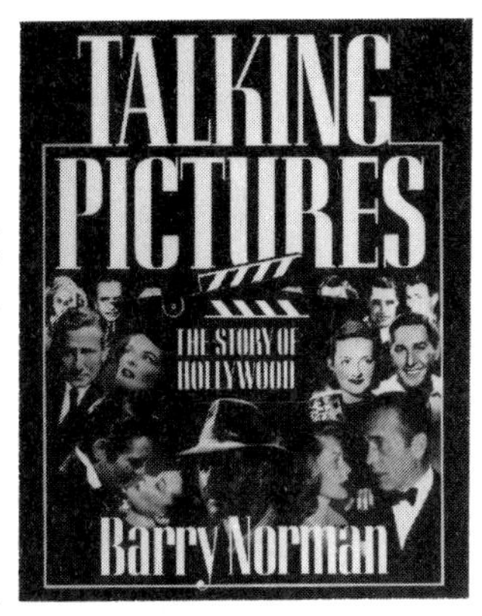

Barry Norman *(BBC/Stodder)*

Less useful is *Talking Pictures* which is simply yet another re-run of the conventional view of Tinseltown. Based on the BBC television series of the same name, the text was clearly spoken rather than written. The result is the 'chatty', put-down, style of Norman's weekly TV show, and it quickly grates. The book's other limiting factor is its over-reliance on interviews, resulting in too many partial views. This is particularly noticeable in Norman's treatment of the studio system, a subject on which there has been a lot of research in recent years. Rather than making use of this, Norman and his researchers merely flesh out the conventional wisdom (tyrannical bosses and recalcitrant stars) with interview-based anecdotes (and not even the best ones at that!).

THAT WAS HOLLYWOOD: THE 1930s

Allan Eyles *(Batsford)*

Slimmer, but more useful, *That Was Hollywood* offers information rather than views. Its accounts of the films are little but capsule descriptions, but the films described are the most popular of their times. Even more usefully, the films are arranged chronologically (and month by month within each year), thus allowing us to see the pattern of production and release, while, in the introductions to each year, Eyles gives us thumbnail sketches of the major events of the year (the merger of Twentieth Century and Fox, the opening of New York's Radio City Music Hall and so forth). The result is a helpful reference book, full of minor but interesting facts: Did you know *Bringing Up Baby* was a flop and the all-but-forgotten *Navy Blue and Gold* was a hit?

SILENT MAGIC

Ivan Butler *(Columbus)*

Silent Magic does not aim to re-evaluate silent films but to describe 'how they appeared to film-goers of their period.' In his introduction Kevin Brownlow pays tribute to Butler's remarkable memory, but whereas Brownlow, in his own writings, is able to imbue us with his love for silent films, Butler's prose and enthusiasm for his subject collapse under the weight of forever looking back. The result is a pedestrian book in which the brief descriptions never match the claims made for the films.

THE HOLLYWOOD HISTORY OF THE WORLD

George MacDonald Fraser *(Michael Joseph)*

More enjoyable and aptly-titled, this is a survey of Hollywood costume drama from the Epic to the Western and beyond. Elegantly written, the book makes many sensible points but lacks a general view. Behind the text lies an extended thank-you to Hollywood for having visualized the past so powerfully and somehow made it real. What is lacking is any interrogation of the pasts Hollywood has created. This stems from Fraser's superficial knowledge of film history (in marked contrast to his wide general knowledge). Thus, while he makes an interesting observation that the real Billy the Kid looked like 'a young and half-witted Oscar Wilde', his treatment of Hollywood's favourite outlaw is simplistic because it touches on so few films; there's no mention of *Dirty Little Billy* for instance. Similarly, while Fraser makes the general point that notions of the past change with passing years, the relationship between past and present - why certain pasts at certain times - is left unexplored. But apart from its lack of an ideological dimension, the book is a light-hearted dash through Hollywood's costume dramas every bit as racy as any of Fraser's novels and, like them, it contains enough in the way of odd pieces of knowledge and enjoyable anecdotes to amuse.

BILLY WILDER IN HOLLYWOOD

Maurice Zolotow *(Pavilion)*

Zolotow's account of the strained relationship between Billy Wilder and Raymond Chandler during their collaboration on the script of *Double Indemnity* forms the basis of Otto Friedrich's briefer version in *City of Nets*. Both authors end their story with Wilder at the Oscar ceremonies expecting the film to win at least one Oscar and finally sticking his foot out and tripping up Leo McCarey, on his way to collect another statuette for *Going My Way*. For Friedrich the event is just one of many, but Zolotow makes it into a set-piece. Where Friedrich tells both Chandler and Wilder's sides of the story, Zolotow, as one would expect from a biographer, stresses Wilder's side. However, when it comes to the films themselves, Zolotow is less sure of his position. Some are treated in detail, others less so, but significantly they are all seen as an adjunct of Wilder's life - there is no separate section on the films - and are explained in terms of it. Old-fashioned though this approach is, it has certain advantages. It helps Zolotow sidestep the debate about Wilder's so-called cynicism and bad taste, which engulfs most accounts of *Ace in the Hole* and *Kiss Me Stupid*, for example. Zolotow usefully counterposes the growing domesticity of Wilder's own life, following his marriage to Audrey Young, with the more central roles given to women in the films. While Zolotow probably makes too much of the relationship between Wilder's life and art, his account of the life (especially Wilder's youth in Vienna and Berlin) is the best available. In particular, a long chapter on Wilder's relationships with his co-writers is very revealing.

THE IT'S A WONDERFUL LIFE BOOK

Jeanine Basinger *(Pavilion)*

MARGARET MITCHELL'S GONE WITH THE WIND LETTERS

Margaret Mitchell *(Sidgwick & Jackson)*

A few Hollywood films have become legends. Two such are Frank Capra's *It's a Wonderful Life* and *Gone With the Wind*. Amazingly, considering its current reputation and TV drawing power, *It's a Wonderful Life* was only a moderate success when first released. The book is an invaluable collection of material relating to the film, including sections from early scripts and Capra's dialogue changes. The subject of Margaret Mitchell's letters is the novel, the classic best-seller of the century, rather than the film, but the underlying story it tells is of how Mitchell was overtaken by

her creation. In her letters to the film's producer, David Selznick, one sees her desperately trying to keep her distance from the film. She refused to endorse Vivien Leigh as 'her' choice for Scarlett O'Hara, and declined all Selznick's entreaties for her to become involved in the film-making process. Her letter of 20 Jan, 1939 to Selznick reveals the pain, pride and growing sense of the personal cost to her of her creation: 'I am so very sorry that I cannot help you with this problem. [Selznick had asked for advice on a scene.] No matter how much I might wish to help you, by writing the dialogue or sketching the scene, it would be impossible. I am a slow writer and writing takes time, uninterrupted time. For nearly three years, I have had no time for writing of any kind. With hundreds of letters coming in, with the telephone constantly ringing, with hundreds of people clamouring for "introductions to Mr Selznick" and newspapers bedevilling me for statements on subjects which do not concern me, I have no time to even think about creative writing, much less attempt it.' Not surprisingly she never wrote another novel.

THE MAKING OF IRONWEED
William Kennedy *(Penguin)*

RICHARD ATTENBOROUGH'S CRY FREEDOM: A PICTORIAL RECORD
Richard Attenborough *(Bodley Head)*

It's a Wonderful Life had to earn its reputation over the years (the book comes some 40 years after the film), but in these days of spin-offs and ancillary marketing, the book of the film is generally available on opening night. Hence *The Making of Ironweed* and *Richard Attenborough's Cry Freedom: A Pictorial Record.* Both are little but collections of stills from the films with short introductions. William Kennedy's is at least well written but Attenborough's sadly suffers the overblown pomposity of 'the public statement' - 'Donald and Wendy Woods are two of the most courageous people I have ever met.'

THUNDER IN THE DUST
John R. Hamilton *(Aurum)*

STRIKING POSES
Richard Schickel *(Pavilion)*

And then there's straightforward nostalgia, for the Western (*Thunder in the Dust*) and for the star system itself (*Striking Poses*). Of the two, *Thunder* is the better. The thin ribbon of text is lightweight, but the photographs are mostly wonderful - some 30 years of Western film-making captured in glorious colour. Horses in mid-stride in mid-stream, grizzled weather-beaten faces, directors at work, Monument Valley (complete with John Ford) and the process of film production are all magnificently captured by John R. Hamilton. A must for Western addicts. *Striking Poses* is more camp. 'Don't laugh' are Richard Schickel's opening words, inviting us to do just that at photos of stars with flowers, with telephones, the American flag, and even Lassie with a collection of old bones. A book of momentary and decidedly minor pleasures.

THE CLASSICAL HOLLYWOOD CINEMA
David Bordwell, Janet Staiger, Kristin Thompson *(Routledge)*

As an antidote to the nostalgia, this account of the development of the classical Hollywood style, now published in paperback, could not be bettered. Bordwell describes how the narrative strategies of Hollywood result in a cinema that is 'excessively obvious', but the book is fair-minded in acknowledging the strength of the tradition and how alternative styles have defined themselves in relation to it: 'The historical and aesthetic importance of the classical Hollywood cinema lies in the fact that to go beyond it we must go through it.' The book's value lies in the thoroughness with which it explores the inter-connections between economic, industrial and technological factors, and its demonstration of how these perpetuate a relatively homogeneous Hollywood style.

EMOTION PICTURES, THE WOMAN'S PICTURE
Hilton Tims *(Columbus)*

WICKED WOMEN OF THE SCREEN
David Quinlan *(Batsford)*

Once dismissed as little but camp, the woman's picture has recently become the subject of much interest and theoretical writing. Most of the latter has passed by Hilton Tims, whose *Emotion Pictures* is an easy-going essay in nostalgia. The text is un-demanding, consisting of little more than plot synopses enlivened with a steady supply of adjectives. Less specific in orientation but equally lightweight is David Quinlan's *Wicked Women of the Screen.* The book uneasily straddles the divide between a dictionary (half the text is an alphabetical listing of stars

with comments) and a thematic study (the second half is constructed around a series of essays in which the actresses are grouped together as 'Gun Girls', 'Vamps' and the like). Quinlan's tastes are genuinely catholic, thus he finds space for such interesting curiosities as Anthony Mann's *The Great Flamarion* and Edgar Ulmer's *Detour*, but the comments themselves are virtually interchangeable with Hilton Tims's, only the adjectives are different.

HOME IS WHERE THE HEART IS

Christine Gledhill *(BFI)*

THE WOMEN WHO KNEW TOO MUCH

Tania Modleski *(Methuen)*

For a more considered view of the subject of women's pictures one must turn to *Home Is Where the Heart Is.* This collection of essays is useful both as a guide to contemporary thinking about melodrama (the genre which encompasses most women's pictures) and to the repercussions within film theory once melodrama was admitted as a subject of study. Introduced in the early seventies by critics interested in narrative, because of the excessively heightened narrative that is generally associated with melodrama (*Written on the Wind* is a good example), and feminists who were interested in how women (traditionally the central characters of melodramas) were depicted on film and how women consumed those images, the debate about melodrama has become a central issue in contemporary film theory. Many of the issues raised in *Home Is Where the Heart Is* are difficult to follow, but they are important. More irritating, but still of value, is Tania Modleski's *The Women Who Knew Too Much.* Subtitled 'Hitchcock and Feminist Theory', it examines a number of Hitchcock films (but surprisingly not *Psycho*) with the aim of showing that, far from providing passive images of women for male consumption, Hitchcock's representation of women is far more complex. Some of the essays, particularly the one on *Rebecca*, are both convincing and exciting to read, but the book is overbalanced by Modleski's (obsessive) desire to obliterate Laura Mulvey's 1975 article on 'Visual Pleasure and Narrative Cinema'. Clearly, the second generation of feminist film theoreticians need to 'kill' their mothers as much as Hitchcock's characters. The unfortunate result of this is that complex arguments about female spectatorship and desire become even more difficult to follow.

'RONALD REAGAN', THE MOVIE

Michael Rogin *(University of California Press)*

Lastly (and why not?) Ronald Reagan. Psycho-history has a chequered past. For all the insights it has produced on the likes of Woodrow Wilson and Richard Nixon, the results have been spotty. Quite simply the facts behind the traumas these historical figures have been described as working out in their public lives have been difficult to ascertain, and the analyses equally difficult to evaluate. That said, the attempt remains fascinating, especially when the subject is Reagan, someone for whom the gap between reality, publicity handouts and other people's words has never been clearcut, either as an actor or a politician. Michael Rogin, in his book of essays *'Ronald Reagan', the Movie,* doesn't quite attempt a full-blown psycho-history (but don't worry, sure as eggs is eggs, that's coming). Instead, starting with the already proven point that Reagan often quotes lines from movies in his speeches, Rogin suggests that, in his movies (particularly *Knute Rockne* which, unusually for the time, he initiated) and later commercials, Reagan unconsciously established a persona that would form a perfect platform for the larger dramatic stage of modern-day presidential politics, in which saying the lines with conviction, looking good on camera and, above all, emoting the American Dream, were more important than having a political vision or making political judgements. After all, the implicit assumption of the lengthy essay is that an American President, like a middle-order actor in Hollywood in the forties, has no power. That belongs to the faceless generals and bureaucrats of Washington. It's an appealing point of view and largely well argued. But (because he's a political rather than cultural commentator) Rogin casts his net too narrowly.

PHIL HARDY

WHO MADE THIS MOVIE?

How can you write about a film director? Some argue for a separation between the person who is also a director and the person who makes films. Commonsense has prevailed over the notion that an individual can be the autonomous creator of a film. And yet, however difficult it may be to do so with conceptual rigour and total confidence, there remains a sense in which it seems meaningful to talk about a Polanski, a Fellini or a Bertolucci.

THE FILMS OF CAROL REED

Robert F. Moss *(Macmillan)*

The weakness of this book on Reed, director of three of the most enduring classics of British cinema, lies in its failure to work out any sort of framework within which to analyze its subject. Moss argues for a re-evaluation of Reed, but he lacks the information necessary for a detailed examination of the director's influence on particular projects. Confronted

by such a minor work as *The Man Between*, Moss reluctantly acknowledges that 'Reed was dependent on the quality of the script he was given, regardless of his own sometimes enormous creative input.' Otherwise, Moss hangs his argument around the hardly startling observation that Reed suffered from the ups and downs of the British film industry, and more particularly from the death of Alexander Korda in 1956. None of this adds up to an explanation of how a director who reached the heights with a trio of films made in the late forties - *Odd Man Out*, *The Fallen Idol*, *The Third Man* - came to put his name to *Flap* and *The Public Eye*. There is a clue, however, in the suggestion (made in passing) that Reed didn't enjoy reading books and hadn't done more than browse through Conrad's *An Outcast of the Islands* before making it into a film.

ROMAN POLANSKI

Virginia Wright Wexman *(Columbus)*

Just as political commentators argue as if an American Vice-President should agree with his President on all key issues, film critics seem to consider that a fruitful writer-director collaboration is necessarily based on shared assumptions and values. It is, however, often more revealing to look at such relationships in terms of conflict, negotiation and the search for a synthesis. Virginia Wright Wexman sees Polanski's creative development as a response to the way his films were received by audiences, and confrontations with collaborators. 'The economic realities of the film industry,' she writes, 'have had a beneficial effect on his art. They have encouraged him to lay aside eccentric personal preoccupations and to communicate fantasies that have a cultural as well as a personal significance. Collaboration has had a similar effect, forcing the director to synthesize the contributions of different talents.' Although this leads Wright Wexman to the difficult position of arguing that *Chinatown* is a better film than *Cul-de-Sac*, rather than just a different sort of picture, her analysis of the way in which the conflict between writer Robert Towne's romanticism and Polanski's cynicism led to a much richer and more interesting version of *Chinatown* than either could have achieved without the other is convincing. The book ends with *Tess* and it is difficult to know how the author would fit *Pirates* and *Frantic* into her argument. I suspect she would have to say that Polanski has obtained too much creative freedom at budgets which allow for excessive creative indulgence at a time when the director has travelled too far away from his 'roots' in surrealism and the theatre of the absurd.

FEDERICO FELLINI

Frank Burke *(Columbus)*

FELLINI: A LIFE

Hollis Alpert *(W. H. Allen)*

Polanski drifted away from a modernist position, towards the Hollywood mainstream: Frank Burke's account of Fellini's early work shows the director moving from neo-realism towards an approach to cinema which leads to him being described by Burke's commissioning editor as 'the artist who belatedly brought to film the modernist sensibility as Joyce had at the beginning of the century brought it to fiction.' Fellini's style arose out of a desire to tell the stories of increasingly autonomous characters with the strength to shake off convention and the 'wombed world of unconscious existence.' This process led Fellini away from plot towards more complex narrative structures. Burke's study concludes with *La Dolce Vita*, and a later tome will pick up the story with the great leap forward represented by $8\frac{1}{2}$. Hollis Alpert's book provides a straightforward account of Fellini's life and careers, but he has nothing original to say about the films.

BERTOLUCCI BY BERTOLUCCI

Bernardo Bertolucci (Enzo Ungari, Don Ranvaud) *(Plexus)*

The Italian director's words to his interviewers collected in *Bertolucci by Bertolucci* come across as sometimes silly, often infuriating. But throughout he seems honest, particularly when talking about collaborators. Most revealing is his account of the role played by editor Franco Arcalli in structuring *The Conformist*, which Bertolucci had filmed as a continuous narrative but re-structured in the editing room because it was dull. The experience changed his views on editing, but the greater lesson about dramatic structure does not, on the evidence of subsequent films, seem to have penetrated. Bertolucci looks back nostalgically to the early films of Godard and pleads for a similar 'shock to the system of cinematic communication that would give way to the creation of a new, deeper relationship with the audience,' but it is surely from the discovery of new ways of shaping narratives so to involve viewers again in the sort of deep emotional experience they seek from cinema that such a shock must come.

THE CINEMA OF ANDREI TARKOVSKY

Mark LeFanu *(BFI)*

If there is any director whose status as an author cannot be in doubt he is Andrei Tarkovsky. Mark LeFanu's unnecessary caution in this matter is indicative of the care with which he approaches such modern masterpieces as *Mirror*, *Andrei Rublev* and *Solaris*, as he tries to coax out their meanings. Since Tarkovsky is regarded by many as an obscure and difficult artist, this approach is a useful one. Also, LeFanu succeeds in his wider intention to place the films in 'as wide and sympathetic a cultural context, as possible,' pointing to the evidence in the films that Tarkovsky had studied the works of Buñuel, Bergman and Kurosawa, and showing his debt to classical painting.

What the book does lack is any perspective on Tarkovsky's technical mastery. LeFanu alludes to the 'mysterious poetic assonances' of *Ivan's Childhood*, the 'ability to conjure up, in piercing epiphanies, that magical submerged world of wonder which forms the adult's later imaginative capital,' but the mechanism isn't explored. He discusses the dramatic problem of characters whose goodness makes them somehow lifeless, without showing how Tarkovsky solves the problem with his camera, making us feel empathy with the person on the screen. Tarkovsky used his moving camera both to articulate his profound vision and draw viewers into an intensely emotional experience. Open the beautifully-illustrated Bertolucci book and sometimes the still images seem to have a force they lacked in the film. Look at a Tarkovsky image and you can only long to experience the film anew.

THE MAGIC LANTERN

Ingmar Bergman *(Hamish Hamilton)*

Ingmar Bergman may still have more admirers than Tarkovsky, but the Swede has no hesitation in acknowledging the Russian as the modern master: 'All my life I have hammered on the doors of the rooms in which he moves so naturally. Only a few times have I managed to creep inside.'

Tarkovsky's work realizes Bergman's aspirations towards a cinema that goes 'straight to our emotions, deep into the twilight room of the soul.'

A medley of memories and thoughts, Bergman's autobiography has irritated some who wanted to hear more of his thoughts on cinema. That is to miss the point. While ranging over his childhood, cultural experiences and romantic relationships, Bergman *is* talking about his cinema, just as when he expatiates on his nervous stomach, the reasons for his fear of improvisation, the love of reflection, the hatred of tumult: 'I want calm, order and friendliness. Only in that way can we approach a limitless world.'

THE LAST OF ENGLAND

Derek Jarman *(Constable)*

Bergman directs considerable bile at the Swedish tax authorities who caused his period of exile in Germany. Film financiers escape his scorn: 'I have always appreciated the honest brutality of the international film world.' Derek Jarman, by contrast, directs his rancour at every moving target. He is unwilling to go beyond a purely visceral reaction to things. Jarman considers big budget cinema immoral. Why then is Julien Temple, who spent millions on *Absolute Beginners*, held up as a paragon of independent cinema while Peter Greenaway comes in for derision? What are Jarman's reasons for asserting that cinema is finished? And how does he justify the assertion that his latest film, which shares a title with the book, 'makes the work of my contemporaries pale into conformity'?

It seems that Jarman now rejects the compromises necessary to get *Caravaggio* onto the screen. He doesn't give his reasons. Jarman creates images as well as he writes - brilliantly - but he seems unwilling to open himself up to the ideas and experiences that would enable him to develop as a film-maker. There's lots wrong with British cinema, but Jarman can't get up the energy to analyze those faults.

STILL DANCING, MY STORY

Lew Grade *(Collins)*

Derek Jarman's father was a kleptomaniac, Lew Grade's a chronic gambler with no head for business. The respective memoirs of these two men are as vivid an illustration as you could hope to find of the gap that can divide the creative film-maker from the film executive or producer.

Jarman's account of his early life is a moving record of pain and anguish, Lew Grade's a story of deficient powers of observation. His family flees Russia but young Louis learns nothing of the pogroms that caused their flight. Having become the World Solo Charleston Champion, he set himself up as a professional dancer and visited Germany in the thirties, but didn't see any evidence of Nazism.

Not every wheeler-dealer wants to tell how he does it, but Grade's memoirs are peculiarly bland, containing little that couldn't have been culled from press cuttings. The book does, however, demonstrate again why those who attacked Grade for ACC's philistine film-making policies during the late seventies and early eighties failed to touch their target. He was unable to perceive a film as anything different from an act for the London Palladium. Suggesting, for example, that two scenes in *Raise the Titanic* justified the price of admission shows zilch understanding of how films draw their audience through the careful development of narrative structure. They cannot be saved by a few set-pieces.

SPIEGEL

Andrew Sinclair *(Weidenfeld)*

THE MAKING OF THE AFRICAN QUEEN

Katharine Hepburn *(Century Hutchinson)*

Andrew Sinclair's biography of Sam Spiegel is more interesting. It does describe how various projects were set up, and the problems that attended their production; and Spiegel was anyway a fascinating character. The apocryphal stories that attached themselves to Lew were good for after-dinner chat, those accruing to Spiegel have bite. His formative years were spent in Galicia - a market town near the Russian border - Vienna and Palestine, before he became involved in the film business, in Germany

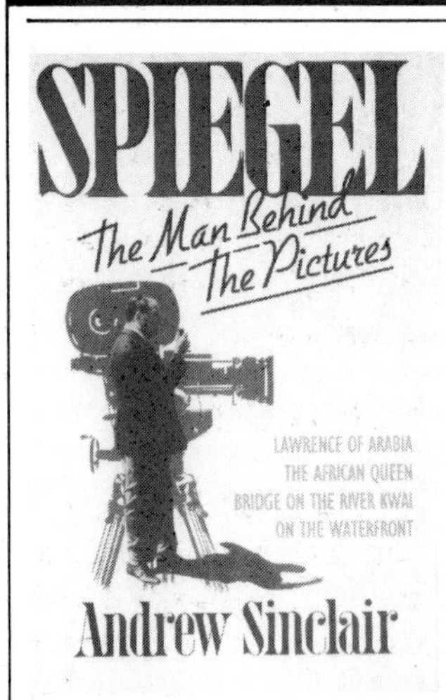

and Sinclair doesn't have sufficient biographical skills to analyze the complex personality that evolved out of these experiences, but he does show that Spiegel was someone who would fight to ensure the films he was involved in had quality.

British director Adrian Brunel reported Spiegel as having said: 'Only films which are produced in strife have any outstanding merit,' and it was Spiegel's willingness to work through conflicts with writers, together with a seemingly instinctive story sense, that led to the brilliantly-constructed scripts for the classic films with which he established his reputation: *The African Queen* and *On the Waterfront*. The various writers caught in Spiegel's maw probably responded in more complex ways than Sinclair gives them credit for (Harold Pinter has questioned the book's account of his working relationship with Spiegel on *The Last Tycoon* and *Betrayal*, suggesting that it was less a case of antagonism than an 'open and active working relationship'), but Spiegel's tough-minded willingness to fight through his sense of structure put him in a class apart from today's timid producers.

Curiously, Katharine Hepburn spent most of the time between being engaged for her part in *The African Queen* and the first day of shooting trying to find someone to whom she could articulate her worries about the script: 'It seemed to me utterly dull and I kept falling asleep over it. What a mess.' Although claiming credit for the kiss that follows the rapids scene, she doesn't say whether the script was changed in response to her complaints, or, as seems more likely, John Huston brought her round to accept what James Agee and Peter Viertel had created. Spiegel had charmed Hepburn from their first meeting, but the actress was initially suspicious of the 'over-male' Huston, whose habit of arriving late or disappearing infuriated her. It took an inspired discussion about the role to transform her feelings to deep and lasting affection.

Beautifully printed pictures in this handsome book provide a counterpoint to Hepburn's tale of distraught kidneys (she's a urologist's daughter), intestinal problems and embarrassment over early morning visits to the toilet. She does not appear to have been aware that, according to Sinclair's account, Huston deliberately encouraged some measure of discomfort, believing that the hardships of the actors would give character to the finished film.

A DREAM OF PASSION

Lee Strasberg *(Bloomsbury)*

Directors are sometimes reproached by actors whom they attempt to 'trick' into giving a particular performance. Lee Strasberg's account of the development of The Method sufficiently suggests the difficulties involved in getting an actor to think the emotional experience of any scene to justify any director who tries to help things along. Although he doesn't focus on the problems of cinema, Strasberg's account of his researches into acting method is also, as he claims, relevant to the problems of artistic creation in general. The actor for every performance, just as the screenwriter or the director at the moment of creation, has to find a point of entry to the emotions of their characters, reaching to a parallel emotional memory that will enable them to create something which carries conviction to an audience. The actor's performance cannot be an imitation of emotion, it has to swell up from the depths of being if it is to move people. Strasberg's summation of his life's work makes it easy to understand the devotion he won from his pupils.

ELIA KAZAN: A LIFE

Elia Kazan *(Deutsch/Knopf)*

One of those devotees who later turned sceptical was Elia Kazan, who remarks in his autobiography that Strasberg had 'the aura of a prophet, a magician, a witch doctor, a psychoanalyst, and a feared father of a Jewish home.' The importance of Group Theatre to Kazan lay not only in the perspective it gave him on acting, but also the sense of belonging it provided along with a series of ideas about theatre's political role.

One comparison suggested by this discursive, sometimes platitudinous, tome is between Kazan and Bergman. Both were men of the theatre; Kazan directed the first performances of *A Streetcar Named Desire* and *Death of a Salesman* back-to-back. Both found that their careers put a distance between them and their children. Both were also men of considerable sexual appetite who, while they regretted the mendacity and pain-to-others their philandering caused, argue (rather repetitively in Kazan's case) that infidelity was an integral part of their creative life. Kazan, eight years older than Bergman, says his bed-hopping kept him 'curious, interested, eager, searching, and in excellent health.'

But it took Kazan over 40 years to discover what Bergman always knew, that 'my best and truest material was my own life.' Always an 'outsider', he had played by the Hollywood rules until his testimony to HUAC in 1952 cut him off from many of his close friends. The resulting pain, together with a determination to show that he still had it in him, was directed into his work. For a convincing (and very different) account of Miller's withdrawal from *The Hook*, readers should turn to *Timebends*, but it was Kazan's good fortune to find a writer, Bud Schulberg, who had been working on a similar project which became *On the Waterfront*, and a producer in Spiegel whose 'infuriating insistence paid off.' There followed such pictures as *East of Eden* and *A Face in the Crowd* before he turned to novel-writing. Kazan writes out of a sense of wonder that he has made so much of his life, and reflects on such casualties of his time as Orson Welles and Clifford Odets.

UNHEARD MELODIES

Claudia Gorbman *(BFI/Indiana)*

Gorbman's book asks why films need music. The score is, after all, alien to classical cinema's determination to convince an audience that it is seeing something 'real'. But music takes listeners to a different level of consciousness and helps to render 'the individual an untroublesome viewing subject' by lessening defences against fantasy. The book reflects on the way in which music helps the viewer to define the emotional content of the image and opens the way to acceptance of high emotion (Gorbman makes the point that audiences might not have laughed at John Gilbert in 1929 if there had been background music). These themes are explored in studies of the work of Max Steiner, and the scores for *Sous les toits de Paris*, *Zéro de conduite* and *Hangover Square*. But the book is marred by the author's distaste for the way in which music 'greases the wheels of the cinematic pleasure machine by easing the spectator's passage into subjectivity ... the hypnotic voice bidding the spectator to believe, focus, behold, identify, consume.'

OZU AND THE POETICS OF CINEMA

David Bordwell *(BFI/Princeton)*

CURRENTS IN JAPANESE CINEMA

Tadao Sato *(Harper & Row)*

Yasujiro Ozu has many admirers in the West. In this rich and comprehensive analysis of Ozu's career, his place in Japanese culture and films, David Bordwell argues that Western directors and critics have worked with a narrow interpretation of Ozu's work, which was not so much rooted in 'traditional' Japanese culture and Zen Buddhism as influenced by a variety of cultural elements that included a vibrant contemporary popular culture, and Hollywood movies. Also, rather than being the aesthetic minimalist of some critical accounts, he produced uniquely 'replete' films, capable of engaging audiences at numerous levels because they drew upon the narrative codes of classical 'Hollywood' cinema and art-cinema, while still experimenting with form.

Ozu's ability to synthesize the styles of Hollywood cinema (watching *Fantasia* during WWII, he is said to have remarked that Japan would lose the war because 'These guys look like trouble') into something distinctly 'Japanese' is also a theme of Tadao Sato's book. This veteran of film criticism shows how the earliest Japanese film heroes derived either from the strong Samurai type of Kabuki drama, or the softer romantics of contemporary Shimpa plays. The history of Japanese cinema is seen as a series of re-workings of these models until the influence of American movies and pressure from the Occupation authorities created a synthesis, which led in turn to the *yakuza* movies of the sixties. Sato's book usefully sets the works of the Japanese masters alongside the mainstream work of their contemporaries, and changes in Japanese society.

EISENSTEIN WRITINGS VOLUME 1

Ed. Richard Taylor *(BFI/Indiana)*

If Ozu should not be judged by the very partial and limited way his work is alluded to in the films of such as Jim Jarmusch or Wayne Wang, even more so must one avoid assessing Eisenstein by the standards of those whose humourless and unimaginative works were made with reference to a 'Soviet' model. But this collection of writings (the first of three) from the period 1922-34 is not likely to turn the sceptical into followers of the great Russian theorist and film-maker. These are texts rooted in the conditions of the USSR just after the Revolution, and they often seem over-dogmatic and hectoring. Eisenstein's project at the time was nothing less than a change in Soviet consciousness, which could only be achieved through an 'organized' cinema. Such a project is bound to seem alien in our less ambitious times, as is the quasi-scientific quest for 'a cinema of extreme cognition and extreme sensuality that has mastered the entire arsenal of affective optical, acoustical and biochemical stimulants ...' But what sets Eisenstein apart from many of his followers is recognition that cinema is an emotional experience. The concern to produce a work that 'is correctly conducted in Marxist terms and results in an ideologically valuable and socially useful product' may seem unartistic, but it is always tied to a recognition that the film only works through 'the maximum intensification of the emotional seizure of the audience.'

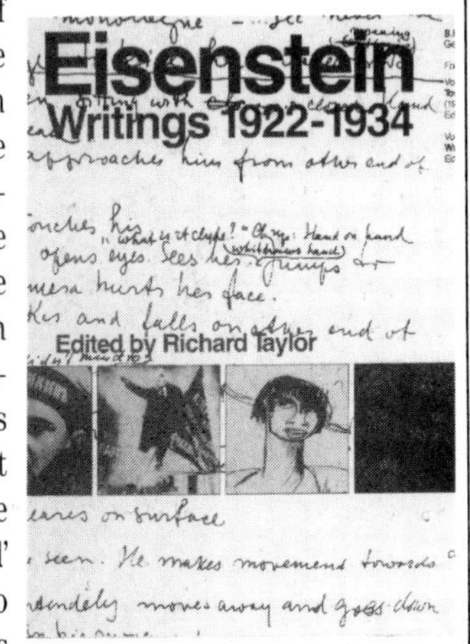

JAMES PARK

FILM AND SOCIETY

Crudely speaking, the world can be divided into Hollywood and the rest. About Hollywood we know quite a lot, about the rest of the world much less. Indeed, many of our conceptions of non-Hollywood cinema are fixed and static. Only recently have we begun to re-evaluate the key moments of non-Hollywood film history.

THE FILM FACTORY

Richard Taylor, Ian Christie *(RKP)*

A case in point is the Soviet cinema. The established view is that the Russian cinema of the twenties was Eisenstein, Vertov, montage and a highpoint of state-sponsored experimentation which only too quickly, under pressure from Stalin, collapsed into what Godard termed Hollywood-Mosfilm. *The Film Factory* attempts to redress this balance. The most comprehensive collection of documents about the Russian cinema between 1896 and 1930 ever published in English, the book makes clear that the politics of Russian film-making were far more complex than is generally thought.

The conventional view is best summed up in the famous 1926 memo by David Selznick to his superiors in MGM: '[*Battleship Potemkin*] possesses a technique entirely new to the screen, and I therefore suggest that it might be very advantageous to have the organization view it in the same way that a group of artists might view and study a Rubens or a Raphael.' He concluded 'the firm might well consider securing the man responsible for it, a young Russian director named Eisenstein.'

Selznick highlights the area of technique as central to Soviet film-making. Later histories of Russian cinema of the period stress collective organization and intellectual debate. The great virtue of Taylor and Christie's collection of documents is that it pulls together these different perspectives. In doing so it demonstrates how much more fragmentary and faction-ridden were the debates and the organization that supported the achievements of Soviet film-making. The resulting picture is one of struggle rather than agreement, and further of a struggle in which Eisenstein and Vertov were merely players (rather than rule-makers) and of a struggle that continued into the thirties (and eventually re-surfaced in the eighties). It's not an easy book to read (it's easier to skip through, find bits that fascinate one and then read around them) but it is an important book, and, unlike most histories, is relevant to the present (ours as much as the Soviets).

THE FRENCH THROUGH THEIR FILMS

Robin Buss *(Batsford)*

This oddly structured (but well titled) book is rather like Stanley Ellis's writings about British taste. Thus there are chapters on family and geography as well as history (but no mention of *The Battle of Algiers*). The result is more an account of the French and less of French films, a book to dip into for the odd sociological/cultural reference, but little else. 'The French Through Their Cultural Artefacts' might be a useful book, but this is not it.

THIRD WORLD FILM MAKING AND THE WEST

Roy Armes
(University of California Press)

Roy Armes' introduction to Third World cinema is an invaluable work. Its major failing is that it is limited in its scope. Thus, there is no mention of the recent widespread western interest in African music or the issues that such an interest has raised. While these lacks don't devalue Armes' account and the useful information he supplies about the film industries of the Third World, they do limit it. What is needed is an account of the cultural interchange between the Third World and Hollywood, in terms of film, television and music.

THE 1988 FILM GUIDE

Peter Cowie *(Tantivy)*

The same criticism can be made of *The 1988 Film Guide*, with the difference that Cowie contains all those vital Third World phone numbers and addresses. Thus, unless you've managed to clip the appropriate pages of *Variety*'s special issues, you need it. As an added bonus, for this Silver Jubilee edition of the guide, Cowie includes a number of interesting lists of Top Ten Movies.

MASS OBSERVATION AT THE MOVIES

Jeffrey Richards, Dorothy Sheridan *(RKP)*

And then there's the British cinema, the byways of which have been under scrutiny in a clutch of books. The most intriguing is *Mass Observation at the Movies*, a collection of documents from the archives of the Mass

Observation movement, which attempted an anthropological picture of Britain at work and play during the thirties and into the war years. The charm of *At the Movies* is the 'rawness' of the data it collects together, in the form of comments by cinema-goers about the films, both in detail and in general. (People's tastes range from plaintive pleas for 'more cowboy films' to denunciations of American accents.) But the book is more than merely charming, it offers the best general picture of Britain's cinema-going habits in the war years. A rewarding and engrossing read.

THE LAST PICTURE SHOW?

David Docherty, David Morrison, Michael Tracey *(BFI)*

Less engrossing is *The Last Picture Show*, a detailed examination of the decline of the cinema-going habit in Britain since the war. Based on extensive surveys conducted by the Broadcasting Research Unit, the authors paint a depressing and all too familiar picture. The statistics which form the basis of the book are leavened by a cine-literate text, but it's not much of a read.

THE BRITISH LABOUR MOVEMENT AND FILM 1918-1939

Stephen Jones *(RKP)*

This plugs yet another gap in British film history, reminding us that film distribution and exhibition between the wars was not entirely dominated by either the major film studios or film clubs with their different emphases ('entertainment' and 'art' respectively) and of the serious debates between those on the left about how to use the medium of film. Some, like the question of whether films should be shown on Sunday, are issues that only touch on filmic matters, but others, the attempt at creating regular 'socialist' newsreels and the workers' film societies that sprang up, hark back to debates within Russia in the twenties and forward to contemporary debates.

CINEMA, CENSORSHIP AND SEXUALITY

Annette Kuhn *(RKP)*

Even more limited in scope, Kuhn's detailed account of the early years of censorship in Britain is not, as one might imagine, only for the specialist historian. The section detailing the saga of *Maisie's Marriage* (1923), a story 'specially written for the screen by Dr Marie Stopes' which suggested that marriage would be even happier for a woman if birth control were more widely practised, is fascinating. The film itself is coy enough - the central message is spelled out in a parable about roses in which after each pruning 'though the roses were fewer, each bud turned into a perfect flower' followed by a dissolve from a perfect flower to the face of a baby - and, although the film was on occasion promoted in such a way as to suggest it was far more 'explicit', the debate about the film was similarly less than frank. A fascinating study.

PHIL HARDY

OBITUARIES

Compiled by Tim Pulleine
1 July 1987 – 30 June 1988

IRVING ALLEN

Polish-born, he made a start in the American cinema as an editor and subsequently moved into short film production. After the war he directed several second features, then produced some rather more prestigious pictures, including *The Man on the Eiffel Tower* (1949), and came into his own in England in partnership with 'Cubby' Broccoli, with whom he founded Warwick Films. The company's output began with *The Red Beret* (1953) and included several examples of superior hokum, generally featuring American stars like Victor Mature, and came to an end with the more ambitious, if lower budgeted, *The Trials of Oscar Wilde* (1960). Allen continued as a producer in both the US and Britain, notably with the successful Matt Helm series initiated by *The Silencers* (1966), his final picture being *Eyewitness* (1971).

Died Encino, California, December 17, 1987, aged 82

LESLIE ARLISS

A cousin of celebrated actor George Arliss, he started out as a journalist and drama critic in Johannesburg, and in the early thirties began a screenwriting career which took in credits on several George Formby and Will Hay vehicles as well as more ambitious undertakings like *Rhodes of Africa* (1936). He graduated to directing at Gainsborough during the war and achieved temporary celebrity as maker of some of that studio's best remembered pieces of costume hokum, including *The Man in Grey* (1943) and especially *The Wicked Lady* (1944), which, whatever its shortcomings, achieved headline status via American alarm at the depth of Margaret Lockwood's *décolletage*. His later directing career took in an even more bizarre costume extravaganza, *Idol of Paris* (1948), but ended with a second-feature farce,

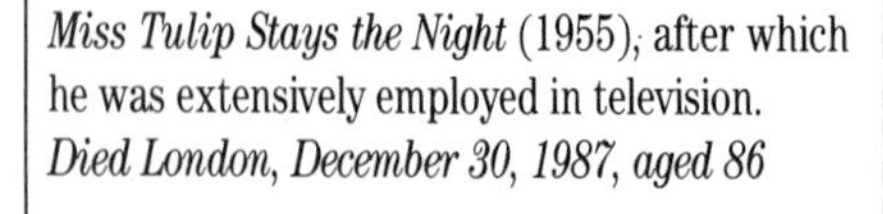

Miss Tulip Stays the Night (1955), after which he was extensively employed in television.

Died London, December 30, 1987, aged 86

MARY ASTOR

'If only Olivier had invited Miss Astor to play Gertrude,' regretted *Sequence* magazine in a paean to the actress which also suggested, with perhaps slight exaggeration, that she had contrived to steal *The Great Lie* (1941) from Bette Davis 'without so much as the roll of an eyeball.' Astor (born Lucille Langehanke) entered films young after being pushed into beauty contests, and by 1942 had achieved the status of John Barrymore's leading lady in *Beau Brummel*, as well as apparently becoming his lover. She went on to a career in some of the best films of the thirties and forties, despite the travails of alcoholism, four marriages, and an affair with the playwright George Kaufman which caused a scandal when it came to light during divorce proceedings instigated by her second husband in 1936. Perhaps her most celebrated role was as the dissembling Bridget O'Shaugnessy in *The Maltese Falcon* (1941), but it would be closely followed by her imperiously comic performance in *The Palm Beach Story* (1942) or her graciously maternal incarnation in *Meet Me in St Louis* (1944). In 1959 she published a far from reticent autobiography, and continued in occasional film roles until *Hush, Hush, Sweet Charlotte* (1964), after which failing health pushed her towards retirement.

Died Woodland Hills, California, September 25, 1987, aged 81

Mary Astor

ALFIE BASS

One of the stalwarts of the British cinema's roster of Cockney character actors, he was born into the Jewish community of the West End and made his stage début with the Unity Theatre. Of his many film appearances, those in *The Lavender Hill Mob* (1951) and as one of the leads in the prize-winning short feature *The Bespoke Overcoat* (1955) are among the best remembered. But he was also active in the

theatre, to greatest prominence when he took over from Topol the leading role in the West End production of the musical *Fiddler on the Roof*, and on television, as the put-upon Bootsie in *The Army Game*, and in a double-act with Bill Fraser in its civilian sequel, *Bootsie and Snudge*.
Died London, July 15, 1987, aged 66

CLARENCE BROWN

Director of seven Garbo movies, Brown trained as an engineer (which he claimed aided him in grasping the principles of cinematic construction) and was working in the automobile industry when he successfully applied for a job as assistant to the director Maurice Tourneur. Of Tourneur, he later said: 'I owe him everything... if it hadn't been for him, I'd still be fixing automobiles.' Noteworthy early films included *The Eagle* (1925) with Valentino, and in 1927 he moved to MGM, where, with the sole exception of *The Rains Came* (1929), he continued to work until his retirement in the early fifties. His Garbo pictures included *Flesh and the Devil* (1927), *Anna Christie* (1930) and *Anna Karenina* (1935), and he was said to be the director with whom she most liked working. Among his later films were *National Velvet* (1945), a great box-office success, and *Intruder in the Dust* (1950), a much admired Faulkner adaptation. In 1971, he donated land valued at $300,000 to his alma mater, the University of Tennessee, and helped to establish a theatre bearing his name there. At his death, *Variety* reported that he had reached the most advanced age of any major American film director.
Died Santa Monica, California, August 17, 1987, aged 97

MADELEINE CARROLL

Born in the Midlands, she graduated from Birmingham University, then joined a touring theatrical company, playing a French maid in a play called *The Lash*. A film test led to her making a début in *The Guns of Loos* (1928), and by the mid-thirties she was a leading British screen star, becoming, in *The 39 Steps* (1935) and *The Secret Agent* (1936), the first in a long line of Hitchcock's 'ice maiden' heroines. She went to Hollywood in 1936, and the following year was a memorable Ruritanian princess in *The Prisoner of Zenda*. Some of her later pictures were indifferent, though she evinced a light touch for comedy when partnering Bob Hope in *My Favourite Blonde* (1942). Following the death of her sister in the London blitz, she returned to England and was active in war relief work, briefly resuming her film career but opting for retirement following *The Fan* (1949).
Died Marbella, Spain, October 2, 1987, aged 81

NAT COHEN

Perhaps the last of the British film industry's relatively few contenders for the term of mogul, he grew up in London's East End and first ventured into the film business as proprietor of a cinema in Teddington. He subsequently moved into distribution, beginning in a small way with re-releases of Hal Roach comedies, and then into production. During the fifties he and Stuart Levy were partners in Anglo-Amalgamated, which churned out scores of supporting features, including the Edgar Lustgarten and Edgar Wallace programme-fillers. Anglo-Amalgamated was also behind the first films made in Britain by Joseph Losey and it inaugurated the *Carry On* series (which later passed into other hands). Cohen went on to more prestigious films in the sixties, and was behind, among others, *A Kind of Loving* (1962) and *Poor Cow* (1967). He took over as head of production at EMI in 1971, and presided over money-spinning pictures like *Murder on the Orient Express* (1974), continuing as an active force in production until the Cannon buy-out of 1986. *Clockwise* (1985) was the last film with which he was associated. Away from films, he was a racing devotee, and was the owner of the 1962 Grand National winner Kilmore.
Died London, February 10, 1988, aged 82

ANDREW CRUICKSHANK

Best remembered for his role as the irascible Dr Cameron in the popular TV series *Dr Finlay's Casebook*, which ran from 1959 to 1966, Cruickshank established a stage reputation in the thirties, notably as a member of the Old Vic company from 1937 to 1950. After the war, he continued to be active in both the classics (he was in the Stratford company of 1950) and in many modern plays, among them the West End productions of *Dial M for Murder* and *Inherit the Wind*. He appeared, generally in minor roles, in a large number of films, including *The Cruel Sea* (1953), *Richard III* (1955), and *El Cid* (1961). In later years he was seen in several National Theatre productions, and at the time of his death was playing the judge in the West End success *Beyond Reasonable Doubt*.
Died London, April 29, 1988, aged 80

JEFF DONNELL

An actress who seldom achieved more than subsidiary billing, she provided an attractive presence in a number of Hollywood films of the late forties and fifties, occasionally appearing in more recent productions. The androgynous style in which she was re-named (her real name was Jean Marie Donnell) testifies to the *jolie laide* manner she tended to be called upon to project, in parts such as those in *Easy Living* (1949), *In a Lonely Place* (1950), or *The Blue Gardenia* (1954). Perhaps her most noteworthy role was as Tony Curtis's long-suffering secretary in *Sweet Smell of Success* (1957). Later appearances included a small role in *Tora! Tora! Tora!* (1970). Her husbands included actor Aldo Ray.
Died Hollywood, April 11, 1988, aged 66

RICHARD EGAN

With the sort of impressively muscled physique which inevitably attracted the description 'rugged' in the captions to publicity photos, Egan started in Hollywood in the late forties (after a brief earlier career as a teacher of public speaking) and was later signed up by Fox, as one of the last generation of contract players. For a few years he played leading roles in a variety of adventure movies and romances (*Seven Cities of Gold*, *The View From Pompey's Head*, both 1955), leaving a rather stolid impression, but made more impact when cast against type, notably as the ruthless villain of *These Thousand Hills* (1959), but from the mid-sixties onwards, his appearances on the big screen became infrequent, and he was more often to be seen on television or in 'road show' theatrical productions.
Died Santa Monica, California, July 20, 1987, aged 65

BOB FOSSE

Born into a vaudeville family, he became a dancer and subsequently choreographer in both Broadway and Hollywood productions, featuring to inventive effect in dual capacity in the movie *My Sister Eileen* (1955). In the cinema he choreographed *The Pajama Game* (1957) and *Damn Yankees* (1958), and his first directorial work was in the 1959 Broadway show *Redhead*, which starred his then wife Gwen Verdon. He went on to direct a succession of musicals, among them *Sweet Charity*, and made his screen directing bow with the 1969 film version of that show. His 1972 film of

Cabaret achieved widespread popular and critical success and won him the best director Oscar. His three further films were *Lenny* (1974), *All That Jazz* (1979) and *Star 80* (1983): the second was an elaborate, semi-autobiographical musical fantasy; the first and third were non-musicals which nevertheless continued his preoccupation with show business themes. But none achieved wide popularity, and latterly he was more regularly engaged in theatre work.
Died Washington DC, September 23, 1987, aged 60

GEORGES FRANJU

The co-founder in 1937 of the Cinémathèque Française with Henri Langlois, with whom three years earlier he had co-directed a short film, *Le Métro*, he was an archivist and critic, before becoming in the post-war decade probably the leading French exponent of the short film. Beginning with *Le Sang des bêtes* (1949), a hideously unflinching view of a Paris slaughter house, and going on to such works as *Hôtel des invalides* (1951), these were films that challengingly transcended the constrictions of the documentary genre. His first feature, *La Tête contres les murs* (1958), confidently extended his preoccupations into the realm of fiction, and several of its successors, like the horror story *Les Yeux sans visage* (1959) and his tribute to Feuillade, *Judex* (1963), confirmed the quality of his vision. But his later films were frequently disappointing in both conception and execution, and his latter years were said to have been marked by increasing bitterness over what he perceived as his neglect by the critical establishment.
Died Paris, November 5, 1987, aged 75

LORNE GREENE

Burly Canadian-born actor who remains forever identified with the patriarchal rancher Ben Cartwright in the TV Western series *Bonanza*, in which he appeared for the length of its run (1959-71). He subsequently performed in two other shorter-lived series, *Griff* and *Battleship Galactica*, and numerous TV movies. In the fifties he played secondary roles in several films, usually as characters of the unsympathetic kind (*Tight Spot*, 1955; *Autumn Leaves*, 1956), and occasionally returned to the cinema thereafter (*Earthquake*, 1974).
Died Santa Monica, California, September 11, 1987, aged 72

IRENE HANDL

A stalwart British character player, mostly associated on the screen with Cockney and working-class characters, a trait which belied her own upper-class origins. She did not embark upon an acting career until she was in her thirties, but met with rapid success in the theatre, particularly as Madame Arcati in Noël Coward's *Blithe Spirit*. Her first film was in 1940 and numerous subsequent pictures included *The Belles of St Trinian's* (1954), *I'm All Right Jack* (1959), and *Heavens Above* (1963), and probably her most substantial role in the cinema was in *Morgan* (1966). She also made many appearances on the stage and TV, and when over 70 embarked on the new departure of writing fiction, becoming the author of two admired novels.
Died, London, November 29, 1987, aged 85

TREVOR HOWARD

By any reckoning one of Britain's leading film actors, he achieved a stage reputation before the war, notably in the long-running comedy *French Without Tears*, and made his first film, *The Way Ahead*, in 1944 after being invalided out of the army. He fully established himself on the screen as the shy doctor of *Brief Encounter*

Trevor Howard

(1945), and his playing of the intelligence officer in *The Third Man* (1949) demonstrated in its laconic authority the obverse of the vulnerability he had shown in the earlier film. Throughout the fifties he played leading roles, with his performances in *Outcast of the Islands* (1951) and *The Heart of the Matter* (1953) representing variations, respectively raffish and repressed, on the persona he had incisively established a few years before; but he also showed a readiness to venture into more flamboyant, or even disreputable, material, by taking on parts like the feline criminal boss of *Interpol* (1957). He was mainly committed by this time to the cinema, though he appeared in the 1953 West End production of *The Devil's General* and the following year played Lopahin in a revival of *The Cherry Orchard*, but began to be edged towards a less rewarding miscellany of character roles in international movies. However, he was an imposingly hateful Bligh in the remake of *Mutiny on the Bounty* (1962), a performance which in some respects prefigured his caustic, bullying Lord Cardigan in *The Charge of the Light Brigade* (1968). It is a pity that during the seventies he was often wasted in mediocre parts, but he subsequently made impressive appearances in such offbeat films as *Light Years Away* (1981) and *Dust* (1985). Married since 1944 to the actress Helen Cherry, he listed his recreations as cricket and travel, though he perhaps might have added the periodic quest for alcoholic refreshment.

Died Bushey, Hertfordshire, January 7, 1987, aged 71

John Huston

JOHN HUSTON

Huston directed his first film, *The Maltese Falcon*, in 1941 and by the end of that decade had probably become, save for the rather special case of Orson Welles, the most celebrated American film-maker of his generation. But though this reputation rested partly on the strength of *Falcon* and even more on his post-war *Treasures of the Sierra Madre* (1948), his fame was perhaps more widely based on his off-screen personality. Certainly Huston led a colourful early life. His father was the actor Walter Huston, but before embarking on a screenwriting career in the late thirties (his credits included *Sergeant York* and *High Sierra*, both 1941) Huston had been a hobo and a boxer and had briefly held a commission in the Mexican cavalry, as well as dabbling in painting and writing. He began to appear, not just in the tone of his work but more particularly in his flamboyant self, as something of a cinematic approximation to Ernest Hemingway; and for a few years it looked as if their parallel might be an unhappy one, with Huston the craftsman vanishing inside Huston the hard-drinking, good-living media legend. In the fifties he became a peripatetic figure, producing the splendid *The African Queen* (1952) but following it with the trite *Moulin Rouge* (1953). His grand-slam attempt at *Moby Dick* (1956) was almost inevitably no more than a half-success, though probably underrated, while the one Hemingway adaptation he embarked upon, *A Farewell to Arms* (1957), reached the screen with another director as a result of differences between Huston and the producer, David O. Selznick. Yet at the point when critics were ready to consider Huston a talent destroyed, his career suddenly regained momentum; and during the sixties, when contemporaries like Wilder and Mankiewicz found it increasingly difficult to get projects off the ground, Huston went from strength to strength. Ambitious work like *The Misfits* (1961) and *Freud* (1962) rubbed shoulders not only with trivial efforts like *Sinful Davey* (1968) but with intrepid and by no means impersonal excursions into the blockbuster, such as *The Bible* (1966). During these years his white-bearded presence in both his own and other directors' films gave him a visible embodiment as a grand old man of the cinema. The early seventies brought one of his most critically acclaimed pictures, *Fat City* (1972), and a few years later came the fruition of a long-cherished project, *The Man Who Would Be King* (1975), which was on a grand scale but no less intimate in its preoccupations. Huston carried on regardless, alternating potboilers with personal subjects, and sometimes combining the two, as in *Prizzi's Honor* (1986), and finally signing off with the grace-note of the miniaturist *The Dead* (1987), set in Ireland where he had for many years made a home and featuring his daughter Anjelica in a leading role. Huston may well have been the last embodiment of the old Hollywood director; but be that as it may, though for many years he had worn the mantle of an old master, he had somehow contrived never to seem like an old man.

Died August 28, 1987, aged 81

ALF KJELLIN

Swedish actor who achieved early success in films, making his first movie at 17 and gaining local fame as the lead in *Frenzy* (1944). He went to Hollywood on the strength of this to play Léon in the MGM version of *Madame Bovary* (1949), under the pseudonym of Christopher Kent. He reverted to his own name for appearances in various American as well as Swedish films, without achieving star status, and during the

sixties directed several movies in Sweden and later one or two nondescript US pictures (*The Midas Run*, 1969; *The McMasters*, 1970), but he was more prominent as a director of TV movies and series episodes.
Died Los Angeles, April 5, 1988, aged 68

JESSE LASKY Jr.

Son of the Hollywood pioneer Jesse Lasky, he grew up surrounded by famous names but came to be primarily known as a contributing screenwriter to numerous De Mille movies, from *Union Pacific* (1949) through to De Mille's swansong *The Ten Commandments* (1956), though he also had script credits on many less prestigious pictures, such as *Mission Over Korea* (1953). His later years were spent in London, where he was active in television, and he was also a prolific writer in other spheres, notably including a humorous autobiography, *Whatever Happened to Hollywood?*
Died London, April 11, 1988, aged 77

MERVYN LEROY

The director most readily associated with the hard-hitting 'social conscience' movies produced by Warners in the early years of sound, LeRoy made *Little Caesar* (1931), one of the most influential of the early gangster pictures,

Five Star Final (1931), which confronted the tactics of the gutter press, and above all *I Am a Fugitive From a Chain Gang* (1932), as powerful a piece of crusading journalism as the cinema has produced, and one which was responsible for prompting penal reforms in the southern US. LeRoy could boast a comprehensive show business background, having been a child actor and vaudeville performer before entering the movies and working his way up from lab technician to assistant cameraman and then comedy writer. He began directing in 1927 and remained at Warners until 1938; in the forties he worked at MGM, where he became identified with very different material. The best remembered of his MGM films are lavish, and undeniably resonant, weepies like *Waterloo Bridge* (1940) and *Random Harvest* (1942), and in 1951 the studio entrusted to him the biblical blockbuster *Quo Vadis*, one of the cinema's most expensive undertakings to that time. From the mid-fifties until his retirement a decade later, most of his pictures were made back at Warners; but these were mainly bland adaptations of stage successes, the chief exception being the dynamic musical *Gypsy* (1962), appropriately set in the pre-war years of LeRoy's own heyday.
Died Beverly Hills, California, September 13, 1987, aged 86

JOSEPH E. LEVINE

Perhaps the last example of the traditional movie mogul, he began as a Boston clothier, then went into film exhibition and subsequently into distribution. His company, Embassy Pictures, made huge profits by buying up Italian spectaculars like *Hercules* (1957) for peanuts and then spending generously on promoting them. He

Joseph E. Levine

moved into production, and his company was responsible for a varied selection of films, among them *The Graduate* (1967) and *Soldier Blue* (1970). In the late sixties he sold his interest in Embassy to Avco, but remained as president of Avco-Embassy. In 1974 he resigned to form another company, which had a stake in the war epic *A Bridge Too Far* (1977).
Died Greenwich, Connecticut, August 31, 1987, aged 81

ROUBEN MAMOULIAN

An innovator in both theatre and cinema, who to some extent suffered the traditional innovator's fate of being overtaken by events he helped to set in train, Mamoulian, born in Tiflis, worked at the Moscow Art Theatre, and arrived in the West as something of a boy wonder, making his directorial début on the London stage when he was only 24. But though the production which established his name there was in a style of studied realism, it proved no pointer to his future. He crossed the Atlantic and became, significantly enough, a director of opera and operetta, and then in 1927 was responsible for the landmark production of *Porgy*; fittingly, he would a few years later win even greater success

with the musical version of the same material, *Porgy and Bess*. By the early thirties, he was also established as a film-maker. His first feature, *Applause* (1929), took his employers aback to the extent that, having been hired as a stage expert, he adventurously chose to exploit cinematic means for virtually expressionist purposes. The films that followed in rapid succession - *City Streets* (1931), *Love Me Tonight* (1931), *Dr Jekyll and Mr Hyde* (1932), *Queen Christina* (1933) - spanned sundry forms but were all distinguished by audacities of technique and style, and it was appropriate (though in fact a matter of fate, following the death of Lowell Sherman) that Mamoulian should have been assigned to make the first feature in three-strip Technicolor, *Becky Sharp* (1935), which evinced a pioneering use of colour for dramatic resonance. On the whole his films of the late thirties and early forties were less personal, and it was in the theatre, especially with his staging of the Rodgers and Hammerstein musicals *Oklahoma!* and *Carousel*, that he was most to the fore. He returned to the cinema with a splendidly assured musical, *Summer Holiday* (1947), but what might have looked like a new beginning proved to be a false start and he was destined to make only one more film, *Silk Stockings* (1957), being denied the chance to direct the film version of *Porgy and Bess* (1959) and losing the job of directing *Cleopatra* (1963) when initial production was aborted.
Died Woodland Hills, California, December 4, 1987, aged 90

Lee Marvin

RICHARD MARQUAND

Early death terminated a promising career for a British director who had established an international reputation. Brother of the politician David Marquand, he won repute as a director of television documentaries, notably with the series *Search for the Nile* (1971). His first work for the cinema was a nondescript horror movie *The Legacy* (1978), but his next film *Eye of the Needle* (1981) marked him as a storyteller of great skill, and on the strength of it he was signed by George Lucas to direct the third instalment of the *Star Wars* saga, *Return of the Jedi* (1983). The courtroom drama *Jagged Edge* (1985) gained him further Hollywood success, although its successor, *Hearts of Fire* (1987), made in England with Bob Dylan, unhappily closed his *oeuvre* on a note of anti-climax.
Died September 5, 1987, aged 49

LEE MARVIN

An actor of imposing presence, he made his first film in 1951 and for over a decade was a reliable supporting presence in an impressive number of Hollywood movies. Almost invariably cast as a heavy, he was perhaps most memorable as the gangster henchman in *The Big Heat* (1953), vengefully throwing hot coffee into his moll's face, and as one of the hick-town thugs of *Bad Day at Black Rock* (1955). But he was on the right side of the law in the TV series *M Squad* (1957-9) and in the sixties moved into bigger screen roles, exploiting his capacity for comedy, and winning an Oscar in the process, as the boozed-up gunslinger of *Cat Ballou* (1965). For several years he was a major star, in such films as *The Dirty Dozen* (1967), and he even essayed a musical in *Paint Your Wagon* (1969), achieving pop record success with his rasping version of 'Wandering Star'. But during the seventies his roles tended to be less rewarding, sometimes verging on self-parody, and in his later years he achieved less publicity for his acting than for the long-running legal action in which the woman he had lived with for six years sued for half his fortune.
Died August 29, 1987, aged 63

COLLEEN MOORE

One of the biggest stars of the twenties, associated in particular with jazz-age flapper heroines, she was the niece of the Chicago newspaper editor Walter Howey and apparently was given a chance in films as a *quid pro quo* for Howey's helping D. W. Griffith to get *Birth of a Nation* (1915) past the Chicago censors. She made her first film in 1917, and went on to play opposite Tom Mix in several Westerns. The first

of her three husbands was production head at First National, and she herself was a shrewd businesswoman, retiring from the screen on the strength of her investments in 1934. She published an autobiography, *Silent Star*, in 1968.
Died Templeton, California, January 25, 1988, aged 85

POLA NEGRI

The first of the screen's great 'exotic' stars, she was born in Poland and made her film début there in 1914, having studied ballet in Russia and then gone on the Warsaw stage. She went to

Berlin in 1917 at the invitation of Max Reinhardt and became a leading figure in the early German cinema, starring in several films by Ernst Lubitsch, such as *Carmen* (1918) and *Madame Dubarry* (1919). Hollywood offers ensued and she began to appear in US films from 1923. She continued the association with Lubitsch in films like *Forbidden Paradise* (1924), and garnered widespread publicity through her romance with Rudolf Valentino and successive marriages to a count and a prince. Her popularity was on the wane by the time sound arrived and in the thirties she returned to Europe and appeared in a number of German films. She went back to the US at the outbreak of World War II, and appeared in one minor film there in 1943, subsequently making a one-off comeback in a cameo role in *The Moonspinners* (1964).
Died San Antonio, Texas, August 1, 1987, aged 92

RALPH NELSON

A director who came out of the 'golden age' of American live television and made his feature bow with *Requiem for a Heavyweight* (1962), a big screen version of a play he had earlier handled on the small one. His subsequent output was eclectic, not to say erratic; but, though his films gained Oscars for Sidney Poitier (*Lilies of the Field*, 1963) and Cliff Robertson (*Charly*, 1968), few achieved much widespread popularity, the exception being the controversially violent Western *Soldier Blue* (1970). Nelson, who started out as an actor, played small parts in several of his films.
Died Santa Monica, California, December 21, 1987, aged 71

PAUL OSBORN

American playwright and occasional screenwriter, whose best known play, the pre-war *Morning's at Seven*, was successfully revived on Broadway in 1980. His other plays, some adapted from novels, included *The World of Suzie Wong*, and among his screenplay credits were *The Young in Heart* (1938), *Portrait of Jennie* (1949), and more memorably two Elia Kazan movies, *East of Eden* (1955) and *Wild River* (1960).
Died New York, May 12, 1988, aged 86

ANTHONY PELISSIER

Son of the actress Fay Compton, he was mainly active in the theatre but had a brief spell as a film director, beginning in 1949 with two enterprising literary adaptations, *The History of Mr Polly* and *The Rocking Horse Winner*. He made several lesser films over the next few years, the last being the Ealing comedy *Meet Mr Lucifer* (1953). His widow is the actress Ursula Howells.
Died Seaford, Sussex, April 2, 1988, aged 75

EMERIC PRESSBURGER

Pressburger might fairly have been called a citizen of the world, yet in collaboration with Michael Powell he created a body of films well-nigh unique in their response to nuances of British temperament and culture. Born in Hungary, he studied in Germany and later scripted films in Berlin, among them early works by Siodmak and Ophuls, before moving to Paris and in 1935 to London. He became a protégé of his fellow-countryman Alexander Korda, who effected his initial contact with Powell. The latter directed *The Spy in Black* (1939) and *Contraband* (1940) from Pressburger scripts, and in 1942 the two men bravely formed an independent production company, The Archers. Over the next 15 years they collaborated on many films, taking joint credit as writers, producers and directors, though the prevailing belief is that Pressburger's predominant contribution was at the scenario level; among them were some of the most ambitious and stylish the British cinema has produced, such as *A Matter of Life and Death* (1946), *The Red Shoes* (1948) and *Gone to Earth* (1950). After the partnership amicably ended in the mid-fifties, Pressburger produced one film, *Miracle in Soho* (1957), but mainly turned to writing novels: one of these, *Killing a Mouse on Sunday*, became the basis of the 1964 film *Behold a Pale Horse*. In 1983 Pressburger became, with Powell, one of the first recipients of a BFI fellowship.
Died Suffolk, February 5, 1988, aged 85

PIERRE PREVERT

The younger brother of the celebrated French screenwriter Jacques Prévert, he entered films in 1928 and worked as an actor and assistant director. As early as 1932 he directed a film in the idiom of eccentric comedy, *L'Affaire est dans le sac*, but despite its inventiveness it failed to attract much popularity and his subsequent directorial career was sporadic: two further comedies, *Adieu Léonard* (1943) and *Voyage surprise* (1947), which were distinctive but similarly lacking in widespread appeal. He subsequently directed several short films.
Died Paris, April 6, 1988, aged 81

JOHN QUALEN

A small and wiry character actor who appeared in well over 100 films, quite a high proportion of them Westerns, he was of Norwegian stock but was in fact born in Vancouver. He reached

Broadway in 1929 with a part in Elmer Rice's *Street Scene*, and made his Hollywood début in the 1931 movie version of the play. He later played in several of John Ford's films, perhaps most memorably as Muley in *The Grapes of Wrath* (1940) and in *The Searchers* (1956). Later film roles included *Anatomy of a Murder* (1959) and *The Sons of Katie Elder* (1965).
Died Torrance, California, September 12, 1987, aged 87

ELLA RAINES

With her mane of hair and deceptively sleepy demeanour, she was a near-emblematic presence of the forties, though somewhat in the mould of Lauren Bacall, understandably so in that like Bacall she was a discovery of Howard Hawks and was initially signed up by a company formed by Hawks and Charles Boyer, making her screen début in *Corvette K-225* (1925), which Hawks produced. She was subsequently given a contract by Universal, and starred to memorable effect in *Phantom Lady* (1944), going on to feature in several other prime instances of the *film noir*, such as *Brute Force* (1947). But she dwindled into lower-case pictures at Republic and elsewhere and made her final movie appearance in the British-made *Man in the Road* (1956), before devoting herself to marriage and domestic life.
Died Sherman Oaks, California May 30, 1988, aged 66

Ella Raines

ALBERT S. ROGELL

A veteran of the vanished form of the B-feature, he entered the industry as an assistant cameraman and by the early twenties was directing low-budget Westerns. Over the next three decades he helmed innumerable minor films in assorted genres. Probably the best known was *The Black Cat* (1941), an engaging example of the semi-comic Universal chiller. His last film was the British-made *Before I Wake* (1954).
Died Los Angeles, April 7, 1988, aged 86

RUSSELL ROUSE

After starting out as a prop man, he formed a writing partnership in the forties with Clarence Greene. They scripted *D.O.A.* (1950), one of the most essential examples of the *film noir*, and subsequently formed an independent company with Greene producing and Rouse directing. This was responsible for an ingenious if self-conscious attempt at a film without dialogue, *The Thief* (1952), and an effective gangster movie, *New York Confidential* (1955). But on the whole their output, as represented by films like *A House Is Not a Home* (1964) and *The Oscar* (1966), was undistinguished.
Died Santa Monica, California, October 2, 1987, aged 74

RENATO SALVATORI

He rose to popular success in Italy during the fifties as a star of youth comedies like *Poveri ma Belli* (1956), then went on to comedy roles in more ambitious films such as *I Soliti Ignoti* (1958), then made an unexpected impression when cast as the boxer turned murderer in Visconti's *Rocco and His Brothers* (1960). He continued to play regularly in Italian, and occasionally in French, films over the next 20 years without ever fulfilling his early promise. His wife was the French actress Annie Girardot, his co-star in *Rocco*. Cause of death was cirrhosis of the liver.
Died Rome, March 27, 1988, aged 55

DENNIS SANDERS

On the strength of the evocative Civil War vignette *A Time Out of War* (1954), directed by Sanders and produced by his brother Terry, which won an Oscar as best short subject, the brothers went on in the same capacities to make a couple of enterprising low-budget features, *Crime and Punishment USA* (1959) and *War Hunt* (1961), which respectively contained the first screen performances of George Hamilton and Robert Redford. But Sanders' subsequent fictional films were sporadic and of less interest. He also made television documentaries and a couple of non-fiction features, including the concert movie *Elvis - That's the Way It Is* (1970).
Died San Diego, December 10, 1987, aged 58

STENO (Stefano Vanzina)

A former cartoonist, he had a prolific career, starting in the war years, as a screenwriter. In the post-war decade he formed a writing and

directing partnership with Mario Monicelli, responsible primarily for comedies, often featuring the comedian Toto, of the sort which were not widely exported. The partnership broke up in 1953, but Steno carried on making films in a similar vein, among them *Mio Figlio Nerone* (1956) and *Il Trapianto* (1970).
Died Rome, March 12, 1988, aged 73

PAOLO STOPPA

Starting on the stage about 1930, he went on to found with Rina Morelli a theatrical company for which Luchino Visconti directed several plays. He began appearing in films in the mid-thirties, and became a prominent supporting actor in French as well as Italian movies. Small and wiry, he possessed a flexibility of style, and was effective in both comic and unsympathetic roles. Notable appearances included the opera director of *Les Belles de nuit* (1952), *La Loi* (1959), *Rocco and His Brothers* (1960), and the parvenu landowner in *The Leopard* (1963).
Died Rome, May 1, 1988, aged 81

ALICE TERRY

Working in films from 1916, she married the director Rex Ingram, and was the star of many of his films, probably being best remembered as Rudolph Valentino's leading lady in *The Four Horsemen of the Apocalypse* (1921). In the mid-twenties she and Ingram moved to Nice, where Ingram set up his own studio, and Terry appeared in such films as *Mare Nostrum* and *The Magician* (both 1926). However, the coming of sound marked the end of both their careers. Following the release of the film *Valentino* (1951), she took legal action against the producers over the portrayal of her relationship with the actor.
Died Burbank, California, December 22, 1987, aged 88

LINO VENTURA

A stocky, deceptively granitic screen presence, something of a natural heir to Jean Gabin, he was born in Italy but his family moved to France when he was a child. After early experience of such jobs as garage mechanic, he became a boxer, and his physical impact in that capacity doubtless facilitated his transition to acting, initially in minor roles in films like *Touchez pas au Grisbi* (1954). Associated mainly with crime movies, he achieved top billing in *Classes tous risques* (1960), and from *Le Deuxième souffle* (1966) onwards, starred in several films directed by Jean-Pierre Melville. Although the many films he subsequently starred in were of variable quality, he was equally at home on either side of the law, and was seldom less than imposing. He guarded his private life fiercely, but was known as an active campaigner on behalf of mentally handicapped children.
Died St Cloud, France, October 23, 1986, aged 68

Kenneth Williams

EMLYN WILLIAMS

A man of many parts in the performing arts, he achieved fame as the author of numerous plays, the most successful including *Night Must Fall* and *The Corn Is Green* which were both filmed more than once, as well as by performing in many of his own plays and those of others. In the post-war years, his celebrity widened with his solo performance as Charles Dickens, and also as Dylan Thomas and Saki, though he continued to make other stage performances (he was, for instance, in the 1962 New York production of *A Man for All Seasons*). In the cinema, he was the writer and director, as well as the star, of *The Last Days of Dolywn* (1948), set in his native Wales; but elsewhere, although he acted in a wide range of films, these had the air of being peripheral to his other concerns. Film appearances included *Jamaica Inn* (1939), *Ivanhoe* (1950), *The Deep Blue Sea* (1955), and *The L-Shaped Room* (1962). He was also the author of several books, including volumes of autobiography and a study of the Moors murderers.
Died London, September 25, 1987, aged 81

KENNETH WILLIAMS

An actor whose extraordinary gift for camp exaggeration and vocal mannerism made him a natural for radio, in such shows as *Round the Horne*, he had an impressive multi-media career. He made his stage début in Singapore, and, after repertory experience in England, achieved roles in West End productions, including playing Elijah in Orson Welles' 1955 staging of *Moby Dick*. Probably his most notable stage appearances were in revues such as *Share My Lettuce* and *Pieces of Eight*, though he was in the original production of Joe Orton's *Loot* in 1965, and much later directed revivals of both that play and *Entertaining Mr Sloane*. In the cinema, he had a few minor roles in the early fifties, but will be indelibly remembered as one of the key members of the *Carry On* stock company, achieving a kind of apotheosis as Julius Caesar in *Carry On Cleo* (1965).
Died London, April 15, 1988, aged 62